EIGHT-WHEELED WARRIORS
AND GRUNTS

EIGHT-WHEELED WARRIORS AND GRUNTS

U.S. Marine LAV and Infantry Operations,
Spring 2004

LIEUTENANT COLONEL DAVID E. KELLY,
USMC (RET.)

CASEMATE

Pennsylvania & Yorkshire

Published in the United States of America and Great Britain in 2024 by
CASEMATE PUBLISHERS
1950 Lawrence Road, Havertown, PA 19083, USA
and
47 Church Street, Barnsley, S70 2AS, UK

Hardcover Edition: ISBN 978-1-63624-492-1
Digital Edition: ISBN 978-1-63624-493-8

A CIP record for this book is available from the British Library

Printed and bound in the United Kingdom by CPI Group (UK) Ltd, Croydon, CR0 4YY
Typeset in India by DiTech Publishing Services

For a complete list of Casemate titles, please contact:

CASEMATE PUBLISHERS (US)
Telephone (610) 853-9131
Fax (610) 853-9146
Email: casemate@casematepublishers.com
www.casematepublishers.com

CASEMATE PUBLISHERS (UK)
Telephone (0)1226 734350
Email: casemate@casemateuk.com
www.casemateuk.com

Contents

Dedication

Special thanks to all those who made my return to active duty possible and provided support throughout that time:

The late Colonel John Ripley, USMC, then head of the Marine Corps History Division at the Washington DC Navy Yard, who gave me great latitude and guidance in composing my Letter of Instruction for this deployment.

Colonel Nick Reynolds, USMC, officer in charge of the Marine Field History Detachment, whose 2003 phone call invited me to deploy to Iraq.

The late Colonel Dave Waters, USMC, also of History Division who kept in touch with me overseas, and with my family back in Lansdowne, Pennsylvania.

Major John Piedmont, USMC, my "wingman" during our deployment to Iraq. His upbeat, can-do attitude allowed us to work as an efficient team. He arrived in Iraq weeks prior to me, and helped me to navigate through the myriad of commands so we could create a systematic interview collection effort.

Finally, to my wife Terrie, and daughters Donna Kelly Romero and Rosie Kelly Sullivan, who supported my decision to accept the chance to return to active duty and deploy to a combat area.

Preface

Along with Major John Piedmont, I was one of two Marine Corps field historians deployed to Iraq in the spring of 2004. We were both Reserve officers from the Marine Corps History and Museums Division located in Washington, DC. Our Letter of Instruction, the official document that outlined our mission, was clear: To travel throughout the Marine Area of Responsibility (AOR) in Iraq, and conduct field history interviews with Marines and sailors. We had no quotas to meet. We did not attach to any individual unit. This allowed us the freedom to meet with Marines at all ranks and staff levels, to try and flesh out official reports with the words of these Marines. My work output was over 190 formal interviews and countless talks with Marines throughout Al Anbar Province. Major Piedmont conducted over 200 interviews. Future researchers and historians may find this information valuable as they reconstruct the events in Iraq during 2004.

Once in Iraq, I began my work as a field historian, using Camp Fallujah as my base of operations.

What made this work possible was the cooperation that I met at every level of command in the 1st Marine Expeditionary Force (IMEF). The command gave us access to meet with Marines in every part of Iraq. Use of the military internet and land line phone systems allowed us to inform units that we were inbound, and gave them time to select key individuals for us to interview. As the senior member of the field history team, I created a matrix of all of the major command elements under IMEF, and attempted to visit each command at least once during our five-month deployment.

Once Major Piedmont's deployment ended, I continued my field history work alone for another month. I've selected the interviews in this book from my work to highlight actions by Marines deployed with elements of the Light Armored Reconnaissance units, and Marine infantry units in Ramadi.

Introduction

This volume presents stories told by Marines in oral interviews that took place within days or weeks of the events described. These Marines served in both infantry units and Light Armored Reconnaissance units during the first half of 2004, mostly in areas ranging from the Al Anbar provincial capital of Ramadi out to the western areas bordering Syria and Jordan.

In March 2004, a smoldering insurgency erupted throughout Iraq, starting with the slaying and defiling of the bodies of American contractors in the city of Fallujah. By April, a full-scale insurgency broke out in many parts of that nation. Planned Security and Stability Operations were put on hold as American forces began to conduct full-scale military operations. As Regimental Combat Team 1 surrounded the city of Fallujah, elements from Regimental Combat Team 7 based at Al Asad moved units to isolate that city from surrounding areas.

These interviews highlight operations with Marines in two Light Armored Reconnaissance (LAR) battalions, and infantry units from 2nd Battalion, 4th Marines, (2/4) and 2nd Battalion, 7th Marines (2/7). The Light Armored Reconnaissance units deployed at that time possessed a unique combination of speed and firepower, working with their own infantry scouts and attached infantry support. These vehicles ride on eight wheels, hence the reference in the title of this book. Delta Company, 2nd LAR Battalion supported the efforts of Regimental Combat Team 1 in the area of Fallujah. In western Iraq, the 1st LAR Battalion, in support of Regimental Combat Team 7, had an attached infantry company and patrolled a huge area on the borders with Jordan and Syria. The presence of these wheeled vehicle assets oftentimes deterred insurgents from initiating fights against Marine forces in western Iraq. The 1st LAR Battalion drove from the border areas to Fallujah to support Operation *Vigilant Resolve* when Marine forces isolated the city in April.

An infantry company, Fox 2/7, supported the efforts of 1st LAR that operated out of a small outpost in western Iraq, known as Korean Village, near the town of Ar Rutbah. This Fox Company also dispatched two of its infantry platoons to supervise border crossings with Syria and Jordan. During Operation *Ripper Sweep* outside of Fallujah proper, Fox redeployed to operations in and around the city of Karmah before returning to the border areas.

In the city of Ramadi, insurgents created a hostile environment for the Marines of the 2nd Battalion, 4th Marine Regiment, almost as soon as the battalion took over responsibilities from U.S. Army units there. Fighting was near daily, culminating in a particularly violent April day for the Marines of Echo Company, 2/4.

In April 2004, the First Marine Expeditionary Force (IMEF) had massed forces from Regimental Combat Team 1, along with reinforcements from Regimental Combat Team 7, to surround Fallujah. Before a full-scale invasion of Fallujah took place, however, a settlement of sorts was negotiated, with city authorities agreeing to allow Iraqi security forces to take responsibility for the city. In the rest of Iraq, Marine forces continued to engage in multiple operations against insurgent forces.

Each Marine's story in this book creates a picture of the events as they happened from his perspective. The field history audio recordings are history "in the raw," made within weeks of the events. Not every Marine in every unit witnessed the same intense combat. In fact, several of the interviews here were with Marines in supporting roles that made combat possible for those on the "front lines." The narratives are created by a combination of notes made during each interview, my personal transcriptions of the audio, and observations in my field history personal journal. The result is that a lot of this book is written in "Marine talk." An updated glossary helps to explain many of the terms used by these Marines. Acronyms for terms in everyday use by all branches of the military, useful for those who need to use them for brevity, may slow down a non-military reader. Even military veterans of different eras may find the glossary useful, as terms and equipment used change rapidly over time. I retain the acronyms in direct quotes and try to use more familiar terms in other parts of the stories.

I hope that this approach will allow the reader to gain an appreciation for the dedication and accomplishments of these Marines who served in Iraq, as well as the effort and teamwork in these actions far from home.

Maps

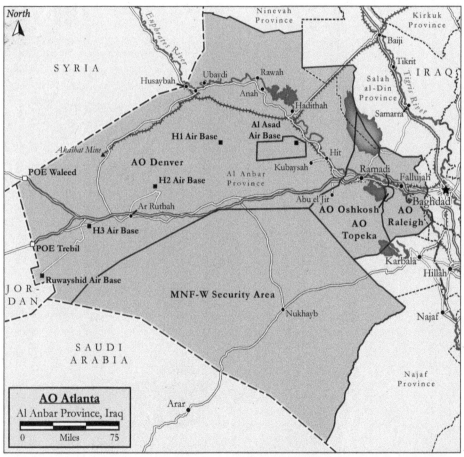

Ar Rutbah—Fox Company, 2/7, attached to 1st LAR Battalion at FOB Korean Village near Ar Rutbah, provided camp security and infantry platoons to supervise border crossings at Al Waleed (Syrian border) and Trebil (Jordanian border). Al Asad—2/7 provided camp guard for the Al Asad Air Base, and sent Echo Company, 2/7, for operations around the city of Hit. Ar Ramadi—Marine battalion 2/4 conducted security and combat operations in the provincial capital. Fallujah—Focus for IMEF's Operation *Vigilant Resolve* in April 2004. (Map by Edward Alexander)

April 2004 unit dispositions at Fallujah. Delta Company, 2nd LAR Battalion, provided support for 2/1, 2/2, 3/4, and U.S. Army special operations forces during Operation *Vigilant Resolve*. (Map from *US Marines in Iraq 2004–2005: Into the Fray*, by Lieutenant Colonel Kenneth W. Estes, USMC (Ret.), History Division)

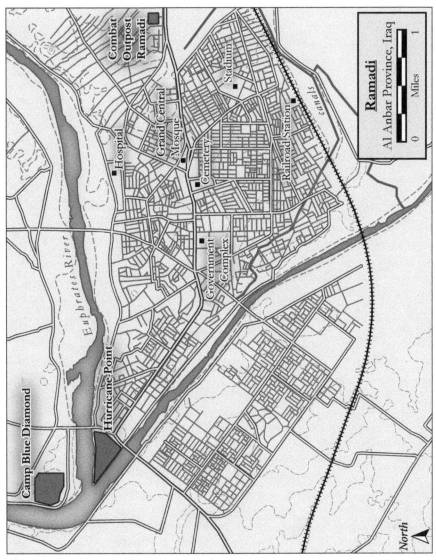

1st Marine Division headquarters at Camp Blue Diamond, 2/4 Battalion headquarters and Weapons Company at Hurricane Point, Combat Outpost Ramadi with Echo and Golf Companies. (Map by Edward Alexander)

CHAPTER ONE

Meeting the Marines from Delta Company, 2nd Light Armored Reconnaissance Battalion

Camp Fallujah

I first arrived in Iraq on April 10, 2004, at Baghdad International Airport. In a few days I got to Camp Fallujah via a nighttime helicopter ride on a Marine CH46. By the end of that month, I had a sense of operations throughout the area, and established a collection plan of Marine units to visit where I could conduct interviews.

Since neither Major John Piedmont nor myself were attached to any single unit here, we had several ways to ensure that our visits would result in productive interviews. Doing this with the units when they were at Camp Fallujah was relatively easy. When possible, we would attend morning briefings at 1st Marine Expeditionary Force (IMEF), or Regimental Combat Team 1 (RCT1) to put faces to names. Sometimes we arranged interviews with face-to-face requests. Most often, we sent emails to the various operations officers at battalions, companies, and squadrons weeks in advance of our trips away from Camp Fallujah. One of the meetings that helped make this possible was meeting with the MEF Staff Secretary, Lieutenant Colonel Mike DiNardo on April 21. He sent an email to all staff advising them of the presence of the field historians, and our desire to meet with Marines and sailors throughout Al Anbar Province.

I would always send a copy of our Letter of Instruction (LOI) created at History and Museums Division when I contacted units to apprise them of our planned visits. This LOI outlined the mission of the Field History Branch, and how the field historians would conduct interviews. Another factor that helped was the fact that during the 2003 operations in Iraq, most of the Field History Division's officers had been attached to invading Marine units. Staff and individual Marines had some familiarity with the field historians and their mission.

Camp Baharia, Monday June 21, 2004

I attended the morning Regimental Combat Team 1's Operations Briefing today. My name was up on Colonel John Toolan's appointment calendar for an interview.

Major Piedmont and I had already made arrangements to meet with Marines from Delta Company, 2nd LAR (Light Armored Reconnaissance Battalion). After the RCT brief, we met with Lieutenant Walker of Delta Company 2nd LAR and got a ride to nearby Camp Baharia where they were based. Delta Company was from the 2nd LAR Battalion, headquartered at Camp LeJeune, North Carolina. Marines used the LAV 25 (Light Armored Vehicle) as its main vehicle, an eight-wheeled, lightly armored vehicle with a 25mm chain gun and 7.62 machine gun. They were used for a variety of missions, can travel over land, and are fully amphibious.

After meeting with Captain Ladd W. Shepard, Delta's commanding officer, we went to work. Our procedure was to split up at every unit visited to maximize the number of Marines we could meet. I had four interviews that day, the longest taking over an hour. Very well-spoken Marines, and Captain Shepard sent Major Piedmont and me the Marines with varied experiences: The deadly VBIED (Vehicle-Borne Improvised Explosive Device) hit on an LAV 25; an ambush in Al Karmah where the LAV section had ridden through a small arms ambush three times; and operations near Fallujah.

The LAR vehicles have been used for a wide variety of missions—to screen for infantry, search for Improvised Explosive Devices (IEDs), run raids, go as a Quick Reaction Force, and so on. They have been used throughout the RCT's area of operations (AO) very effectively. Captain Shepard provided some office space in his Combat Operations Center (COC) area for the interviews—it was out of the sun, and the air-conditioning made it a comfortable place to sit and listen.

Sergeant John Denton Leuba
Scout Squad Leader/Platoon Sergeant, 3rd Platoon, Delta Company, 2nd LAR Battalion

Much of the pre-deployment training prepared these Marines for Security and Stability Operations when they entered Iraq in March 2004. Insurgent resistance changed the conditions in Iraq. The Marines of Delta Company have been used in a wide variety of missions due to their speed and weapons systems. Leuba outlined many of these high-intensity encounters, from raids to full-scale combat on highways and inside Baghdad and Fallujah. His most trying day came when another LAV in the company was destroyed by a suicide bomber in a vehicle-borne IED attack, killing several Marines he knew.

Sergeant Leuba came to 2nd LAR in September 2000. Before that, he was with 2/8 (an infantry battalion), and has been deployed to Haiti, Okinawa, Greece, and countless training evolutions in the United States and other areas of the world. In 2003, he deployed with the 26th Marine Expeditionary Unit (26th MEU) for Operation *Iraqi Freedom 1* (OIF1). "It's been an interesting time, sir," he said. He has been a Marine for, "Seven years and nine days." "I had just returned from the 26th MEU. It was October 26th [2003] when we returned. I found out weeks after that that we were gonna deploy, Delta Company come over here [to Iraq] to deploy."

He said that the training was rushed, but his platoon remained pretty much intact from the previous deployment. There was a lot of Security and Stability Operations (SASO) training, but he would have liked more small unit training. In a way, the training was really done before the 26th MEU deployment: A year of training, then an eight-month deployment, then getting ready for the current deployment. With very low turnover in the unit, in his opinion most of the Marines formed a tight, well-trained unit, "I have an extremely seasoned platoon now, which I had never seen. This is definitely the most-trained platoon I've ever been with."

Once the company flew into Kuwait, they stayed and trained there for a few weeks. They then moved north into Iraq in March 2004, and the move was much different from his move into Iraq in 2003. This time Delta Company came up with the infantry companies from 2/1 and acted as a security element for the move. The LAV 25 vehicle was well-suited to this role, especially in the move through large desert areas of Iraq. However, there were no threats during this move. They skirted Baghdad, and then drove into then-Camp Volturno, now called Camp Baharia.

I asked him to explain his current role in the platoon. Normally the platoon sergeant is a staff sergeant (E6). "My permanent duty is scout/squad leader, I'm filling in as the platoon sergeant, due to the fact that my platoon commander was wounded on April 30th, with shrapnel wounds to the vehicle from an IED. His wounds were a little bit too much for him to stay here, they needed to get him out and take some shrapnel out of his arm, they were impacting some nerves and muscles. So they sent him back to the States. I'm the senior sergeant in the platoon, so as an additional duty, it was pushed down. I mostly deal with personnel issues and gear issues as platoon sergeant. We have another sergeant in my platoon, Sergeant Henrickson, who is an actual 0313 [The Military Occupational Specialty for LAV crewmen]. I'm an 0311 [Infantry Rifleman], so my experience with the vehicles, my knowledge with the vehicles is pretty limited. I know their capabilities, I know what they can do, [but] I don't know how to fix them. I don't really want to know, so that's their job, they take care of that."

"As a scout/squad leader, my job is to train, maintain accountability of, and ensure the safety and security of the scouts. We have four scout teams in the platoon, so I have three other team leaders and myself, as the fourth team leader. My main role actually comes into effect when we're on the deck [the ground], maneuvering forces around, and employing it [the LAV 25] as the ground force leader."

Sergeant Leuba said that when they first arrived at this camp, there were some Army Rangers and soldiers from the 82nd Airborne here. He said LAVs have a "tenuous" relation to the Army's Bradley fighting vehicles. However, he noted that the Light Armored Vehicles (LAV 25s) are very lightly armored, and their strength on the battlefield is their maneuverability and firepower, but they can't sit there and take a beating like a Bradley can. Bradleys have much thicker armor. Both the Bradleys and the LAVs have the same chain gun (M242 Bushmaster 25mm chain-driven autocannon), and the LAVs were given many of the missions of the departing Bradleys in this area. The first mission for the LAVs was Main Supply Route (MSR) security.

"When we first got here, we were tasked with clearing the routes. When the vehicles came up, they'd cross the roads, line up, and then the scouts'd get out, we'd deploy them in echelon, and we'd sweep the roads for IEDs [Improvised Explosive Devices]." He noted that these dismounted IED sweeps were a rough mission for the scouts. "I personally don't mind doin' it. I'm willin' to go and take my risk, but, you know, these younger guys, they're, it's rough telling a man to go kick for an explosive device."

The Army units had been here for over a year, and Leuba said that he could see the fatigue with the soldiers. They had gone over the same roads repeatedly, and it showed in their performance and lack of enthusiasm for the job. "It is a hard battle to maintain the kind of enthusiasm you have to maintain." At the time of the interview, he and his Marines had been here for about three months, and the deployment was expected to last for seven months total. But he said that he really doesn't keep track of days. He said that he would actually like to stay here longer, because in his opinion it takes about six months to really get a feel for an area, but that the Marine Corps can sustain a presence with the seven-month deployments. However, staying for a year may dull the sharpness of the Marines.

While the Army was still here, there were no enemy contacts: No IEDs or mortar attacks. Then it started slowly building up into the attack on Fallujah in April 2004.

"They [insurgents] started mortaring our base, they started setting up IEDs, were making small contacts here and there. And then it just erupted. That was the most productive time we've had here. Where we were actually going out, hunting out the enemy, finding him, killing him, destroying him, capturing him. It was exactly how things needed to be going. We'd find people here that were bad, go in and hit them, letting the good people go and take care of their lives. I thought that was the best thing we'd done in Iraq. I wished we'd maintain it, from my vantage point, my view, there was no better way to conduct what we're doing here. Immediately after that, we had no problems. The people, they respected power."

Sergeant Leuba described the first actions: "The first contact we made, they [Marine forces] just started the attack on Fallujah, started securing Fallujah, piece by piece. The company came out, they were sitting in a coil, pretty far north of Fallujah proper." (A coil is a 360-degree formation of vehicles that is ready to deploy into action quickly.) The Headquarters and Service (H&S) element of the LAR company took and received fire, and pushed an insurgent force back.

"That night, we went out and ran through a stretch of Route 10, that apparently had some sort of insurgent force on it. They received RPGs [Rocket-Propelled Grenades] from it. That was the first contact we were in, really. It was mostly a drive-by."

Leuba was towards the front of the pack. He saw a muzzle flash and put a 40 mike mike (launched 40mm grenade) on it, and kept driving through. When they got through it, he saw a bullet hole through a backpack on the outside of the LAV, and that pack was right next to his head! His SAW (Squad Automatic Weapon—M249 light machine firing a 5.56mm round) gunner, Lance Corporal Walsh, was on the other side of the pack. "We were like, wow, we almost got taken out." Leuba said that the insurgents are bad shots in the daytime, and even worse shots at night.

In mid-March, an Army convoy heading into Baghdad came under mortar and rocket-propelled grenade (RPG) fire. Leuba's platoon had been on company operations that whole day. The attack was about a 40-minute drive from this camp.

"It was almost like they ran into two simultaneous ambushes, and they were really, they were in trouble. So they called up two of our platoons, we went out, found the (Army) unit that was in contact. They had been out of contact for a while, but we rolled up. There was a Humvee there that had taken a catastrophic hit from an RPG right in the front right quarter panel in front of the door, definitely American wounded that had been inside. There was blood throughout. It was a really rough thing to see." It was the first time that many of his Marines had seen friendly blood, and the aftereffects of enemy contact. The leaders helped to talk them through it afterwards.

One of the CONEX boxes (large intermodal shipping container) on one of the Army trucks had been hit by an RPG, and it was full of mail that was now on fire. Leuba said that this burning mail also made many of his Marines mad. All Marines over here knew how much they looked forward to getting their mail. This was mail that would never get delivered. The LAR platoons then escorted the convoy to a base somewhere in Baghdad. The platoons stayed there for the rest of the night.

The next morning as they left Baghdad, another convoy came under fire, and the LAR platoons pushed up into the kill zone near a bridge with two overpasses nearby. On one side was a large field with some sort of stadium, on the other, rows of houses with a large building off to the left of the road. Leuba said that it was about five to six hundred meters to the bridges. Off to the right side was a large wall about 20 feet high that had about a three-foot gap in it.

"As soon as we came in, we took some fire, don't know if it was friendly or enemy, but they were just shooting the hell out of the bridge we just came underneath. And, so, me and the other scout in the back, were just scanning furiously back and forth, trying to figure out what they're shooting at. There was absolutely nothing there for them to engage, and [we] had no idea what they were doing. So, we're just looking around. All of a sudden, the VC [vehicle commander] comes over, he tells my SAW gunner, Lance Corporal Walsh, 'Hey, we got a guy out, far, by the stadium.' And I was using the squad advanced rifle [SAM-R, a specially modified M16 with optical sight] so I popped that up. I scanned over and I saw a guy in a green shirt, he was behind a large pillar. I saw him look around, so, you know, they're saying, 'Engage him! Engage him!' I look out, I say I got an AK, low, low ready. So I took one shot at him. I had ranged it at like 600 meters, I hit a little bit low and right. I readjusted my shot, and when I shot, I came off target. You know, standing position, moving vehicle. I shot, I came back down, as I came back down, and looked hard in my sights he was falling down, I guess his hands going up in the air. I'd aimed right for the head, so, most likely where I hit him."

"Scanned over, we were scanning around, and as soon as we came into it, we could see it was a mess. Two contractor vehicles had come and jack-knifed right in the center of the road."

The only way past this on the road was a small gap on the left. Their (Number) 4 Vehicle pushed through this gap and got engaged in a firefight on the other side of the tie-up. Leuba's platoon commander came to him and told him to try to get the contractor vehicles off the road to allow a convoy through. Sergeant Leuba took his fire team out of their vehicle and used one of the trucks as cover as they began to try to gain fire superiority. Enemy fire was only sporadic. One of his Marines used his ACOG (Advanced Combat Optical Gunsight) rifle sight to engage and take out an enemy shooter in a building about 300 meters off the road to the right.

Then they directed their attention to the rows of houses off to their left. "I had a guy [enemy] who was running right in front of the houses with an AK [AK-47, Soviet-designed rifle]. I took a shot, hit him in the chest, he went down. There wasn't really a whole lot left in the area, so at that point we started trying to move the vehicles out. The Army guys, they're pretty scared. I mean they're Army convoy guys, not wanting to be out there [being] John Wayne or anything. So, they're pretty well freaked out, we're just trying to get everybody calmed down, everything moved out. One of the contractors had been hit, and they had already evac'd him."

There were two Army trucks and another Army vehicle that had taken some serious hits. The Marines found some Army drivers who could get the trucks to move. Leuba told them that the Marines would provide them cover. One truck got started and drove away. Soon a wrecker truck came to move the other truck out. The Marines kept providing cover fire and engaged targets to protect the trucks. Finally, the second truck was chained up and began to be moved away. One truck was left.

"Finally, a tank rolled up, and it was awesome, because they sucked up all the fire. I have no idea why a guy with an AK is gonna spend 50 rounds trying to shoot at a tank that he cannot destroy, instead of shooting at the guys running around with M16s. However, they did, so I was happy to see it."

Sergeant Leuba said that some RPG rounds started coming in towards the tank, but it was some of the worst shooting he had ever imagined! One RPG shot aimed at the tank instead hit a support structure some 40 feet above the ground. "So we shot that guy."

He continued, "Throughout we're engaging targets, putting people down, and it's amazing how calm you can be in the middle of the worst, you know, firefight.

It was working out really well, our guys were moving. So, eventually, I'm moving around, and I find the guy that's in one of the trucks, and there's a contractor [a civilian] hiding in the back of a truck. And I'm like, hey, I need you to help move one of these vehicles. He was really scared, he wanted one of our vehicles to come with him and escort him out. I was just like, hey, it's just not gonna happen. All you gotta do is just travel that way, you're gonna run into all the other trucks, there's plenty of walls, once you clear this bridge, you're fine. It's no problem, but right now you're in a kill zone." So the driver got into the truck and drove out of the area. "At this point the fire almost completely dies down."

By now, Sergeant Leuba had seen several people die through his rifle's sight. He continued to scan the area, and looking towards another vehicle, he could see 10 enemy dead there. The Marines in the other LAV were all doing good, with only minor scrapes. He told them to watch out for any counterattacks. As Leuba returned to his area, gunfire started up, Sergeant Counter [sic] got shot. The round went through his right side, but missed any vital organs.

By his estimate, they were there for a good two hours. He was checking on ammo as the firing began again.

During one of the firefights, he saw rounds hitting the ground near the feet of one of his Marines, and Leuba spotted the shooter at the three-foot gap in the 20 foot-high wall that was some 600 meters away. He began to make plans to go to the wall and take out the guy, but word came from the platoon commander that they were moving out. One of his Marines, Lance Corporal Goucher [sic] had about a three-inch groove on his Kevlar helmet, with the spent brass round embedded in it. "He came about a half inch from having his head blown off," said Leuba. "He was really amped up, really excited, really happy about what was going on, and then he noticed that and he's like, 'I don't feel so well right now.' Yeah, go ahead, sit down, open your flak up."

"I get back, I'm looking, I'm just scanning the area, as I'm waiting for this counterattack to start up. And, I see this head pop up, pops back down. I'm like, oh, what is that? So I put my scope up, and I'm lookin' through it, and I see a head come up, I see a head go down. So I'm sighting in, I'm trying to figure out, okay, is someone trying to spot us? You know, what's goin' on here? I see a blue shirt come up, and lay over a line. It's two ladies doin' their laundry, right in the middle of a firefight!" He then laughed, and said, "It was the funniest thing I'd seen!" [And I thought that it was lucky for the two women that he was so careful before taking a shot!]

As they left the overpass area, they received random AK fire that passed over the tops of the LAVs. It was over 600 meters away, so the shots were just randomly fired in their general direction. They got to an old factory off the side of the road and watched the Army vehicles that were still stuck in the kill zone. A crowd of people came out to loot the vehicles, and the insurgents fired RPGs at the vehicles, killing some of the looters. The LAVs then pulled out of this, their first real engagement of 2004.

"That was the most productive engagement we had been engaged in. I was really proud of how my men performed. They did exactly what they needed to do. My team was the only combat ground force, in effect. We were constantly shooting and moving." One Marine, Sergeant Counter, was hit, and not severely. He got to go back home and see his family.

The most notable engagement since then was in Al Karmah. "We rolled into an ambush. We actually came into it backwards of where they intentionally set it up. Immediately the lead Victor [what he called the vehicle] saw movement through his thermals [sights]. So he zeroed in on it. They saw somebody with RPGs and AKs, so they immediately opened fire. So from that, it was just 'game on.' We came in, started engaging targets, rollin' through. At this point, I was using M16, with 203 [M203 is a single-shot 40mm grenade launcher attachment], and I had the AN/PVS-17 Delta attached, which is a really good piece of gear. It's a night vision sight, it's a four-and-a-half-time optical sight, NVG [Night Vision] capability. It's got a little red dot right in the center."

He had not been able to zero-in the sight, only bore sighted it, but it worked well. "We kept moving through. I was engaging with 203 at the beginning. We had large targets, behind walls, in little nooks and crannies. So we threw some 40 mike mike on 'em. My set was the right side, and it had a lot of buildings on it. I wasn't really getting a lot of targets through there. However, my left side machine gunner was covering, and he was getting a lot of muzzle flashes, getting a lot of engagement on the left side."

They worked to avoid crossover of fire. Towards the end of the kill zone, the enemy had set up 10-foot-tall Jersey barriers. The first vehicle backed up and rammed a barrier. They also shot coaxial (25mm machine gun) and 240 (240 Golf 7.62 machine gun) fire on it to blow the barrier apart and just drove through.

Sergeant Leuba was in the back of his vehicle and heard the noise but did not know what had happened. Then he got his only sure kill of this action: "This guy comes running along a ledge, he comes running on the side. So I just put that sight right on him, pull the trigger five times, and all five went right into him. And spun around, hit the deck, didn't move."

Leuba fired 56 rounds total in this engagement. "Nothing ridiculous" he noted. After making it out of the ambush, he checked on his Marines. No one was seriously hurt. "One of my guys, Lance Corporal Hoffa, he was an engineer attachment, he took a round through the sleeve. Right by his shoulder area, no wound, just one of those lucky shots that didn't hit him."

Leuba anticipated that they would be sent back into the ambush, but on this occasion, they were instead sent back to the base.

On Route Mobile, there was an area that they called RPG Alley, but they themselves never saw RPGs when they traveled it. They have done a couple of raids. A company raid north of Karmah went without incident. Intel had reported that there were enemy elements and bomb makers in five buildings there, but no enemy or weapons were found. The inhabitants were cooperative, even though their doors had been knocked in during the raid.

"The people were really nice; they were actually waving to us when we came through later. It was incredible. It really shows that we actually are getting something accomplished here. If you can raid somebody's village, and break so many things, peek in their doors. They still understand, they still wave, they still support. It gives me an incredible feeling that this is actually working out, that we really are winning hearts and minds. In spite of the fact that we don't always get a lot of waves when we're on the highway."

Sergeant Leuba bragged that the LAR company is a raid element all in one. They are mobile, and can provide their own security and assault elements for a raid. They have gone out with Recon a few times, but are mostly assigned as a Quick Reaction Force (QRF) for the battalion. "I've fought some pretty bad people and put 'em away. That's great. No end to the joy that that brings."

Operation Iraqi Freedom 1

I then asked him to reflect on OIF1. In 2003 Sergeant Leuba was here with the 26th MEU, and was inserted into Mosul in northern Iraq. "Entirely different area, different mind frame, different everything." To get to Iraq then, they had gone into Crete and spent a few days at an airfield there waiting to go into Iraq. Sergeant Leuba was the second-senior sergeant in the platoon. They had normal issues of ammo, but not extra 203, SAW rounds or extra 240 Golf ammo. There was a problem with weighing the LAVs, also, and a concern that they might not be moved on the C-130 aircraft. Leuba's team flew into Iraq with Recon. Once they flew over Iraq, he looked at his newly issued desert cammies (MARPAT digital utility uniform), desert cover for his Kevlar, and brown boots, and saw nothing but green fields below! Recon told them that the airfield was not secure and that they would probably be coming in under fire. The plan was to get off the aircraft as quickly as possible and secure some nearby buildings.

"So we hit the deck, and I've got two teams. So we immediately come out of the back of the vehicles. They had to unload all of the personnel prior to the vehicles. As we were comin' out, we immediately set up into a hasty 360 around the back of the aircraft. The IPADs [*sic*] come out and just take off. I'm looking up at these IPADs [*sic*] takin' off across the tarmac and I'm like, 'Shit! What is goin' on?' We jump up and we're trying to chase the vehicles down, and we're trying to communicate with security. And we had no idea whatsoever what's going on. Finally get there, get everything set up, get set in. You know, claim a piece of the giant pie of defense."

They did virtually no LAR operations at this point. There were 25 Marines on the ground along with their lieutenant and the Navy Corpsman. He had four security posts dug in, and the Marines were acting as dismounted infantrymen. They did get involved in a firefight, captured a Fedayin fighter, and got their Combat Action Ribbons.

Back to Current Operations

Leuba said that it was completely different from operations for him and his Marines this year (2004). The people, the enemy, the day-to-day operations, and the heat, were all different. The Mosul area was green with foliage, there were no overt hostilities other than occasional sniper fire and the one firefight. Sergeant Leuba expected much of the same this year, but it has not been that.

Sergeant Leuba liked being a dismounted infantry leader, but also appreciated the cover that an LAV can provide, with only his elbow exposed when he was shooting at people. He said that there was a high tempo of operations now, even though it seemed that they were not doing a whole lot. For the past two nights there have been engagements by the Cloverleaf east of Fallujah. There were some ICDC (Iraq Civil Defense Corps—After June 30 known as Iraqi National Guard) units there and the Marines were letting them take more responsibility. Leuba really wanted to go into the city though, and destroy the insurgents.

2nd LAR was now on a six hours on, 18 hours off rotation. They had been on a five on, 10 off rotation. Their tents don't have air-conditioning, and during the daytime it's too hot to sleep in the tents, so his Marines go out and find a shady area where they could rest and grab a smoke.

Sergeant Leuba said, "It's good to be here. I volunteered to come here. I'm glad that I did. I volunteered to stay here. There's a lot that we have to accomplish here. I'm really glad I came here with the Marine Corps."

He also added that he was glad that he didn't join the Army, as the Marines are so much more professional. "Our guys are eager for combat, love it, excel at it. I'm really proud of my platoon, proud of this unit. Doing good things. Glad to be here."

VBIED Blast (Vehicle-Borne Improvised Device)

Sergeant Leuba gave details about the deadly VBIED attack that happened on April 30, 2004.

They were operating south of Baghdad, near Abu Ghraib, on April 30 and had taken a patrol out on zone reconnaissance, looking for areas where there might be threats or restrictions on road movement. A Marine vehicle stopped as it spotted several howitzers in a large open area. The vehicle's scouts dismounted and approached the weapons. Sergeant Leuba went up to several Iraqis who seemed to be working on the howitzers to find out what they were doing there. He finally learned that they were cutting up the weapons to sell for scrap. Leuba marked this on the map and went with several of his Marines to take pictures of the weapons. They continued to push ahead and find more of the pieces. By this time, he and his Marines were about 900 meters away from their vehicles.

Sergeant Leuba then said, "At that point I hear a tremendous explosion, a heat wave. I spin around, my immediate first thought was that something happened. Maybe that there was a loaded shell in one of the howitzers, and it blew. So I spin around, and I can see a vehicle, just black, smoke and flames just everywhere. And I see the howitzers still intact, and just no idea whatsoever what just happened. All I could think is, could that have possibly been a mortar? You know, was it a rocket? How was it fired? It didn't make any sense. It sounded wrong, it looked wrong. You know, it wasn't the clean, black explosion that happens with enemy ordnance. It wasn't that bumping, cracking, bang. It was just like a pushing explosion-ey, movie-thing going on."

He thought that they must be under some type of attack. He ran and was scanning the area, trying to figure out what was going on. He'd run 100 meters towards the vehicle, stop, scan, then continue towards the vehicle. "As I'm closing on the road, I'm running right towards the artillery piece, because there were two Iraqis there. So, my first thought was, you know, we do have people inside the line, so I have to make sure these aren't the ones who found something." The Marines had four LAVs out there at the time.

"So I come running up and could see pieces of metal all over the ground. And I hear, I don't even know who it was at the time, yell, 'Wilfong's dead, Wilfong's dead.' Corporal Wilfong, Corporal Joshua F. Wilfong, was one of our engineer attachments from CEB [Combat Engineer Battalion]. About that time, I looked down at my feet, and I could see the scalp of a man laying right in front of me. Obviously not Corporal Wilfong, 'cause it was long, and black, and just peeled straight off the head. You know, that's how I'm looking at the vehicle [an LAV 25]. Can see the vehicle's been pushed, covered in black, it's burning. And I run around, and I'm running with my friend, another team leader, Corporal Hall. And, I find out that it's staff sergeant's vehicle that's been hit. And the team leader that's on it is Corporal Scott Vincent, a good friend of mine, been with me forever."

Vincent was Leuba's SAW gunner during their first deployment in 2003, and went to Mosul with Sergeant Leuba. Pretty much every day that Leuba was with LAR it was with Corporal Vincent.

Sergeant Leuba ran to the back of the LAV and saw Wilfong and Vincent lying on the ground there. "I could see Vincent; he was just staring up at the sky. His mouth was open, eyes were wide. And I yelled to him, you know, thinking he was in shock. I'm, 'Vinny, Vinny, what's up?' And I ran round, and as soon as I got next to him, I could see that his face was just covered in glass, and dirt. And I pretty much knew right there that he didn't make it."

Leuba could hear screaming coming from the other side of the vehicle. He closed Corporal Vincent's eyes, then went to see what was going on the other side of the vehicle. He looked inside the vehicle, and saw that it was a mess. It was black and charred, the glass had blown out of the vision blocks in the back. Wilfong and Vincent had been in the back, facing outboard, and it pretty much ripped Wilfong's head off. Vincent had been thrown from the vehicle by the explosion, and a piece of metal had ripped off the back of his head, and his helmet was a couple of hundred meters away. Wilfong's flak jacket was shredded off his body.

Doc Ferguson was working on Lance Corporal Thiel, a SAW gunner with the vehicle. Thiel had massive bleeding from his head. Sergeant Leuba cut off Thiel's pants leg to expose a wound there, and then held a bandage on his bleeding head.

Leuba continued, "During this time, I'm also yelling at people to get a defensive perimeter set up, so if there is some kind of counterattack, we can deal with it. So, I'm talking to Thiel, you know, tellin' him he's gonna be okay. I know I have to get off. I have to stop talking to him. I have to stop dealing with [him]. I have to make sure everybody's safe. I have to make sure I get the defense set up."

"So I started to kinda take my hand away, from the bandage on his head, to get it to pass it on to somebody else. And I just see this massive, gaping, wound channel through his head. And, uh, it's really bad to see. I knew that is this situation, as bad and as awful as it was, there's nothing you can do, other than make sure everything's okay. You know, you have to step up. You have to be the leader. You have to take care of the business at hand, because, you know, the men are really, really, upset. They're my friends, too. But the ability to be able to distance yourself from the emotions, from the feelings, and take care of what needs to be taken care of, falls under those who lead."

So Sergeant Leuba began to organize what had to be done. About this time, elements from 2/1 who happened to be traveling through the area, came and helped them with their defenses. Leuba said, "It was awesome to be able to get them there, because I could put them on the security." Leuba briefed these Marines on the area, so they could set up defensive fields of fire. These Marines also fired at approaching vehicles to keep them away from the blast area. Leuba said, "For some reason, in Iraq, you set up a roadblock and every vehicle will come up, wanting to get through." Once shots are fired in their direction, the need to come through the area disappears.

Sergeant Leuba said that he then checked on Doc Ferguson, who had some wounds on his leg, and Lance Corporal Thiel was still being worked on. A medevac was en route, but just not fast enough. The medevac finally came in, and the helicopter evacuated the wounded.

Then Leuba said, "I'm just sittin' there, waiting for the QRF to show up, to turn the site over. And, I just sat down with my friend, just died, and just smoked a cigarette, sat there and said goodbye. I have to say that was probably the worst day I've ever been in. That was April 30th. We hadn't had any contact in like 30 days. We weren't lax, but you just don't see that coming."

The incident began when his staff sergeant had popped up out of the hatch and told an Iraqi vehicle to just go through. He got back inside the vehicle and this suicide bomber just blew himself up.

"The force of the explosion was so great, it put a hole in asphalt [that] was 15 feet in diameter and a good four feet deep. Almost vaporized the car. The engine block was pushed about 500 meters forward. It blackened the outside of the vehicle [the LAV], tore it apart. It actually breeched the hull. There was a crack inside the hull. Destroyed weapons. Killed my friends, sent three guys home."

Leuba said that the Marine vehicle driver and the gunner escaped without any injuries. But every Marine in the back of the LAV sustained some kind of injury. The force of the explosion pushed this 16-ton vehicle five feet off the road.

Sergeant Leuba said that in the immediate aftermath of the explosion, he ran around making sure everybody was all right. As a leader, he had to just make himself all right in order to do his job.

I then asked him if he was all right himself, if he had somebody to talk to. He replied, "Yes, sir, I'm all right. I mean, I don't have any lasting issues with it. I talked to the platoon, we all talked together about it. It comes up frequently. I talked to Vinnie's mom, she's a great lady. It's incredible they're going through this the way they are. Yeah, it was just a rough day." He said that this is why they were so eager to get back out there and do their job again. "We haven't had any contact since then."

Leuba said that his Marines got through that day, and nobody seems "messed up" about it since then. "They're strong men. We came here with the understanding that we might not leave, that not all our friends are gonna leave here. That's something that you face as a combat troop, that's something that you face as a Marine. It's our job to deal with it."

In about a week, I would get the opportunity to interview Sergeant Leuba again after he and his Marines had been engaged in more combat operations. That next interview was on June 28, 2004.

Sergeant Michael Irvin Honigsberg II
LAV Crewman/Gunner, on LAV 2, 1st Platoon, Delta Company, 2nd LAR Battalion

Sergeant Honigsberg described the two most harrowing actions during this deployment: A nighttime firefight where two large convoys were attacked by insurgents, and a near-fatal accident when the LAV he rode in slipped into an irrigation ditch, nearly drowning the crew. He also knew the Marines killed in a suicide VBIED attack.

Sergeant Honigsberg is an 0313, an LAV crewman. He joined the Marine Corps right out of high school, reporting to recruit training on June 5, 2000. He attended SOI (School of Infantry) at Camp Pendleton, California, then had a choice to become an LAV crewman. He joined the Fleet Marine Force (FMF) at Camp LeJeune,

North Carolina, on January 3, 2001. His LAV is a TOW (Tube-Launched, Optically tracked Wire-guided anti-tank missile) carrier vehicle.

He participated in a Combined Arms Exercise (CAX) in California, then went on the 24th MEU (Marine Expeditionary Unit) for a nine-month deployment. He went to Kosovo, then the United Arab Emirates, Djibouti, and finally 33 days in Iraq during OIF1. He then returned home.

His original Expiration of Active Service was June 2004, but he voluntarily extended his enlistment for six months to come back over to Iraq for a second time. His platoon sergeant at the time was Gunnery Sergeant Rosswell, who helped convince Honigsberg to stay on active duty. Rosswell was now the company gunnery sergeant. "A lot of Marines wanted to follow where he went, so a lot of Marines voluntarily extended with me, to come back over with him." Sergeant Honigsberg was currently debating whether to reenlist. "When we first got here, it was February 28th, I picked up sergeant March 1st, which is pretty neat, picked that up in Kuwait. We came here to Fallujah, Iraq, and did a turnover with the Army, which went pretty good."

Around April 4 to 8, the whole company was on a Traffic Control Point (TCP), north of Fallujah. They stopped vehicles traveling along the Main Supply Route (MSR), and checked them for weapons and explosives. A couple of convoys went through during the day without incident, but one nighttime convoy was ambushed from both sides of the road. The LAR company commander decided to send 1st Platoon up to run through the ambush site.

"We went through there, we got about the middle of it, we received no fire. We didn't see any people. All of a sudden, I was lookin' through my thermals [sight] when an RPG hit on the right side, within five to 10 meters of my vehicle. My staff sergeant, which was the VC, vehicle commander at the time, started firing in that direction. I slewed onto where he was firin' at, 'til I got the RPG team with 25mm [machine gun fire]. And then right after that, we had six more follow-on RPGs all at once. And then, all hell broke loose after that. Went through RPG Alley, maybe I'd say about half a click long [about 500 meters]. Stopped, regrouped kinda, reloaded ammo if needed. Went through it again. Took fire again from both sides. Got to the end of where we [originally] started. And then our company commander decided he wanted to go out with us. We turned, went through again. There's no contact at that time." They then went back to the Traffic Control Point.

After the next day, they went back through RPG Alley, and got fired on again. Honigsberg's LAV got a jam in the 25mm gun. He had to switch to single-shot firing, using a manual hand-crank, and then got the gun operating in automatic again. For the next three days, he said that they took a lot of fire running through this area. Over the next few weeks, they sat in overwatch of this area to prevent ambushes.

One day on overwatch, Red One, the platoon commander's vehicle, was under a bridge and began to take sniper fire. The gunner found the sniper in a house, and sent three rounds of 25mm fire into the house and "took out" the sniper. Since then, there have not been any ambushes from that northern part of Fallujah.

During a raid in mid-May, his LAV fell into an irrigation ditch. It was so dark that even the night vision goggles did not provide a lot of vision, and the road along the ditch was very narrow.

· "We started taking on a lot of water, maybe we had fallen in a lake, or just a canal. So the VC [vehicle commander] popped out real quick. Otherwise he woulda been cut in half. There was a tree stump [that] actually stopped the vehicle from going completely upside down. He buttoned down real quick, everybody was okay. One of the scouts in the back hurt his wrist, but he was all right. When I tried to get out, the tree stump was stopping me from getting out. I had to take off my flak, got stuck between my hatch and the stump. And I was basically sittin' on top of my VC. And he was basically under water, and I yelled for one of the scouts to pull me out. If he hadn't pulled me out when he did, the VC coulda drowned."

He detailed how they got out of the LAV: The driver went out through the emergency hatch on the left side of the vehicle, Sergeant Honigsberg, the gunner and the VC got out through the gunner's hatch because the VC's hatch was blocked by the tree stump. The scouts got out through the back doors. Honigsberg said that later he saw that the water was about chest high. "That was a little bit different than your average day," he added.

All seven (one Corpsman, three scouts, and three crewmen) got out of the LAV and got the ammo and serialized gear out also. The next day, an Amphibious Assault Vehicle (AAV 7) came up and pulled the LAV out of the canal. Back at Camp Baharia, they had to switch out the engine, change the fluids and oils, and the vehicle was up and running again.

For most of the Fallujah siege in April 2004, 2nd LAR was involved in route security, raid support, QRF missions, and making sure that IEDs were not being emplaced.

At the time of this interview, his platoon was on a six-hour on, 18-hour off rotation. During the six-hour periods, they patrolled roads, and were on call for any units that needed their support. His platoon patrolled from about 1400 to about 2000. He said that many of the Marines were veterans who were in Iraq last year. The leadership in the company has played a big role in this. "There's a lot of good guys in our chain of command."

"I personally think you can't have any other job better than being a Marine. What better job could you have, you know, helping defend an entire nation?"

He also noted that the pay over here is a lot more than normal, and Marines who are getting out can get out with a large chunk of change. But, "A lot of them [Marines] do it because they can come over and help make a difference."

I then asked him to discuss last year's deployment to Iraq. He said that the 24th MEU got here when the war part was pretty much over, and he only had one firefight at a checkpoint. One vehicle took some machine gun fire, and returned fire but couldn't find the shooter. They did a lot of searches of houses and found weapons and mortar rounds.

This year they have gotten a lot more weapons firing at them.

He felt that the morale level was high as they get to the midpoint of their deployment. He also said that now they have internet and phone access at Camp Baharia, so they can easily communicate with people at home. They get mail on a regular basis, too. And they just recently got ice! The chow hall was not too bad, he said, and they now had air-conditioning in the sleeping areas.

On the downside, he spoke about the LAV that had been hit by a VBIED. "I knew one of the guys, Corporal Vincent, he was from Oklahoma, which I'm from." That LAV was in a different platoon, and two Marines were killed, and several injured. Honigsberg said it was kind of a shock, because Marines in the LAVs often feel that they can't be hurt in them.

Lance Corporal Keith Allen Bridges
LAV Crewman, Weapons Platoon, Delta Company, 2nd LAR Battalion

Bridges rejoined the Corps in 2003 after a two-year break. He participated in two weeks' worth of action in "ambush alley," and later helped to pull dead Marines from the LAV destroyed by a suicide VBIED attack.

Lance Corporal Bridges began, "Oorah! In May 1998, I joined the Marine Corps, went to boot camp, San Diego, California."

After the School of Infantry (SOI) he went to LAV crewman school, and then reported to Alpha Company, 2nd LAR Battalion, in December 1998. In July 2000, he deployed with 2nd Platoon of Alpha Company on the 26th MEU, and returned from the deployment in December. In December 2001 he left the Marine Corps, but re-entered the Corps on October 23, 2003, rejoined 2nd LAR and became part of Delta Company. They left Camp LeJeune, North Carolina, in late February 2004 to deploy for OIFII (Operation *Iraqi Freedom II*)

Shortly after he returned to the company, it began to do its workup to return to Iraq. The Marines did MOUT (Military Operations in Urban Terrain) training, SASO training, and got spun-up on customs and religion of the Iraqis. All in all, the training attempted to get them ready for any situation here.

Weapons Platoon in the LAR company consisted of 81mm mortars and AT-variant LAVs (AT = Anti-Tank). The AT variants have better sights than the LAV 25s. The company utilized the mortars for indirect fire support and the superior TOW sights on the AT variants for various missions.

For the convoy up into Iraq, he said, "Usually what you want to do is tuck the mortars in behind the 25s, so you'll stagger 'em. You'll put them generally in the middle of the convoy." The rest of LAV 25s ride in the convoy itself. However, since being in Fallujah, Bridges has been on several scouting missions in the LAVs. They have studied the terrain, swept Alternate Supply Routes (ASRs) and MSRs to ensure that they are trafficable and free from IEDs.

When he arrived in this area, he said that the turnover with the Army units here was very professional. "They took us out, for the first month, I'd say, on their patrols. So that we could get a feel for the Op tempo [Operational Tempo] and some of the things they were doing, and things to look for. They were really helpful."

When the Army left, the LAR units began IED sweeps of the roads in the area, and setting up Traffic Control Points (TCPs) and Vehicle Check Points (VCPs) in the area to control the flow of vehicles, and to set up blocking positions for 2/1 when it began to cordon off the city of Fallujah.

"In the beginning, I was a driver for the LAV 25, for the platoon commander. The driver is primarily responsible for the vehicle and the safety of the crew. My job is to report to the vehicle commander any problems that the vehicle might be experiencing, or any terrain we might need to negotiate." Then Bridges moved to the AT-variant LAV. The driver's mission does not change in this vehicle. He next became a scout to provide security on the mortar-variant LAV. During the siege of Fallujah, LAVs were near the Cloverleaf to the east of the city, in an overwatch position due to their speed and the weapons sights on the vehicles. They could respond quickly to incidents in the city.

Once the siege ended, his company began patrolling the MSRs between Fallujah and Abu Ghraib along with some of the ASRs and service roads. They have done IED sweeps, looking especially for loose dirt along roads. This kept the supply lines opened for resupply.

There have been a few incidents where they have found IEDs. "Just the other day, as a matter of fact, I want to say it was the 18th of June, we were conducting an IED sweep. It was approximately 1830, on the ASR between here and Abu Ghraib. And we come across some UXO, which is unexploded ordnance, and we had to call out EOD [Explosive Ordnance Disposal] to dispose of it." He said that this was a short distance off the ASR. The EOD Marines arrived in about 45 minutes.

Of late, the enemy had started to set up IEDs along these lesser-used roads. Lance Corporal Bridges said that depending on the size of the device found, they would cordon off the area 100 meters or more, and set up security around their vehicles to keep civilians away. When EOD arrives, the LAR Marines provide security for them. The mission will resume once the IED is disposed of. In his experience there have not been any incidents where an enemy has used these IED disposal operations as an opportunity to attack the Marines.

Lance Corporal Bridges said that there has been only one occasion where he has been under fire. He called the area "Ambush Alley."

"There, for about two weeks, it was pretty heavy. It seemed like every time a convoy would roll through there they would hit 'em with everything they had. So we spent a lot of time up there, setting in security, and conducting convoy security through that area. For some reason, they like to target our vehicles (the LAVs)."

In early April, they were hit by the small arms and RPGs, returned fire, and also called in close air support from the Cobra helicopters. Bridges himself fired a few rounds during this firefight.

He said that currently his platoon was on a six on, 18-hour off tempo. Vehicles have to be maintained, Marines have to PT (Physical Training Workouts) to stay fit, and they also take first aid classes from the Corpsmen. The actual time of each mission rotates within the company. Weapons Platoon goes out as a regular platoon to keep the men sharp and the vehicles running. He added, "You're pretty much on alert all day. We have a sign-out log, that you sign out any time that you go anywhere." They could get called out almost any time. Marines can't go too far on this camp, and they can be ready to launch in less than an hour.

Lance Corporal Bridges then described events of April 30, 2004. "April 30th, 3rd Platoon rolled out, with a couple ATs, anti-tank variants. And we were conducting some zone and route reconnaissance in a new area that we hadn't had eyes on. And, I guess it woulda been, southeast of Abu Ghraib, we were patrolling up around a water treatment facility. We'd stopped, there was some locals, which were crowded around an artillery piece. So we stopped just to see what they were doing around the artillery piece."

He believed that it was an old Iraqi artillery piece. "That area had been known for heavy IEDs. We were making sure that they weren't setting an IED up."

"While we were stopped, a vehicle approached, with a foreign national in the driver's seat. The vehicles [LAVs] were set up in like a staggered column, along the MSR, and had halted, and had provided basically local security. When the man in the vehicle pulled up next to one of the 25s, LAV 25s, and started shouting something at the VC. The VC looked down to see what the foreign national was trying to say. And at that point, the vehicle detonated. Ah … the explosion … threw the chassis and the engine approximately 150 yards in front of the LAV 25. Knocked all the tires from the right side of the vehicle out. Knocked the marine-driver propeller off … taillight … I believe one of the scout hatches … it actually pushed the vehicle sideways. The crater was, more than waist-deep, and approximately 10 feet across."

The Marine vehicles around there pushed out their scouts for security, and the Navy Corpsman started to provide first aid to the wounded. It was hard for Lance Corporal Bridges to get through at this point, and he now spoke slowly.

"Unfortunately, we suffered two KIA [Killed in Action], four WIA [Wounded in Action]. Once the platoon commander was able to radio up to higher, called in for air medevac. At that point, another unit, I believe it was Recon, came down the road, and offered any assistance they could." They helped with local security. The air medevac arrived within 20 minutes of the call. A ground medevac moved those wounded to Camp Fallujah.

Lance Corporal Bridges was ahead of the explosion area when it had happened. When he popped out of his LAV after the explosion, he looked back and asked the VC if it was one of theirs. The explosion also pushed another LAV in front of the LAV that was hit forward, too. A Quick Reaction Force (QRF) from 1st Platoon, Delta Company, also arrived on the scene.

It had been relatively quiet since their first months here.

Once the recorder was off, Lance Corporal Bridges explained that he had lost a good friend in the VBIED attack, and found it hard to talk about. He also helped to pull some of the Marines out of the LAV that was severely damaged by the VBIED.

Corporal Jeffrey John Bertch
Scout Leader, Bravo Section, 2nd Platoon, Delta Company, 2nd LAR Battalion

Early during this deployment, Bertch participated in continual searches for IEDs along roads in the area. In late April they rolled through an ambush area twice, taking and receiving small arms fire. Bertch silenced shooters hiding behind a bunker with 40mm grenades.

Corporal Bertch entered the Marine Corps in June 1998, about 20 days after he graduated from high school. He completed recruit training at San Diego, then became an 0311 infantryman. His first duty station was at the Marine Barracks in Washington, DC, where he was one of the ceremonial marchers. In 2001 he went to 2nd LAR Battalion at Camp LeJeune, and joined the Surveillance and Target Acquisition (STA) Platoon for one year. He then became one of the infantry scouts on an LAV 25. He's done a couple of deployments with Bravo Company.

Corporal Bertch was with Bravo Company before transferring over to Delta Company when asked if he would volunteer to come out with the company to Iraq. He only had about three days with Delta Company before deploying to Iraq.

"While I was in Kuwait, I was pretty much just a team leader on one of the vehicles in the Alpha Section. I spent the time in Kuwait just trying to get to know the Marines that were in the company. They were all pretty much just new faces to me." He became tight with his crew.

When they left Kuwait, his LAV was the lead vehicle for the whole convoy into Iraq. He said that at every bridge that they came to, he and his team had to go up, or over, or around the bridges to ensure that they were clear of any insurgents or IEDs. It was clear the whole way up and it was a smooth-running convoy. Once in Iraq, they drove into Camp Baharia, their current location. They slept near their vehicles as the tents had just recently been put up, and still did not yet have wooden floors or air-conditioning.

The Army was still in the area, and he went out to shadow them on their IED sweeps along the roads. The Army rode in their Bradley fighting vehicles, and the Marines rode along in their LAV 25s.

"Once they left, we continued with IED sweeps the way the Army were doing it: Get out alongside the road, set in a skirmish line, using the vehicle as our base. Pretty much sweep down through eight or nine kilometers of roadside, check and make sure that overpasses and roads, guardrails were safe of all IEDs."

Bertch said, "During April, the tempo picked up quite extensively. Got into a couple little ambushes we rode through."

They were then doing less IED sweeps and more mounted patrols. They were trying to intercept insurgents coming into the Fallujah area, and also some who were trying to flee that city. In April they rolled through a large ambush near the town of Karmah. It was a small road, with houses close-in, and people were running away.

"We had three LAV 25s, and one Log variant, logistics variant. All the people were scattering, we started takin' small arms fire, from [the] park side of the city. And that followed by several RPG shots. Quite extensive small arms fire, some light machine guns fire. We ended up rollin' through it, and then turned around, came back through it, reloaded, went back through it. Turned around again, and came back through it, and then came on back. Which was kind of odd, because up until then, they would ambush us, and then they were gone." He said that on this ambush it seemed that the enemy was there to stay and fight, as they had fortified positions on top of buildings.

During this ambush, the scouts inside the vehicles did not dismount. The team leader and assault gunner popped up in the back of the LAV to provide rear security. They watched the flanks of the vehicle during these moves through the ambush. He and his SAW gunner fired a lot of rounds. Bertch estimated that he fired four magazines of M16 ammo (about 120 rounds total), and the SAW gunner fired two drums of ammo (200 rounds per drum/magazine). When they reloaded, he and his gunner swapped out with two different scouts.

Corporal Bertch said that the enemy was using old cars on the ground, and bunkers on buildings, and he fired two 40mm grenades into one bunker, and hit one vehicle that insurgents were hiding behind. After his second shot on the bunker, all firing from it ceased.

During most of the Fallujah operations in April, his unit was screening outside of the city, making sure that no one got out of the cordon as the Marines were flushing them out of buildings. They also did what he called some "rolling screen lines" to cover a larger area from time to time. "We stopped vehicles that were trying to leave, checked their vehicle, made sure they didn't have any weapons or anything suspicious on 'em." Bertch didn't find any weapons himself, but said that sometimes they came across individuals with large amounts of American money. These individuals were detained and taken to Camp Fallujah's detainee facility.

Around mid-April, some of the LARs were attached to 3/4 (a Marine infantry battalion), and helped that battalion in its efforts to clear out the town of Al Karmah. They went through in the early morning, and one of 3/4's 7-ton trucks turned over into a canal there. As Bertch was setting in his team as security while they waited for a wrecker truck for the 7-ton, they began to take sniper fire from a shooter on a rooftop. The Marines returned fire, and the shooter left the rooftop. "Later we heard him shouting and screaming, he was wounded, and couldn't get to his friends, or his friends couldn't get to him." Bertch tightened up the security perimeter near the truck.

A Marine sniper on top of the ICDC (Iraqi Civil Defense Corps) building in Al Karmah saw insurgents running near a wall about 1,100 meters away, far beyond the range of his M16. He gave a call to see if anyone had a SASR, a .50 caliber Special Application Scoped Rifle. Corporal Bertch's platoon sergeant called back and told that Marine sniper that they did have one, so two scouts from Alpha Section came back and escorted Bertch to the ICDC building. He went onto the rooftop along with Sergeant Rowe, the platoon's chief scout. One of the scouts had the designated marksman rifles, and Bertch the SASR.

"It looked like that the insurgents were comfortable, we couldn't engage them as far out as they were running. So they were just pretty much, just freely walking about. So between myself and the other sniper that was up there for 3/4, we were engaging targets. Anywhere from 600 to 1,100 meters out."

The Marines on the rooftop were taking pretty consistent small arms and machine gun fire from a mosque about 200 meters from their position. The insurgents were also firing mortars from behind the mosque. "They would sneak around the back of it, take RPG shots from our right flank, which would ultimately sail over our head. They weren't very accurate with them. This went on for probably about an hour. They started walking mortars in, they had a spotter as well, in the mosque."

Bertch called back to Lance Corporal Ingal, who was on the radio, for fire support onto the mosque. The LAV 25s fired high explosive 25mm rounds into the mosque, without effect. Six to 10 gunmen remained inside the mosque and continued to fire on Bertch and the other Marines on the rooftop.

"Ultimately the decision came from higher that they were to bomb the mosque, using the JDAMs [Joint Direct Attack Munitions], we had 500-pound JDAMs."

The Marine sniper teams were pulled off the roof and a "fast mover" (Air Force jet) dropped a 500-pound JDAM and completely leveled the mosque. A tower remained standing with some insurgent snipers firing inside. Another JDAM took that tower down. Lance Corporal Dabb returned to his vehicle while Corporal Bertch and his spotter, Lance Corporal Ingal, moved back up on top of the roof. 3/4 continued moving into palm groves near Al Karmah, engaging insurgents there for two or three hours. The battalion called for several F-18 strafing runs and artillery fire on the insurgents in the groves.

As insurgents tried to flee the palm groves, Bertch and the other LAR Marines fired on them with the 25mm guns, as well as long-range sniper fire.

"There was an orange dump truck, comin' through, dumpin' off insurgents." He said that about five at a time would pile out of the truck. Bertch identified this target for one of the LAV 25s, and the LAV engaged the truck with 25mm fire and took it down. The insurgents ran away from the truck into the palm groves. By about 1700 that day, the gunfire died down, and they could see some insurgents going out of the back end of the palm grove, headed into Al Karmah. The Marines got word to pull back. Tanks came in and fired at a downed Marine 7-ton truck to demilitarize it.

At the end of April, they went into Al Karmah without any small arms fire at them. He said that it was a quiet town after the initial engagement.

Since then, they resumed their IED sweeps, although fewer of these were dismounted. They were no longer being mortared on a daily basis as they had been before April, and there has been very little enemy activity. It has only been in the last week or so that random mortar fire resumed. An LAV in another platoon was hit with an IED that did not do any serious damage. The company was now doing a lot of patrolling on the roads to see if there was any activity in the area.

Then just two nights before today (Saturday June 19, 2004) there was an ambush that engaged a convoy along Route Mobile on the northeast side of Fallujah near the railroad tracks. The insurgents fired small arms, machine guns, and three RPGs at the LAVs. The LAVs engaged with their 25mm guns, and Marine Cobra helicopters came in for close air support, clearing a group of insurgents from behind a berm. Several more convoys came through without any shooting. The AC130 Spectre gunship was also operating in the area. Bertch's section stayed in the area until about 0430, and then returned to Camp Baharia.

The LAVs get tasked out to different units. They worked with both 2/1 and 3/4 when they have gone into the city for meetings at the mayor's office there. Corporal Bertch said, "We basically set a tight coil around the mayor's cell. They go in, have their meeting, we watch the streets. They have ICDC and Iraqi police, Fallujah Brigade out there as well, to kinda control the streets." When the meetings end, they pull back out.

Normal patrols run from four to six hours. When a platoon gets tasked out to support other operations, this increases the length of time the remaining sections go out.

Corporal Bertch felt that his platoon likes his leadership style. They have become a real tight group since they have gotten in Iraq. "Our platoon as a whole, is real close knit, probably do anything for any of them. We all know our jobs."

Thursday, June 24, 2004

Events were constantly overtaking my scheduled interviews with Colonel John Toolan, the busy commander of Regimental Combat Team 1. I was able to interview Marines from 9th Communications Battalion, starting with the battalion commander, Lieutenant Colonel Loretta Reynolds, and tried to nail down a time to meet with General Richard Kramlich, commanding general of the 1st Combat Service Support Group out at Camp Al Taqaddum. I also sent messages to RCT7's S3 Officer, Lieutenant Colonel Nick Vukovitch about meeting with Marines near Camp Al Asad.

I was scheduled to get a ride to Camp Baharia to continue meeting with Marines from Delta Company, 2nd LAR Battalion this morning. After the RCT1 briefing, I was supposed to meet up with Lieutenant Walker of Delta, but no one from Delta was at this briefing.

It turned out that 3rd Platoon from Delta Company was at the time engaged in a firefight on the outskirts of Fallujah near the Cloverleaf east of the city. However, when Major Piedmont and I walked to the parking area, a driver and Humvee from Delta was waiting for us.

At Camp Baharia, we met with Delta's first sergeant, and thought that our scheduled interviews might be canceled due to the fighting nearby. Instead, they had five Marines ready to talk with us. They took us to the sleeping areas of the commanding officer and executive officer to be away from the busy company command post (CP).

Sergeant Travis Dean Madden
Vehicle Commander, Alpha Section, 2nd Platoon, Delta Company, 2nd LAR Battalion

Most of Madden's time here has been spent on security patrols outside of Fallujah, or providing escort for Marine infantry forces. He has twice entered the city during General Mattis's proof of concept patrols to the Fallujah mayor's office, riding at the head of the convoy in his LAV 25. "So, we were basically going into the mayor's house to see if we got shot at or not! That's what they told us." A large Quick Reaction Force was coiled outside the city in case shooting erupted. This QRF had about 10 tanks, 15 Amtracs (AAV 7s—Marine Amphibious Vehicles), and a battalion's worth of infantry Marines from 3/4 ready to come in and snatch them out if needed. He also outlined how the company was currently organized for combat.

Sergeant Madden entered Recruit Training in San Diego, California in October 1994. He originally trained as a Dragon gunner, 0351, and did his first tour with 2/3 on Hawaii. He later served on Okinawa. In May 1997, he received a hardship discharge due to an accident in his family. By 2000 he had gotten married and had a child, and decided to resume what he had started in the Marine Corps. He was able to return with his prior rank, lance corporal. He said that he was then an "old" lance corporal. He got on-the-job training as a driver for the LAVs, then was promoted to corporal and became a gunner. He became a vehicle commander (VC) while on a Combined Arms Exercise (CAX) at 29 Palms, California. Since then he has been a vehicle commander.

In September 2002 he deployed from Okinawa to Kosovo and Greece, went through the Suez Canal and spent time off the coast of Northeast Africa: Djibouti, and the United Arab Emirates. He was in the Persian Gulf on reserve status during the start of the war in 2003. They got word that they would land and join in the war. He said that they were anxious to go to Iraq. They landed in Kuwait in April 2003, and mostly did escorts up to the battle front so that the supply lines stayed secure. They only spent a month on this mission, then cruised back home on Navy shipping.

A few months after the end of that deployment, he learned of the plans to return to Iraq. He and his platoon sergeant were sent to California for Security and Stability Operations (SASO) training. (The lights went out in the building at this point, and I continued to take notes using my Maglite flashlight.) They received a week of training in everything from room clearing techniques to doing mounted and dismounted patrols. They then trained their platoon for several months to prepare for the return to Iraq. Sergeant Madden also explained that their company, Delta Company, was the only LAR company from 2nd LAR Battalion to deploy to Iraq on this tour. All of the 1st LAR Battalion from Camp Pendleton was currently deployed to western Iraq.

"They had put the vehicles on ships probably a month and a half before we came over. So, they sent an advance party that came, probably two weeks early, to off-load the ship, get the vehicles read to move." The rest of the company flew into Kuwait and got some briefings there and rode to Camp New York where the vehicles were already staged. They spent two weeks getting acclimated in Kuwait. The company was split into two groups for the move into Iraq. Sergeant Madden's platoon of LAVs provided the security for the headquarters element of the infantry battalion, 2/1. The trip into Iraq took two days.

The Army was still at the camp when they arrived. All of the units had housing except for the LAR company. They pulled up to an empty parking lot and one big tent at Camp Baharia. Each platoon took over a different area of this large tent. They were still in the tent, and the air-conditioning still did not work in this tent. He joked, "I guess at night the air-conditioning keeps the cool night cool, and during the day it keeps you from sleeping, or something!"

While the Army was still here, a Marine vehicle commander would go out with a section of the Army's Bradley fighting vehicles for the Left-seat, Right-seat transition. Two LAVs full of section leaders would also follow the Bradleys. "They would teach us how they were doing things, which was basically IED sweeps along the highways here, MSR Mobile and MSR Michigan." Two weeks into this, the Army would send an observer with the Marines as the Marines started to take out their own LAVs on patrols. They have patrolled as far north as the Thar Thar Bridge, and just south of the Baghdad Airport.

During the height of the tensions at Fallujah, the LAVs were kept on the outskirts of the city along MSR Mobile. They did security escorts for infantry companies moving to another part of the city. "We're not scary as a tank, and we're pretty bulletproof, and we have a pretty big weapons platform." The vehicles are well-suited to moving quickly in open areas outside of the villages and towns. The only time that they have gone into Fallujah was during the two proof of concept patrols to the mayor's headquarters there. I had personally watched the progress on maps inside of the RCT1 command post during one of these rides when General Mattis went into Fallujah.

He described one of these rides: "When they told us that we were going into Fallujah, we thought for sure it was going in to pick a fight, or to stop somebody from fighting. So, we were all pumped up about it. When they told us it was just gonna be our platoon and five other Humvees, that the general (Mattis) was gonna be in one Humvee and the colonel would be in the other Humvee, and the convoy commander, which was at the time, a lieutenant, it kinda made me skeptical of what we were actually gonna do. And then they broke it down, saying that the general just wanted to see if the Fallujah Brigade was able to take over the city, or control the city. So, we were basically going into the mayor's house to see if we got shot at or not! That's what they told us."

"We take our five LAVs, 'cause we were augmented with a fifth LAV, a usual platoon is only four LAVs. We had a LAV L, which is a log variant for logistics, full of reporters that wanted to see what we were doing." They drove along with the five other Humvees. "In among our section were the Iraqi police vehicles, as well as ICDC vehicles, which were full of their soldiers. So if anybody was gonna shoot at us, they were gonna shoot at them also." Madden said that it was to show the Iraqis that this was not an attack.

They sat around for about an hour before entering the city of Fallujah. He described it as more of a parade, with people out on the streets watching the vehicles drive through the main street. After they passed the Cloverleaf east of the city, there was either an ICDC soldier or Iraqi policeman facing outboard every 10 feet for the entire two-and-a-half to three-mile trip to the mayor's house.

General Mattis only stayed at the mayor's house about a half hour before starting to exit the city. Reporters took lots of pictures there.

While this was going on, there was a large Marine reaction force in waiting outside of Fallujah in case there were any problems. Sergeant Madden said that this QRF had about 10 tanks, 15 Amtracs (AAV 7s—Marine Amphibious Vehicles), and a battalion's worth of infantry Marines from 3/4, ready to come in and snatch them out if needed. He wasn't sure, but thought that there may have been a QRF on the west side of town, also (I could not confirm this). There were helicopters flying overhead, and jets were also on station.

I asked Sergeant Madden what the plans were if his unit had gotten shot at inside of the city. He said, "If we were at the mayor's house, the house has some barriers around it. It was up to the convoy commander, mission commander, to decide whether or not we were gonna 'go firm' and stay where we are, or risk trying to come back out. [Or] We stay where we were, just call in the QRF. They come in and help us out. Or, if we get hit on the way out, or on the way in, then how many vehicles were knocked out of commission would determine if we would get out on our own or call in the QRF."

Then he talked about the second time they went into Fallujah, about two weeks ago. It was a whole other infantry battalion, 2/2, ready to go in as needed on QRF. "This time, we did a lot of rehearsals," he said. "The first time was more a by the seat-of-your-pants. Second time was more of a let's prepare, let's do rehearsals, let's get it down to the 'T.' Everybody knows their position, know everybody else's position. So we did probably a week's worth of rehearsals, going to the mayor's house. Actually set up a mock mayor's house over on Camp Fallujah. We practice going down the street, settin' in at the house. Practice goin' down the street and getting hit with an IED, you know, reaction drills. We'd practice with an angry mob in front of us and what we'd do. We'd practice with calling in the QRF taking over. We'd practice with casualty drills."

The second move to the mayor's house was canceled about four times, but the rehearsals continued. "What we got out of it was that the enemy was in control of the city again. And … the Fallujah Brigade, or whoever it was that gave the go-ahead for us to go in or not go in, finally told us that they did not have control of the city. That, if we came into the city, that the bad guys just gonna say, they're gonna shoot at us. And they knew they were gonna shoot at us, and in return they knew that we were gonna return fire to get superior fire, and a lot of them were gonna be killed, die, or hurt."

After a few more days' delay, the Marine force was able to go into the city again. The ICDC and Iraqi police had come onto Camp Fallujah and took part in the rehearsals in a mock city there so that everyone would know what to do when they went into Fallujah. "We thought for sure that we were gonna get hit this time, because they came out and said they didn't have control of the city. So we thought for sure there was at least one person that was gonna shoot at us to start something."

Madden said that a lot of Marines from the company volunteered to take part in this. "So, we set up early in the morning. QRF was in place, with all their tanks." The LAV Marines were the only ones who had been in the city before, so they were chosen to go back in. He said that it was about 10 in the morning. They were led by Iraqis, either ICDC or Fallujah Brigade, to show that the Marines were not assaulting the town. As they went past the barriers into Fallujah, the streets were lined on both sides with ICDC and Iraqi police and uniformed people on top of buildings a block or two away from the street. Sergeant Madden said this made the Marines suspicious, since they were not sure who these personnel were. The Marines were not allowed to engage anyone unless fired upon.

"We go into the town, we pretty much know where we're going. I was the lead vehicle in the platoon, I was the lead vehicle in the last patrol that went into town. So, there was no chance of a wrong turn or gettin' lost. The street was wide open, no traffic. All traffic had been stopped by ICDC and IP (Iraqi Police). We pull up to the mayor's house, everybody goes in exactly how we practiced. We set in. We'd said it'd take us an hour for the meeting. And then we were coming out, it was real hot, two and a half hours later. We're wondering where's everybody at, how come they haven't come out yet. We still get word every once in a while, you know, 'They're wrapping it up, they're wrapping it up.' Probably two hours of wrapping it up, three hours total. Started gettin' the word to mount up the scouts, mount up all the people in the vehicle, lead again."

Sergeant Madden said that it was real tense for the Marines there, as they were waiting in the heat, and had no one to act as reserve. They were on alert the whole time they waited. They stayed alert, drank water and didn't want to look weak to the enemy who they knew were watching them. He explained that the three crewmen, the driver, the gunner, and the vehicle commander stayed inside the vehicle and monitor the radio, the weapons system, and the mobility of the vehicle. The four scouts who ride in the back provide security for the LAV, making sure that no personnel came close. The scouts went out and blocked a gate to make sure that no vehicles came close. To get shade and rest, Madden had them rotate one at a time into the back of the LAV. There were crowds of Iraqis gathering about two blocks away, but Madden said that the Iraqi police did a real good job of keeping them back. His Marines did a good job of staying vigilant and reporting all suspicious people in the area.

Once they got word to pull out of town, they followed Iraqi police who were carrying the Iraqi flag. Madden was told that there might be some "celebratory fire" while they were leaving, and unless there was accurate fire on their vehicles that they could not return fire. "I never heard any," he said.

Outside of town he saw the QRF waiting by the overpass, ready to get them if needed. Madden said, "In a way it was a letdown, preparing for action and the action never comes. But it was a true success, as in, nobody got hurt, and the general [Mattis] was able to get in and talk to the mayor safely, as long as he felt he needed to. And he wasn't rushed around or pushed around." Madden noted that this ride wasn't as covered by reporters as the first ride into the city had been.

For most of April and May, his platoon was attached to Kilo Company, 3/4. "We went on three missions, total, with them. Twice to Karmah, and once, not really to a town, it was south of Fallujah." They had been taking harassing fire—day and night mortar and rocket fire. The counter battery intel was figuring out where the fire was coming from. At Karmah, east of Fallujah, the LAVs were the point element for Kilo's assault. They moved up Route Chicago, and the enemy had erected a set of barriers (cement barriers, spike strips, dirt berms) near Karmah. An AC-130

Spectre gunship was flying overhead and found an alternate route for them to use. "I switched over to his net [the gunship's radio network] and he walked me through the bypass. Since I'm the point man, I do all the navigation." Kilo Company was following in trace.

Once in Karmah, they crossed two canals and Kilo dismounted and went through the town. The Marines were fired on. Madden's vehicle provided support for the infantry units that needed it. The infantry would point out where they needed to engage targets, and the LAV weapons systems can penetrate many walls with their firepower. The LAVs are "bulletproof" up to a 7.62 round. Even some RPG rounds will bounce off, or even if they detonate, not penetrate the hull. Kilo and Madden's platoon spent about four or five hours in Karmah while the nearby barriers were cleared.

To this point, his platoon has not taken a casualty in Iraq.

About two weeks later, 3/4 again requested Sergeant Madden's platoon. One section went with 2nd Platoon. His section, Bravo Section, was down to two vehicles and went with 3rd Platoon. The mission was to search a farm area that was the origin of RPG and mortar fire. What had started out as an eight-hour operation turned into a three-day mission. They continued to find RPG rounds, mortar rounds and ammo in the area. He said that there were weapons caches almost everywhere. Mortar and rocket fire subsided some, he felt that the capture of the weapons was the cause.

The next mission towards Karmah also involved 2/1, but was very uneventful. The locals told them that the enemy had left the town as a result of the earlier fighting there.

About four days ago while on patrol, they were providing route security along Route Mobile, from north of Fallujah to the area of the Abu Ghraib prison. "We do continual, 24 hour a day patrols up and down the route." 2/2 was also assigned this area. The rotation was six hours on, 18 hours off. "My patrol goes from 2000 to 0200."

A few days ago, he got word that an observation post (OP) under a railroad bridge outside of Fallujah was fired upon. Enemy inside the city were shooting at passing convoys. The LAVs went along with a convoy that was being fired upon, and they then went into an overwatch position to protect the convoy. Madden's vehicle fired about six HE (High Explosive) rounds into Fallujah, and shortly afterwards a Marine Cobra helo appeared and hit enemy positions inside the city.

Madden said, "If you've never seen a Cobra fire, that's the best laser light show you'll get to see!" One problem for Madden's Marines was that this convoy drove between their position and the city, making it difficult to fire into the city. When there was a gap in the convoy, his gunner fired at an enemy machine gun position and guys with RPGs there. Then all fire from the city stopped. They stayed there until about 0500 that morning.

Sergeant Madden said that the advantage of working at night is that you can see where weapons were being fired. (At this point the power to the room went off again, the air conditioner shut down, and the lights went out. We continued the interview in the pitch dark, with me again taking notes using my mini-Maglite, neither of us missing a beat.)

I asked how the Marines in his section were performing. There were only three who were not here last year. Some were even *Desert Storm* veterans. Most came into Iraq this time with Combat Action Ribbons. "Those that weren't under fire the first time, performed very well this time." He credited good leadership in the platoon for the performance of his Marines.

Sergeant Madden then reminded me that I had wanted to know how his platoon is set up. Before he did so, he said that some of my questions had helped him to remember many things that he had not thought about. "Me, I'm not a good storyteller," he said.

While on float, the platoon is big. There are six LAV 25s, and a Log (Logistics) Variant with the platoon, and about 45 to 50 Marines, big for LAR. He said a standard LAV platoon normally has four LAV 25s, with about seven Marines per vehicle. For call signs they currently go by color and number: 1st Platoon is Red Platoon, 2nd Platoon is White Platoon, 3rd Platoon is Blue Platoon, Headquarters is Black, and Weapons Platoon which has the TOW/Mortar-Variant LAV is Gold Platoon. Alpha Section for 2nd Platoon is White One, and his wingman, Sergeant Madden, is White Two. The platoon sergeant is White Three, and his wingman is White Four. White One is the senior sergeant, in charge of navigation, and he travels in the front.

Madden said, "In the brief before the patrol, there'll be a route discussed, and it's his job to look at all the [map] grids and make sure that the route is either navigable or to find an alternate route. And bring that up to the platoon commander before you take off. That's my job in the platoon. I'm the senior sergeant in the lead vehicle. After me is White One, the platoon commander, he likes to be in the front, so he makes the decisions if he wants to change the route at this time." Contact usually comes from the front.

There are four scouts in the back of the vehicle, and the platoon commander has an engineer among them to advise him when they come across an IED, or to check out a bridge before crossing it. White Four has the mechanic with him as part of his scout team. If any of the vehicles break down, this vehicle in the rear can move forward to repair the vehicle ahead of it. This way, the vehicle with the mechanic doesn't have to turn around and go back to repair another vehicle.

Recently the LAV with the platoon sergeant and Corpsman inside was hit with a vehicle-borne IED, so of late the platoon has changed the position of the vehicle with the platoon Corpsman riding inside.

There were 28 Marines in the platoon, broken down into seven per vehicle: Three crewmen, four scouts. The scouts carry the 203, M16s, and the SAW. They also have AT4s (Disposal 84mm anti-mech rocket), SMAW rockets, and the 40mm grenade launchers. Madden claimed that the LAV platoon has more firepower than a regular infantry company.

As for the LAVs themselves, Madden said, "The LAV 25 has the Bushmaster Chain gun, it shoots a high explosive round, as well as an amour-piercing round. Can flip back and forth, depending on how the situation fits. You also have a Coax-mounted 240 Golf, which is your secondary weapon in case you have a jam in your main gun, you have a machine gun right next to you."

The vehicle commander also has a 240-machine gun mounted next to him. The LAV AT (Anti-Tank) has the "Hammer Head." It has twin-mounted TOW missiles and a 240 Golf for the vehicle commander. The LAV mortar-variant has an 81mm mortar mounted inside the vehicle, so that the vehicle can stop, and the mortar crew is able to fire quickly without dismounting. The Log variant has the vehicle commander's 240 (machine gun). Madden also noted that there used to be an AD version—an Air Defense variant with a five-barrel 25mm Gal on it.

During operations, the scout team leader stands in the rear of the vehicle with his M16 and a 203 launcher on it. He is in communication with the vehicle commander. The M249 SAW gunner stands next to the team leader. A SMAW (MK153 Shoulder-launched Multipurpose Assault Weapon) gunner and a regular rifleman (with an AT4) sit inside the vehicle. When they dismount, they have a good amount of firepower to engage a bunker or approaching armor vehicle.

I asked if he had any "Saved rounds" at this point, Sergeant Madden replied, "I've talked more now that I've talked in the past three months." He then added, "I struck my cobwebs free there. I'm empty." We both laughed and I ended the session which took nearly an hour.

A Firefight in the Distance

While Sergeant Madden and I were talking, I could hear Cobra helicopters flying nearby, and about 50 minutes into the interview, I could hear what sounded like impacts of bombs in the near distance. Once the interview was done, I went outside the building to try and figure out what was going on.

There were two Marine helicopters, a Cobra and a Huey flying in the distance about two clicks away, and I could hear gunfire, or rather machine gun fire. Then I heard another impact and saw a large plume of smoke rising from the west. I asked one of the nearby Marines what was going on, and they said that there was still fighting in Fallujah that had started that morning about 0700. I looked for a better vantage point, and saw the commanding officer, Captain Shepard, on the roof of his headquarters building. I climbed up the ladder onto the roof in time to see another bomb impact in the city. The blast kicked up a column of dirty black and gray smoke. The Marines on the roof of the building cheered. Most of the LAR company was watching the fight from the tops of their vehicles behind the company headquarters. They were loaded up and ready to get into the fight if called on.

A lieutenant showed me where to find the Cloverleaf and the outer edges of the Fallujah. It was maybe two or three clicks, maximum. The Cobra and Huey worked together attacking targets. Then I saw a really huge black explosion and seconds later heard the blast. I learned that Marine Harrier Jets were dropping GBUs (guided bombs) on targets. That one had to be a 500-pounder, as it seemed much larger than the others.

It was very hot on the roof, but the dozen or so Marines there didn't mind at all. They knew that the air strikes were aiding Marines in a platoon from their company. Reports that had come in listed two Marines wounded, neither seriously, and five or six confirmed enemy dead by mid-morning. By the looks of those blasts, there are probably many more enemy dead who will never be counted because there will not be anything left to count. Captain Shepard watched the fighting with his field glasses, and had a TOW sight brought onto the roof for a better view.

About an hour into the fighting, there seemed to be a lull—the choppers had temporarily pulled off station, and we could still hear the jets, but not see them in the bright sky. Another bomb hit and more smoke rose into the air from the city. Suddenly we saw a streak of smoke and what looked like a bright orange-red flare heading towards us at Camp Baharia, and it went over the wall about 150 meters to my left (the south). It was about 150 feet in the air. Shortly after it passed over the wall, there was an explosion, and then what looked like a red flare kept going forward. After about two seconds, the flare exploded with a large noise. One of the Marines there said it was probably an enemy SA7 ground-to-air missile. Whoever fired it had no target—the choppers were not there at the time and Marine Harriers and Air Force jets were operating way too high to be hit.

During all of this, a platoon of Marine tanks rushed by the wall just on the other side of us, along with several other vehicles. I guessed that they were headed to the area of the Fallujah Cloverleaf.

Finally, about 1230, things seemed to quiet down some, and Major Piedmont and I spoke with the company executive officer (Lieutenant Walker) and arranged to ride back to Camp Fallujah. We also told them that we'd return in a few days to try to get the story from 3rd Platoon about today's fighting.

Back at Camp Fallujah

Back on Camp Fallujah, I went to the work tent and checked messages to learn that this morning a Marine Cobra helicopter had been hit by an RPG outside of Fallujah, and it had landed safely near Camp Baharia. Nine minutes after the Cobra was hit, the fixed-wing assets hit the building that had shot the RPG round with a GBU guided bomb!

The fighting had begun sometime before 0800 with some small arms fire on the 3rd Platoon's patrol, and also the Traffic Control Point (TCP) near the Cloverleaf received small arms fire and RPG fire. Both of these actions had been happening regularly in that area—an exchange of fire, and that would be it. The city of Fallujah is supposedly under the control of the Fallujah Brigade, and they were supposed to be disarming insurgents. But few weapons have ever been turned over to the Marines, and the city was not under the Fallujah Brigade's control by any stretch.

On my way to chow, I saw Sergeant John Leuba, platoon sergeant for 3rd Platoon of Delta Company. He was talking to a group of Marines clustered next to his LAV 25 parked on the street near the Camp Fallujah main chow hall. His platoon was in on all of the action earlier today. I learned that the LAR patrol went out at 0200, and was due back at 0800, a planned six-hour patrol. When the patrol received small arms fire from Fallujah, they fought through it and then turned around and drove through it again. Leuba said that the Marines from 2/1 fought well, also. Injuries to his Marines were minor, and he estimated at least six enemy dead. He was still "amped up." It was like a kid after a well-played football game. This platoon had lost two Marines to that VBIED in April, so they were itching to fight.

Intel reports were warning about a possible rise in violence as the end of the June arrived, and it becomes time to turn over sovereignty to the Iraqi Interim Government. There were supposedly Saudi suicide bombers in Fallujah, and they are/ were planning to hit Baghdad soon. There was violence in many Iraqi cities today, and given this intel, it may have been an opportunity for the USMC to hit known targets in and around Fallujah. I don't really know—this is pure speculation on my part. But I saw three to four large guided bombs hit the eastern area of the city of Fallujah, and this may give the Marines a reason to stop and search all vehicles leaving or entering the city—since the Fallujah Brigade does not have a handle on it.

A truly amazing day to experience. All day long I could hear the sound of the jets flying overhead. Hear them only, as they were very hard to see in a bright, sunny sky. I will try to get the details of who all fought and the results at the RCT brief in the morning.

Monday June 28, 2004

Easy morning for me—Online I checked the SIPR (Secure Internet Protocol Routing) site for the IMEF (1st Marine Expeditionary Force) brief, then all my personal emails. I checked in at the MHG Embarkation tent to get a ride to the landing zone (LZ) tonight. My hope was to get on the helicopter to TQ (Al Taqaddum air base) to interview General Kramlich. Staff Sergeant Sagredo from Bravo 1/5 was in the EFCAT (Enduring Freedom Combat Assessment Team) tent talking with combat cameraman Staff Sergeant Carter. I had interviewed Sagredo when I was out at their "Firm" base at Al Shahabi two weeks earlier. He and his platoon were now back here at Camp Fallujah. I told him that I would look up his Marines on Wednesday for some interviews about the patrols that they had run in the Al Karmah and Shahabi areas this month.

IRAQI SOVEIGNTY TODAY!

I learned that the government authority was transferred from the Provisional Governing Authority to Iraqi officials at about 1100 local time today. It was done quietly, I guess to disrupt the plans that insurgents might have had to cause trouble on the June 30th or July 1st. We'll see what happens.

I managed to get in a few unexpected interviews today out at Delta Company, 2nd LAR Battalion.

I contacted the executive officer from Delta Company, and got a ride over to the Delta command post area at Camp Baharia for interviews. Captain Shepard was my first subject, and in my notes I wrote that this interview of over an hour gave a great perspective of how the LAVs have been utilized in current operations in Iraq.

Captain Ladd Wilkie Shepard
Commanding Officer, Delta Company, 2nd LAR Battalion

Delta Company, 2nd LAR was formed about a year before the deployment, and was the only LAR unit from Camp LeJeune on this deployment. On arrival, the company was attached to infantry battalion 2/1 for operations in and around Fallujah. They first received hostile gunfire and mortar fire during a meeting of leaders in downtown Fallujah in March. By mid-April 2004 they were detached from 2/1 and placed in general support of RCT1. Mobility and fire power make the LAVs a much sought-after weapons system.

Shepard began, "I enlisted in the Marine Corps Reserves in September of '90, went to boot camp in May of '91, graduated in August. Attended North Carolina State University."

After his freshman year in college, he received an NROTC (Naval Reserve Officers Training Corps) scholarship and he left the Reserves. He was commissioned a second lieutenant in December 1995 and completed The Basic School (TBS—The Basic School for all Marine officers) and the Infantry Officers' Course (IOC) before attending the LAV Leaders' Course. He completed a deployment with the 13th MEU, BLT 11 (Battalion Landing Team) in February 1998. He next served as executive officer and weapons platoon commander with H&S Company. At Parris Island, South Carolina, he was a series officer and also a company commander. During his last year there, he was the aide to Brigadier General McMenamin.

In June 2002 he went as a United Nations observer to Ethiopia and Eritrea. He returned to Parris Island in January 2003, and then joined the 2nd Light Armored Reconnaissance Battalion at Camp LeJeune, North Carolina. Assigned as the battalion logistics officer, he deployed to Kuwait that month in preparation for Operation

Iraqi Freedom. He served with the battalion during the war, and assumed command of Delta Company in August 2003, after return from Iraq.

Captain Shepard said that last year, Delta Company did not exist. Delta Company was re-established in August 2003. "We started from scratch, no vehicles, no equipment, when we got vehicles and equipment it seemed that it was everybody's broken stuff."

He said that in late November, early December 2004, word came that the battalion might be sending the company to Iraq. The decision to send one LAR company for a seven-month deployment was firmed up in the December time frame. He informed his Marines about this at that time. He encouraged everyone to take normal Christmas leave, and he went to the Security and Stability (SASO) conference hosted by the 1st Marine Division. "I think I spent most of Christmas trying to figure out how in the world we were going to get ready to embark on the sixteenth of January, after returning to work on the seventh of January!"

Christmas leave ended for his Marines on January 7, 2004, and the company began to get ready to deploy. "The focus was getting the vehicles ready." They also received some vehicles that had to have the gun systems test fired on ranges. After a weekend with the vehicles, they packed up gear for two days, then had an inspection that Wednesday. On January 16 they moved their vehicles to Wilmington, NC, to be staged for embarkation. Then Captain Shepard started to prepare his Marines for operations in Iraq. He had sent some of his Marines to California for training. They developed a three-week training package: Two weeks of classroom work and one week at the MOUT (Military Operations in Urban Terrain) facility in Camp LeJeune.

With SASO training done, his Marines battle-sighted (BZO) their M16 rifles, and those with ACOG sights got familiar with them. Marines also got Wills and Powers of Attorneys completed, medical records updated, and all admin details taken care of.

Shepard said, "By the time we had finished that up, the advance party was headin' straight out the door. I believe the advance party left somewhere around the 18th of February." This group included his company gunnery sergeant, his ramp chief—Sergeant Flaherty, and some of the drivers and vehicle commanders. They would get the vehicles ready to move from the port to "marry up" with the Marines of the company, who would meet them at Camp New York in Kuwait.

The company flew into Kuwait on February 29, 2004. "All the Marines got on the vehicles, did SL3 (Stock List) inspection. We did preventive maintenance checks and services. They started runnin' the vehicles, runnin' the thermals, running the communications, going through all of their operations checks, and kind of making the gremlins happy. These are the types of vehicles you have to run, or they break."

Captain Shepard and his senior enlisted staff attended staff briefings. The company was attached to 2/1, in direct support. At the Camp Udari range his Marines did a bore-sighting with the 25mm guns, and fired all of the coaxial machine guns.

Around March 4 they moved into staging area outside of Camp Udari, Kuwait, with all of Battalion Task Force 2/1, and conducted convoy rehearsals. The company executive officer had flown into Iraq to begin turnover briefings with the Army unit that they would be replacing. One of his platoons provided security to the Headquarters and Service Company of 2/1.

Shepard said, "I was the convoy commander with the remainder of the company, for the Log [Logistics] Trains and Combat Trains, Second Battalion, First Marines [2/1]. We conducted rehearsals over a number of days, received certification from Division G 3 that we'd met all of the requirements to move north, and we were authorized to move north, on the 15th actually." They moved outside the wire on March 12 and began the move north on March 15.

They made the 400-mile road march from Camp Udari to Camp Baharia in about two and a half days, with two stops en route for sleep breaks. At Camp Baharia, his company gunnery sergeant had a nice big lot ready to stage their vehicles. The Marines established a temporary camp since the large Arab-style "hadji" tents had not yet been erected.

On March 19, Shepard, Lieutenants Nunley, May and Snipes, along with the rest of the battalion's company commanders went to downtown Fallujah to the Fallujah Provisional Authority (FPA) Council meeting. 2/1's battalion commander also attended. The company commanders observed how "One Panther" (the U.S. Army's One 504) secured this compound. Shepard said that he met with his platoon commanders in the back of a Humvee and was taking notes on signs of some complacency on the part of the Army unit that was getting ready to leave. He also noted a whole lot of things that the Army had done well.

Shepard said, "It was shortly after that that the compound started receiving fire. Mortar, small arms, and rocket-propelled grenades. Again, we were sitting in the middle of this open compound. All the vehicles were parked in the middle of this compound, and my lieutenants and I were sitting by our vehicle, talking. And we were saying, 'This is a good time to get out of the open area!' So we started to move towards some cover, some of my lieutenants were running. There was [an] Iraqi police compound just off to our right. I yelled to the lieutenants to stop running, that it would look like we were scared."

"Right then a mortar round landed around 15 meters in front of us. Exploded, hit Lieutenant Nunley and myself with some small pieces of shrapnel. Big black cloud, people on top of a building, watching. It was kind of funny 'cause we're just kinda moving towards the building, big black cloud, then all of a sudden all of these guys were running away from that spot. So we ran right back to the Humvee where we started out, just kinda stared at each other, picked the shrapnel out. Decided that we hadn't made any progress, we needed to still find some cover. So we ran back to the south wall, ran into an Army medic, [he] took a look at us, patched us up, then he left to take care of some wounded soldiers. So we decided we all needed to take up positions along the south wall, 'cause everybody had pretty much disappeared from back there. So we all hopped in the back of one Humvee, the high-back Humvee that had armor plating on the side of it. I was like, all right, we can't just all stay together. So we sent two lieutenants to another position, and myself and another lieutenant stayed right where we were. Between the four of us we had two M16s and two Mark 19s [Mark 19 40mm grenade launchers]. So the plan was, when the guy with the M16 gets hit, next guy picks it up. That was an interesting day downtown!"

Captain Shepard continued: "We headed out of there at a high rate of speed. Avoided any further casualties. That was kind of the beginning of the downfall here, here in Fallujah."

Over the next few days his Marines started going out with Attack Company, 1-506, (U.S. Army) doing the turnover with the "Left-seat, Right-seat rides." The Army unit shared its TTP (Tactics, Techniques, and Procedures) for how they swept the MSRs for IEDs, techniques for trying to catch those emplacing IEDs, and counter-mortar, counter-rocket patrols. Shepard said that it was good information for him and his Marines to learn, "Some solid procedures that we absolutely plagiarized."

On March 23, Shepard's LAR Marines assumed authority of the MSRs in the zone, and began their own sweeps. They conducted several patrols from then until April 3, providing security for Task Force 121. These were USOF (U.S. Army Special Operations Task Force) forces going in to hit targets inside of Fallujah. One evening they were hit by an IED as they were leaving the town. Shepard said, "We secured their Exfil [Exfiltration—or exit], secured a landing zone for them. They had some wounded that they had to get out. And [we] turned around, re-staged a majority of the company to go back in, and support them in prosecuting some targets inside of town, and give 'em some payback. Uh, that mission was canceled. Kinda stood down, and 2/1 decided to take the eastern edge of the town ... right up against MSR Mobile. We established some Traffic Control Points, north, south and east of Checkpoint 45, which was the Cloverleaf, while 2/1, Echo and Fox companies went through and cleared that eastern portion of the city."

After a couple of days there, his Marines came back. Over the next few days, they returned to and held the Cloverleaf several times. That ended his company's work with 2/1. They detached and returned to general support for RCT1 (Regimental Combat Team 1). They performed a variety of missions while Fallujah was being besieged by the Marines:

"First, we started off by establishing a Traffic Control Point to the north of MSR Mobile at the very far west of the Regiment's AO [area of operations]. We established a Screen Line to the south of Fallujah, with one platoon." Another platoon was near the Cloverleaf east of the city.

Most of his company was about four to five clicks east of the Thar Thar Bridge. That night they noticed a convoy rolling by, southeast of their position, just about dark. That convoy was ambushed between the two bridges in Saqlawiyah. Shepard sent a platoon down to reinforce the convoy and help them to get through the ambush. The convoy pressed through the ambush with no casualties and no damage to its vehicles.

"My platoon, 1st Platoon, pushed down, through the ambush, got to the east of the eastern bridge in Saqlawiyah, turned around, and staged. Sent 3rd Platoon down. 3rd Platoon drove through the ambush site, no contact. So 1st and 3rd turned around to come back up. And, they started taking contact again from the left side of the road, or the southern side of the road, MSR Mobile. So I grabbed my vehicle, my wingman, the two platoons and some Cobras [attack helos], and went back through the ambush site and, no contact that time. Kinda found that the air [helos] tends to scare 'em away. The rest of that night we didn't have any contact. We stayed at TCP 12. Put the company in a coil. And stayed there for the next three days."

Shepard said that the ambush site was active during those next three nights, and his vehicles would go down and "Pump 25mm rounds into it." He said that when Marines searched the area in the daylight, they did not find much there in the way of spent brass casings, a sign of a disciplined ambush force of anti-Iraqi forces. Only once did they find some bodies that had been left behind.

Captain Shepard noted that they began to get a myriad of taskings on about April 7. 2nd and 3rd Platoons were sent to assist an Army HET (Heavy Equipment Transporter vehicle) convoy along ASR Lincoln in the northern portion of the AO. He lost contact with 3rd Platoon for about 12 hours. It turned out that 3rd Platoon had been tasked to escort a civilian KBR (Kellogg, Brown, and Root) convoy to Tadji Air Base, and then returned with it through Baghdad. On the return trip the convoy was ambushed near Abu Ghraib. The civilian drivers abandoned their trucks. The convoy was taking hits from small arms, mortars, and RPGs. One section of 3rd Platoon got cut off from the rest of the platoon. That's when Delta Company had its first casualty: Sergeant Calendar. He was shot in the gut.

Shepard described Calendar's actions. "Sergeant Calendar, shot in the gut. Magnificent bravery from that Marine. Here he is, he's already been hit in the hand, with some shrapnel. And still directing the fire with his 25 (LAV 25). Cut off from the rest of his platoon. He's maneuvering his vehicle, he's talking on the radio with the platoon commander. He gets shot in the gut, and, continues on, maneuvering his vehicle to safety, maneuvering out of the kill zone. Tremendous job. But unfortunately, he didn't get to come back to us. He had to get on a plane, got evac'd to Germany. They did some surgery, and he's back in the States convalescing."

Captain Shepard found out that Combat Service Support Brigade (CSSB) had tasked his 3rd Platoon with this mission. The regimental S3 (operations officer of RCT1) stopped this kind of tasking after this incident, so that the RCT would have positive control over attached units such as Delta Company.

Shepard said, "We've done everything from running Traffic Control Points, to escorting convoys, to conducting raids." They also have provided direct-fire reinforcement, and have been attached out to "Just about everybody except 1/5." They were with 2/1 during the siege of Fallujah, and had a platoon attached to 3/4 that went into Al Karmah. One of his scouts called in an air strike on the tower next to a mosque there. The tower had been used as an insurgent spotter's lookout, and Marines observed weapons being taken into the mosque as well. One platoon was attached to Recon Battalion to help them with sweeps of some large areas. They went on a raid and captured the Tadji brothers.

Delta Company was at one point attached to 3/4 on a sweep of the northern security area of the area of operations (AO).

On April 30, Lieutenant Riles's platoon was hit by a Vehicle-Borne Improvised Device (VBIED) while conducting zone reconnaissance along the flanks of Recon Battalion. "3rd Platoon had been out doing the zone reconnaissance south of MSR Mobile, and, uh [he paused slightly], that's when the VBIED hit. Killed two Marines, instantly. Two scouts, one was part of Delta Company originally. The other was on loan to me, engineer from Second Engineer Battalion, Corporal [Joshua] Wilfong. [Corporal Scott M. Vincent was the other Marine killed] The back of the vehicle, the vision blocks in the back, kind of a very cheap aluminum bracket that holds 'em in place, which blew right out. That big vision block shattered. The block itself, came back and hit Lance Corporal Field in the head, cracked his, had a severe bulge in his head. Hit the Corpsman, with some shrapnel, some flying debris in the vehicle. The platoon sergeant who was the vehicle commander, flames, some burning to his hands and face. Whole bunch of shrapnel in his right arm, right side. And then another Marine, who was in the anti-tank variant, the loader's hatch about 200 meters down the road. That was a rough day for us."

"We ... once we got everything done, got everybody back here, at the base camp, had the chaplain in 2/1 come over and do a memorial moment for us. Something immediate to address it, ah, while we waited for the opportunity for a memorial service, more fitting memorial service down the line. I don't know that that memorial down the line was actually more fitting. I think that that immediate closure that came from the immediate memorial was the best handling that we could have had. And I mean all we did was gather all the Marines in the company around, the chaplain said a few words, I said a few words, first sergeant said a few words. Lit candles. Had a moment of silence. Picked up the sand from underneath our feet, put it in a container with some sand from where the vehicle had blown up. And that was that. And provided a lot of healing. A lot of healing."

Captain Shepard said that the Corpsmen constructed a makeshift memorial to those Marines outside of the Battalion Aid Station at Camp Baharia

The constant activity had worn down his men and his vehicles, so at that point they took about five days to do a maintenance stand-down. Shepard said, "We took about five days to really go through the vehicles, get a good LTI [Limited Technical Inspection] of all of our equipment, all of our optics, and our weapons, and the vehicles themselves. Give them some loving care."

He then discussed some of the raids his company was involved in. The first was the mission that never happened. The company had been attached to Recon Battalion. The planned mission involved an intel report about a "Mujh" staging area near the cluster of camps around Camp Fallujah. But as they began planning for the raid, recon reports came back that there was nothing in the area. There were some boots and helmets in an old camp, but Shepard said it looked like this gear had been there since last year [2003].

The next was a mission to raid a mujahideen training camp. "That was the LAR company proper. I had a platoon of tanks attached, and a scout-sniper team attached. I had a HET [Human Exploitation Team] Marine. I had two Marines from the Regimental 'Deuce' [S 2—Intel Section] shop. I had a military working dog team." As it was a fairly large objective that needed to be covered, they took a different approach to this raid. There were three different clusters of houses that needed to be searched, and a large palm grove about a click (1,000 meters) square that also needed to be searched.

"So what we did was take all of the scouts from all of the platoons and kinda formed them together into a scout platoon. They usually work, you know, 16 scouts per platoon. They usually work independently and usually by sections, so usually eight work together." Shepard had them rehearse for a couple of days, refresh their shooting skills. They then went to the objectives.

They started on the first of the houses and found some suspicious people, but did not have anything to really pin on them. "Found that the police chief from Saqlawiyah lived behind one of these houses. Just didn't find anything there." They swept the entire clusters of houses and the palm grove also, but didn't find anything. Shepard called it a "Giant Dry Hole." His Marines were disappointed.

They did their next raid with Recon Battalion, going south of Abu Ghraib, going after six high-value targets (HVTs, or sought-after suspects). "We went in on the battalion Objective Bravo, and captured one of the high-value targets. Bravo Company, First Recon Battalion hit Objective Alpha, and caught two of the four they were looking for. So that was a success. Marines were really pumped up about it. You know, it was done in the middle of the night, and they'd done a lot of preparation. Lot of rehearsals. Lot of night shooting with night optics, and things like that. And everything went down very smoothly, just like clockwork. And it was good. It was finally a good payoff for the Marines."

The company has sent detachments to work with 2/1 and 2/2 on small raids.

On May 10 and in mid-June, General Mattis, the division commander, went into Fallujah. Bravo's 2nd Platoon was attached to 3/4 when they did the "proof of concept" patrol into Fallujah in May. The same platoon was attached to 2/2 when it did its "proof of concept" into Fallujah in mid-June.

Captain Shepard said that, "Currently, we're working MSR security. Runnin' up and down MSRs Mobile and Michigan. Conducting IED sweeps, conducting counter-mortar, counter-rocket overwatch. Watching for IED emplacers." He said that the enemy has adapted its techniques. He said that they got good at emplacing IEDs but, "We got really good at finding them." Now one insurgent technique is to precede LAR's patrols and throw out the IEDs 10 minutes in front of a patrol. Another was to follow a patrol and emplace IEDs for when the patrol returns on the same route it went out on.

He also said that the insurgents have also gone to VCIEDs (Vehicle-Concealed Improvised Explosive Devices). They will conceal the explosives in an abandoned vehicle. "There was one that hit General Mattis's convoy. We just had one that hit us about two days ago. Hit 3rd Platoon. They were lucky. They had driven down, driving east on Mobile. They noticed a car in the west-bound lane of Mobile. They turned around. They came up the ASR, heading west. Stopped, dismounted some scouts to check out the area. Got to a canal. The scouts were trying to find a way around the canal when the vehicle blew up. Maybe the guy [insurgent] got worried. He didn't know where the scouts were, so he just went ahead and blew it."

Shepard said that for all of the IEDs and VCIEDs, the enemy has line-of-sight to them. "It's hard figuring it out. It's hard when something explodes not to duck your head. Or look at the explosion. We're trying to condition the Marines to not do that, because we're losing precious seconds. We're missing something that happens." He added that it was frustrating to be missing these triggermen.

"The Marines are amazing. They're doing extraordinarily well. I really have to hold them back in. There's no kickin' 'em to go out the door. They're excited. They're full of life. They enjoy what they're doing. I've had platoons that will go out on patrol, they'll drive through an ambush site three or four times until they run out of ammo. And I've gotta make 'em come back and get more ammo before they go back out and finish off the site."

His Marines have seen a lot of combat and a lot of different missions in addition to their usual reconnaissance and security missions. They have worked with 2/1, 2/2, 3/4, the Regiment, Task Force 121, Task Force 626, assisted Army convoys, worked with the ICDC highway patrol, and Iraqi police.

It is hot here, and the Marines and their vehicles run hard. "All in all, the Marines are very resilient. I've never known men like this. I always tell everybody that they're the best men I've ever known. There's not a day that goes by that I don't think about Corporal Vincent, Corporal Wilfong. And, the Marines here think about 'em all the time. And every time we drive out, we see that memorial, and we see a sign that's by the front gate, 'Complacency Kills.' Reminds us [that] you gotta stay on the ball here. There's peaks and valleys. Sometimes it's intense combat for days, and other times for weeks nothing will happen. And you go out there and patrol the same stretch of road day after day, hour after hour, in the heat."

"It's miserable, it's hard on the Marines. We haven't had air-conditioning here at our camp. Just got that taken care of, got that runnin' now. That's four months these Marines have been without air-conditioning. Tents are 110 [degrees] now, the tents are actually hotter. The headquarters tent's, a little bit smaller tent, doesn't have as big [of a] ceiling as the other one, and the other day [the] temperature measured 136. And they're out there on patrol, it's 108, the exhaust from the engine blowing on you the whole time. And the Porta-Johns around here, it's the stinky sauna. So they [the Marines] have no refuge."

With all of this, Shepard said his Marines are having the time of their lives. "It's a really good bunch of Marines. A lot of very good people." He said that feels fortunate to have this opportunity to steward these guys.

I then said to Captain Shepard, "I can't let you go before I ask you about last week, when I was here to interview some of your Marines. They were putting on a show for us out across the desert at Fallujah. Could you tell how that started, how that evolved?"

Shepard responded: "How it started. The incident in which you're referring to ties in with a number of attacks which happened across the Iraqi countryside earlier last week. How it started for us, the people say it's in response, their attacking us is in response to some air strikes that we've made. General Mattis had received some information that there were some high-value targets in and around Fallujah. And that Task Force 66 was gonna prosecute 'em. There were some precision air strikes that took place. And I guess about two days later, that was one evening, so it was the next full day, the next morning. A platoon of mine was at the Cloverleaf, heading south on MSR Mobile. Get just to the southeastern portion of Fallujah near the highway patrol station, when they started receiving small arms fire. They continued to push down, called Regiment, made coordination to find out whether or not any units from 2/1 were in the area. And whether they were free to maneuver to engage. They got the clearance, they started maneuvering into this, kind of open desert area between the city and the police station. And this giant car lot, semi-trailers and what not. It appears that some of these anti-Iraqi forces, anti-coalition forces had established some fighting positions underneath these vehicles. It took a while for 3rd Platoon to figure out where they were getting' hit from. They weren't seeing the muzzle flashes, they were just hearing the rounds come and hit the side of the vehicles. Figured out where it was coming from, they returned fire with the main gun, started doing some damage there."

Shepard estimated that his Marines were involved in this fight for about three hours. They killed seven of the anti-coalition forces. One of his vehicle commanders was shot in the arm and another vehicle commander received shrapnel from an air burst RPG round, and one scout was wounded going into a housing area.

Captain Shepard continued: "I sent 1st Platoon out there to relieve them. They'd been out on patrol for about 12 hours. Didn't know where this was gonna go, but it was early morning, it was about 7:30 when it began, so, now we're talkin', it's 11:30, 12 o'clock." Once 1st Platoon took over, they noticed people running back and forth between buildings in the area. At the same time, all of the eastern portion of Fallujah erupted. These forces were firing at coalition convoys, Iraqi civilians, Iraqi police, AKs at the tanks, firing at everything.

"Strange event. People just started to gravitate to this area. One RPG gunner would pop out and try and take a shot, and we'd blow 'em up with a 25mm round. And another guy would come out of the same building with to the same spot, and make his try at it. So, we tried to start working an air [support] package, get some air in there. Had a hard time talking two F16s on to a target, so I sent out three anti-tank variants [LAVs] to reinforce that platoon. Because by now, they'd been goin' on about three hours, four hours, and we're just slayin' cords of people, at these two buildings. We need to drop these two buildings 'cause they were holding up in there."

"So, pretty much marked [the building] with a TOW. We took a TOW missile, shot it in the building, pilot said, 'Roger,' he had a tally. He came in, dropped some 500-pound bombs, and leveled the building. Did the same thing on the second building. And then things just really all of a sudden just quieted down. That was a—that was an interesting show that day," said Shepard.

The LAR platoon then moved south of the city and stayed out there overnight. Things quieted down over the next few days. And the mayor came and spoke with Colonel Toolan with excuses for the actions. Shepard said that there was no "typical" day out here. His Marines were always called to do "something else" because of the capabilities that they bring with them.

One night his Marines were tasked with going to the Fallujah hospital to verify a reported 65 bodies that were supposed to be there in the morgue. It turned out that there were no bodies, and also that the hospital did not have a morgue!

When Captain Shepard issues an Operations Order (Op Order), and conducts rehearsals, he and his Marines know to be ready for events to overtake plans. He said that during the heavy fighting in Fallujah, he barely had time to make notes in his small green notebook before executing an operation. In looking back on the SASO training to prepare for this deployment, he felt that perhaps he could have spent more time preparing for combat. A lot of the company attacks and raids were done for the first time here in Iraq, without practice stateside.

I noted that I had to ask hardly any questions to get him to detail the events of his company. I then said, "Just one question at the end: Any saved rounds, final thoughts that you may not have touched on?"

Captain Shepard replied, "I think I can just talk for hours. I've been horrible about keeping my own journal, I'm just so far behind now. I try and do that, I try and reflect on each day. The only thing I can say is that, you know, I was at Parris Island. We used to have the 'Killer Tomatoes' come down there, all the 'red hats'

[Older veteran Marines wearing red USMC hats]. And so many times I heard derogatory comments towards the training. Oh, you know, 'We had our crucible, and the lights went out.' You know, things like that. There's a lot of concern from the old Marines that we weren't keeping the faith. That we weren't doing things right. And I knew that we were."

"But, I really saw it out here. I don't have a lot of really young men that have not seen combat. The vast majority of the company either's been here last year, with OIF1. Or they were in Kosovo. Or they were in Afghanistan. And some of them have been in all. I don't think that there has been a more difficult environment for Marines to operate. We've gone up and down and back and forth. We've been here four months. We've seen General Krulak's three-block war. We didn't realize we were in the second block, tryin' to think about how we were gonna help these people out. In reality, we're taking IEDs, we were rocketed and mortared every night for six weeks when we first got here. And then we went into Fallujah and went totally kinetic, and then pulled right back out."

"I don't think we've ever fielded a better group of warriors who were able to work independently to make well thought-out decisions. Young men, young corporals, young NCOs, that are, as General Mattis says, the 'Strategic Corporal.' Making decisions, avoiding the tipping point of turning things bad against us. Their dignity and compassion, killing only those that need to be killed, not becoming murderous out of memory for those friends of ours who we've seen wounded, maimed, or killed. To me, that's the closing thought, how, how tremendous my Marines are, the Marines are in general here, in the environment that they're in. Able to turn it on, turn it off, and shift missions and, it's just amazing. It's awesome, it's good to be a part of that."

"Sir, I think that's about it," ended Captain Shepard.

Sergeant Gaw Sekou Jones, Junior
Squad Leader, 1st Platoon, Delta Company, 2nd LAR Battalion

During OIF1, Sergeant Jones deployed with Alpha Company as a liaison/translator for operations in Liberia, his native land. On return to Camp LeJeune, Alpha Company Marines were given the opportunity to join the newly forming Delta Company to deploy to Iraq in 2004. He has been in firefights and on successful raids to capture high-value individuals. Outside of Fallujah, he used a sniper rifle to take out an insurgent about to fire an RPG.

Sergeant Jones joined the Marine Corps in May 1998, after spending two years in college. He entered a week before his brother, who joined at the same time. After initial training, Jones went to a sea berth, while his brother joined 3/6 at Camp LeJeune. Sergeant Jones joined Alpha Company, 2nd LAR in February 2002, and his brother joined the battalion later in the same year.

During OIF1 (on a Liberian Deployment) Jones became a scout section leader in 3rd Platoon of Alpha Company. His platoon then was sent on the 26th MEU (Marine Expeditionary Unit) with BLT 1/8 (Battalion Landing Team). After a year's workup they sailed for a Mediterranean deployment. So, while the rest of the 2nd LAR Battalion was getting ready to deploy for OIF1, his platoon was on a "Med cruise," and he said that the Marines there were not happy about this. They had done all of this training, but were not going into combat in Iraq. By this time, his brother was a sergeant with 2nd LAR and deployed to Iraq. Jones said, "Most of our focus was to come over here [Iraq] and do some real operations after all the training we had done."

However, "The MEU got called up to Mosul, we stopped in Greece to fly into Mosul." But only a few of these Marines got to go into Iraq before the offensive operations were stopped. "So I just sat at an airport for about two weeks, while the other Marines flew back from Mosul. And we got on a ship for Albania for some training down there in Albania."

After leaving Albania, they sailed through the Suez Canal and did training in Djibouti, then were called to go to Liberia on the opposite coast of Africa! Sergeant Jones is a native of Liberia, so I asked him how it felt to be off the coast of his original homeland. He replied, "That was one of the, I would say, the highlight of my Marine Corps career for me. So far, for me, it was an opportunity, be originally from there, and seeing what had happened. That was back there in 1990, when the war, the destruction and stuff, go back, as men from our country to help restore peace—that was a great opportunity."

He got to work as a liaison/translator, worked with maps, and gave briefs on what to expect in Liberia. "I had to go ashore for about three weeks, to see my mom and sisters [who] I hadn't seen in about 13 years."

Jones said that many of the Liberians he spoke with were thankful for the Marines to have come and helped to calm things down there. "When the MEU first got there it was like a ghost town, but after they found out that the Marines were there, [in] about a week's time, things were back, I won't say normal, but things were running in a new phase. I mean there were people out in the streets, taxis were running, and people had places to go and buy without worrying about getting shot at or beaten up."

This was all personally touching for him, to see things getting to some degree of normality in the country where he had been born. He even got to see a couple of friends from when he was in the first grade!

"I hadn't changed," he laughed, "I just grew up and got bigger. They knew who I was, they just recognized me." So I asked Sergeant Jones if he had a mustache (as he does now) in first grade. He laughed, "No sir, I did not, sir!" He said that he does resemble his dad, though. I remarked to him that this Liberia deployment was really a unique experience for a Marine to have, and he agreed.

Sergeant Jones said that he recently read in the *Marine Corps Times* that some Marine teams were being sent to Liberia to help train the military there, and he wanted to be a part of this if he could in the future. He said he would do it if his wife allowed him. I asked if she was Liberian, also. He said no, that she was from Chicago, and a former Marine herself. He said that this was a blessing. Because of her own military experience, his wife was understanding about deployments.

Sergeant Jones returned from Liberia in late October 2003, and Delta Company was forming up to go to Iraq. Marines in Alpha Company were given the opportunity to remain in the States since they had just returned from an eight-month deployment. But Jones volunteered to join Delta Company for the return to Iraq. He added, "Didn't tell the wife I volunteered, though. I told her I got *VOLUNTOLD*."

I laughed at this newly-coined word that I had not heard before.

Sergeant Jones said he volunteered to come over to Iraq because he didn't get the opportunity the first time. His brother had told him about his own experience in his 2003 Iraq deployment. "I wanted to experience it myself. It's as if, going to college, and earning a degree, and not being able to use the degree." He says that now, after five or six years in the Marine Corps, he finally got to use the training he had received.

OIFII

Delta Company left the United States on February 29, 2004, and got to Kuwait. On March 16, they crossed into Iraq. Sergeant Jones felt the significance of crossing from a peaceful area, Kuwait, into a much more hostile one, Iraq. "This is what you're here for. There's no turning back. You have to do the job, hoping to do it right."

He spoke about the first IED he encountered. It was on March 24, when they had to escort some forces back from Forward Operating Base Al Taqaddum. Along the route, he took pictures of likely choke points in the area. While he was putting his camera away, an IED went off on Route 10. He took a picture of the explosion that was about 150 meters away from him. "We got out of the vehicle, spread out, stopped traffic." No shots were fired when this IED exploded, and a team came to remove the damaged vehicle.

On the 25th, there was a Marine convoy going through Fallujah. They lost one Marine. It was an ambush along Route 10. On March 26, the killing of the civilian contractors took place. Jones's platoon was sent up to the Cloverleaf outside of Fallujah. They next went to Check Point 12 to set up a Traffic Control Point (TCP) close to the Thar Thar Bridge.

Sergeant Jones then jumped to June 6, his birthday. He said that he wanted to have a firefight on his birthday! He was now laughing about this wish. It was near Saqlawiyah, an area he referred to as "The Gauntlet." Convoys kept getting ambushed in this area. 1st Platoon was sent out sometime after 2400 to take care of the ambush site.

"That was my first fight. Even though it was dark, it was up close and personal—enemy about 200 meters away. And, just shooting at muzzle flashes that were coming towards us, taking care of the outfit. We drove down, stopping at the ambush site, drove down slowly, drove around. Reloaded, and re-uploaded the gun, and came back in and slowly, started firing again. And that was it for that night."

Sergeant Jones said that this happened for about three or four nights in this ambush zone. Army convoys would get through the zone and be ambushed, and 1st Platoon would go back into the ambush zone to deal with the enemy there. He wasn't sure how many of the enemy they killed, but said that on the last morning there, they saw a couple of bodies lying around. The net result of these actions was a significant reduction in ambushes in that area.

Next, they moved to a blocking position west of Karmah. They set up TCPs and checked vehicles in the area. Sergeant Jones said that the local Iraqis seemed to want them there. He said that there were about 50 to 60 kids around their vehicles. It was a Friday evening, and Jones and his Marines noticed a lot of people leaving the area. They asked the people if an attack was coming, but were told that it was the start of a holiday. At 0200 they got word to pull back to the company position.

Since that time, the missions have been mainly security and IED sweeps up and down Route Mobile. His scout Marines complained about the IED sweeps because it gets boring, walking along looking for IEDs. They actually wanted to get into a fight! Jones says that he doesn't look for a fight himself, but was prepared to get into one when it happened.

The company's first raid mission came north of Saqlawiyah, in a palm grove area where there was believed to be a weapons cache or mujahideen staging area. The platoon scouts were in charge of security and the searches of four houses. They found an Iraqi soldier and a police chief, but there was nothing there, no evidence of any weapons or training areas. He said that the local kids went with them as they swept through the area on line. The Marines then apologized to the people living there, and told them that payment would be made for any damages. Sergeant Jones said that these Iraqis were very understanding. He said that the Iraqis said, "We can't wait for you to actually take care of the bad guys. They don't use their area to fight, they go into other people's area, away from their families to do the fighting."

One local asked him, "Where were these guys when Saddam was in power? Why didn't they get rid of him if they wanted to fight. Why, after he's gone, now they want to mess the country up." This Iraqi understood that the Americans wanted to get things settled down, and then get out of the country.

Another mission took place near the Abu Ghraib prison. They got reports of several high-value targets (HVT) there. Sergeant Jones's team was given one house to raid. "So we did have about five or six days of rehearsals, just for that objective." When they got to the house, there were two older men sleeping on the lawn, and the

Marine flexi-cuffed them. The Marines then stormed into the house, and found the individual HVT in about 30 seconds.

"I was the first one to enter his room, and he was kind of stunned, he didn't know what was going on. So, it was good. He didn't put up any fight, [or] any resistance. We got him flexi-cuffed, and after 30 seconds we called the HET team in, the interpreter, and they didn't believe we had, had gotten the person in 30 seconds!"

The guy was still sleepy and dazed. The Marines then searched the rest of the rooms and the roof. They found several women and some babies. The interpreter told everyone to remain calm. The Marines found an AK rifle and the allowed 50 rounds, along with the proper paperwork.

On June 15, an IED exploded. Sergeant Jones had just observed several men by a white vehicle which looked suspicious, park on an Alternate Supply Route (ASR) near the Main Supply Route (MSR). The IED was set on an incline, and because of its angle, the explosion did not do any serious harm. The lesson he took from this was to never get complacent.

On June 20 near Checkpoint 84, a Marine riding in a vehicle spotted a 155mm round that was wired to a small battery. It looked like a trash tube alongside the road. They called in an EOD squad to disarm the explosive device using a robot.

He was involved in a firefight near Fallujah on June 24. 3rd Platoon was initially involved in a firefight there, and Jones's platoon had just come in from an overnight security patrol. As the fighting continued, his platoon got their vehicles ready to move in and assist 3rd Platoon, if needed.

(Note: I had happened to be at the camp doing interviews when this June 24 firefight was happening, and I told Sergeant Jones that the Marines in his platoon looked like they were getting ready to get into a football game as they waited around and on their LAVs. Those on top of the vehicles had been looking over the wall of the camp to see the fighting near Fallujah, just a couple of clicks across the desert.)

Jones said that eventually they got called in to relieve 3rd Platoon, and 3rd Platoon oriented them as to what had been happening there. 3rd had been engaged from about 0400 until 1200, and were physically tired. Jones took a SASR Sniper rifle, and used the scope to try to spot enemy shooters who were over 1,000 meters away. He was letting one of the LAVs know where the enemy was.

Sergeant Jones then said, "There was some guys that had the audacity to leave the edge of the city and advance towards us with RPGs and other things. Vehicles engaged [a] couple of them, and then one of them stood up with an RPG, which I called in, to Lieutenant Smyth. Said, 'Sir, there's a guy with an RPG.' And I take him out. [I] actually got down behind the SASR [Sniper Rifle]. It seemed like it took forever. He was standing up too long. I think it was about five seconds, but to me that was too long. Took my time, sighted in, and shot my round. And as I shot my round, he was shooting RPG almost at the same time. But my round got him, and he kinda jerked back, and caused the RPG to tilt forward and hit [the] ground. Exploded about 50, 100 meters in front of him. I looked back and he was knocked out, going around."

Jones said that the enemy fighters were about 2,000 meters away at first, too far for them to effectively engage the Marines. He said that they seemed stupid to come out closer to the Marine force there. They did try to spread themselves out among the buildings on the outskirts of Fallujah. He stated that the Marines killed a lot of these fighters. "I don't know why they kept on coming. Seemed like there were vehicles coming and dropping them off, and trying to pick up their wounded." When one vehicle came to pick up wounded, Jones did not order his Marines to engage them as he felt this would not be following rules of engagement.

Jones's lieutenant was on top of a vehicle, and told him that he could see an enemy fighter about 150 meters in front of them. Jones did not have sight of this enemy. "So I stood up, and there was a guy walking around in a daze. Lieutenant says next time he gets up, shoot him!" But when this Iraqi did not get up, the lieutenant felt that he may be valuable as an Enemy Prisoner of War (EPW). So Jones and two other Marines went to try to capture this Iraqi. When they got close, they saw one dead Iraqi, and this other Iraqi was laying on the ground, with shallow breathing. There were RPGs on the ground in the area, too. The Marines flexi-cuffed the insurgent, but Jones told the lieutenant that he didn't think that the man was going to make it. The next thing Sergeant Jones knew, they were under fire, and had to leave the position [and the wounded insurgent] there.

When they got back to the vehicles, a mortar round landed about 20 feet behind him. One of the Marines there received minor shrapnel wounds. Other mortar rounds were impacting around them. The Marines called in some air strikes to destroy some of the buildings in the area. His part of the firefight lasted about four to five hours. Things quieted down, and they stayed east of Fallujah until about 0200 the next morning when they were relieved by 2nd Platoon. While they were out there, they observed convoys getting shot at near the Cloverleaf. An Air Force Spectre gunship was called in during the night, and took care of the problem.

Johnson heard that just about a day before this interview, 3rd Platoon got hit with a Vehicle-Concealed Improvised Explosive Device (VCIED) as they were going up to check a vehicle. This is why he hates to check vehicles. One never knew when the vehicle was a VCIED.

The most common mission now was MSR security.

Sergeant Jones felt an important thing for Marine units that would be coming into Iraq was language training for team leaders and those who will be making contact with the Iraqis. He knows a few words that he tries to use on TCPs.

He works to stay alert and focused on each mission.

About the younger Marines out here, he said, "Sir, they are doing great." He would have liked to have more training with his Marines, he had only joined the battalion last December. He says that the Marines wanted to do more than

MSR security. Jones reminds them that they have a main job to do, and part of what they want to try to do is to change the minds of Iraqis to help themselves, and rebuild this country.

He hoped that the Iraqis would put down their weapons, and realize that the foreign fighters from outside the country were here to help Iraq.

Sergeant John Denton Leuba

Scout Squad Leader/Platoon Sergeant, 3rd Platoon, Delta Company, 2nd LAR Battalion

(Second Interview) Sergeant Leuba was in the thick of the firefight outside of Fallujah that I saw from a distance on June 24, 2004, and I used today as a chance to have him give me the details of what happened at that most recent fight.

Sergeant Leuba: "Couple of days ago, we were on a zero two [0200] to zero eight [0800] shift, conducting MSR security. We were driving down Route Mobile, Route One. Pretty much our area of operations was from the Cloverleaf down to Abu Ghraib. We were cruising up and down from there. It was about seven-thirty, we were closing in with the Cloverleaf when we took some fire."

He said that they had gone up to the Cloverleaf and turned around, when they began taking gun fire from a truck stop near there. They got permission to begin to assault the enemy forces there. They closed in on the enemy with massive suppressive fire. "We were taking some fairly good hits on our vehicles."

No Marine was hurt, and it was hard to see where the enemy was firing from among all the trucks there. Leuba was using a 9-power scope, and was having a hard time identifying targets, so he switched his weapon to full automatic and sprayed down some areas on occasion. When he did identify a target (enemy fighter), the enemy would quickly move to cover, and Leuba was not able to get good shots.

"I was just directing my SAW gunner on. Quite a few times a hail of fire would just come on us from nowhere, everybody'd be kinda ducking and weaving around, trying to figure out where they are, exactly. During those first 10 minutes, the only thing going through my head was, where are they? Where are they? Where's this fire coming from?"

The Marines pushed another LAV up to get better lateral fires on the area. The enemy began to move back from the truck area where they had begun the engagement. The enemy moved to an area that looked like a strip mall—little houses surrounded by walls. Leuba was also concerned about security to his rear, as Iraqi civilian vehicles were still moving along the MSR there. He said that his vehicles were not taking serious fire at this time. They had been taking AK and RPK (a 7.62mm Soviet-designed machine gun) fire, as well as RPG fire. Leuba said it was easy to tell the AK fire from the RPK fire, as the RPK fire is much more rapid.

"The first thing I see, is a guy running with an AK, and he's a good 1,500 meters away. Really made me mad that I couldn't hit him. Had my SAM-R, [M16 rifle with modified sight] but I hadn't re-zeroed. Wound up switching lots, just through firefights we'd been in, so then my LC nine nine's [a .50 cal machine gun] going away, which I originally zeroed with."

Leuba said that he was coming close with his shots at this insurgent, but wasn't hitting him. Leuba's Marines had killed two insurgents near their vehicles. The lieutenant wanted them to take pictures of these dead insurgents and their weapons. He then told Sergeant Leuba to go into a building where they had killed another insurgent.

Sergeant Leuba went to a building on the far right, with a low wall outside of it. "So, I took myself and my machine gunner, uh, my SAW gunner, Lance Corporal Walsh, myself, Lance Corporal Freddy Behr [sic] and Lance Corporal Wheeler. We closed in, and I never, when it comes to that kind of thing, nobody's ever dead. So, we went in tactically. I went in. I was number one man, punched to the far wall. Everybody else came in. I went to the corner, I swept, and let 'em know, hey, right side's clear. At which point, he said, 'Hey, he's still moving! Still moving!' At that point, the guy popped up, and fired up a burst of his AK, so we immediately turned around and started emptying rounds at him. I immediately pulled everybody back outside the initial engagement area, right there in that courtyard. And I thought we'd just go ahead and put some 25s [25mm cannon] on it. But the vehicles were a little bit far away from me to let them know what I wanted."

Sergeant Leuba was hoping to get some Marine infantry into the area, because he felt that his Marines did not really dominate the ground. There were lots of defilade positions that the enemy could use as firing points. At this point they were about 2,000 meters outside of the city of Fallujah proper. Leuba fired some rounds at targets (fighters) out of the range of his scope, but he felt that at least this was preventing any enemy fighters from approaching any closer. He did fire on a fighter hiding behind a wall about 750 meters away, and after that did not see this fighter again. Leuba felt that this was a definite kill. He remarked, "It was a weird fight, because it went from being so close to so far."

When helicopters approached, they received enemy SA7 (Surface-to-air missile) fire from the ground. He said that this shooting was intense, but not close to their positions. The LAV platoon was there from about 0730 until 1300. 2/1 was heavily engaged up near the Cloverleaf area. Leuba heard that there was an infantry platoon out of 2/1, and that morning they were engaged with three waves of about 25 fighters each time.

Leuba saw a Marine Cobra helicopter just after it got hit and was heading towards the ground at a 45-degree angle. He was watching for a secondary explosion. But over the radio, he learned that everybody on the chopper was fine, having only minor injuries.

"It was great having the air there. They'd come over, they'd [the enemy] start shooting at them, you know, they were the guys we were engaging. They'd [the helos] flare up, put some good missiles on target! Great to see! It was a pretty intense fight, but it wasn't ridiculous. We weren't taking excessive shots. They're definitely getting better with their mortars. We had mortars come close. We had three injured in that firefight." One Marine took shrapnel, a vehicle commander got a small piece of shrapnel in his neck, and a turret got hit, and the sergeant inside of it got some shrapnel.

That night another platoon from Bravo Company went out and got engaged in a pretty heavy fight. Leuba felt that if he had had infantry with them that morning, they could have eliminated the threat.

The next day, they set up a Traffic Control Point (TCP) south of the Cloverleaf and received some ineffective mortar fire. A day after that, while patrolling near Abu Ghraib, they went out to check out a stopped vehicle near them. As he dismounted from the LAV and went out towards this stopped vehicle, he saw that it was on the other side of a canal. He walked alongside the canal instead of going directly at the vehicle. Corporal Hall, on another vehicle, was approaching, and called up on the radio. As they were talking about how to approach the vehicle, "BOOM!" It went up in a large explosion.

"It was one large explosion to begin with, and it just twisted the vehicle inside out." Leuba told his Marines to run back to their vehicle. He was anticipating an attack with enemy small arms fire. Then there was a secondary explosion from the vehicle. None of his Marines were hurt. Had they reached the stopped vehicle, Leuba was sure that he and several of his Marines would have been killed.

"It was pretty nerve-rattling, because every time you see one, every time you do an IED search, every time you look in a vehicle, the thing that goes through your mind is that this thing can blow up any second. And when it actually does, you just, it reminded me of when we lost our other guys in that vehicle-borne IED, you know, it came so close."

This day, no one was touched, and they all began to scan the area to try to figure out where the triggerman was. A Marine questioned a shepherd who said that a man had left the vehicle there that morning.

Sergeant Leuba said that he was the only sergeant in the platoon who had not been injured.

Since that incident it has been fairly quiet. Now when they get calls to check out IEDs, he gets nervous, as they have to allow civilian traffic to continue. That was how the Marines were killed in the VBIED explosion in April. One Standard Operating Procedure (SOP) that they have changed was that now the scouts come out of the vehicle when checking suspicious vehicles.

Memorial Service for LAR Marines

After evening chow on July 18, I had the most solemn and sad moments since I've been here. Back on July 6, 2004, Marines from Delta Company, 2nd LAR hit IEDs/mines. Four of them died on that day: Corporal Jeffery Lawrence, Lance Corporal Scott Dougherty, Lance Corporal Justin Hunt, and Private First Class Rodricka Youmans. I made it a point to go to the memorial service held for them today in the Camp Chapel, since I had gotten to know many of the Marines in the Company through three interview sessions at their camp and a lot of individual interviews. The company was a tight, motivated group of Marines.

I entered the chapel/auditorium at about 1850 and sat in the back with Major Troy Landry of the EFCAT team. In a minute or two, Lieutenant Walker, Delta's executive officer, came up and said that Captain Shepard asked for me to sit up front with him. I was honored, a little reluctant, but he insisted. Captain Shepard shook my hand when I got to the front row.

The front of the auditorium had four small platforms on the floor, each with a pair of boots, an upended M16, a pair of dog tags on each rifle, and a helmet with goggles on top of the rifle. These are the symbols of fallen warriors. Behind these was a stand with the American flag and the Marine Corps flag. On the back wall was a large screen projecting the emblem of the 2nd LAR Battalion.

This was the first memorial service that I attended here, and since I knew many there, I did not feel like I was intruding their mourning. I could join with them and show my support. The Chaplain, Commander Stephen Pike, USN, opened with an invocation. Then Chaplain Lieutenant Scott Radetski, USN, did the first reading from Ecclesiastes 3:1–11. Company First Sergeant Sprague did the second reading, Psalm 23, and Staff Sergeant Woods did the third reading from Luke 9:51–56.

Chaplain Pike's Pastoral Reflection was comforting, saying that these young men who had died had given their all, doing what they loved. The life well-lived. After playing a recording of "Amazing Grace," friends of the deceased Marines came forward to read their remembrances of the Marines. These were simple, yet elegant and well-spoken memorials to their friends. As each Marine was memorialized, his picture appeared on the screen. The wife of Corporal Lawrence gave birth to a daughter four days after he was killed. Another Marine was the father of two, with a third on the way. The other two were very young men, just starting out in life.

Captain Shepard had the difficult task of talking about these Marines. This gave his small company a total of six Marines killed during current operations. Finally, Colonel John Toolan, the regimental commander, spoke about honor and how these young Marines had lived honorable lives.

Chaplain Radetski gave the Benediction, and then all sang "Eternal Father," a traditional Navy/Marine Corps hymn used when asking protection and in mourning.

First Sergeant Sprague then read a short roll call, calling each fallen Marine's name three times before going to the next name. He called the company to attention as "Taps" was played.

Finally, we were asked to file in front of the boots, rifles and helmets representing the departed comrades. I did not take any photos—I felt that this was a sacred and private time for the men of the company, and my words would be my memorial. It was a sad evening, but I think that it helped the Marines say goodbye to those with whom they have shared so much. Their sacrifice is not in vain.

2/7 Marines at Al Asad

Saturday July 3, 2004

I checked on transportation for tonight, and submitted an Assault Support Request (ASR) for a trip to Camp Blue Diamond in Ramadi the following week. I finished up both of today's summaries, packed and brought travel gear back to the EFCAT tent. Then I left with Major Piedmont and we walked to the MHG tent at 2200. We only had about a 45-minute wait at the LZ as our helos arrived early! We landed at Al Asad about 2400, and a corporal from RCT7 was waiting there for me. John Piedmont had preceded me to Iraq by a few weeks back in March. He helped me to settle in at Camp Fallujah, and we worked as a team whenever we traveled away from the camp to visit Marine units all over Al Anbar Province—a history "wingman" for me. He had been out-processing for a few days, and today was beginning his trip to Kuwait, and then home. I said goodbye to John and wished him a cold beer on the flight out of Kuwait. I'd be working with him in August when I got back to DC. John then went to the waiting area for a flight from Al Asad down to Kuwait. I went with a Marine driver from RCT7 who had a key for me to a nice room in the tin city of trailers. I hit the cot right away and had a great sleep.

Sunday July 4, 2004

Al Asad Air Base. I got up early and showered, had chow, then went to RCT7, and met with Major Zeman (S3 Alpha) and Major Adams (the air officer). I checked on travel arrangements to 2/7 and Korean Village. Visiting 2/7 was easy, as it's located here at the Al Asad Air Base, on the other side of the flight line. Echo Company, 2/7 was at Korean Village, which would be a helicopter ride later this week.

Two Marines drove me in a Hummer to 2/7's command post area where I met Master Gunnery Sergeant Wolterding. They had a room ready for me there. "Top" Wolterding had Marines ready to sit with me for interviews, and I went straight through with six Marines, from lance corporals to gunnery sergeants. By now, if I had a group to see, I first explained to them all how I would conduct the interviews, my purpose in getting these for History and Museums Division use, and where the interviews would be kept. This saved time when I met with each Marine individually. I also let them know that it might take a while before I met with each one today, but none seemed to mind waiting and relaxing for a change! 2/7 provided me with a private room where I could sit and conduct the interviews.

Lance Corporal Robert Anthony DeLuca, Junior
Ammunition Technician, H&S Company, 2/7

Lance Corporal DeLuca enlisted in August 2002, and in two weeks was en route to boot camp at Parris Island. In Iraq he ensured that units had the ammo needed for BZO of weapons and fam (familiarization) fire. He also worked to have outgoing units accountable and ready to leave when it's their time. He has been on several convoys and patrols in the area.

Before becoming a Marine, Lance Corporal DeLuca had worked at FedEx for five and a half years. He said that he got tired working the "same old job," and decided that he wanted something new. It happened in August 2002: "Walked in on a Saturday morning, told them [the Marine recruiters] just to sign me up. Following Monday, told me to come back. Came back, roughly at noon, lunchtime. He said, 'Well, we can take you down to Little Rock, couple hours away, get you tested.' I said, sure, called in to work, told them I wouldn't be there. Went and took my test, got sworn in the following day. Came back, none of my family knew about this. None of my friends. Everyone knew I was thinking about it, but never knew I was going to make the big jump."

What was supposed to be a delayed entry program turned into three weeks from swearing in to arrival at boot camp. The recruiter told him it would probably be about seven months before he was called up, but in two weeks he called and told DeLuca that he had four days to pack and go to Parris Island!

"It's been a wild ride, it's been a great ride," he added.

After basic training, he attended his MOS (Military Occupational Specialty) school in Huntsville, Alabama, graduating in February 2003, and then reported in to 2/7 at 29 Palms.

Rumors of this deployment to Iraq began in October 2003. Official word came by the beginning of November. From October to November, the pace was a normal, casual pace: Marine Corps Ball, Thanksgiving leave. But in December, the pace picked up. He would often work from 0630 until 2300 getting HESCO containers (Mesh barriers to be filled with sand or gravel) loaded for shipment to Iraq. Everyone had classes to prepare for deployment, and powers of attorney to complete. The battalion was busy doing lane training, going from 0300 until 2400 most days. DeLuca had a broken foot at the time, so he worked in the S4 shop, assisting with transportation and supply requirements. Training continued at March Air Force Base, and there he helped to guard ammo being used for training.

The battalion packed up and left for Kuwait in early February. Lance Corporal DeLuca said that due to the stress fractures in both feet, he was not sure if he would deploy with the battalion. Lieutenant Colonel Phil Skuta asked him how he felt, and said that he would try to keep him off his feet over here until his feet healed properly. So he was on his way on the last plane out for 2/7 on February 18. He said that when they got on the plane, "You could tell the people who haven't been over [to Iraq], the first time, you know, eyes wide open. Still playful, knowing that they're with the battalion, still looking, for what's to come." Marines who had been over in OIF1 told what it was like for them.

The plane stopped over in the Czech Republic before going into Kuwait. Once they landed in Kuwait, they had the in-country brief, then waited for the busses to Camp Udari to meet up with the rest of the battalion. No one fell asleep. He described the feeling of being lost at Camp Udari, "Not knowing nothing." They were looking for the rest of 2/7 in the huge camp. Everyone there was in good spirits, he said.

During the two weeks of getting the Marines and vehicles ready for movement from Kuwait into Iraq, he went to work to make sure that ammo was ready for everyone who needed it. Prescribed combat loads were issued. His workdays were very long. Because of his stress fractures, he flew up to Camp Al Asad instead of moving with the convoys. Once at Al Asad, he was able to get to an internet café and tell the folks back home that he had arrived safely. The next morning, he got up early to get familiarized with the base and find out where the Ammunition Supply Point (ASP) would be.

Army units here were happy to be going home after their year-long tours. He said that the Army units were great to work with, they were very helpful. It was an interesting time on the base as Marine units took over from their Army counterparts.

Then his real work began, checking with units in the battalion, learning the policies of the Wing, Division, and Regiment. At first, they did not have air-conditioning or running water out here. Over at the main side of the base, he saw many Iraqis working. After about two months here, DeLuca got to go out on his first convoy.

There was going to be a four-day convoy patrol east of the Euphrates River. DeLuca was told 30 minutes before the convoy pulled out to pack his bags. He would go as a driver. "It was great. I really got to see first-hand what it was like, to go out. To be a part of the 03 [Infantry], the actual patrol." It was dark when they went out, but they drove with headlights. They first went to resupply an infantry platoon. Then his part of the convoy went to a house suspected of making IEDs. He was told that he would help provide security for the vehicle. Other dismounted Marines went ahead to the house and searched the house and area.

They slept near an Iraqi Civil Defense Corps (ICDC) checkpoint by a mosque. The sound of the morning prayers woke him up. The patrol left about 0800 on its mission for that day: Looking for mortar and rocket sites. He estimated that they patrolled a 30 square mile area over the next two days. People waved at them as they drove by. In one town, the people said that it was the first time that coalition forces had visited them. "Little boys and girls were coming out, thumbs up, you know, 'It's good, good. U.S. good.'" Marines in the patrol handed out extra snacks from their MREs (Meals Ready-to-Eat) and extra water bottles.

During one mounted patrol, the lead Humvee got lost, and a little Iraqi boy came up and knew where to take them to get them back on the main road. There were also suspicious times, for instance once when a patrol stopped by a bridge over the Euphrates. DeLuca said that several Iraqis on mopeds drove by them. One in particular came back to observe them more than once.

More recently he has gone on a logistics train to the Combat Outpost at Hit. He said that it took several hours in total to get ready, rehearse, and drive out to the company outpost there. Once a week the battalion sends chow, ammo, water, and even delivers the laundry to Echo Company. DeLuca saw the austere conditions for the Marines out there, and this made him appreciate life at Al Asad Air Base. He even spent a full week there to do ammo inventory, but felt bad knowing that he would soon return to the relative luxury of life on this base. "They eat T-Rats [Tray Rations heated in the field] twice a day. No cold water. They just recently got their showers working." He said that the Marines out there took care of their own morale. When not on missions, they relaxed by playing football or soccer, or playing cards.

Currently Lance Corporal DeLuca was beginning to get ready for the turnover to the units that would be coming to relieve them in about two months. They don't have forklifts, so everything that has to be moved has to be moved by hand. He was looking forward to getting back to the States, but realized that he might return seven months after that.

I asked him about the IED situation in this part of the AO. He responded, "It always crosses your mind. It could be that time, you know, IED goes off in that convoy you're on. I was in the turret of this 7-ton [MTVR 7-ton Capacity Truck], I was there just for the extra space. And then, we're going down this main MSR [Main Supply Route], going down to Hit. Everyone's thinking, nah, it'll never happen to us. The thought's still there—it could be us." Then the convoy commander told him to watch out for fertilizer bags stacked on the side of the road. DeLuca saw them, and reported that they were right alongside the truck. That was his biggest scare. The bags did not detonate, but looked very suspicious. He said that when they first got to Al Asad, some mortar rounds had landed a couple of hundred feet from their sleeping area, but seeing these fertilizer bags on the side of the road was more disturbing. When the convoy finally got to the Combat Outpost at Hit and was unloading, they heard a big boom coming from the area that they had just passed 15 minutes earlier.

As an ammo tech, he said that he "plays" with ammo every day, but he always takes precautions. But he never thought he'd be going along with mortars in his path, mortars laying between the tires of a vehicle going on a road. Or seeing minefields along a road.

He said it's fun to go out on a convoy and see what's out there, but it is not fun worrying about IEDs. He said he'd rather be in an ambush than having an IED go off.

Currently he had a lot of responsibility with the ammo as his non-commissioned officer (NCO) was on guard duty. He ensured that units have the ammo needed for BZO of weapons and familiarization (FAM) fire. He also worked to have outgoing units accountable and ready to leave when it's their time.

When he first got here, they worked in an open area near the C-130 flight line. They loaded the ammo back onto 7-tons (trucks) and looked for a better area to work from. They found an old radar station that looks like a concrete Quonset hut about a half-mile from where we were now sitting. It had good air flow, two-foot-thick concrete walls that stay cool—important for an area where the temperatures get to 120 degrees. Cook-offs of ammo is a potential problem with high temperatures like that. They spent a couple of days cleaning it up, and when Lieutenant Colonel Skuta (2/7's battalion commander) gave them the okay, cleaned it up and began to unload the ammo there. DeLuca said that it looks like the building was hit by some kind of air strike during the Persian Gulf War, but it served its purpose now. There was an old radar control system inside that they wanted to move out. Also, it does not look like an Ammunition Supply Point (ASP).

Lance Corporal DeLuca said that the ammo techs work to prepare the ammo out of its cases for quick distribution to the units when they need to draw it.

When 2/7 leaves, he would probably be one of its last Marines here. As units prepare to leave, they will leave ammo here, and new units will draw ammo as needed until the turnover is complete. One thing that would make his job easier when he returns home was that most of the ammo was staying here except for some 5.56 ammo. He concluded by saying, "It's been a wild experience, sir!"

Corporal Samuel Frank Dyche
3rd Section Leader, 81mm Mortar Platoon, Weapons Company, 2/7

Dyche attended a four-week Arabic language course prior to deployment, and has used this skill during interactions with some locals. During an escort convoy for an EOD team, his truck was hit by RPK fire, and several Marines were wounded. One died from a bullet wound to the head. Within minutes, a Huey helicopter arrived to take the wounded Marines for treatment. He said his "stupidest" moment was when he reached to touch a large IED in a plastic bag.

Corporal Dyche joined the Marine Corps in January 2001, and said that he was honor man of his platoon. He also was top mortarman at his MOS school. He wanted to be a mortarman when he entered. He joined 2/7 and later went to Sniper School in Quantico, Virginia and went back to 2/7 at 29 Palms. During OIF1, he was with 2/7 on Okinawa.

Once they found out that they would deploy to Iraq, they began training. One part of it was a two-week Security and Stability Operations (SASO) course at 29 Palms. Marines from 1/7 gave classes on everything that they did in OIF1. Once in Kuwait, they did convoy training, as they had a 150-vehicle convoy for the move into Iraq. They also continued SASO training. Before the deployment they had been told that mortars would rarely be used, only in offensive operations.

The convoy north into Iraq was uneventful. They settled into tents at Al Asad. They even set up a rec room in a tent. It was cold when they first got to Iraq.

The Army was still conducting patrols at the time. He and another Marine squad leader went out on an Army patrol to the Hit area to get familiar with it. The soldiers showed them where they'd had contact and been ambushed.

On March 9, they began patrols without the Army. They were headed down to Forward Operating Base (FOB) Hit to cut off a vehicle suspected of carrying an insurgent mortar team that had been firing on the Marine outpost.

They were headed south when they took gun fire from some buildings. SAW gunners fired at a building. When they got inside, there were three Iraqi electrical workers inside who said that they thought they were being attacked by robbers. As Dyche had taken a four-week Arabic course, he was able to talk with them a little bit. (He said that since he has gotten here, his mom bought him some CDs and a book from Amazon, and he continued to study Arabic.) The Human Exploitation Team (HET) then arrived with a fluent Arabic speaker to talk with the workers. Dyche had his Corpsman give some Advil to the sick son of one of these Iraqis.

Since March 17, they totally took over from the Army in the area. There was still an Army EOD team available, and often Marines would run what they call "Samurai," or EOD escort when a team was called to disarm an IED or weapons cache. The unit that finds the IED will maintain its security, and the Samurai team provides security for the EOD team.

The first few weeks here, there were frequent mortar attacks at night, but fortunately none of the rounds landed near any personnel areas.

On April 2, they were doing an EOD escort to Husaybah, taking the team to a site that was supposed to have 30 or 40 155mm rounds. "We get to a little curve and we're going down the road, start to turn left, and we start to take contact from an RPK about 10 feet off the road. Just lights the truck up. I can see sparks coming off the truck, but I can't see the shooter, where he's at. I immediately stop the truck, and I jump outta the truck. Everybody else jumps outta the truck, set up security. I'm trying to get my assault team in there, found out we had two guys hit."

He sent the Corpsman to treat them. One was wounded in the arm, and the other was supposedly hit in the shoulder. "I went back to where he was layin'. Says to the doc, search for the bullet hole? You see one in his shoulder? [Doc] Starts to take off his Kevlar, and [the] bullet just drips out the Kevlar. Doc said he was hit in the head."

They called in a medevac, and Dyche said it was the most amazing thing he had seen. "It had to be two minutes after we got contact, we're calling in a medevac. And, as soon as we call it in, in comes one of the Hueys [helicopters]. He drops down, right behind my vehicle. And I'm waving him, he comes in perfect, comes in, slides around with his door right there, facing. Picked up my buddy and carried him to the helicopter, tell the crew chief it's a head shot, and the pilot takes off. I mean, not even five minutes after we take contact, pick him up, take him to Al Asad."

They took the Marine wounded in the arm to FOB Hit. A Combined Anti-Armor Team (CAAT) took over the mission with an AAV. Later Corporal Dyche found out that the bullet had entered the Marine's arm and then lodged in his hip. He was sent to the States to recuperate. The Marine with the head wound, PFC Dustin M. Sekula, did die. He had only recently turned 19, and Dyche said that he was a good kid. Dyche paused and then said, "I'm going to see his family when I go home."

As for the weapons cache, they did find 30 155mm rounds right behind where they had been shot from, and EOD destroyed them. The shooter disappeared into thin air, though, and the Marines never found him. Dyche searched the area and saw no footprints or shell casings.

"Shoot! That was harsh, not being able to get this guy that killed one of my buddies."

Then around April 12, 2/7, along with the rest of the regiment was sent down to assist with the offensive operations around Fallujah. Dyche said, "Basically the regiment just picked up and went down there." They did gun drills for two days straight to get ready for the move.

"We were told there were going to be 1,000 to 1,500 insurgents in one spot, Al Karmah. And, ended up, Golf Company, Echo Company, ran through the whole city. Got shot at *one* time, and people ran off. Other than that, they searched every house in the whole city—found nothing more than the norm. Couple [of] hospitals had some bloody bandages, and stuff like that. Nothing, nothin' like what we expected."

At another spot, Al Hillah, they expected to encounter 1,000 of the enemy. At the city, they had their mortars in one spot, AAVs to their right, tanks to their left. Golf Company went into a compound but only found kids and women there. The insurgents had left the area.

The mortar Marines were staying up all night during this time, waiting for fire missions from the mortar platoon.

On a map in the room, he showed me the movements of 2/7 during this time. The CAAT vehicles were moving with the dismounted Marines, and the tanks behind.

The mortars stayed about 3 to 5 clicks away so they could provide support if it was needed.

Corporal Dyche said that the Arabic course he took allowed him to personally talk with local sheiks and police chiefs in the area. He was grateful to have this ability. One thing that he learned was that many Iraqis had lost their jobs when the U.S. disbanded the Iraqi Army. They told him that there were no new jobs for these men to do.

His next combat was down south where they set up a Vehicle Check Point (VCP). A local vehicle came speeding through the VCP and got tangled in concertina wire and then hit a Marine Hummer.

Later, a big convoy was going south to Ar Ramadi and had contact just south of Hit. A 7-ton truck got hit with RPG fire, flipped on its side and caught fire. Most of the Marines inside got out safely and the convoy continued on its ride. When the convoy got to Ar Ramadi, they discovered that one Marine was missing—he had been burned in the truck at the ambush. This led to one of the longest missions that Dyche has been on.

They rode back out with a HET team to the area and talked with the local ICDC force. After returning the HET team to base, they escorted an EOD team to the site to blow up any unexploded ordnance on the damaged truck. Dyche and his Marines were there all day as EOD cleared the area of IEDs. On the way back, on what he called "IED bridge," an IED exploded as an EOD vehicle approached it. The explosion caused the truck to hang over the side of the bridge. Dyche said, "These two guys are the luckiest guys I've seen. They come out: One guy had a broke[n] arm; The other one had shrapnel wounds, shrapnel to his face, his arm."

Dyche said that it was only two wounds from five African-made (artillery-IED) rounds. They saw an Iraqi riding a bike on the opposite side of the bridge who they thought was the IED trigger man. The Marines "opened up" on him, and he took off running. Marines went into a palm grove and found a man there who fit the description of the bike rider. He was sent to FOB Hit to be detained and questioned.

Dyche and his squad stayed by the truck until a contact team came to haul the vehicle back to the base. His day had begun at 0300, and he got back to the base after 2000.

He said that the HET teams would talk to locals, and evaluate whether they thought that the tips about suspicious activities were legitimate. Once they decide to act on a tip, Dyche's team would escort an EOD team if it involved disposal of an IED or weapons cache. Dyche said that some of the informants were doing it for money, and he suspects that some of them set up an IED and then report it to get the money. Dyche said that some of the informants come up to a gate on the base and report their information there. It then gets relayed to the battalion command post. However, he said that only a few informants have been civilians, most have been either Iraqi police or ICDC.

Two nights ago, the squad went out and relieved a Hunter Team. The vehicles from that team headed back along the route that Dyche had just traveled. When the team got about 500 meters from him, it hit an IED, resulting in four WIAs. Dyche and his squad drove to the site and found the four WIAs and started to get the medevac to FOB Hit. Dyche then went to the local police station that was only 500 meters from their station. He asked why no one was keeping watch over this area.

Dyche then went to where the IED had gone off, and across the road found a plastic bag. He then did what he called "The stupidest thing I've ever done." He rubbed his hand across the bag, and felt a large artillery round. Another IED! He ran and yelled to clear the area, and to get EOD up there. He said, "That's about the closest I've ever been to dropping a load in my pants!"

Dyche said that an EOD Marine told him that he should have checked out the bag from behind it, that is, away from the road, because usually the IEDs were set to blast towards the road. If someone stays down doing this, they are less likely to have the blast hit them at head level. When EOD checked out the IED, it was made from a 160mm mortar round! He said that the truck that had been hit by the IED on the other side of the road had its entire console destroyed by that blast. Had this one detonated, he knew that he would have been dead.

I asked him how the four Marine WIAs from the IED explosion were doing. He said that they were doing well. At the time of the blast, they were in shock. They had shrapnel wounds, but should be back in the field in about a week.

Half of the 12 men in his squad are new Marines, straight from the School of Infantry. He likes being a section leader because he can teach them the right way. He said that they were a lot more mature now and have learned a lot. They react well to every situation that they face. "They are doing a good job." Losing one Marine hit them all hard.

I also asked if he had been able to use his sniper skills. He said that once he left the sniper platoon, he has become a mortar section leader. He wants to lead his mortar section. "I got the ACOG on my rifle. That's the closest I get [to being a sniper]."

His big concern now is ensuring that his Marines get the recognition that they have earned, especially those who have earned the Purple Heart.

Gunnery Sergeant Troy Antoine Barlow
Company Gunnery Sergeant, Golf Company, 2/7

Gunnery Sergeant Barlow said that the toughest thing about deployment was that there was no way to prepare Marines for the loss of life that they would encounter in combat. The younger Marines were especially affected by it. After returning from operations near Fallujah, Golf Company has been involved in training local Iraqi Civil Defense Forces (ICDC).

Gunnery Sergeant Barlow enlisted in 1989, and his first duty was as a security guard at the U.S. Naval Academy at Annapolis, Maryland. He served there for two years, and then went to 3/7 for about four years where he learned a lot about leadership. He then served as a recruiter in the Bronx, New York. He taught at the School of Infantry (SOI) at Camp Geiger, North Carolina. He then went to 2/7 at 29 Palms. And here he was now in Iraq a year and a half later.

During OIF1, 2/7 was deployed to Okinawa, Japan, in a seven-month deployment that stretched out to 10 months. He said he enjoyed his time there. "Because of the extended deployment, [on return] we lost a lot of Marines who were EAS, PCS, so we were down to nothing. At one point the company was down to about 50-odd Marines."

He said that around October 2003, they learned that they would deploy to Iraq. The company began to receive many new Marines just out of SOI. "Preparation was definitely a challenge when we got the word we were coming over."

There were lots of unanswered questions then: How long they would deploy; what gear they would deploy with and use. Would they take their own gear? Or would they fall in on gear in Iraq?

There were lots of training requirements, also. But it was tough to train without a fully staffed company. They did some things two or three times to make sure that every Marine was ready to go. As company gunnery sergeant, he had a big concern over the serviceability of the gear that his Marines would have. Some of their vehicles were not in the best of shape to deploy after just recently returning from the long Okinawa deployment.

The company began its SASO training, with Marines from OIF1 acting as the teachers. Marines from the most recently returned battalions shared insights about how some of the Iraqis appreciated what was being done for them, and how the environment there had begun to transition from the offensive operations to the start of the Resistance. These Marines talked about the culture and the individual Iraqi. This gave his Marines a little insight into the culture of the area they would be in.

They did lane training, allowing the company's Marines to learn how to deal with different scenarios, and then move on to new scenarios. Gunny Barlow said it let the Marines get proficient at it as they moved on. It developed their confidence to face unknown challenges here in Iraq.

However, he said: "The one thing in training, I don't think that, actually prepares you for, there's probably no way you can prepare for it, but just, the loss of life. Individuals that you're sitting right next to, a day-to-day basis, and then the next thing, that individual might not be there. Encountered a few casualties that we've had, a lot of young Marines that are directly affected by it. Because this individual was with them at SOI, or this individual was their best friend back home. That was the one thing there was absolutely no way to prepare 'em for."

The culmination of the SASO training came at March Air Force Base, with personnel acting as Iraqis—everything from town dwellers to "sheiks" and local "officials." Marines practiced setting up Firm Bases, rotations of security forces, contact personnel, etc. They learned how to spread load the responsibilities within the company.

After the intense training, the battalion granted what he called "max leave," and there were very few problems for the Marines as they took leave. Everyone made it back on time, many were even early. They were eager to go to Iraq. Barlow called it a "determined focus."

Barlow said that he couldn't prepare the Marines for the emotions that they would feel here. The first Marine killed in the battalion hit everyone hard.

Gunny Barlow said that the more senior Marines seemed to be able to handle it a little better. He speculated that it may have been because they had been in the Corps for longer times, and had often times made friends that they never saw again once they changed duty stations. It was harder for the younger Marines to "let it go" when a friend died. "In my mind the only thing that kept them going was a structured lifestyle. Waking them up in the morning, 'Hey, you're still going on patrol!' Don't give them the opportunity [to dwell on losses]." Barlow said that he wants them to continue working hard to do the mission that they came here to do.

Gunny Barlow said that when they first got to Iraq, and took over responsibility from the Army, they began to conduct business differently. The Army had ridden its Bradley fighting vehicles into the towns, and did not do dismounted operations. The Marines came in on Humvees and unarmored 7-ton trucks, and conducted dismounted operations.

"Initially when we got here, there seemed to be a rise in activity. I believe it was the way we conducted business. We found more IEDs within the first nine days, than the Army found in 45 days. We had a lot more interaction with the locals, the young children, the middle-age[d] males and females. And a lot of that part was due to their being able to see [Marine] faces." His Marines became known to people in the area they were working in.

"We started with the city council members, trying to establish a budget." This was in the town of Baghdadi, just outside of Camp Al Asad. Barlow described the political problems in the town—a very young (30 something) mayor who didn't get along with the police chief. After a lot of what he described as "tea drinking and cigarette smoking" at meetings, they began to hammer out some decisions. Many of the local leaders asked for money to get things done and get the local economy moving. But Barlow also said that often the leaders would use the word "I" when asking for a car, or supplies, rather than saying "we." There was corruption—often contracts that had been let out would not be completed. Barlow said that the local officials may have gotten used to money being given to them before the Army left.

The locals felt that the Marines were stricter and more demanding than the Army. But after about a month, realized that the Marines were there to help them, also. Barlow said that the First Marine Division's motto, "No Better Friend, No Worse Enemy," has been effective. Even after firefights, Marines would still give out items to children, and provide minor medical care.

2/7 participated in Operation *Ripper Sweep* near Fallujah. They cordoned off the area, and looked for anti-coalition forces. In his opinion, he felt that the enemy realized that it made no sense to go up against a large force. When Marines went to areas to engage these forces, the forces vanished. For about three weeks, the battalion was constantly moving, but had few engagements. In the town of Karmah, for example, where there had been lots of small arms fire and IEDs, but when 2/7 got there, the town was abandoned by the civilian populace, and any anti-coalition forces.

On return to Al Asad, Golf Company became the trainers for ICDC forces here. Battalion (2/7) set up the headquarters for the training. One Marine platoon went to help train an Iraqi ICDC battalion. That is where they have had lots of contact with Iraqis. Barlow said that the Iraqis seemed fascinated with how the Marines operated. It was performance-based training. Each stage of training had to be mastered before a new skill would be taught and practiced. Marines would teach small numbers of Iraqis, who would then go to their units and train the other Iraqis. Barlow described the Marines' training mentality here as "Crawl, walk, run."

Barlow said that corporals and sergeants would teach various skills. Many are former instructors from the Marine School of Infantry. Staff NCOs and officers also provided instruction.

"I went down and conducted a [rifle] range, a BZO range. And at the end of it, at the end of the day, just as Marines do, we're like, okay, it's time to police call, get all of this trash up. Get it out of here, put it on the vehicle, we're going to take it away. They just looked at me and said,

'Well, but it's trash! What are we gonna do with it?'

'Like look, you take it, you burn it, don't care what you do with it. But you will pick it up.'

'Well why? It's just some range.'

I said, 'I like the area clean. So you know that any time that Marines are around, if you get done doing something, just take your trash around, dispose of it appropriately. Burn it, put it in the trash can, something.'"

Barlow said that after about three days of yelling, it became a normal routine for the ICDC.

These Iraqis respected the fact that the Marines were trying to learn their language, and would teach them what they could. Barlow said that he has often come across Iraqis who he has helped to train.

The rest of the company continued to check the Iraqi forces at various checkpoints, and train them on how to set up various types of VCPs, ECPs (Entry

Control Points) basic fire team offensive measures, mounted and dismounted patrols, etc. ICDC (now ING—Iraqi National Guard) personnel who had been trained by the Marines would go to small units throughout the area and train other Iraqi forces.

Patrols in the area were now joint; Marines working with Iraqi forces. ING forces have been involved in firefights, and search vehicles at checkpoints.

Barlow explained how the training was organized. The Marines trained 11 Iraqis on the BZO course, and they then trained their fellow Iraqis in their company. One platoon from each Iraqi company was trained on fire team tactics. About a platoon and a half from each Iraqi company was taught mounted and dismounted patrols. He described this as "spread loading" the information to small groups so that they could train their peers. The trained Iraqi soldiers were now experts in that area.

"Right now, Golf Company isn't running anything, at all, by themselves. Everything is joint." Patrols through palm groves and cities are joint patrols. The Marines go with the Iraqi National Guardsmen, and pair-up just about one-to-one. They have done raids and patrols together, and check points also.

I asked about the equipment that the ING has received. Gunny Barlow said that it has been an issue, but that the Iraqis use some of the equipment they have in different ways from the Marines. Information flow is often slow from the Iraqi-manned check points. They needed to learn how to properly maintain the gear that Marines have given to them. Some of the vehicles have been driven hard.

Gunny Barlow said that there is a new Iraqi commander, a Colonel Faahd, and this officer was serious about getting his soldiers trained properly. "He's a demanding individual, he's a no-nonsense kind of guy. And, if he can just help convince his staff to be the same way, I think it'll be beneficial in the long run."

Barlow felt that some of the local Iraqi officers had not yet "bought into" what was happening with the training from the Marines. Also, the Iraqi non-commissioned officers (NCOs) are not used to the responsibilities that Marine NCOs have. They see the way that Marines conduct business, and Colonel Faahd has told the Marine company commander that he wished he had a staff as good as the captain's.

Barlow concluded, "One of the biggest things, sir, is my frustration, with the journalism, the news. There's a lot of good that's coming out of what we're doing over here. The difference between four months when we actually stepped on deck, and took over the area, and, the point that we're at now, no one sees that. And it's kind of frustrating when I call home, or the younger Marines call home. 'All I've seen is all this horrible stuff.' They're reporting the truth, but by not reporting some of the information, I think the American public is getting a slanted view. Of what's going on. [Of what] The sailors and soldiers are doing over here."

The battalion has built playgrounds, brought clothes to kids, assisted with hospitals. Barlow said that these good things should also be known about back home.

Corporal Christopher Michael Bowles
Acting Admin Chief for 2/7

On return from a 2003 deployment to Okinawa, Bowles was heavily involved in the administrative challenges as 2/7 ballooned from 400 to 800 Marines in a matter of weeks. The battalion sergeant major told the newly arriving Marines that they would be going to Iraq in six weeks. After arrival in Kuwait, half of the battalion flew into Iraq, and the other half drove up by convoy. Bowles also served as driver for the battalion executive officer in meetings with local Iraqi officials. Constantly moving creates huge challenges in keeping track of administrative records for his section.

Corporal Bowles entered the Marine Corps on October 10, 2001, and went to Personal Administration (PA) school after recruit training. He wanted to go overseas right away, but instead was sent to 2/7 and immediately participated in their Combined Arms Exercise. He was then meritoriously promoted to lance corporal. He next deployed to Okinawa, Japan where he worked in the admin section, but also attended a one-week long Jungle Warfare Training Course. He then did mountain training in Korea.

Around January 2003, rumors started to swirl in the battalion as plans for the Iraq invasion began. The battalion was extended indefinitely on Okinawa. He didn't mind being in Okinawa, and there was still a possibility of deploying to Iraq. He said that Marines in 2/7 were getting upset that they were stuck on Okinawa, and did not do much of any training. There continued to be rumors about going to Iraq. "We wanted to be in the fight as much as everyone else."

In June 2003, 2/7 learned that it would return to the United States. After block leave, a whole new command structure was put in place. Major General Mattis spoke to the battalion and told them that there was a good chance that they would go to Iraq. Rumors continued from September 2003 on, but regular training continued. Bowles attended the Corporal's Course at Camp Pendleton, graduating as honor grad. He met a corporal who worked in G4 who told him that there was a still a good chance that they would go to Iraq. Around the time of the Marine Corps Ball (early November), the Marines of 2/7 learned that they would definitely deploy to Iraq in the January to February 2004 time frame.

Bowles noted that as an admin clerk, he doesn't spend the time in the field training, but for several months his workdays went from 0600 until 2100 in the office, and the shop was short-handed. They did the lane training and SASO training. They also did a battalion Field Exercise at Camp Pendleton. After return from Christmas block leave, the training went seven days a week most of the time. During this time, Corporal Bowles became the battalion executive officer's driver.

I noted that there had been a massive influx of new Marines into 2/7 at that time, and I asked him what effect this had on the admin Marines in the battalion.

Bowles said that the battalion had gone from 800 to 400 Marines when they got back from Okinawa. "As soon as we found out we're going, the job of the S1 shop, we had to do a DSR, Deployment Status Report. Says, this is how many people we have, for each MOS. This is how many people we rate. We send that up to Headquarters Marine Corps, especially in a situation like this. We're about to get deployed, they'll start shooting Marines our way."

2/7 began to get "drops" (joins) of 150 Marines at a time. The battalion sergeant major would greet them, and tell them they were getting ready to go to Iraq in about a month and a half. "That added to our work all day, all night, because they'd come in at 2000, and you'd have to check 'em all in, you have to make sure they have orders, you have to make sure everything's ran on 'em." Corporal Bowles said that the admin section had to worry about Marines' Service Record Books (SRBs), make sure that all of their entitlements were in, and update next-of-kin information for accurate Personnel Casualty Reports (PCRs).

Bowles flew into Kuwait with the battalion, and stayed in Camp Udari for about two weeks. Half of 2/7 then flew up into Iraq, while the other half, along with the battalion executive officer (XO), and Bowles as his driver, convoyed up. He said that it was about a two-and-a-half-day drive. Once they crossed into Iraq, it was about a 70-vehicle convoy traveling north. This drive was uneventful. When they drove past Fallujah, the Army had the city blocked off, so 2/7's ride-by was safe.

Corporal Bowles said that on arrival at Al Asad, he took over responsibilities as battalion color sergeant, as that Marine had to stay at home due to medical problems. They did the turnover with Army's Third ACR (Armored Cavalry Regiment). The Marines had to follow Army PCR procedures during the turnover time. "The second week we were here, we had our first rocket attack … since then it's happened five or six times."

The battalion executive officer had to travel around the local area, establishing contact with the local sheiks. Bowles drove him into the towns of Hit and Baghdadi. During these meetings, Bowles would stand security outside with the rest of the Marines. During one meeting in Baghdadi, there was an explosion about a block away.

The XO would also go to attend school openings: Two in Hit, and one in Husaybah that was for boys only. He and Bowles also attended some playground openings. Sometimes they had to ford local streams to avoid areas with IEDs.

During Operation *Ripper Sweep*, Bowles drove for the XO near Fallujah. Bowles said that the whole RCT (RCT7) went down to Fallujah, and took some less obvious routes to do it. What was usually a two-hour drive took much longer. En route they stayed at Al Taqaddum for a night. The Combat Operations Center (COC) kept track of movement of all 2/7's Marines. At Al Amariyah, the battalion did operations and captured an HVT (High-Value Target individual).

In the city of Karmah, Marines found six daisy-chained IEDs before they could be detonated. Karmah was quiet when they moved through it. The battalion set up a command post outside of the city. The line companies (infantry) were searching the town, but things were quiet and there was no fighting. When he was not driving, Corporal Bowles said that he stayed in the vehicle and tried to sleep when he could, because he never knew when he would be moving again.

Bowles said that 2/7 did not have much enemy contact, had only a couple of PCRs to report, and no deaths in the battalion. When things quieted down in Fallujah, 2/7 returned to Al Asad. Currently Bowles does little driving and was mostly working on base at Al Asad. The XO rides in vehicles with the infantry companies. Bowles kept track of 2/7s Marines at Al Asad. He was in charge of awards, and up until about a month ago, awards were slow in coming. The Marine Commandant had recently said that the awards should be pushed through for the Marines here. Bowles said that pay problems are worked through an IPAC detachment sent out from 29 Palms.

There is an infantry company from 2/7 out at Korean Village near the Jordanian border, and their admin comes through 2/7's shop.

I asked about the newer Marines in his admin shop. There were four brand-new Marines, learning on the job. Many came without SASO training because they joined the battalion just weeks after finishing their admin schools. Some were also assigned temporarily onto camp guard.

Bowles said that sometimes there was a "Groundhog Day" feeling here, as he often had to retrain and reteach the same things. He has been able to get a routine to get in some PT, showers, and he also runs a remedial PT program for Marines who need it. Chow was good, and conditions better than most Marines expected.

I asked him if he was able to give breaks in the schedule for his Marines. Most of his Marines were able to get a day off once a week. He makes sure that his Marines get their time off to stay fresh. He concluded, "My job and my stories are not, probably as exciting as some of the others, but I do my job, and I do it well. I think we're doing pretty good out here."

I remarked to him that if he didn't do his job, a lot of things would not get done.

Sergeant Lorenzo Mathis Young
Communicator/Radio Operator, H&S Company, 2/7

The battalion Communications Platoon handles all types of communications, including radio, wire, and internet/computer connections. Young has only been outside the wire of the camp twice since he arrived by convoy, and worked with 60 Marines to provide communications for the entire battalion.

Sergeant Young joined the Marine Corps in 1996, and received his discharge in November 2000. He said, "I was out for approximately five months, when I decided to come back in, which was approximately April 2001." He had picked up sergeant while he was on terminal leave, but when he returned, he was a corporal. He worked as a recruiter's assistant while he waited for orders to 2/7. During his first enlistment, he spent his entire time at 29 Palms, California.

Sergeant Young was a cook with 3rd LAR. A first sergeant there fought to get him sent to communications school. He was now getting ready to take over as radio supervisor because one of the staff NCOs is getting ready to leave. He said that right now he couldn't be happier to be here in Iraq with 2/7.

He said that deployment rumors were rampant in the battalion, he called it the "lance corporal's network." Once word about the deployment became official, they began lane training and SASO training. They practiced patrolling, mounting and dismounting vehicles. They trained at 29 Palms, and then went to March Air Force Base for final training. They interacted with actors to prepare for situations that they might encounter in Iraq.

That done, they began to pack their gear over the next month. In dealing with a large number of new Marines in communications, he said that it was not a problem, but just a matter of getting them ready to come over here. He noted, "They came at a time where they were able to get their training, so they weren't too far behind." They got a good shipment of Marines for the Communications Platoon, and they now had about 60 Marines for the platoon. "They're doing great, they're doing awesome, even though they're new. Some are scared, but we talk to them and, it's almost time to go home, so we're happy for them."

He explained that the Communication Platoon is broken into parts: The radio side; the wire side; and the tech/izmo side. The wire side sets in phone lines and comm cables. The tech guys fix the man-packed radios and radios on vehicles. The "izmo" guys deal with data nets and computer issues.

When he takes over the radio Marines, he will supervise about 30 Marines.

After leaving March Air Force Base, they flew into the Czech Republic and stopped for about an hour, then flew to Kuwait and stayed there for two weeks. The battalion moved into Iraq by ground and air. Half the battalion flew up to Al Asad. Sergeant Young was in the ground convoy that drove from Udari, Kuwait up to Al Asad. The convoy was broken up into three parts, or "sticks," and Young was in the third part. His radiomen provided the comm support for the entire convoy.

Once at Al Asad, he participated in "Left-seat, Right-seat" training for about 10 days with the Army units that were here on camp. They observed what was working for the Army, and applied some of the ideas to their own unique comm setup.

"Some of the challenges? Wow! For me being a communicator, whoo! Trying to have everyone talk to each other. Finding loopholes. Sometimes comm doesn't work, depends on terrain, the weather, you know, this heat out here. Power grids." He said it took about two months to get everyone talking to each other. He explained a term "Loop Back." Radios away from the camp will sort of relay radio signals to radios further away. It's a mobile setup and the radios use the same frequency. They also used retrans, where the radios use different frequencies. To help me understand the concepts, Sergeant Young used the chairs and couch in the room to represent the different radios and how they would interact on loop backs and retrans.

He went out in April for Operation *Ripper Sweep* to help clear roadways for convoys that were coming through. He was in charge of communications on a TACC (Tactical Air Command Center), which he explained was a Combat Operations Center (COC) Mobile that controlled the fight. These were the only two times he has been outside the wire here at Al Asad.

As Radio Supervisor in Comm Platoon, he was also responsible for getting the turnover ready for the incoming Marine battalion that would replace 2/7. This included all of the records for the communications gear and ordering of repair parts.

I asked him about some of the smaller squad-type radios I have seen in use here. He said that the PRR (personal role radio) is a British-made radio that some platoons are using. The Marines also have a small radio called an ISR Radio that is used for intra-platoon communication. Some infantry companies also have small, privately purchased radios that they use to communicate within platoons. Sergeant Young said that these small radios do not interrupt the comm platoon's radios at all.

When Regiment decides a need to change the radio Crypto settings, the Comm Marines do it. Sergeant Young said, "I came over here with a bunch of new Marines, and they're all grown up, and doing awesome things out here. They're not only doing comm things, they're also doing security things. They're going out on security forces. They're escorting people around, and, they're just doing a great job out here."

H&S Company provides security on the base. So his Marines work both on and off the camp. They have also delivered playgrounds and provided security for higher-ups.

Sergeant Young again praised his Marines, saying that without them, he couldn't get the job done.

Lance Corporal Craig Richard Bowden
Machine Gunner, 81mm Mortar Platoon, Weapons Company, 2/7

As a formally trained machine gunner, Bowden's skills were needed for missions run by the mortar platoon. He has been on a variety of raids and convoys in the area around Al Asad, but had not seen direct combat action. Some missions allowed interaction with Iraqi police and civilians.

Bowden entered boot camp on June 16, 2003. "[I] Just had a blast at boot camp. Everybody always told me how hard it was, but, I always took the best, the best thing out of it every day. Really helped me a lot, becoming a man, things like that."

He graduated top of his class as a machine gunner at the School of Infantry (SOI). He then found himself in the fleet the day before Thanksgiving. He got to go home on Christmas leave, and when he returned, 2/7 began lane training and SASO. Corporal Bowden was at first assigned to the CAAT platoon, "Killer Two," and he learned a lot about Marine Corps leadership and the Marines in the platoon. Along with several other Marines, he was selected to be part of a squad to accompany the battalion commander and VIPs.

About a week before deploying to Iraq, battalion decided that it needed machine gunners to be a part of the Quick Reaction Force (QRF), which was created from the 81mm mortar platoon. As a school-trained machine gunner, he was selected and transferred to the 81mm mortar platoon/QRF. So, after only three months in the fleet, Bowden found himself in Iraq.

He left the United States on February 12 from March Air Force Base, describing it as a long, long, flight. It was a commercial 747 jet, not a military transport. After an hour-long stop in Prague, the jet continued on an eight-hour flight to Kuwait. In Kuwait, they received Rules of Engagement briefs and went to Camp Udari. They spent about two weeks at the camp. He did PT every day except Sundays, and thought the chow hall was excellent. The battalion also reviewed lane training and did convoy rehearsals. Marines who had wartime experience shared their down-to-earth combat experiences.

At the end of February, they loaded up onto vehicles at Camp Udari, did a few last rehearsals, got intel briefs, and had a 24-hour stand-down. They then drove 12 hours to the Iraqi border. Corporal Bowden saw his first camels outside of a zoo during this drive. After a night on the border, they got up about 0400 and then went into Iraq. They stopped at a small camp en route. During this drive, he was part of the assault element.

They arrived at Al Asad, and got to know the area of operations near the base. The Army began to load up for leaving about 10 days after the Marines arrived. Bowden participated in "Samurai" operations, which was two days on extra security patrols, or to reinforce other patrols in the area, then two days on QRF, and two days of stand-down to rest and recover. Bowden said that mainly when he went on Samurai it was to escort EOD when they went out to dispose of IEDs or UXO (Unexploded Ordnance) piles. Also, it was sometimes to bring supplies to FOB Hit.

The first mission he went out on was to escort fuel trucks bringing fuel to FOB Hit. On an EOD mission there was an IED made out of a propane tank and gunpowder. "It was the first time I had seen an explosion that wasn't fireworks, or something like that. It was kind of cool."

"Shogun" was the name for the QRF. Another platoon from the company was hit by an ambush along the side of the road, and Bowden lost one of his best friends from SOI. The ambush consisted of an AK-47 and an RPK. "I just remember them coming in after the mission, about two o'clock in the morning. Getting woken up, them telling me about my friend, because they knew I was really good friends with him."

Bowden knew that he had a job to do while he was here. His section often escorts Navy Seals to provide security while the Seals did cordon and knock operations.

Sometimes on Samurai they themselves go on cordon and knocks. Bowden got to go on one raid at the home of a former Iraqi general as part of the breaching team. They found weapons, but missed catching the HVT general they were after.

He said that the schedule for Samurai, Shogun, and CAAT squad was changed about three weeks ago: Now each assignment was for seven days, instead of two days. He got to go out on patrols and interact with the Iraqi people. However, one recent mission involved going out after an IED explosion to look for the remains of Marines who were killed. While on the mission, an Iraqi farmer offered the Marines some produce that he had grown. Kids came out and played around with the Marines. Then later, Bowden learned that one of the Marines killed by that IED was one of his best friends from boot camp.

On his second patrol out, he got to get some pictures taken with some Iraqi children, and showed more Iraqis that the Marines were there to help. A boring patrol was an IED sweep along Route Bronze, and they stopped at a couple of Iraqi police stations. He said that the police try out their English skills on the Marines, and compare family pictures.

At a police station in Hit, he traded for some Iraqi cigarettes. And some of the police there offered them whiskey, which the Marines had to turn down!

Lance Corporal Bowden said that the worst missions for him have been the ones he has had to do with little sleep, or for extended times. One patrol that was escorting an EOD team had received small arms fire and mortar fire. He said that the enemy mortar tubes were so close he could hear them dropping the rounds into the tubes. He had stopped for a moment to adjust his gear when a piece of shrapnel from a grenade whizzed by his head. "It was probably a good thing that I stopped to adjust my gear, because I probably would've been hit by that shrapnel on the side of my face otherwise."

Bowden said that when he was down at Echo Company's base (outside of Hit) as part of a QRF for the company, the best thing about it was that the waiting lines for the internet and phone were really short! It was always guaranteed that he could get on and talk to his family.

Just about as Lance Corporal Bowden was wrapping up, a Marine knocked on the door, and Bowden had to leave on a mission.

Chow with 2/7's Commanding Officer

When I got done the interviews today, I went to the 2/7 chow hall, and sat with Lieutenant Colonel Phil Skuta, 2/7's very calm battalion commander. He seemed genuinely interested in the history program. The food was good, and I was very hungry on top of it, so it tasted even better.

After our meal, I sat in on Skuta's battalion commander's evening brief. His staff sections all reported using PowerPoint slides projected onto a screen. Lieutenant Colonel Skuta had a professional, relaxed way of running the meeting. The officers and staff NCOs were eager to have the right information for the colonel. He held briefs at 0800 and 1830 every day. A reporter from the *Los Angeles Times*, John Bowser, a former Marine (Vietnam era) himself, chatted with me for a few minutes, and asked if he could *interview me* (!) the next day. I agreed to meet him in front of the battalion headquarters at 0715 and do the interview during breakfast.

Monday July 5, 2004

I met the *LA Times* reporter John Bowser outside of 2/7s chow hall and did the interview with him as we ate breakfast together. He was intrigued that a high school history teacher would be doing the field history work. We'll see if it ever appears in the *LA Times*! (To my knowledge it never did.) He asked if he could sit in on one of MY interviews and get a couple of photos. I readily agreed.

I attended Lieutenant Colonel Skuta's morning brief at 0800. Again, professional and well-paced. All staff got right to the point. Afterwards, back to interviews—I got four in this morning, a gunny, lieutenant, captain and a major. More emphasis on civil affairs and intel than on combat actions in these interviews.

Captain David Wendell Palmer
S2 Officer, 2/7

The constant presence of Marines in the area surrounding Al Asad has provided the battalion intelligence officer with lots of information from locals. His team gathers information for Marine units to conduct operations locally. Workdays are long, but his Marines remained motivated.

Captain Palmer began as a Marine reservist, completed the ten-week Officers' Candidate School (OCS) program and received his commission in 1997. He went to The Basic School (TBS) in June 1998 and completed the Signals Intelligence Course. He served two and a half years with 2nd Radio Battalion at Camp LeJeune. In 2002 he trained at the MAGTF Intelligence Officers' Course. He joined 2/7 in May 2002.

In August 2002, 2/7, deployed to Okinawa, a deployment that extended from six months to 10 months due to the start of Operation *Iraqi Freedom*.

As the battalion intelligence officer he explained, "Mostly we collect information from various sources in the battalion, and we have many attachments now, in support of the battalion task force." They fuse this information into useful products that they provide to the elements of the battalion, adjacent units, and higher headquarters. They also provide information for force protection. Captain Palmer also served as security manager to safeguard information and personnel with access to it. Twice a day he produces intelligence briefs. Weekly they conduct "target meetings," where they take information gathered the previous week and determine the best way to use this information. He uses the assets available to develop intelligence for the SASO environment.

To prepare for this deployment to Iraq, his section began to plan how they would gather and use information. To deal with local Iraqi civilian, police and military officials, they developed reporting formats. The Army's Third Squadron from the Third Armored Cavalry Regiment (ACR) was in the Al Asad area, and Captain Palmer established contact with them prior to 2/7 arriving in Iraq. The 3rd ACR also left computer files and data bases here.

On arrival, his Marines met with, and shadowed the Army personnel here. They also went on patrols to get a feel for the area of operations over a two-week time period. Captain Palmer attended the 3rd ACR's meetings to help him understand the area. They did "Left-seat, Right-seat" familiarization, too. They were comfortable when the Army left on about March 10.

With the Army gone, the local enemy began to test the Marines. The Marines expected that this would happen. The enemy studied the Marine battalion's TTP (Tactics, Techniques, and Procedures).

The Intel Section conducts twice a week Targeting Meetings, attended by the battalion commander, the operations officer, the officer in charge of the Human Exploitation Team (HET), a representative from the Civil Affairs Team, a representative from Information Operations (IO), members from Special Forces, and when possible, the infantry company commanders.

Captain Palmer has 10 Marines in his section, most of them augments. Two of them were Marine reservists. The 10 were spread out into different areas. One was with Fox Company operating with 1st LAR. Some have operated at FOB Hit. He explained that the towns in the area had varying degrees of cooperation with the Marine forces.

When asked if he saw any trends developing in the recent May to June time frame, he responded, "For the most part, all the way across the board, we've seen successes." There has been a general decline in the amount of enemy activity, especially when compared with events in April. He said that the enemy had attempted to use significant dates for activities, for instance, April 9 was the one-year anniversary of the fall of Baghdad, and that was when the insurgency heated up this year. The enemy used stand-off tactics. Marines sent out regular patrols day and night, and have been able to defeat the enemy on many fronts.

The turnover of sovereignty was a week old at the time of this interview, and Captain Palmer said that there had not been any significant disruptive events since the new Iraqi government took over. There had been an expectation that the insurgents would try to disrupt Iraqi security forces, take over government buildings or hospitals, or critical resources such as water treatment plants or electrical generation facilities. None has happened to date.

Palmer said that some locals have shared information with them through various methods, not always in public. Often time patrols gather information, or Iraqis send it in by phone or by coming onto the bases. The Marines ensure that the providers of this information are not made public. He said that there is such a constant presence of Marines in the area of operations that it makes it easy to talk with merchants, police, and people on the street. It can look like they are just chatting with the Marines. Often intel specialists go out with squads. "We stress to the Marines and sailors that anyone can collect information." He added that now that the Marines know what is normal in the area of operations, they can become more observant and realize when things are not normal at various times of the day.

Captain Palmer said that his section has worked well together. They have put in lots of long hours, 12 on, 12 off. This translates into 15 hours a day with turnover and briefings. His Marines have stayed motivated. They were now finding out what their responsibilities are now that the Iraqis have taken on more responsibility.

Last year in Okinawa, Captain Palmer had only a four-man section, and his focus was on terrorist groups operating in Southeast Asia, and studying the countries in that part of the world. Force protection was a big issue then, too. Now he has many more sources of information in an active situation, and is generating intelligence products in his section. They push information up, as well as use products provided to them.

The Tactical Fusion Center has been stood up at the MEF level to generate intelligence. Captain Palmer can access this information on a regular basis.

He was now beginning to prepare for his own turnover with incoming units. Palmer said that it will be a big task because there is so much information to give to incoming units. He wanted to help the relieving unit to better understand the area of operations. A Marine Reserve unit would be coming in, and there will also be a different regimental headquarters.

"The mission that we've had here, has been a real good mission for us. We've had successes all the way across the board here."

His Marines have kept up their motivation levels. Success generates success, he noted. "Marines believe in the mission that we're doing here. They feel like they're making a big difference for the people. And it gives them a sense of pride. Comparing what we've been able to achieve here, and other areas as well, all the way across the board, we're seeing the Marine Corps making a difference."

When the finishing the interview, Captain Palmer discussed how his Marines have gotten better at conducting debriefs of Marines. He said that it is a skill that grows with practice.

Lieutenant Junwei Sun
81mm Platoon Commander, Weapons Company, 2/7

Lieutenant Sun has been with 2/7 since completing his officer training. He reconfigured his mortar platoon into a basic infantry platoon for the planned missions in Iraq. His platoon has served on convoy escort, as a Quick Reaction Force for 2/7, and other escort missions. They have also provided security for Army Special Forces units.

Lieutenant Sun graduated from college in January 2001, and entered the Marine Corps via the Officer Candidate Course. He completed The Basic School (TBS) and then the Infantry Officer's Course (IOC) in December 2001. He joined 2/7 in January 2002, and made his first deployment to Okinawa from August 2002 until June 2003. About the time of the Marine Corps Ball in November, he learned that 2/7 would be deploying to Iraq. He deployed to Iraq in February 2004.

Originally, he led an infantry platoon with Fox Company, but has led the 81mm mortar platoon since March 2003. However, he said, "Once we found out we were going to Iraq, and the job we were going to be performing over here, which is Security and Stability Operations [SASO], the mission has changed. I had to transform my platoon to a basic rifle platoon. And I got the word, at the time, that the platoon was going to be performing as the battalion Quick Reaction Force, QRF. And also, my platoon was tasked with convoy escort, and any kind of escort mission that comes down the pike."

Regiment and battalion established training programs to ensure that all the Marines would be ready for the environment that they would face in Iraq.

Later, he had to also integrate his platoon with CAAT platoon to conduct mounted patrols along the Main Supply Routes (MSRs) in the area of operations. So his platoon now had three missions: Battalion QRF; Convoy Escort; Mounted Security Patrols.

I asked Lieutenant Sun how his mortar platoon Marines reacted when they learned that they would not be firing their mortar tubes. He said that they were not surprised, given the conditions here in Iraq. They knew that there would be more face-to-face contact with the insurgents, and house searches. Also, he said that since half of his Marines were fresh out of the School of Infantry (SOI), they had minimal exposure to the mortar tubes, and did not have to make a transition from mortarmen to riflemen. "And besides, all Marines are 03s [infantrymen] to start with, so they have the basic rifleman skills."

Sun had to reconfigure his mortar platoon to make it an infantry platoon. An 81mm mortar platoon has two sections with four tubes each. An infantry platoon has three squads. He had to redistribute weapons and gear. They trained in live-fire ranges as well as doing lane training. The Marines had to learn to fire only at targets that threatened them, moving to an advanced level in a short time. Training also involved lots of classroom work on Iraqi culture.

The 81mm mortar tubes were currently in the battalion armory, and 81mm ammunition in the Ammunition Supply Point (ASP). During Operation *Ripper Sweep* at Fallujah, Sun got the word to prepare to operate as an 81mm mortar platoon. He did this in 24 hours and the platoon fired six missions at Fallujah. "The transition was very smooth, because I have a very experienced core of NCOs."

He explained that the fly-in portion of the deployment involved Marines and their personal gear. The heavier equipment, including Humvees and mortar tubes came by ship. The ship-borne gear left well before the fly-in echelon. In Kuwait, they were billeted in Camp Udari for 15 days, waiting for their heavy equipment to arrive. The battalion advance party then flew into Iraq. The rest of the battalion conducted a two-day convoy up to Al Asad. There were four separate convoys. All were uneventful, with no enemy actions against the convoys. Sun said that units operating in the areas that they traversed also provided protection. With so many convoys moving at the same time, there was sometimes problems with coordination. "It was a big deal. They [U.S. Army forces] wanted to get relieved. They didn't want the relief to get shot at."

The U.S. Army's Third Armored Cavalry Regiment was operating out of Al Asad. The day after 2/7 arrived, they began the Left-seat, Right-seat turnover with 3rd ACR. The Army ran the patrols and the Marines rode along on the right-hand side of a vehicle. The soldiers showed key areas in the area of operations (AO,) types of IEDs and enemy TTPs. Then the Marines conducted the patrols with the Army along to provide assistance if needed. The turnover took place on March 15. Sun said that the Marines were eager and excited to go out into the AO. "Every Marine wants to have the chance to go out."

In the early days here, Lieutenant Sun said that his Marines did not get called out often in their QRF role, but they did do a lot of escort duty. They would go out two or three times a day, usually during nighttime hours. He said that the insurgents would be actively emplacing IEDs each night, usually from 1900 to about 0100. His escort Marines would take the EOD Marines out to disarm IEDs that had been found along roads. The platoon got called out on an observation post (OP) mission one night when FOB Hit was getting mortared.

In mid-April, they got called down to Fallujah after the civilian contractors were killed there. Division called for 2/7 to go to Fallujah, and Lieutenant Sun said, "To restore courtesy there, in General Mattis's words."

Sun said that he fired 81mm illumination rounds near the town of Karmah in support of Marine snipers. They also set up OPs to provide security for other Marine units operating in the area.

I asked him to explain the capabilities of the illumination rounds fired by the 81mm mortars. "Okay, sir, once you fire the illum, it depends on the distance. As you know 81s, 81mm mortar can reach out to 5,500 meters. The time in flight depends on how long, how far you're firing. But the illum itself burns a minute. We assume the round will burn for 55 seconds." Each round will illuminate an area of about 100 by 100 meters up to an area 500 by 500 meters, depending on the height. Sun's Marines fired the rounds about every 50 seconds to provide continuous lighting.

Sun said that they did receive a warning order that the Marines were going to clear the city of Fallujah. About April 23 they were told to pull away from Fallujah when a deal was struck with local Iraqi security forces. 2/7 then returned to Al Asad and resumed their former missions. The 81s Marines cleaned the mortar tubes, returned ammo, and resumed the prior missions.

Third Battalion, Fourth Marines (3/4) stayed in the Fallujah area, so 2/7 now had to cover a large area near Al Asad on its own. Missions were now longer duration for the 2/7 Marines.

Sun said that the missions for the infantry companies of 2/7 has not changed much since the turnover of sovereignty at the end of June. "We're still doing MSR security, we're going up and down the roads, going into cities and towns." He said that before this, in May and June, they did a lot of cordon and search missions, where they searched entire city blocks from house-to-house, looking for weapons caches and insurgents. And often, his platoon gets sent out to perform on-call missions when the CAAT platoon can't get ready as quickly.

I asked him about missions he has been directly involved in where a high-value target was captured. He replied, "The only high-value target I can think of is when we went out with ODA, Operational Detachment Alpha, Army Special Forces. We were providing support for them, and according to them, they captured some guy down in Hit. But I didn't really see the guy, because we established the outer cordon for them. They were the ones who [were] going into the houses, snatch the guy. So, they don't really tell us a whole lot, because they're Special Forces. They don't feel the need to tell us anything. They just say, 'All right, we're done. Let's get out of here.' We just know we [have] done our job, 'cause they conduct their raid safely, nobody really mess[es] with them, so our job's done. We usually hear from the [S]3 that, either they did it or no."

Sun said that a lot of the raids that they went on were "dry holes" because the intel expires fast, as the person is gone when the Marines get there. He said that the Marines understand that it takes a lot of raids to capture a high-value target.

Lieutenant Sun noted that when his Marines have a big mission coming up, they get really motivated, but when they sit around for a couple of days, or don't see anything on a patrol, they get a little bit bored. Sun said that he thinks that the battalion commander, Lieutenant Colonel Skuta, keeps the Marines well-informed, and this helps to keep morale high. He helps the Marines to see the big picture in the area of operations (AO).

"Once they're on a mission, they put their game faces on. Out the main gate, everybody's Condition One, locked and loaded." The Marines stay professional and complete the mission. Before they came out here, Sun imagined that the Marines would get tired and let their standards drop. But they have not let up.

Sun sees the progress in the AO. He sees the local people and the combat environment. He especially sees how fast his Marines have matured into men in the few months that they have been in Iraq. They have seen fire fights, and see fellow Marines and buddies wounded and killed. The day after, they continue their mission. The Marine Corps has instilled this pride and discipline into these young men. "Whatever the Marine Corps' doing, they're doing right."

Lieutenant Sun said that even though they are conducting SASO, the Marines still need to train for combat operations and keep the aggressive combat arms mentality.

Gunnery Sergeant Bradley Scott Everett
CAAT Platoon Sergeant, Weapons Company, 2/7

Each squad in his platoon has run about 90 missions to date, ranging from route security, to raids, to operations outside of Fallujah during Operation Vigilant Resolve. *Without threats from enemy armor, the Weapons Company Marines have adapted to a variety of missions to maximize their mobility and weapons systems. Young Marines have taken up leadership positions when more senior Marines were not available for some missions.*

Gunnery Sergeant Everett entered the Marine Corps in 1990, right out of high school. He served at Subic Bay, Philippines, one of the last Marines to serve there, and was there when the Mount Pinatubo volcano erupted. He has served as an instructor at the School of Infantry (SOI) and the Advanced Infantry Training Company, on the Inspector Instructor staff for 1/24, and has had five separate platoons within 2/7 over the past two and a half years. He noted that he is one of the few gunnery sergeants who has not done either recruiting duty or a tour on the drill field.

Everett said that this deployment was atypical. After returning from Okinawa, his platoon was at about a 40 percent effective level. Many of these Marines were senior lance corporals and other NCOs who were frustrated that they, the desert fighters, had not been deployed to Iraq in 2003, and were instead training in the jungles of Okinawa.

In November 2003, they received word to begin preparing for deploying to Iraq. They had to retrain for this new mission. Their regular mission as a CAAT (Combined Anti-Armor Team) platoon is to destroy enemy armor. The main purpose of the CAAT platoon is to screen the battalion from enemy armor threats. Now, without these types of threats, they had to train for a new environment. They had to train new Marines, as well.

Everett said that the training prepared them for Security and Stability Operations (SASO), much different from the normal mission of destroying a clearly defined enemy. They learned a lot about the culture and conditions over here. Gunny Everett said that many of the older NCOs had trained and fought in places like Somalia and Kosovo. The focus of many new Marines had come in a post-September 11 environment, expecting larger scale fighting. But the current fight was mostly a small unit leader's fight.

Everett said, "There's never, never, never enough time to effectively train to what you want to." They only had about three and a half months to get ready for this deployment. He emphasized how important the decisions were at even the low levels of leadership. He said that the environment when they first arrived was over-cautious.

The Marines got lots of briefings from many sources, and it overwhelmed some of them for the first month in country.

When asked about the turnover with the Army, Gunny Everett responded: "The turnover with the Army was about … as effective as two completely different services, probably could make it. Not only did we change over with the United States Army, you know, infantry-infantry side, there's gonna be a lot of crossed wires based on terminology and doctrine. But we crossed over with Army armored cavalry regiments." His company turned over with the Army Avenger Company. Its vehicles and personnel fit the Army's doctrines. For instance, their vehicles had fewer soldiers in them than equivalent Marine vehicles. He said that the Army tended to be more top-rank heavy on their patrols, where the Marines have many more junior enlisted.

"I can't fault the Army, the Army had been here for a year. They were exhausted. You could see it by their actions. You could see it by how they cut corners in things such as pre-combat inspections." Everett said that they were tired, but they gave the incoming Marines a lot of information about the area.

Gunny Everett said that the Army cavalry regiment that had been here had about 800 soldiers, but only about 300 of them were combat soldiers. The rest were support and logistics soldiers who maintained the tanks, and M1 and M2 vehicles. As a result, they could not generate the same level of combat power that the Marines can. The Marine squads could dig out things that the Army platoons had not been able to find.

"We were able to flood all of the zones, and basically disrupt the hell out of the enemy." The Marines also went across the Euphrates River into towns that the Army had not been able to get to. The Marines encountered enemy who did not expect them in area. Firefights and IED attacks increased due to this increased Marine presence. Everett said that the pattern developed where there would be increased enemy activity in an area for two or three weeks, then would taper off as the enemy resupplied itself or reassessed its efforts.

In April, the battalion went to Fallujah as part of Operation *Ripper Sweep* to pick a fight with the enemy fighters that were there. Gunny Everett feels that "Nobody in their right mind is gonna stand up to a reinforced Marine regiment with combined arms capabilities." Especially an insurgent force. "A regiment sweeping through an area, they're [the enemy] are just gonna simply get outta the way." When Weapons Company went down to Fallujah, they split his CAAT platoon into four sections to support different infantry companies there. Each section has four vehicles with Mark 19s, TOWs, and .50 caliber machine guns that can traverse the battlefield quickly and lay down a lot of firepower. They were not called on to actually fight in Fallujah, however. He said that his Marines were skilled at maintaining fire discipline in difficult situations. After about two and a half weeks at Fallujah, they returned to the Al Asad area and resumed their prior missions.

The platoon elements have been going on patrols that last from eight to 18 hours. There have been Main Supply Routes (MSR) security patrols, snatch missions of high-value targets, cache raids based on intel, and helping infantry squads from Echo and Golf Companies. They have also delivered supplies to Iraqi civilians in Baghdadi and other small towns. Missions have ranged from guarding a playground swing set from IED emplacements prior to a playground dedication, to snatching a suspected insurgent sheik. Each squad has had at least 90 missions, and they had two months left here. "They have done admirably. I can't speak highly enough of these NCOs." He added, "These guys are capable of doing things, I doubt I would have the ability to. Not only tactically but technically, too."

Gunny Everett said that it has been a small unit leaders' fight. He admires the hell out of his four squad leaders. He and the other staff NCOs go on patrol with them once or twice a week, and allow the squad leader to run his squad. "They know so much more as a lance corporal than I did!" He said that even some of the Marines who are laggards in garrison situations have turned into outstanding Marines in this combat environment. He has seen them making decisions that he had hoped that they would be capable of. He said that the junior officers have also performed admirably.

"I brought 86 individuals into this country. When I first joined the platoon in October of last year [2003], I had 29 [Marines]." The large influx of many brand-new Marines came in November and December, along with new NCOs. One sergeant who came from the Air Wing has achieved MOS proficiency as an 0351 [Machine gunner]. Everett said that this sergeant is just an outstanding NCO, and wanted to be an NCO in charge of Marines rather than a technician that he had been with the Wing. Everett said that when the platoon returns to the States, it will have a solid core of about 50 to 60 Marines to train the incoming Marines. He said that there were at least 15 Marines who will be good squad leaders on the next deployment.

Cross training has been a big concern for the platoon. Thanks to concerted training, they now have Marines cross-trained with the TOWs, Javelin Missiles, and machine guns. They first trained everyone with the machine guns, as they are the primary weapons system in the CAAT platoon. They also have learned to use the night sight capabilities of the Javelin Missile launcher. Each squad takes a variety of weapons with it, and all Marines train in all of the weapons. They have also cross-trained the vehicle commanders. He would like to have had more time to do even more training, but the operational tempo has controlled what they have been able to do. The techniques are easy to teach, tactics take more time in his opinion.

"Machine guns we use all the time. The .50 cal, the Mark 19, and the 240 Golf, and the Squad Automatic Weapon (SAW), which in this battalion is considered a light machine gun. We have fired one TOW missile in this area of operations. One of my squads was being suppressed by three, possibly three, RPK machine guns.

After possibly gaining fire superiority, the machine guns quieted down, and then opened up with another burst. The TOW gunner was tracking, using his night sight to possibly identify where that came from." He saw tracers coming from a window, and the TOW gunner fired the missile towards that window. "Lo and behold, all three of those machine guns, and the entire surrounding area, not a thing was heard from them for about two days."

Everett said that the .50 cal round will go about two-and-a-half miles, and is a precision weapon. There is very little here in Iraq that will stop this round. The TOW, on the other hand, is a precision-guided weapon with a shaped charge. It makes a smaller hole, but is precise. It will stop when it hits the building, unlike a .50 cal round that keeps on traveling through several walls. The CAAT platoon ends firefights very quickly due to its massive fire superiority over insurgent fire.

"My platoon has 11 Purple Hearts." Three were from shrapnel from large 170mm rockets. Four other wounds were caused by a triple-stacked IED, which also killed a platoon sergeant. Three nights ago, another double-stacked IED went off and wounded four more Marines. Everett said that the paperwork was not yet complete on all of these combat wounded Marines. Other injuries have been broken bones, a broken jaw, broken eardrums, and two or three concussions. "The mines and the IEDs do cause fear."

When Staff Sergeant Markman was killed three weeks ago, it really affected the entire company. Everett said that it shocked the Marines. But they have had several contacts since then, and have sucked it up to perform well. Many injured Marines have been quick to return to action. Everett said that they wanted to go back out there and be there with their Marines. These are junior Marines, including corporals and lance corporals. Everett said that when he is in the rear and listening in to contacts on the radio, it is gut-wrenching for him. He wants to be with them, but cannot always be out on patrol. The lieutenants and staff NCOs cannot go out with every patrol every time, he said.

Gunny Everett said that today's Marines are considerably smarter than when he first joined the Corps. They want to see the big picture. They want to know why they are doing the operations. They don't like to be patronized, either. They want to know how their one little piece fits into the big wheel. He said, "You give them a why, you get much more performance out of them."

Operations are physically and mentally challenging. The Marines do it for themselves, their buddies, and their immediate superiors. Sometimes they get frustrated with the enemy's ability to hide behind the local populace. "They're doing it correctly to keep themselves safe." In Gunny Everett's view, this has probably not changed in the past two thousand years for fighting men. He feels that they want only to be appreciated for what they are doing.

Gunny Everett wanted to emphasize the faith that he has gotten about the abilities of the young NCOs he has had the pleasure to work with. They have excelled.

He then apologized for not having more to share: "That's it, sir, I've been up for 32 hours!"

Major John Richard Smith, Junior
Civil Affairs Officer, 3rd Civil Affairs Group, Serving with 2/7

The Marine Corps' Civil Affairs Marines are all reservists. 2/7's initial goal was to get the local Iraqi security forces to do their job. Once that would happen, efforts at Civil Affairs reconstruction projects could commence. 2/7 augmented Smith's team to create a 9-Marine Civil Affairs Group. The team faced the challenge of working with local contractors and engineers on projects, as well as helping to create local security forces. His goal was to work Civil Affairs out of a job by having the local officials take on more responsibilities in security and rebuilding.

Major Smith goes by "Rick," among friends. He was commissioned an officer in 1988 via OCS, and became an infantry officer after The Basic School. He did his initial active duty with 3/9, and served as a platoon commander during Operation *Desert Storm*. After a deployment to Okinawa, he left active duty in 1992. He returned to Phoenix, Arizona, and joined a Marine Reserve reconnaissance company in Albuquerque. In civilian life he is a police detective in Phoenix. He was recalled to active duty after September 11, 2001, with Joint Task Force Civil Support, at Fort Monroe, Virginia. Shortly after joining the 3rd Civil Affairs Group (CAG), he went on active duty for this deployment. He had only done two reserve drills with the unit before getting orders to what he called "CAG University," an intense five-day civil affairs course. He was then sent to join 2/7 as the civil affairs officer.

He flew overseas with the CAG, then met up with 2/7 in Kuwait. Four days later he was with them in Iraq. He said that Lieutenant Colonel's Skuta's priority in Civil Affairs was to get the local Iraqi security forces to do their job. "So we didn't focus on civil affairs projects themselves. We had a dual mission, of actually looking at the Iraqi police, and the Iraqi National Guard (ING), and find out what they needed to do the job. What they were short of, and come up with ways of getting them up to speed."

Smith said that training was a big concern for these Iraqi forces. They had previously received a five-day training course. Lieutenant Colonel Skuta said that he wanted to establish a joint training facility for the police and the Iraqi Civil Defense Corps (ICDC) who were now the Iraqi National Guard (ING). Smith took his Civil Affairs Group to survey a facility, an old Iraqi army building at Camp Hit, just north of the town there. They came up with a plan to use the buildings and facilities there to include motor pools, training ranges, etc. He held weekly meetings with the local Iraqi police chief, the local head of the ING, and the city council members to discuss all of their concerns. All of the Iraqi leaders said that they needed help in getting their security forces up to par.

Major Smith's team originally consisted of himself, a gunnery sergeant, two sergeants and three corporals. "I was very fortunate in that 2/7 had a lieutenant who was a tanker, and an NBC [Nuclear, Biological, Chemical weapons] warrant officer, that Colonel Skuta basically said, 'They can help you out.' So that was it. The nine-man team became a conglomeration of the CAG team I brought out here and a couple of officers from the battalion."

His team had to learn how to work with the local Iraqi contractors and engineers. They remodeled the existing buildings at FOB Hit, created classrooms, a motor pool, and ranges. It was an ongoing process. However, the essential elements—firing ranges and command post facilities—were now complete. Barracks were not yet done, and road paving was ongoing. It was now the JCC, Joint Command Center, for the Iraqi police, ING, and Marine staff.

Major Smith outlined the type of training that the local forces had received previously. He explained the ICDC training. "One type, you had traditional training through the Iraqi military system. There were very few of those because the thought back in OIF1 was to not use too many of these prior military men. So there was a very small number of those men." "The other group were basically civilians, they found out that they were hiring, went through the five-day training course." Since then, different groups have joined, along with some officers who have had prior training. Those who denounced their Baath Party ties have been allowed to join.

Major Smith said that beyond security, the priorities of the local leaders were not the same things that he would expect when he got here. He said, "For example, we had several towns that had no electricity, dirty water, open sewage running through the streets. Those are the types of projects that I anticipated getting from the city councils. What I started to receive after the first few weeks here, I started to get projects dealing with renovations of buildings for the city council members. I got requests for furnishings, so they could hold meetings. But we also got several projects for mosques and schools." He began to get concerned because he wasn't getting requests for the infrastructure-type projects that he had expected. He said that it has been a balancing act to set priorities on the projects.

Also, in the Hit area, there are several smaller towns such as Baghdadi, and these towns needed to get everyone a fair share of the funds to rebuild. Outlying towns also felt that Hit was getting too much of the resources for the projects. After a few months, Lieutenant Colonel Skuta decided to have the city councils come to him with their requests.

Major Smith explained how the projects get approval and how payments were made. "I thought it was a very simple process when we got here, but it wasn't. We had to adjust." At first, the city council would identify a problem. The CAG would ask for an Iraqi engineer who was part of the council to go and assess the cost of the project. Then, CAG would look at it and decide if they would fund it. Council was then asked to identify contractors to bid on the project. For projects of greater than $10,000, three bids were required. Smith's lieutenant would review the bids with the Iraqi engineer, then the CAG would choose the contractor. Regiment would then send the project request to Division for approval of funding. Then the contractor would begin work. The contractors would get an initial payment of about 25 percent of the cost. Engineers photographed progress on the project, and payments continued. Final payment came after a member of city council inspected and approved a project.

Smith said that there was sometimes a problem when a non-local contractor was the only bidder and got the contract. The local council could then approve or disapprove the project.

Smith has task-organized his Civil Affairs Marines. He takes the meetings with the local leaders himself. His lieutenant and warrant officer handle project management with so many projects going on at once. The lieutenant also works with the four local Iraqi civil engineers who would come to the gate of the base to discuss projects. His gunnery sergeant would send teams out to inspect progress on local projects.

I asked him to outline projects in just one of the towns in the area. He responded: "Mahmudiyah is a pretty small town, [so] they ended up not getting many projects, but the projects that we did give them are important. I think we only had three or four mosques in there. The two mosques that were in the worse shape, one of the first things we did, we went ahead and renovated those mosques. The people of that area said that was the most important thing we could do for that area. We said, okay, that's what we'll do. They only had three schools, and they were having to split the day, the boys and the girls. And that was causing a problem there. So we, and this just recently go approved, we never did finish this, but we will finish this before we leave, is repairing the two schools so they can facilitate more students. And actually we built them an old school, that they hadn't been using, to give them another school, so they separate out the boys from the girls."

Smith said that they had also renovated the police station in Mahmudiyah. A water project, costing over $100,000, will become part of another water project that Division has for the area.

There was also a jobs program, where the town could get 30 workers for each of three projects, for a total of 90 workers for projects such as trash cleanup.

4th CAG would be taking over when 3rd CAG returns to the States. The money for projects has been significantly reduced. The Iraqi government now controls most of the money formerly known as the CERP (Commander's Emergency Response Program) funds for projects. The CAG had a small amount of money, about $250,000 a month through September 2004, and they were currently trying to finish off important projects.

There were several ongoing projects. One was a playground factory, to provide for schools in the towns in the area. Another was the Al Anbar jobs program which employed about 700 Iraqis. Also, money for a free local newspaper, *Al Furat*.

When 4th CAG arrives, he will explain what has been done here and near-term plans. On his return to the States, Major Smith foresaw using these experiences to help train future CAG teams that come out to Iraq.

Everyone in Smith's CAG team were from other MOS's. His junior Marines are actually artillerymen. When they return to the States, they will return to their reserve units and leave active duty. Major Smith's orders have him on active duty until January 2005. He anticipated that he would complete after-action duties before then.

"The tempo was very fast, especially when we first got here. With the whole focus on stability and stabilization operations, and security, we were incorporated in every operation that 2/7 did. Our ultimate goal was to basically work ourselves out of a job, to where we didn't have to go to every city council meeting, we didn't have to go down and run the ING training facility. And we didn't have to go out and do the same thing basically with the police." He said that the civil leaders now hold meetings with CAG when they need to, not every week. The tempo has definitely slowed down.

Lieutenant Colonel Skuta has told Major Smith that he was happy with how Civil Affairs has supported 2/7's goals. Skuta understands that every dollar put into the community lessened the possibility of a terrorist working in the area. He sees the positive effect of Marine Corps civil affairs. Smith noted that both of the two Marine Corps Civil Affairs Groups are reserve units: 3rd CAG on the west coast, and 4th CAG on the east coast.

CHAPTER THREE

Echo Company, 2/7, at Forward Operating Base Hit

Ground Convoy to FOB Hit

Interviews complete at Camp Al Asad, I got ready to convoy to Forward Operating Base (FOB) Hit. This would take me to Echo Company, 2/7. It was very hot, and I had to meet with the convoy commander, a staff sergeant, around 1300. He gave a thorough convoy brief to everyone about to ride in the convoy—the Marines out here realize that this is a dangerous area, and every convoy is thoroughly briefed. Part of the preparations for the drive beyond the wire were rehearsals. Even though all of the Marines have repeatedly done this, they readily go through the rehearsals without complaint. They know that this convoy is different from any other, there are different Marines in each vehicle, different vehicles, and it's a new day. Before leaving Al Asad base, we did two drills, one where we dismounted and simulated receiving an attack, and then an attack and medevac. And it got hotter! We were all in full flak jacket and helmet. Near the gate, we dismounted and loaded our magazines into our weapons. I was in a Humvee with a gun mount, and the Marine there manned an M240 machine gun. I had an M16 rifle and a 9mm pistol. I loaded them both.

After leaving Al Asad, the convoy went on some main roads and also some dirt roads off the main track. I kept alert, as this was only the second time I've really been outside the wire on the ground (my short convoys to Baharia and Camp Abu Ghraib near Camp Fallujah don't really count). This convoy had seven vehicles, either up-armored Humvees or 7-ton trucks. We traveled without incident, and I was relieved when we dismounted and cleared our weapons inside FOB Hit. The FOB is a former Iraqi army base just north of the town by that name.

Echo Company's first sergeant met me and got me a room—really a large squad bay with concrete slabs for beds. The Marine engineer unit that had used it until recently had left a mattress, so I knew that I would have a good night's rest. The company staff allowed me to take a needed nap in the air-conditioned room, and I then went to dinner at 1800. Interesting setup. Echo Company commander Captain John Kelley used this mealtime every night to have all of his staff and officers sit at a long series of tables pushed together in the rectangular room. After the meal, he conducted a company staff briefing. He called on all of the company staff, and each platoon commander. The word gets passed one time to the leaders. Also, this gets the staff out of the hair of the enlisted Marines of the company for an hour or so, so it ensured that they have some quiet time. Captain Kelley introduced me and told the staff what I would be doing.

My interviews began after chow and went until 2230. I started with two sergeants who each ran a "Backup Alert Force" (BAF) for the company. This FOB was an hour and a half drive from Al Asad, and was responsible for operations in and around this part of the Al Anbar Province. It was almost an independent command, and Captain Kelley ran it like a mini battalion. Sergeants Jonathon Graham and Timothy Day explained their jobs and what the forces do—they were formed from the company's Weapons Platoon. Next came HM3 Eric Delano Giles, Corpsman for 2nd Platoon. He was badly wounded in an IED attack, but after spending time in a Baghdad hospital, with an opportunity to go home, returned to duty with the platoon. A very remarkable young man! His arm was still healing, but he was doing his Corpsman duties. He said that part of why he came back was to help the morale of his platoon. He spoke glowingly of the Navy Corpsman–Marine bond. The battalion surgeon, Navy Lieutenant Robert Gould was the final interview for the night. He was serving as a surgeon to the company, and he explained that he was there because the company was so far from the battalion at Al Asad.

Sergeant Jonathon Jarrett Graham
Backup Alert Force (BAF) Commander, Echo Company, 2/7

Echo Company's BAF was a unique force. It performed lots of missions, everything from route clearance, to reaction force, to observation posts (OPs), to reinforcement, to escorting the company commander to meetings in the area. It was Echo Company's own reaction force. They have run a variety of mission in the Hit area, and served outside of Fallujah during Operation Vigilant Resolve.

Sergeant Graham is a machine gunner, currently serving as the BAF commander for Echo Company here at Camp Hit. He entered the Corps in 1992 at Parris Island, South Carolina, and served with Charlie Company, 1/1, at Camp Pendleton. He then did a lateral move into the Combat Photography MOS. He returned to the infantry, serving at Quantico before coming to 2/7.

During OIF1 he and 2/7 were serving in Okinawa. On return to the United States, many Marines left the battalion, and in the three months before coming to Iraq, 2/7 joined many new Marines right out of the School of Infantry (SOI). Between Thanksgiving and Christmas they learned that they would be coming to Iraq.

They did SASO and lane training at 29 Palms, led by 1/7, learning from that unit's experience. They spent a week at March Air Force Base to learn about conditions in Iraq. They did patrols, searched for weapons cache sites, and so on. Graham said that here the training for the new Marines was different from what they had learned at the School of Infantry.

They arrived in Kuwait in mid-February, then convoyed from Camp Udari, Kuwait up to Al Asad in Iraq. Half of the company had flown into Al Asad. The convoy itself was uneventful. Once Echo Company linked up together at Al Asad, it began the ride-alongs with the U.S. Army units here. They also met with local Iraqi sheiks and leaders.

He explained that the Backup Alert Force was the company QRF, called BAF for short. It's comprised of Weapons Platoon assets: A squad of machine gunners; Two teams of assault Marines; A team of mortarmen. He said, "Gunners man the guns on the vehicles, pretty much react to anything."

They began patrols around the city of Hit, and set up their firm base here at the FOB. He explained current operations: "Basically one platoon has firm base for three days, one has patrolling, and then one has local QRF of the firm base. BAF reacts to everything, basically, out in town. The QRF reacts to local security stuff. It's kinda changed lately, 'cause we got four platoons out here."

They had two significant fire fights during this early time here. 3rd Platoon was at a traffic circle. "The town was quiet, we were settin' up VCPs [Vehicle Control Points], all over the place, due to insurgents comin' out of Fallujah. 3rd got in their fire fight, and as the backup force we got called out for them. Basically came there, point team, supporting fire. Shortly after that we had a firefight with just the BAF, Backup Alert Force, which was on the northern side of Hit. One of the two major conflicts we've had here besides IEDs and mines."

He estimated that the firefight involving 3rd Platoon was probably from an insurgent squad, the other one was perhaps one or two guys firing AKs.

When Fallujah heated up in April, Echo Company became part of *Ripper Sweep* there. "We were sent down there to help out RCT1. Didn't go actually into the city, we did stuff in outlying areas." One platoon was mounted in vehicles, the rest of the company was in tracs (AAVs). It operated as an armored company. They helped with the cordon outside of Fallujah, northeast of Fallujah, in the town of Karmah. After a few days at Camp Fallujah for refitting, they returned to FOB Hit. 24th Marines had taken over FOB Hit during that time.

Back at Hit, they worked observation posts (OPs), watched the Main Supply Routes (MSRs), and uncovered numerous IEDs. Many OPs were set up along hill 107, where they believed a group they called "Mad Mortarmen" had been shooting at them. "We'd sit up there and watch that hill, so that if they did shoot, we'd respond to it." They also did a lot of route clearance to ensure that roads remain clear for convoys.

Their first two IEDs that they hit were actually mines, and two Marines were lost to them. South of Hit, there was an area that Echo Marines call IED alley. The Marines were getting pretty good at uncovering the IEDs. "Had one go off in the city on a platoon, which they also received gunfire at the same time. The Claymore that went off in the middle of the city. The thing about the Claymore is, they had it facing the wrong way, which is good. So it shot back at 'em. IEDs, were basically 155 rounds. Most of 'em were hard-wired, some type of crank box to make them go off."

More recently the IEDs have become remote-detonated. The insurgents use small radios, like Motorola iCom radios. One Marine company had an IED go off near the Marines when they used their squad iCom radio, as it was on the same frequency as the IED's detonator.

Around the beginning of June 2004, Graham said that they saw an IED that was a sign about six inches square, about three feet tall, filled with plastic explosive, and remotely detonated. They found it before a convoy came along, otherwise it would have hurt a lot of people. When EOD detonated this IED, Sergeant Graham said that he was about 400 meters away, and he could feel a powerful concussion wave from the explosion. Now, the insurgents were starting to stack 155 rounds into IEDs. However, the Marines normally find them.

After *Ripper Sweep*, the number of IEDs found slowed down for a while, but of late, more have been found.

Sergeant Graham said that the ING train with Golf Company, and now Echo Company needed to have ING soldiers when they go into the city of Hit. They have gotten quite good, doing a good job. The ING also had a new commander.

Sergeant Graham estimated that about 80 percent of the company was made up of new Marines. He said that these Marines were performing a lot better than he thought they would. He told about Lance Corporal Figuerola taking control of a patrol when the patrol commander was incapacitated, and kept order. More recently, a PFC Menna was hit by small arms fire, he got up and his first instinct was to set up security even though he was bleeding.

Despite feeling that things were going good, both with his Marines and the ING in the area, Sergeant Graham had a feeling that something big could still blow up. He wondered if the ING would be able to handle it.

When the Army left the area, Sergeant Graham said that the locals were standoffish at first. They were more welcoming now that the Marines have been here for a few months. He thinks these Iraqis would be sad to see the Marines leave.

Sergeant Timothy Curtis Day
Mortar Section Leader, Backup Alert Force (BAF), Echo Company, 2/7

Early during the deployment to Hit, Sergeant Day had one of his Marines killed by an IED blast. In April, Echo deployed to the area outside of Fallujah for 7th Marines Operation Ripper Sweep. *A continuing challenge was fighting complacency among his younger Marines as operations slow down.*

Sergeant Day began, "I came into the Marine Corps in December, '95. First went to FAST Company in Norfolk. Deployed to Bahrain during that time." After two years, he went to 7th Marines, and was discharged in 1999. In 2001, he reenlisted and returned to 7th Marines. When he reenlisted, he kept his prior rank as a corporal, but lost his time-in-grade, so it took him another year before he was promoted to sergeant.

He couldn't remember exactly when Echo Company got the word that it was coming to Iraq, but said that once they got the word sometime last fall, they began lane training. There were lots of new Marine joins—he estimated that half of the battalion was Marines fresh out of the School of Infantry (SOI). The training covered the basics, and the Marines did well during the training. "It was a needed work-up, just to get them prepared, get them mentally prepared to come over here." He noted, however, that a lot of the training was based on the wartime experiences of a returning unit, 1/7, and did not fully prepare 2/7 for current operations.

After arrival in Kuwait, they trained for about two weeks. Then half of his platoon flew up to Al Asad, while his part of the platoon went with the company in a convoy into Iraq. They went right to Hit, and started doing patrols with the U.S. Army units here. The Army shared its knowledge and Echo Marines got a feel for the area.

"The first week, really, we got a feel for what it was gonna be like, because that night we took mortar rounds. Welcome to Hit!" He added that every other night after that, they either got mortared or rocketed.

"March 18th was the first time that we actually lost our first Marine on patrol. Which happened to be my patrol, so, [I] remember that pretty well. We drove over a land mine, drove over it on the passenger side … killed my driver [Corporal David M. Vicente]." He paused.

"There was no ambush. Basically we thought they were using that round for their mortar attacks. That was our first combat loss, that. After that, I'd say, our unit alone, the work got a little bit more busy. Encountered a lot more IEDs, and land mines, right after that. About a week after that, another unit, think it was 2nd Platoon, hit a land mine. Right off the road."

Sergeant Day said that his unit was going out every night. He said that they found an IED along the road just about every day during the time leading up to Operation *Ripper Sweep*. "All the platoons were working pretty hard at that time, first two months. Wasn't really too much off time."

When April came around, they began to run a lot of Vehicle Check Points (VCPs), staying out for six or seven days at a time. Then they went south to Fallujah for Operation *Ripper Sweep*. They traveled to a small town, and there was no action there. He said that they ended up "Smilin' and wavin' for two days." Next, they went to Karmah and did a sweep of the town. After a three-day stay at Camp Fallujah (he called it Camp MEK), they returned to FOB Hit. Most of the Marines were happy to get back to this area, he said. Why? They felt that up here they were actually doing something, they could see the results.

Back in Hit, Echo Company did a lot of sweeps, and found several weapons caches. He described one of them for me: "I think it was about first week we were back, first week in May. Found, couple hundred feet of det [detonating] cord, a lot of improvised explosive devices that were already made. Overall it came out to be one of the largest ones [weapons caches] we'd found to that point." Sergeant Day said that they found this one based on careful observation by his Marines. This cache was in a hole about five feet by five feet, and three feet deep.

In late May, Sergeant Day was tasked with taking out a group of engineers to a site. Day's Marines had been filling in IED holes in the side of the roads. These holes were from IEDs that had already been cleared. "They [insurgents] figured out what we were doing within one day, and they put an IED right next to a previous IED hole. So, when we cleared up to it, our engineers saw the IED. Right when they saw it, they were right next to it, [the IED] killed three of 'em."

Sergeant Day paused before continuing. "Thing about it, they were catching on to a lot of the stuff we were doin', a lot of the route clearance. Which—there's not much—in the leeway on which routes we can take, and vary up what we were doin'. So, it's inevitable that we hit these things. It was pretty bad."

Missions have slowed down since the beginning of June, and since June 24 they had to go out with ING soldiers as part of their patrols wherever they go. Day didn't mind this, "The less we go out, the less they're [insurgents] placing IEDs." The Marines felt that now the IEDs were getting harder to spot.

His section was always on standby in case anything comes down.

His mortar Marines have fired a few illumination rounds, and an HE (High Explosive) round or two, but given the nature of the missions, mortars are not often called on because of concerns about collateral damage to civilians. Mostly the mortar Marines have been acting as basic Marine riflemen.

I asked Sergeant Day to outline the missions of the BAF. He responded jokingly, "We're abused by the company! We're used for about everything. Whenever we're used for the CO [commanding officer], whenever he has to go out, at any point in time, to talk to officials."

They were also used to react to any situation outside the firm base or in the town of Hit. If another platoon gets attacked, the BAF reinforces them. BAF often gets search missions. They set up the cordons during searches for weapons caches. They are one of the more versatile parts of the company. There were usually 20 Marines on BAF out of a Weapons Platoon of about 40. They rotate Marines every three days. While on post, they man guard positions for the firm base. Sergeant Day and Sergeant Graham rotate the duties, also. He said that this has been a long few months.

Day said that the younger Marines have done well at ever-changing situations. They have held their own. "All I can say about my younger Marines is that I've been very impressed by their actions. We got a great group of Marines right before we came over here."

Sergeant Day said that a challenge was to train up the younger Marines to take over leadership positions after they return to the States. They have not had a lot of training opportunities over here because of the tempo of operations. He foresees his biggest leadership challenge to date as fighting complacency in the company as operations slow down.

Hospital Corpsman 3 Eric Delano Giles, USN
2nd Platoon Corpsman, Echo Company, 2/7

On his second combat tour in Iraq, Giles used his combat experiences to help train new Navy Corpsmen and the Marines in Echo Company. During a return from an observation post (OP), he was in a Humvee with six Marines who hit a terrific explosion from an IED. Wounded himself, he immediately began to treat those more seriously wounded, including an officer with compound fractures in one leg. A Marine treated Giles's wound as Giles continued to work on the wounded officer. His own wounds were serious enough to allow him to return home, but he felt that his Marines in Echo Company needed him, and he returned to Hit to recover and return to full duties.

"Doc" Giles had taken some college courses, and after a friend told him about the Navy, he went to the Navy recruiter and signed up to become a Hospital Corpsman. He went to recruit training at Great Lakes in August 2000, and after graduation began training to become a Corpsman. He said that he and a few other graduates of the Corpsman training school were selected to attend Field Medicine school. (Now, he said, all Navy Corpsmen attend this school.)

Giles was then sent to Camp Pendleton, California, for Field Med School, and was in the SAT (Students awaiting Training) platoon waiting for the course to begin. He had the opportunity to work with Marines during an exercise called *Colonel Blitz* at Pendleton. He said, "So I had the opportunity to see how the Marine Corps works from that time. So I was kind of interested, I was on the fence, whether I wanted to do it or didn't want to do it."

He then began Field Med school in March 2001. "You learn to hump [field hike], get yelled at a great deal, you learn the Marine Corps rank structure, because at boot camp they didn't bother too much with that." Corpsmen learn to be a "Doc" for the Marines here.

He got picked to join infantry Marines and went to Alpha Company, 1/7. Navy Corpsmen have to learn to fit in with their Marine units. He worked to ensure that he was in good physical shape, as Corpsmen have to stay up with their Marines. The day after he checked in to Alpha Company, he went on a 13-mile hump, and this helped to build up his confidence. He did a Combined Arms Exercise (CAX) and a deployment to Okinawa with Alpha 1/7. He also did Operation *Cobra Gold* in Thailand.

OIF1

He went to Bravo Company, 1/7, and was then an E3. He said that the company began to do some real heavy training. He suspected that something was up, because a unit just back from a deployment usually would not be training so hard so soon. There were lots of long marches, live-fire exercises, and lots of medical simulations and drills. "I was wondering, like, something's got to be going on. Got a battalion formation, said we're going to OIF1. And then, February 1st, of 2003, 1/7 flew to Kuwait. And from there we're in the desert, we're used to being in the desert from 29 Palms."

Giles said that they had been warned that the war would be a very different type of affair. He and the other Navy Corpsmen in the battalion would get together every day to hold medical classes and drills on how to treat certain types of casualties. They got Marines involved to help them learn how to be combat aidsmen to the Corpsmen. The Marines were also getting restless, as they were there for about a month and a half without any definite word of the start of combat.

On March 28, 2003, word came that they would push off early in the morning. They staged in the Amtracs (AAVs) and moved up the 18 kilometers to the Iraq-Kuwait border. "Our main objective was to go to the Az Zubair oil field. We were supposed to, Bravo Company, 1/7, was supposed to take the Az Zubair oil field to help the Iraqi infrastructure down the line."

When they got there, Doc Giles said that he ran all kinds of scenarios in his head. He knew that this was the "real deal." "Get the word: 'Ramp comin' down!' So the ramp comes down, and we all off-load the trac. The Marines get off. The Marines get on line, as squads, and we start engaging our objective. So we move up, little resistance. Couple guys are out there, the Marines deal with that."

Doc Giles said that there was one unfortunate incident there. The artillery units had prepped the objective area with some cluster bombs. Some of the bomblets had not exploded when they hit. There were some Iraqi kids in the area, and a little boy kicked one of the unexploded pieces of ordnance. This little boy lost his legs, his torso was peeled up, and his face was damaged. This hit Giles hard. He wrapped up the dead little boy, and began to treat the boy's older brother who had shrapnel wounds. Giles was the first one on the scene, and he began to treat the wounded boy. He pulled out the pressure bandages, and applied pressure to stop the bleeding. Giles and another Corpsman started an IV on the boy, who threw up everything that they stuck him with. The Marine battalion commander came onto the scene. He took off his blouse and began to talk to the boy. The boy was then medevac'd and survived the wounds. This helped Giles's confidence.

Giles said that 3/4 was leading the charge, and the Marines in 1/7 were following. Giles did not have to treat any wounded in his company. He mostly treated wounded Iraqis that they encountered. He treated some deep cuts and bullet wounds of these Iraqis.

When the main combat was over, Giles and the Marines in 1/7 thought that they would soon return home, but wound up remaining in Iraq from February until October 2003. They moved to the city of Najaf and worked there for about six months. They patrolled the area and only had a few small fire fights.

They were sent to Babylon to do guard duty for the Marine Expeditionary Force (MEF) that was there. One night, at the end of a patrol, Giles could see shots in the dark. He heard someone yelling, "Doc! Doc!" and feared that he would now have to treat some Marines after having gone through the whole deployment without any casualties. He ran up to the scene, and a Marine there told him that none of them was wounded, but an Iraqi insurgent had three gunshot wounds: One in the wrist, one in the neck, and one in his back. Giles treated him, and along with some Marines, carried the wounded insurgent onto a vehicle. The insurgent survived.

Giles said that it was his job to treat all wounded, but he doesn't like to treat the enemy.

One Marine died at Babylon when he fell off a large building during a night in July 2003. He tripped and fell about 60 feet to his death.

In October 2003, 1/7, went to Kuwait and returned home that month. The battalion granted everyone leave. Then rumors began floating around that they would be returning to Iraq for OIFII. "I'm like in my head, there's no way people that just got back from OIF1 are gonna have to go there. 'Cause 2/7, of course, they were in Okinawa for the whole time." Then rumors came that those who had certain cutoff dates would not deploy.

When Giles returned from leave, he got orders to go to join 2/7. He said it was not fun, as they had to do all the workups and pre-deployments again. Giles recollected that the last two months before deployment of 2/7, they only got two full weekends of liberty. "It was like nonstop working, Monday through Sunday. Getting maybe half of Sunday off, going right back to it on Monday." Now that Giles was an E4, he got to be in charge of some of the medical training. He enjoyed being in charge, and helping to train some of the younger Corpsmen that had not yet been to Iraq. "I actually got to feel that I was a big part of the grand scheme of things," he said. The fact that he was combat experienced gave him more credibility with these newer Corpsmen.

OIFII

2/7 deployed to Kuwait on February 17, 2004. Again, Giles ran different scenarios through his mind as they trained for several weeks in Kuwait. He trained up the Marines in the platoon, and all but about seven were new Marines. He reviewed carries: fireman, low crawl, and flak jacket drag. He also taught them how to splint broken bones and treat wounds, in case he himself was wounded and the Marines had to do first aid on their own.

When March came, his platoon and Weapons Platoon were tasked to go into Iraq on the convoy. The rest of 2/7 would fly up into Iraq. The three-day convoy went off without a hitch. The rest of Echo Company was already in FOB Hit. Giles asked his medical chief if the Hit area was bad, and he told him that from what he knew it was not a bad area.

"The first three weeks, nothing really happened. We'd go out on patrols. We'd be out there doing our jobs, you know." The new Marines were just trying to get used to Iraq, trying to get SASO going. Then in late March, Weapons Platoon lost Corporal Vicente to a land mine. Giles heard this from Sergeant Day of Echo's BAF. Giles knew Vicente personally, and this news hit him hard, the fact that any one of the Marines in the company could be killed any day. This death heightened the alertness of everyone in the company.

"Then March 31st came. We were out on a patrol. It always happens on the end of a patrol, for some reason. I mean, I don't know why. It's always when you're about to come back. We're setting out to OPs for like hours." They were near Route Uranium, making jokes. A buddy of Giles (Lance Corporal Gibson) joked that it felt that they were driving over a minefield. "Right when he said that, BOOM! The Humvee I was in, Corporal Cullen, myself, Lieutenant Diaz, Lance Corporal Gibson, Lance Corporal Pimental, PFC Dion, PFC Bowers, there was about seven of us in the Humvee. Right when he said that, it was uncanny, it was so weird, BOOM! You know, you get that nasty smell, the explosion smell—it's like horrible. Just smells like the stuff they use to make the explosives."

"And, uh, all I hear is this loud screaming. Loud, loud screaming. I'm trying to get my bearings back, 'cause that disorients you a great deal. So we got thrown out the Hummer. I'm trying to get my bearings back, and I feel this pain in my arm, but I didn't think it was nothing. 'Cause one time we were driving, and we hit the brakes hard, and I banged my shoulder up against the cab. I was like, ah, it felt just like that. It's getting more intense, I'm not worried about it. And I hear my lieutenant screaming. The land mine went off right under, he's on the passenger side, right up under him. He had just come back to the grunts, he had got out to go back to college to become an officer. So, he's a brand-new second lieutenant, he was a corporal in the Marine Corps before. So he knew what was going on. [He] Came back in, one of the best people I've ever worked with. He had a wife, kid, just about to have a new kid. And this happened, and I was like, wow. But the good thing, he was still screaming so I knew he was alive. So I find where he is. He gets thrown about five feet in the Humvee. Humvee's just destroyed, like a big shot gun took a hole out of that side, and the inside was just completely destroyed."

Giles said that the lieutenant's rifle looked smashed. His face was peppered with grains of sand, and small pieces of metal. His lip was split and his face was swollen. The lieutenant had bilateral tibia and fibula fractures, open fractures where the bones were sticking out of his legs. "One of the worst injuries I've seen. I've seen some pretty bad stuff, the worst I've seen."

"Trying to treat him, then my left arm, searing pain. I'm like, what's going on? And my buddy Gibson, Lance Corporal Gibson's like, 'Hey Doc, you're bleeding.' At that point I just felt everything. I look, see a hole in my cammies, I'm not worried about it. Trying to treat him [Lieutenant Diaz], just started hurting too bad. Called [an]other Corpsman, HM Bender. He came, pretty new to the Navy, maybe a year and a half, two years in." Bender helped with the lieutenant, then Giles took off his own cammie blouse. Then he saw the hole in his own arm, about three inches in diameter and about an inch deep. Tissue and muscle were hanging out of his arm.

PFC Inglemier treated Giles's wound with a bandage and using the skills he learned from Giles's first aid classes to the platoon. His arm wrapped, Giles went back to help HM Bender treat the lieutenant. Both Corpsmen continued to talk with Lieutenant Diaz until the company surgeon, Lieutenant Gould, came onto the scene. Diaz was talking to the two Corpsmen, fearing that he was dying. Gould came with two other Corpsmen. Gould re-splinted the broken legs. Diaz was then medevacked, his legs were saved, and Giles said that he was currently recuperating back in the States.

Giles said that he didn't know that he could do this until it happened. He also said that that Corpsman–Marine bond is unique and strong. The teamwork saves lives.

I then asked him about his wounds and how he was treated. Giles laughed, then responded: "Me being the hard-headed person I am, I get evac'd to Baghdad. We go to Baghdad, Green Zone, 31st CASH [Combat Support Hospital—pronounced 'cash']." The lieutenant was immediately taken to surgery, and Doc Giles was taken to a treatment room. "They stuck me with a couple IVs." He said that at first, he was telling the Army medics how to do their jobs, but then he calmed down and let them do what they needed to do for him. He was taken to surgery for a deep cleaning of his wounded arm. He then went to recovery and talked to Marines and soldiers who had been wounded throughout Iraq. He was permitted to walk around the facility where he saw many of the seriously wounded, including amputees being treated or in recovery.

Giles said that the medical staff asked him if he wanted to go to Germany, back home to recover, or back into the fight. He told them he had to think about it, as he had been in Iraq both last year and this year.

"I could have easily left and said I served my duty, and not feel bad about it. But for some reason, my mom said about my character, I just care about other people. She was really upset. The final day came down, they asked me again, and I said, naw, I'm gonna go back to my unit. 'Cause I didn't want to leave our other Corpsman, HM Bender, out to dry like that. And also, I didn't want to leave the Marines out to dry. Because I thought it would be a good thing to get their spirits back up, with somebody injured coming back. 'Cause while I was in the hospital, about two or three days after, some of those same guys that were in my Humvee that didn't get hurt, an IED went off. That was a bad week for my platoon, 2nd Platoon had a bad week that week."

On the April 1 IED attack, Lance Corporal Barr, a good friend of Giles, was killed. Barr's uncle had died in Vietnam, and Barr had kept a carefree attitude in country.

On April 2, Giles was waking up in his hospital bed, and he saw a bloody face. It was one of five Echo Marines who got wounded by the IED. Inglemier, one of those who had patched up Giles was also hit, his face peppered with shrapnel and his back torn up. Most of these Marines wound up going home, and Giles said that his helped make his decision to return to Echo Company here at FOB Hit.

Today, his arm had not yet fully healed. When Giles first returned to Al Asad, he came back to the platoon for a visit. They told him that it was an honor for them to have him come back. That day, several of the Marines he knew were out on patrol and hit a land mine, and the rescue vehicle also hit a land mine. No one was killed.

As he was getting ready to return to the platoon, Echo Company got word to move to the Fallujah area as a part of Operation *Ripper Sweep*. They were gone about two weeks. Giles remained at Al Asad, and he said this gave him a good time to heal. "I come back to the platoon. First patrol we go on, another IED goes off! Luckily this time, no one gets hurt. By this time, we're like, explosion veterans. We just handle stuff really good now. No one panics, everyone gets out."

Giles said that now they were on the home stretch.

I asked him about his Navy commitment. He said he plans to get out of the Navy at the end of his five-year hitch. He said that he had said he had thought about staying in if he got to E5. He said that now with a Purple Heart, his two combat tours, and the experience he has gained, he could see himself staying and teaching younger Corpsmen. But, he doesn't know if he wants to come back here for a third time, as his luck may just run out. He says that he loves the Navy and he loves the Marine Corps, but isn't sure about staying.

I said that perhaps if he had a nice Mediterranean cruise, with about 14 liberty ports, in the future, that might sway him to stay. He laughed and said that that was one of the reasons that he had enlisted. He wanted to see Australia, that's what the recruiter said he would probably do. "Haven't been there yet!"

Right now, HM3 Giles said that he had orders to report to Balboa Naval Hospital in San Diego, and he has heard that it is a really cool area. That might encourage him to stay Navy. He's been with the grunts for three years, has seen a lot, and done more than he thought he would do in the military. He never expected to go overseas on a combat deployment. He never thought he would have to do his job in combat, or himself be injured in combat.

He said that people at home should see what the military goes through over here. The military life experience is like a blessing in disguise. He has done so many different things here in Iraq. "I just hope everybody makes it back to the U.S. unscathed."

Lieutenant Robert Joseph Gould, MD, USN

U.S. Navy Medical Corps, Echo Company, 2/7

Normally a physician would work at a Battalion Aid Station. Gould was sent to work with Echo Company at FOB Hit due to its distance from the base at Al Asad. Preparations for deployment included Gould updating the medical and vaccination needs for all of 2/7. His quick response to injuries on Marines from an IED blast helped to save the legs of a badly injured platoon commander. Marines out here rarely go to sick call, as they are busy with real-time missions.

Lieutenant Gould went through Officer Indoctrination school in 1998, prior to attending medical school. He earned his medical degree at Creighton University in Omaha, Nebraska, then went to the Balboa Navy Medical Center where he completed his one-year internship in surgery. He was then sent to 29 Palms, California, for duty with 2nd Battalion, 7th Marine Regiment (2/7) to act as a general medical officer. He was there since July 2001, and there when 2/7 returned from Okinawa in 2004.

Lieutenant Gould said that they began to get hints about the current deployment around November 2003. "What that meant for us was, we always try to maintain a certain level of readiness: Meaning mental readiness, keeping up with immunizations, keeping up with physicals, and whatnot." He worked to get the battalion at least 95 percent ready in the medical area. He also began working to train the Corpsmen to deal with the casualties that they would be likely to see in Iraq. He trained them in trauma care for battlefield injuries and how to evacuate the Marines.

Some of the training was internal: Corpsmen training other Corpsmen, Lieutenant Gould giving lectures and briefings. In Field Exercises at 29 Palms they had what he called "Cherry Pickers," Marines who would act out certain injuries that the medical personnel would then have to treat. Gould said, "Our Chief [Navy Chief Petty Officer] did an outstanding job. We had all the junior enlisted guys, did a really good job. So, the docs can take credit for that." Also part of the check-in process for the newly-joined Marines included the medical screenings and inoculations. Sometimes, though, he would have to grab units and do mass inoculations to get those who had slipped through the earlier screenings.

They left the United States on February 12, 2004, in the early morning. "Had all of our stuff staged, in front of the barracks, we then walked over to this other parking lot, where the Red Cross was out there. I thought that was pretty cool. They had a lot of refreshments, and we were able to get ourselves settled. Busses arrived, we hopped on. We went to March Air Force Base, where we probably were waiting for approximately four hours or so."

They boarded the planes, and stopped in the Czech Republic for a couple of hours. They arrived in Kuwait in the darkness and hopped on busses. After about an hour's drive, they arrived at Camp Udari, still in darkness. After breakfast, they got settled into large tents that each held about 50 people. Gould said that the Battalion Aid

Station (BAS) personnel stayed together and took up about a third of a tent. They began sick call for the Marines in the battalion. When they encountered a really sick Marine, he was sent to a medical clinic on the camp. But there were not a lot of Marines at sick call.

After about two weeks, two-thirds of the battalion convoyed up into Al Asad, Iraq over a two-day period. "There was a group of us that got to fly out on C130s. I was involved with that group, so it took us approximately an hour and a half, which is nice!"

At Al Asad, he rode on one of the shuttle busses and checked in before going to a tent city. Army soldiers were still there, so conditions were cramped in the small tents. In two days' time, he joined Echo Company at FOB Hit.

It is unusual for a Marine Rifle Company to have its own medical doctor. Lieutenant Gould explained: "Because each battalion's supposed to have two physicians, because this area [of Hit], we were expecting to have more casualties, and in fact, that's the way it's been. We've had more casualties here. So they wanted to have a physician out here, so that the points of contact with the physician would be sooner, rather than later. So we'd have higher care, sooner. Since I have a little more experience with trauma than the other doctor, they wanted me to come out here. So essentially that's why I'm out here." Gould explained that FOB Hit is about 31 miles away from Al Asad. A ground medevac takes 45 minutes to an hour.

Gould noted that one good thing was that Al Asad is an air station, so casualty evacuations (CASEVACS) happen real fast. "When we get a casualty out in Hit, for instance, and the BAS responds, we go out there and do what we can, bring 'em back. Lot of times we only have five to ten minutes before the helicopter we're relying on, patch 'em up, get 'em on the helicopter." The response time at this FOB was very good.

"We've had a lot of IED explosions, so we've had a lot of blast injuries. Initially what we saw, the IEDs actually destroyed the vehicles, and hurt the guys inside. Lately, the IEDs have maybe been hurting the vehicles, and but the guys have not been injured, if they've been injured, but not so much." Many of these injuries have been lower extremities. Some of these have been compound fractures, with bone sticking up through the skin. Lieutenant Gould said that the 7-ton trucks were very resistant to the IED blasts, while Humvees suffered more damage, even some of the hardened vehicles. "I don't think I've had a patient in serious condition that was in a 7-ton."

Of late, he said that most of the casualties have been shattered eardrums and shrapnel wounds, but nothing super-serious. There was an up-gunner on a Humvee who suffered a broken jaw when his Humvee hit an IED, and Gould was not sure whether he should have to intubate the Marine at the time. Gould checked the Marine's oxygen levels with a pulse oximeter device, and the levels were good, so there was no need to intubate. There were four other Marines injured by that same blast.

Lieutenant Gould along with his Corpsmen, HM3 Martin, HM3 Webber, and HM3 Maizano, responded to the IED blast that seriously injured Lieutenant Diaz. It was at night when the medical team arrived at the damaged Humvee. Gould didn't recognize the lieutenant in the dim light. The Corpsmen on the scene had already splinted Diaz's leg. They were calling the lieutenant "Sir," and Gould said that this was what made him realize that the wounded Marine was the platoon commander. Splinting one leg helped lessen the pain slightly. Once this leg was splinted, Diaz complained about pain in his other leg. Gould saw that it was also fractured, but the skin was unbroken. Gould began working on splinting that leg.

Lieutenant Diaz was then loaded onto a medevac and taken to BAS, where Gould took off the bandages to provide additional medical care. "This is an incident where we had, basically, five minutes to do what we had to do. So what I ended up doing, I took off the bandages, not completely, but enough so that I could see the feet. Both feet were getting kind of edematous, meaning swollen. And also, the pulse a little bit hard to feel." So he felt around to try and get a better artery to feel for a pulse. He could not find a better pulse. He prepped Diaz for the helicopter ride out of the FOB.

Diaz was medevacked to Baghdad, then to Germany, and was currently recovering in the States. Gould said that Diaz was now walking, and depending on how he recovers, may be able to stay in the Corps. He needs to be able to pass the physical fitness test, and Gould did not know how well along Diaz was recovered. "But he is doing well. He has both his legs, both his feet."

Gould continued, "I haven't had to do any what I would call, life-saving maneuvers. I haven't had to do a chest tube, I haven't had to intubate anybody." Marines have been wounded and Corpsmen have stopped the bleeding in the field. When they get to the FOB, Gould and his team gives fluids and run IVs, to help prevent shock from getting worse. "We try to make sure the bleeding stops. With the SAPI [protective inserts in flak jackets] plates that each Marine has, that prevents a lot of the chest injuries." He has treated rib fractures, but no penetrating wounds to the chest thanks to this protective gear.

Lieutenant Gould said that a lot of the time, the Corpsmen in the field do a great job under difficult conditions, and this made his job at the BAS a lot easier.

The closest that he has come to having to do a chest intubation was when a wounded ICDC/ING soldier was brought in. Initial reports said that he had been wounded in the chest. When he got to the BAS, Gould found that the Iraqi soldier had two small wounds: one to the lower chest and one to the upper chest. They had closed themselves, and the man's oxygen levels were good.

Lieutenant Gould enjoys being the senior medical officer at this remote FOB. Most of the Marines are young and healthy. Gould is able to handle the orthopedic traumas. "Being on my own, being able to make decisions on my own is nice." He has 100 percent access to the Marines under his care. He can ensure that they follow up on his medical advice. He is on call 24/7. Here, there is no place to go, and he has gotten used to the routine.

Lieutenant Colonel Skuta, 2/7's commanding officer, asked Gould if he wanted to remain out here at FOB Hit when another Navy doctor based at Al Asad returned to the States. Gould could have gone to Al Asad, but both he and the battalion commander felt that it was good to have a doctor out at Hit. Gould decided to remain at Hit with Echo Company. At Al Asad, the battalion has an IDC, or Independent Duty Corpsman, who is capable of diagnosing many conditions. And there is higher-level medical care at Al Asad, Alpha Surgical Company, only about 10 minutes away from 2/7's area.

"I don't feel like I am completely alone out here even though I am alone. I do have access to the phone, to email. We have, prior to leaving for Iraq, we had a series of emails, from general surgery, Navymed.com, or something like that." If Lieutenant Gould ran into a problem, there were doctors at Al Asad that he could quickly contact for consults and advice. He said it was nice to have autonomy out here at FOB Hit, but also nice to know that he can get answers to his questions from the physicians at Al Asad. "I think I've been able to practice good medicine out here, despite being in a remote location."

Gould said that at the end of this deployment, he was not looking forward to all of the paperwork he would have to do. There will be extensive post-deployment physicals for the Marines, and discharge physicals for Marines who are leaving the Corps at the end of their enlistments. But he looks forward to driving to work, cooking his own meals, having the bathroom next to his bedroom, etc.

On the plus side, being deployed makes many medical decisions easier. He said there is "A lot less shit out here." Given the fact that here all activities are "real world," it is not like the training situations in the rear (the States). Light duty has not been an issue out here. "Marines do their jobs, and it's a great job. I'll miss that."

I asked him about sick call due to minor injuries. He responded that his experience in this combat situation is that Marines don't come in to sick call, because they're too busy. They don't come in for a cold out here. He noted that a lot of the Marines want to be here.

Lieutenant Gould ended: "I guess I'll close this, I think my experience in Iraq has pretty much been what I expected. I think I'm getting a lot of good experience with trauma care, and I think that will help me with my future career." He has gained more perspective and calmness. He has seen some pretty major casualties here.

Gunnery Sergeant Paul Michael McElearney
Company Gunnery Sergeant, Echo Company, 2/7

McElearney was one of the senior non-commissioned officers with Echo Company. He first outlined preparations for the company's deployment into Iraq. During Operation Ripper Sweep, Echo Company prepared for a big assault into Karmah in support of operations in nearby Fallujah. However, expected enemy resistance there never appeared, and things remained peaceful. Echo Company did sweeps through Karmah to search for weapons and explosives. As company gunny, many of his concerns revolve around quality of life issues for the Marines at the remote FOB.

Gunnery Sergeant McElearney enlisted in 1990, with the objective of getting out after a four-year hitch and becoming a Massachusetts State policeman. But he was enjoying himself, having so much fun that he stuck around. He started out in infantry and he went to security forces first. He spent a year and a half in Naples, Italy. He then returned to duty with the fleet, with 3rd Battalion, 8th Marines. He made two Mediterranean cruises with 3/8. He enjoyed that so much that he went to the "schoolhouse" for Special Operations training group with IMEF at Camp LeJeune, North Carolina. While there he helped trained units deploying. He served as a drill instructor at Parris Island for three years.

Gunny McElearney joined 2/7 in May 2002 and began a work-up for a deployment to Okinawa. The tour was extended during OIF1. "And shortly after returning home, we began hearing about OIFII. They were gonna rotate the units out, get some new units in there, and continue the efforts of the coalition forces to free and stabilize Iraq. All of us in 2/7 were pretty excited about it." They had not wanted to be on the extended deployment to Okinawa during OIF1. They felt let down when they had been left out of that. "We understood, why we were where we were at, North Korea, and all of that." McElearney said that the Marines in 2/7 really perked up when unofficial word came that they would be deploying to Iraq.

"For myself, I was a little excited about it, on the same hand I was a little reserved about it, because I am married, with two children. And I had just spent a year in Okinawa, came home for a few months, and now I'm gettin' ready to go again." The gunny said that the families at home have to accept it, even if they don't understand it. But he said that this is what the Marines joined to do. He felt that now it was his turn to do his thing.

McElearney said that OIFII was a lot different from OIF1. In OIF1, there were clear lines as to where the enemy was, now the efforts were to get Iraq back on its feet and stabilize it. This required them to completely revamp the training of the Marines to redirect their focus. "Marines are flexible, 'Semper Gumby,' so we began our training at 29 Palms." There, the Marines of 1/7 who had been in Iraq, came up with a SASO training package. He said that the lessons taught were invaluable to his Marines. They had classes on civil disturbances to deal with crowds, how to do a snatch of certain individuals. The squad leaders learned a lot during the time at 29 Palms, and all the Marines learned to developed constant situational awareness.

Gunny McElearney said that the Company Commander, Captain Kelley, has had a clear focus on how to prepare for this mission. "The Marines are extremely fortunate to have him as their company commander. All of us. Very level-headed individual, calm, can handle any situation that's presented in front of him." The platoon commanders also get this focus from him.

The next training came at March Air Force Base, in a small unused housing complex. Some British Royal Marines were there to help with this training. They taught their concepts of Firm Bases, and "Trap Doors" from where and how to leave the Firm Bases. McElearney explained the "Bomb Burst" patrol: a foot patrol technique where members of a patrol sprint out of the gate for 100 yards or so, and then quickly take up defensive positions to evaluate conditions. A lot of the training was to learn foot-patrolling techniques. He noted that much of what the company currently did was in vehicles, and that they have adapted some of the patrol techniques to movement by vehicle. Vehicles will speed up before choke points, or change lanes, which will disrupt the plans of any potential trigger man. "There have been occasions where the IED has gone off just after the first vehicle has gone by, or just before the first vehicle gets there." He would like to think that some of this is due to the training that the BAF commander has received. These mistimed IEDs don't kill anyone or destroy vehicles.

When 2/7 got to Kuwait, the Marines were anxious to get into Iraq and apply what they had learned. Company Commander Captain Kelley spent several years in the Middle East, and has a great knowledge of the history, religion, and tribal aspects of the area. Kelley worked with many local civic and tribal leaders, and has tried to convince them that our forces are here to help them develop. When they came to him for assistance, he provided it for them. Kelley has been able to put the Iraqi face on an Iraqi problem. He has made it clear that the U.S. forces are not in this part of Iraq to exploit the country, but to help solve the problems.

Lieutenant Colonel Skuta made the decision to have Captain Kelley operate in the area near Hit, fairly independently of the battalion.

Echo Company replaced two Army units that had been operating there: An infantry unit, Mike Company, which operated out of Al Asad; and Two-Five Field Artillery that was at FOB Hit. The artillery only occasionally fired missions. They provided a great deal of turnover information about the area and how they were operating in it. Lieutenant Colonel Skuta had come over about a month before Echo Company arrived and shared what he learned with the company.

The Army had about 50 or 60 soldiers at FOB Hit, and was training ICDC forces on the FOB. When half of Echo Company arrived, it now had twice as many personnel on site. McElearney worked with his Army counterpart to house the Marines and begin the turnover. Left-seat, Right-seat rides commenced to familiarize the Marines with the "geometry" of the area and share their months of experience with the local people. The Marines had about a week or two to pick the brains of the departing Army leaders.

When the rest of Echo Company arrived, the Marines began "Left-seat" rides, where the Marines were running the patrols, and the soldiers were along as observers.

The Iraqis knew that there were new U.S. personnel here. The new Marine digital camouflage uniforms (cammies) made it clear that this was a new U.S. force.

Things were quiet when RCT7 began to flow in from Kuwait. McElearney's opinion was this was because of the emphasis that General Mattis had put on his motto of "No better friend, no worse enemy," in the First Marine Division. But the Marines expected things to pick up, and they did. Soon they began to receive indirect weapons fire here on FOB Hit. McElearney called it "shoot and scoot," where a member of the anti-coalition forces would ride up, set up a mortar tube or rocket launcher, shoot and drive away. Sometimes the rounds have hit inside the wire, and sometimes go clear over the FOB.

His Marines found it frustrating at times when they could not immediately go out against enemy forces. Captain Kelley carefully gathered data before reacting. He sent Marines out to look for scorch marks on the ground from where rockets had been fired. Locals were not very cooperative in sharing what they knew. In the last month or so, McElearney said that locals have begun to volunteer bits of information about strange vehicles or movements by individuals in the area. Some individuals in the town of Hit don't want to be seen talking with the Marines, even when they have intel that they want to share. McElearney realized that the locals may have a lot to lose if they cooperate with the Marines.

One new program began about six weeks ago, with money that was to be used by local Iraqis for schools, medical supplies, and repair of mosques. This also enabled coalition forces to be seen speaking with locals. Some intel can result from these exchanges.

The HET teams have also been useful in getting information from locals. They worked out signs used by locals when they want to contact the Marines. The HET teams will tell the Marines to detain certain individuals who they believe have information for them. McElearney said, "So, under the guise of snatching this guy up, we can get him out of there, and we can bring him to a safe location, where he wouldn't be identified [as] supporting coalition forces. And then he can give us what he had, and we can react to it."

McElearney said that in working with HET or the Army PSYOPS (U.S. Army Psychological Operations) guys, they need a lot of time to develop local sources of information and intel. Anti-coalition forces carefully observe what the Marines were doing, and develop plans based upon how the Marines operate. He described a VCPs south of here, where after about a week, anti-coalition forces set up firing points across the river to shoot at them with indirect fire weapons. Infantry Marines prefer to keep changing up routines.

The local sheiks have become more helpful for Captain Kelley. This is a tribal area. Kelley and Lieutenant Colonel Skuta have had meetings with these leaders here at Hit.

In April, during Operation *Ripper Sweep*, 2/7 had to move out quickly to the Fallujah area. A reserve infantry battalion, 3/24, came in and assumed 2/7's missions at FOB Hit. They only had a 48-hour turnover. 3/24 did engage someone outside the FOB, but there was no confirmation of enemy casualties. 3/24 continued security sweeps, and also found some weapons caches. McElearney said that the mission at Hit continued uninterrupted.

The Echo Company Marines were excited to actually get into the fight at Fallujah for Operation *Ripper Sweep*. Echo traveled on Amtracs as the mechanized company of the battalion. Most of them had worked with tracs before. Many in the company were new Marines right out of the School of Infantry. "Real young kids. Real, real young kids. I don't ever remember being that young myself! You could see it in their faces, they were pretty excited. A lot of them had a lot of apprehension." McElearney had told these new Marines that they would be going to Iraq when they joined the company.

After a day or two at Al Asad, the Marines loaded up into the Amtracs, McElearney loaded chow and water onto two 7-ton trucks, and they began the move to Fallujah. "It was kind of a rough time for the Marines, because everywhere we went, it seemed like they knew we was comin.'" Echo Company moved on Amtracs, along with a four-tank section, a CAAT section, and Echo's Humvees. "We were loaded for bear. We were ready to go." He said that the move was quiet, as no anti-coalition forces fought with them. At one town, they expected a fight, but LAR vehicles (LAV 25s) had surrounded the town during the night, and things stayed quiet there. Echo Company maneuvered into attack positions, and then word came to shift from a frontal assault to "smile and wave" in the town. His Marines quickly made the transition to smiling and waving. They went into SASO mode throughout the town.

This was a small town, and the men in the town were not friendly. The young kids were friendly, however. McElearney said that this helped to break the ice with some of the parents in the town. He said that at one point, one Iraqi boy threw a flower over a fence that lodged itself in the back of gunny's flak jacket. I remarked that he was the victim of an "Indirect Flower Attack," and he replied, "And I lived to tell about it!"

Echo Company moved out of the town, and moved on to check out the outlying area. The Marines searched buildings that seemed suspicious.

Word came that the town of Karmah was a strong point for anti-coalition forces. So Echo Company went there, set up a plan of attack, issued orders, and started rolling in to the town, from north to south, on the east part of Karmah. Echo Company was to establish a foothold for RCT7 there. 3rd Platoon was in the lead, the tracs in a blocking position, mortars were being moved into position, tanks were on the move. They expected a large number of enemy personnel at this location in well-fortified positions. There was supposed to be a fight there.

"We began, we came to L Hour, we began, 3rd rolled in, we all just kinda sat around the radio, those of us who were back." They were waiting for reports of gunfire to start coming in. "Nothing. Nothing." McElearney felt that the movement of the large number of Marines caused whatever forces had been in Karmah to leave the town before the Marines arrived.

There had been reports of rocket-launching positions on rooftops, and bunkers, but the Marines did not find any in their searches. They searched one building that was six or seven stories tall, and once it was cleared, Captain Kelley gave the word for his Marines to move into it. "War Dog" (the 2/7 command group) set up just outside of this position. Golf Company came down on the west, and both Golf and Echo cleared the town. Locals told them that the town had been full of "bad guys, Ali Baba," just a week prior.

Captain Kelley chose their second objective, the police station, as the Combat Operations Center (COC) for Echo Company. "Then we just began clearing the city. Block by block, cordon and search, cordon and search. Found some stuff, some weapons here, some caches here. The major thing we found was IEDs. When they [anti-coalition forces] pulled out, they're looking to delay [us]." McElearney said that the battalion altogether found between 90 to 110 IEDs within Karmah. All day long, EOD was blowing another IED. Every five or ten minutes they were blowing up an IED. "Even though the Marines didn't get into a good fight, they were able to at least make Karmah a better place for the people of Karmah to live."

2/2 was called in to take over for 2/7 in Karmah. McElearney said that most in his battalion wanted to do a more thorough relief in place than was done. 2/2 seemed to be in a hurry to take over in Karmah. Then they heard that two days later, 2/2 got hit pretty hard in Karmah.

Gunny McElearney said that the Marines in Echo Company work hard at security. They keep their gear on, their helmet straps buckled, flak jacket closed, weapons up, staying alert and attentive. They were not a very easy target. This was what General Mattis told his Marines, to make themselves a hard target. Some of the (outside) convoys that travel through the area were not as professional looking. And these guys get whacked by insurgents.

During Operation *Ripper Sweep*, the Echo Marines did not get into the fight that they wanted. But this meant that they would get to go home, and they would be able to talk about the time in Karmah.

Two Marines from Echo Company have been killed: Lance Corporal Aric J. Barr and Corporal David M. Vicente. A platoon commander was medevac'd early on. Lance Corporal Barr was killed in an IED attack in downtown Hit, and Vicente was killed in a mine strike. Neither knew what hit them.

An attachment of engineers lost three of their Marines while filling in IED holes about a month and a half ago. They were filling in IED holes along MSR Bronze because insurgents were using blast holes to drop new IEDs into. The engineers found an IED in one of these holes, and the IED went off while they were checking it out: Corporal Matthew Henderson, Corporal Nicholas, and Lance Corporal Kyle Codner. The whole BAF was there with them to provide security. "The three of them just basically disappeared when the IED went off." Echo Company's Executive Officer, Lieutenant Benz, was there and had the torso of one of the killed Marines land next to him after the blast.

Gunny McElearney said that since the Transfer of Sovereignty, the company has spent more time inside the wire here at FOB Hit. Also, Captain Kelley talks to the Marines and keeps them informed about what is happening. They have started back into physical training (PT). There is an MWR (morale, welfare and recreation) room at the FOB and the Marines have access to email and phones. He himself has been on prior deployments without this little luxury. He said it was good for keeping morale up.

McElearney and the Marines in Echo Company were wondering if things would soon change now that the transfer of authority has taken place. He realized that his Marines were shaping history right now, and would be able to look back on their accomplishments 15 years from now. He says that they know that they are not just fighting for the Marine on their right or left, but for all of the Marines throughout Iraq. And in some small way they are making a difference in the lives of many Iraqis.

At this point I asked if he had any "saved rounds," and McElearney responded that he had not really talked about himself and his main focus—logistics for the company. "Just like the lance corporals, the PFCs, and the captain, I'm just doing my job. A Forward Operating Base, it's a new beast to me. A company gunny is a real simple thing in a training environment, it's a real simple thing in a patrol base even, 'cause you don't have facilities, you don't have structures. You don't have local nationals, that you're coordinating, dealing with on a daily basis. It's been a beast."

McElearney has had to take care of the Marines' logistical requirements: Chow, water, ammo. Quality of life issues, simple things like taking a shower. The Army had only about 50 soldiers operating here, and now he estimated that the FOB was supporting about 350 individuals. A working shower was a big issue out here. Electricity was also big. The Army had left a generator that had a series of minor breakdowns before conking out completely. A working generator has a lot of issues, too: Oil for lubrication, fuel, heat problems, repair times.

The gunny has said that every day was a challenge, there has not been a "Groundhog Day" for him yet. He works hard to ensure that when the Marines come back in off an eight-hour patrol, they have working showers, air-conditioning in their berthing areas, and chow. Currently only two of the four berthing areas have working air conditioners. Electrical breakers need to be working for all of the AC units to work. McElearney called himself "Tim the Toolman" (after a popular American television character) to explain the home improvements he has supervised on "This Old FOB." His Marines have been good about taking care of the facilities, but things just happen due to heat and dust, and things have to be repaired constantly.

He said that the battalion has been supportive. Today he was expecting a set of free weights for Marines to train with. Somehow the battalion located the equipment needed. He also said that the battalion S4 officer, Lieutenant Cox, would do whatever he could to support Echo Company. For instance, a refrigerator truck for their frozen food broke down, and somehow on short notice Cox got a new refrigerator truck. With the food, soda, "near beer", ice cream, chips, corn on the cob and hot dogs, McElearney was able to put on a nice cookout for the Fourth of July at the FOB.

McElearney pointed out that Lieutenant Cox supports Fox Company, Golf Company, Weapons Company, 3/24, and Headquarters Company every day. At Echo Company, McElearney said he has been given a lot of leeway to do his job, and support from the company commander and the battalion. He said that he has several "go-to" guys in the company that make his job easier. He said that Corporal Warren, a mechanic by MOS, has been invaluable in fixing all kind of mechanical problems. Radio operator, Corporal Douter [*sic*] has been another "go-to" guy to get working parties from any part of the FOB. McElearney joked that the only thing they don't bring enough of is Coca-Cola!

CSSB (Combat Service Support Battalion) has kept the FOB well supplied with water and ice. All vehicles that go out have coolers and ice when out on patrols. There were a number of small refrigerators which McElearney uses to keep small cartons of milk cold, and keep soda cold when it's delivered.

McElearney joined 2/7 in 2002 and originally served with Golf Company as a platoon sergeant. When he picked up gunnery sergeant, he was transferred over to Echo Company. Looking back, he now felt that it was a good move for him. He also said that First Sergeant Harrison Leon Tanksley has been supportive and helped him to grow as an NCO. The staff NCOs also work together well, and the officers and commanding officer as well. Captain Kelley is calm, cool, and professional in dealing with all of the Marines: a true mentor to his men.

Gunny McElearney said that throughout his career, he has been fortunate to work with outstanding staff NCOs and officers.

First Sergeant Harrison Leon Tanksley
Company First Sergeant, Echo Company, 2/7

A seasoned veteran of 23 years, Tanksley served in a wide variety of billets in the Corps. He joined Echo Company in 2003 as it began the work-up for deployment to Iraq. He modestly stated that his main role was supporting the enlisted Marines of the company. He credits the company commander with keeping these Marines on task. Despite its remote location at FOB Hit, Echo Company now has ample showers, and access to phone lines and the internet at the FOB. His opinion is that the Marines and sailors with Echo Company represent the best of American society.

Before we sat down to a formal interview, the first sergeant and I had a very informal talk outside the chow hall after dinner. But once we started the interview, he was all business. I guess he felt that once the voice recorder was on, his personal feelings were off.

"Sir, for the past 23 years I've been a United States Marine. June 22nd, 1981, I arrived at MCRD [Marine Corps Recruit Depot], Parris Island, South Carolina. I was assigned to Delta Company, 2nd Recruit Training Battalion."

After recruit training, he became a basic warehouseman, MOS 3051, and served a year in Okinawa. On return to the States, he served with 2nd Force Reconnaissance Company. After promotions leading up to sergeant, he requested orders to the drill field. At Parris Island, he was assigned to Delta Company, 2nd Recruit Training Battalion, where he had originally begun his Marine Corps career. He was there for two years, from 1986 to 1988. He then returned to supply battalion. He went to 2/8, and deployed to the Mediterranean and Okinawa. On return to Parris Island as a warehouseman, he requested to join 3rd Marine Division, where he served with Combat Assault Battalion. He also served with Marine Security Forces at U.S. embassies in Cyprus, Belgium, and the American consulate in Jerusalem. When selected for first sergeant, he was assigned to Marine Communication Electronics School in 29 Palms, California. After a successful tour there, he requested orders to 2/7, and checked in on January 15, 2004.

Two weeks after First Sergeant Tanksley checked into 2/7, they went to March Air Force Base to commence SASO training. On return to 29 Palms, 2/7 began preparations to deploy to Iraq for OIFII. There was no downtime for him once he checked in.

"We deployed to Udari, Kuwait, where we stayed for approximately three weeks. I, along with the XO, convoyed from Udari to Al Asad, Iraq, via vehicles." It took three days for the 38 vehicles to move to Al Asad. Echo Company then continued to FOB Hit, and jumped into operations immediately.

"We suffered our first casualty, Corporal Vicente. Corporal Vicente's death hit the company hard." Tanksley said that Captain Kelley kept the company focused during this time. 2nd Platoon next suffered a serious injury to its platoon commander, and another death (Lance Corporal Barr) from an IED in Hit. Tanksley also credited Captain Kelley with keeping the company focused after the death of the three combat engineers that were attached to them. He said that the platoon commanders and platoon sergeants continued to lead and guide the sailors and Marines in the company. "As far as my role in this, I would like to think I do minimal. I lead Marines to the best of my ability, always looking out for the Marines and sailors' welfare, and providing steady leadership to any Marine or sailor that is in need of any guidance. I am the company commander's right-hand man. I try to assist him to the best of my ability."

He said that operational tempo has been heavy for the company. In the past couple of weeks, the tempo has slowed a little, and Marines have been able to get some needed rest.

In April, Echo Company participated in Operation *Ripper Sweep* around Fallujah. For 11 days they looked for "bad guys," but did not find any. "Had we found them, we woulda killed them. We would have eliminated any threat posed to the Iraqi people or coalition forces."

"In my time in Echo Company, I can honestly and proudly say, I'd rather be in no company or no other battalion in the United States Marine Corps. Each and every day I thank my lucky stars that I was assigned to this company and battalion. The company commander's outstanding, as well as the Marines and sailors of this company. I am proud of each and every one of them, and there's nothing I wouldn't do for each and every sailor and Marine in this company. I've sweated with these Marines, I've shared my tears in private with these Marines and sailors. The American people have nothing to be ashamed of with these Marines and sailors."

Tanksley said that about 90 percent of the Marines in Echo Company are first-term Marines. Some barely know how to read their Leave and Earnings Statement yet. His first challenge was to get their administrative matters squared away. They needed lots of reinforcement in learning Security and Stability Operations (SASO).

Tanksley said that for Operation *Ripper Sweep* the company started in Al Amariyah, then went to Karmah, did a rest and refit at Camp Fallujah. They were on the operation for 11 days. They did not find opposing forces, but they uncovered IEDs and bomb-making equipment in Karmah. No individual or vehicle was lost.

On return to FOB Hit, 2nd Platoon went to ASP (Ammunition Supply Point) Dulah, to guard an ammo dump there. The rest of the platoons resumed local security patrols in and around the firm base and the city of Hit. The tempo slowed down about two weeks before this interview. From April until the middle of July, they were going nonstop. Now, only one platoon or squad was out during the daytime, and that was in an overwatch position watching Route Page. At night, in addition to this, there was another overwatch position at a bypass on Route Uranium that is used by convoys.

First Sergeant Tanksley said that the expectations of many about the turnover of sovereignty, was that things would go to hell in a handbasket. "But the Iraqi people have held this together quite well, actually. Nothing out of the ordinary has happened. As of right now, the Marines aren't playing a big role in helping any Iraqi [units] right now. The police have stated that they will try to handle all problems, which may arise. If they need our assistance, they will ask for it."

Within sight of this FOB is a camp used for training Iraqi forces. He said that it was for the Iraqi National Guard. Golf Company, 2/7, works with them there.

He said that he felt that the Iraqi forces in the area were now more professional, now that they have been trained by the Marine forces. They have a sense of pride that they are the ones protecting their own people and families.

The challenge for him now was keeping his Marines focused, ensuring that complacency does not set in. He makes sure that they have ample opportunity to stay in touch with loved ones back home. And he works to take care of his company commander. Every Marine needs rest, and he watches out for signs of stress or depression, especially for those who have lost friends.

I asked the "Top" about the arrangements for officer and staff meals in the evening here. I had had dinner with them last night, and noticed that all of the platoon commanders and platoon sergeants sat at one large table, much like a wardroom on board a ship. He responded: "Yes sir, we have it set up, basically, sir, like a wardroom, so to speak. A wardroom slash mess night. The staff and officers get together, a chance for the staff and officers to get together and talk about today's events, tomorrow's events. And for the company commander to pass word. And the comradery, the *Esprit de Corps* you would expect in Marines. It's a chance for us to get away from the younger Marines and talk about some things we wouldn't talk about in front of those Marines. It's the company commander's chance to see all of his platoon commanders, platoon sergeants, and any officers or staff NCOs attached to the company. Because, once they're attached to the company, it is *a company."* It's a chance to unwind and enjoy each other's company.

I noted that it also gives the junior Marines a time when they are not under the supervision of the staff and officers. He agreed. "It gives them a chance to get in the internet café without any interruptions from the staff NCOs or officers."

Top Tanksley described the small internet café here at this remote FOB. It has six operating telephones that can be used to call back to CONUS (Continental United States). There are also 18 computers that can access the internet, available 22 hours a day. Every Marine and sailor can use them throughout the day. The café is closed for two hours each day during chow times, to ensure that they go and get chow. "It's a big morale booster for us to have this here. When I joined the Corps, there were no such animals on a deployment."

He then spoke about the physical comforts that have grown on the FOB. "When we originally got here, we only had six showers for 199 Marines and sailors." Insurgents threatened local Iraqi water contractors with death, and this limited the amount of water available for showers. Marines would often go four days or longer without showers. Even with "Navy Showers," they would run out of water. They now have 12 additional showers. The water contractor was now filling up the tanks twice a day. I noted that this was also a sign that the power of the insurgents had lessened, as it was safe for these Iraqi contractors to drive onto the FOB and provide the water.

Local Iraqi contractors also provide the Porta-Johns and trash removal.

About his Marines: "The first thing that jumps out at you, no matter how tired, hungry, or frustrated they are, those Marines would get off those rusty, dusty, trucks, laugh, tell a joke, and get ready to do it again at a moment's notice. There's no quit in these young men. Not a one. Even after seeing their friends in the platoon injured, in some cases killed, those Marines will mount their gear, get right back on those trucks, and do whatever mission is assigned to them by their company commander, and their platoon commander, and their platoon sergeant."

"It's a tribute to the young men of the company, no matter if they're wearing the Eagle, Globe and Anchor, or the Anchor of the United States Navy. Those young men are a tribute to American society."

Two of the Navy Corpsmen have been awarded the Purple Heart. The Navy Medical officer has also gone right to the front.

He explained the Backup Alert Force (BAF) of Echo Company. It is the company commander's own rapid response force that responds to IED attacks, weapons caches, or any unit in trouble within the company's area of operations (AO). They also escort Captain Kelley to weekly meetings with the battalion commander. The unit was formed from the Weapons Platoon of the company. The Marines from machine gun section, mortar section, and assault section were formed into the BAF. One section was commanded by the machine gun section leader, the other by the mortar section leader.

Finally, First Sergeant Tanksley said, "I really don't believe the American people know what is going on here. There's a lot of positive things that are happening here. A lot of blood, sweat and tears that is happening here." Only the Marines here will be able to share this with their loved ones. The Marines take a lot and go out and do it again. None of them has quit out here.

Staff Sergeant Jon Thomas Brodin
Weapons Platoon Sergeant, Echo Company, 2/7

The main challenge in the Hit area has been the IED threat. There have been very few direct-fire encounters, and Brodin explained that the enemy in the area studied how Marines reacted to the IED threat, and continually evolved their techniques. The first Echo Marine killed in action was from his platoon. When they returned from operations in the Fallujah region, he was on a convoy that was hit with a complex attack. The main missions most recently have been patrolling major supply routes, working with the Hit police department, and transporting Captain Kelley to meetings with the battalion commander or the local sheiks in Hit.

Staff Sergeant Brodin enlisted in 1987, served at "8th and I" in Washington DC, and at the Presidential Retreat at Camp David, Maryland. He deployed with 5th Marines during Operation *Desert Storm* and Operation *Restore Hope* in Somalia. From 1994 to 1996 he was a drill instructor at MCRD San Diego, California. He was with 6th Marines at the early stages of the Kosovo campaign. He served as Assistant Military Officer Instructor at Marquette University in Milwaukee, and then joined 2/7 in June 2002. As an aside, when he was at Marquette, he was able to get some college courses completed, although not as many as he had hoped.

After first joining 2/7, he deployed to Okinawa in August 2002, for an 11-month deployment that coincided with Operation *Iraqi Freedom*. He said that there was some frustration in the battalion that they were left out of that fight last year. On return to CONUS, Staff Sergeant Brodin said that there was a massive outflow of Marines from the battalion. He estimated about 70 percent of the Marines in the battalion left due to EAS (Expiration of Active Service), and routine end of tour assignments. Due to OIF1, there had been a hold on normal EAS dates, and at the end of the deployment, these holds were freed up for a lot of first-term Marines.

"Actually, I lost my platoon, when we returned to go to the company. I remember the company shrinking to about 65 Marines within the first month of our return. That includes staff and officers." As he remembered it, they first got word that they would be deploying to Iraq, then the rebuilding of Echo Company began with an influx of new Marines, staff NCOs and officers.

He continued, "The platoon was reconstituted, Weapons Platoon was reconstituted as a provisional rifle platoon. We conducted SASO training at the regiment level." They had a three-section platoon in the Weapons Platoon, but each section trained as an infantry squad.

The 7th Marine Regiment put together a training package for the return to Iraq. Brodin said that leaders from the regiment got together and created a Mission Essential Task List of what they foresaw the needs for arrival in this theater of operations. "Colonel [Craig] Tucker really assembled an outstanding piece of training with our lane training." 1/7 provided the training environment, instructors, vehicles, weapons systems, training areas, and communication assets. Units like 2/7 did not have their own gear available for the training as they had already begun to embark the gear for transit to Iraq. "It was just a very phenomenal piece of training they were able to assemble, really, in a short amount of time."

"We arrived here somewhere around mid-February, I think it was February 12th or so. Stayed a couple of weeks in Kuwait, Udari." There was an airlift element that flew directly into Al Asad, and ground element convoys that brought the vehicle assets overland. Echo Company arrived at FOB Hit around March 6.

"We saw quite a bit of IEDs, indirect fire, and it really, this is a very intelligent enemy. The IEDs were put out, obviously not well camouflaged. With the intent, I believe, of us finding them so that they can look at our techniques of dealing with Improvised Explosive Device threat. See how we were handling it, and they could expand their tactics and techniques, and put them [IEDs] where they can actually kill us." He said that there has been a very, very limited number of direct-fire attacks that were easily dispatched. The main threat has been the IEDs and indirect fire attacks.

"Our first casualty was actually a Marine from my platoon, Corporal David Vicente. Was killed by an anti-tank mine. It was placed on one of the roads the Army drove by quite a bit, in their mechanized vehicles. One of our Humvees, just happened to strike the mine just right, to send that round up and kill Corporal Vicente." They went a couple of weeks without any contacts. Then came a week where there was a casualty almost every time the Marines went out. IEDs were detonating on them, they weren't detecting them. 2nd Platoon of Echo Company got hit pretty hard. They were the platoon that was patrolling that week.

The platoon sergeant from 3rd Platoon had to return to the States for a medical problem, and Staff Sergeant Brodin asked Captain Kelley to take over as platoon sergeant for 3rd Platoon. "My first day with that platoon, we had gone out on a, [to] provide a Vehicle Check Point [VCP], in the third Hit traffic circle. During that vehicle check point, there was a massing of individuals protesting coalition force activity." Brodin said that this was around the time that Fallujah and Ramadi were cordoned off and put on "lock down." He felt that the people in Hit may have been fearful that Hit was going to be locked down, also. The Marines eventually returned to the FOB.

Later that same day, they were sent out to set up a VCP along the main road through the area of operations. "As we were moving through that, we passed through the first Hit traffic circle, and we were engaged by RPG and small arms fire, at that traffic circle. I think what was different about that patrol and one of the reasons we were engaged is because we were operating with two 7-ton vehicles as part of our patrol." Usually they would patrol with four Humvees, but this patrol had two Humvees and two 7-tons. "I think the ambush was actually sprung early, thinking that we were a convoy that was passing through the AO [area of operations], and not a rifle platoon equipped to go into a fight."

Two RPGs missed, sailing right over the Humvees. Brodin said, "I took one squad through the buildings that were engaging us, cleared those buildings out. All totaled, firefight lasted approximately 48 minutes. From the time receiving the first rounds until we loaded up on vehicles and left the area. No casualties, no friendly casualties."

Following that, they spent about six days out at a VCP. This was about two days before Operation *Ripper Sweep*. There they were engaged a couple of times by indirect fire. Once, the rounds were accurate and landed within the perimeter, but no friendly casualties. The accuracy of the shooting led Brodin to believe that they were dealing with a different, more professional enemy team that night. The last mortar round left the tube before the first round hit. Brodin said it was a very skilled mortar team. "They shot eight rounds in very quick succession," but the Marines were well dispersed. He had about 30 Marines with him at the VCP in defended, dug-in positions. They did not have overhead cover, but the squad leaders had all of the Marines in their holes.

Staff Sergeant Brodin remained with 3rd Platoon for Operation *Ripper Sweep*. The Marines from Weapons Platoon went back to their conventional roles, and machine gun and assault sections were attached out to rifle platoons. The mortar section stayed intact, and their platoon commander moved with them. Sergeant Day ran the Fire Direction Center (FDC) of the mortar section for the operation.

3rd Platoon was the company focus of effort during *Ripper Sweep*. When moving, 3rd Platoon was mounted in Humvees. The rest of the platoons were mounted up in AAVs. 3rd Platoon was near the head of the column, directly in front of the CAAT Section that was attached to Echo Company. The idea was for CAAT to recon, and 3rd Platoon to fix any enemy, and then allow the other two mechanized rifle platoons to destroy the enemy. However, "We were never engaged during that operation. I think we just brought too many heavy assets to bear on any enemy and they chose not to fight us."

Echo Company was south and west of Fallujah for *Ripper Sweep*. They were attempting to locate any enemy that may have left Fallujah. The Marines went into Al Amariyah, and Karmah. "In Karmah, we saw evidence of enemy activity, but no enemy." Brodin said that they expected that they would have to take the city of Karmah by force, block by block if necessary. Instead, they were able to occupy all objectives without a fight. However, at last count, Brodin said that 93 IEDs have been found emplaced along the route that the enemy expected the Marines to use to enter the city. But the Marines did not use that route.

Golf Company stayed in the Karmah area while the rest of 2/7 returned to Al Asad and Echo Company to FOB Hit. Echo had to assume some of Golf's responsibilities in the area of operations (AO), including manning some of the ASPs. Echo Company also returned to "business as usual": Patrolling major supply routes, working with the Hit police department, and transporting Captain Kelley to meetings with the battalion commander or the local sheiks in Hit.

Sometime in May shortly after *Ripper Sweep*, Staff Sergeant Brodin went back with Weapons Platoon in Echo Company. He sent his machine gun section leader, Sergeant Graham, to 3rd Platoon as the platoon sergeant. When a replacement arrived, Sergeant Graham returned to machine guns.

Staff Sergeant Brodin outlined how Echo Company organized its Backup Alert Force (BAF) from elements of Weapons Platoon. Each section was about the size of a rifle squad (approximately 12 Marines) with a machine gun squad attached. The Marines are all machine gunners, mortarmen, and assault men (MOS—0331, 0341, 0351). With the exception of the machine gunners, they were in a rifleman's role. They responded to almost any situation in this AO. If a patrol loses a vehicle, or a platoon is engaged with the enemy, the BAF could respond quickly to reinforce or help the effort. When IEDs are found, the BAF will go out and cordon off the area until the threat is eliminated. Every time BAF is outside the wire, it is because someone needs them. Brodin praised both Sergeant Graham and Sergeant Day, and hoped that they would soon get promoted. He also praised the Marines in his platoon. He said that they have just pinned a second Purple Heart on one 19-year-old Marine who continued to go on missions. In Staff Sergeant Brodin's opinion, NCOs lead the last 100 yards of every battle.

As for what was expected in June, he said, "We were actually expecting quite a bit more resistance, from insurgents. Anti-Iraqi forces, we were referring to them at that point. Forces that do not want to see a democracy succeed in Iraq." But that has not held true in this area of operations. There have not been the coordinated attacks that they expected. But there was stress in the minds of the Marines who expected that. He said that the Iraqi National Guard (ING), formerly the Iraqi Civil Defense Force (ICDC), has stepped up in this area, and were committed to the success of a democracy in Iraq. They were manning their checkpoints. Golf Company was supporting them. This, in turn, has reduced the role of Echo Company in this area. Echo still maintained route security missions and observation posts along routes used by U.S. forces. Iraqi Colonel Faahd is in charge of the Iraqi National Guard battalion in the area, and Brodin said that he was doing a phenomenal job.

Brodin continued, "Right now, our biggest challenge is maintaining a combat mindset, as we pull back within the wire, we limit our operations outside the firm base. Marines are playing football, they're playing softball, they're playing horseshoes. They're getting some rest now." The BAF still goes outside the wire searching routes for IEDs, and makes logistics runs to Al Asad, but the company's rifle platoons have slowed down their operations. Brodin calls the area a "non-permissive environment," not hostile, but an area where the Marines need to be watchful. There was still an enemy out there that wants harm to come to the Marines.

Lieutenant Brian Edward Humphreys
3rd Platoon Commander, Echo Company, 2/7

An older lieutenant, he joined the Corps after spending seven years as a freelance journalist in Russia. His platoon has mainly searched the area roads for IEDs, and was the only platoon in the company to be involved in a direct-fire battle. During Operation Ripper Sweep, *Echo Company prepared several times to encounter hostile fire, but the creation of the Fallujah Brigade stalled any offensive actions for 2/7 there. To date, none of his Marines have been lost in action.*

During college, Lieutenant Humphreys went to the former Soviet Union as an exchange student. After he graduated, he worked there as a freelance journalist for seven years. He said that he tired of writing about store openings in Russia, and wanted to do something more meaningful with his life. It was then that he finally decided to act on something that he had thought about doing when he graduated from high school: Joining the U.S. Marines!

In 2000, at age 27, he enlisted in the Marine Corps on the delayed entry program He began recruit training in October that year, and was then 28, about 10 years older than the rest of the recruits in his company. He enlisted to be a Marine rifleman, but wound up in a Reserve artillery unit instead. After he reported to his Reserve unit, he applied for the Enlisted Commissioning program. He was injured at Officer Candidate School (OCS) in 2001, and spent a year getting back in shape to try OCS again. He completed OCS in December 2002, and was commissioned as a second lieutenant. He then attended The Basic School (TBS) and the Infantry Officers' Course (IOC) at Quantico, before joining Echo Company, 2/7, in November 2003.

Humphreys said that many of his instructors at Quantico had warned new lieutenants that when they arrived at a new battalion to expect to be sent to a unit that had some kind of urgent personnel situation. Sure enough, when he and another lieutenant arrived at 2/7, there was a huge investigation taking place, and all of his Marines were tied down in a "Health and Comfort" inspection that was a part of the investigation. He also learned that all planned training had been canceled as 2/7 had just received a warning order to go to Iraq. "That's my first day in battalion."

Quickly, he was involved in the regiment's lane training to prepare for its Security and Stability (SASO) mission in Iraq. Their trainers were Marines from another battalion in 7th Marines who had recently come back from Iraq. They also taught 2/7s Marines about Iraqi culture and how to deal with the Iraqis, and types of threats they might face, such as IEDs and sniper fire. Humphreys said that he had been training at Quantico throughout 2003, while the Marines in 2/7 were on Okinawa, and all had felt that they had missed out on the combat experience in Iraq. Now it would be their turn.

Training completed, they left for Udari, Kuwait, then into Iraq. Humphreys's platoon flew from Kuwait into Al Asad in C130 aircraft. He was part of the advance party ahead of his platoon. He took part in a Civil Affairs mission west of Al Asad with U.S. Army units. "It was actually my first experience outside the wire in Iraq. First time, [I] made it across the Line of Departure, outside Al Asad. It's very tense for the people [who] haven't been there yet. Army guys, they have like, radio blasting in the Humvee. Smoking cigarettes and stuff [he laughed as he said this]. And a couple of Marines in there with their rifles pointed out the window. Going into "Indian country" for the first time. Go out to Kubaysah and do this mission. And everybody is very friendly, kids are waving. People want their picture taken with us. That's not at all like some of the things we had heard in the media about the way Iraqis were against occupation."

It made Humphreys begin to take a different look at the Iraq situation.

Then about two minutes after they left the town, an IED blew right next to his Humvee! This IED had been buried too deep, and the blast went out instead of up, and no one in his Humvee was injured.

"Kind of an odd moment to have. Army kind of doing their thing, a few Marines around wondering what happens next: Go charging off the road to find out who did this? Sweep the area? Or any number of things. Kind of ready to go with the enemy. I kinda cobbled together a makeshift fireteam with myself, and a Marine sergeant who's part of the CAG [Civil Affairs] team, and grabbed an Army staff sergeant, just one of the Army soldiers who happened to be around. Had our little fireteam, went off-road, snooped around, looked into some thicket shacks, and rounded up a few people who may or may not have had a thing to do with it. Kind of a first little taste of how things go around here."

He said that usually the people rounded up would be released, as wires or caches were not usually found. By this time in Iraq, the insurgents had gone from (wire) command-detonated IEDs to remotely (wireless) detonated IEDs. Humphreys said that the insurgents tended to use a Nokia base station, basically cordless phones, to detonate IEDs. These can be detonated from a good distance from the targets. "You might find the battery, circuit board, talk to the locals, they usually haven't seen anything. If they do, they'll usually give a little gesture showing they don't know anything." Most times the Marines did not have translators with them to get any detailed information.

Humphreys said that they have had a number of casualties from IEDs, and one company Marine killed in action in downtown Hit, in the market. "There's a narrow turn that comes, off one of the main routes as you go down to the bridge, which goes over to the east side of the river. It's a channeling feature, there's only so many ways you can get to the bridge. One of them, they placed an IED behind a wall." This IED killed a lance corporal riding in a vehicle. Humphreys was not at this attack. The attackers were never found.

Most of the injuries from the IEDs have been perforated eardrums and shrapnel wounds. His platoon has been fortunate—they have not had any injuries. "We've had indirect fire at us while disposing of IEDs. We've had indirect fire while working Vehicle Control Points [VCPs]. We actually had a direct-fire situation, ambush down at [the] traffic circle. Which is really the only time someone here has had a firefight, where the enemy stayed and fought." I asked if this was true for the whole company, and he said that this was the only firefight that the company has had.

On a mission to the Mahmudiyah area in early April, his platoon was going to set up a Vehicle Check Point in order to stop traffic from going to Fallujah. They were to stop all traffic, search all vehicles, seize weapons and arrest insurgents. Around this time, Humphreys said that there was an influx of fighters into the area. He believed that some came from Jordan or Syria.

"The night before this ambush occurred, we got intel that several Jordanian terrorists had come into town, and were holed up in the city. And turned out my platoon was gonna go down and conduct a raid. And then that was canceled. Then ODA [Operational Detachment Alpha], which is basically Delta Force, had the mission to conduct the raid with us. Provided security for them. Then the battalion became involved, became a very large operation around these eight individuals that were supposed to be holed up there. A great number of moving pieces going in and out of Hit. Then our intelligence turned out not to be actionable." The operation was canceled. The information about the eight individuals came from a member of the Iraqi police force who was later assassinated.

"The next morning, my platoon was sent to the same general area to conduct a vehicle control point in effort to try to hem them in. If they were at that area, to try and have their vehicles as they left the area. Personally, I suspect that they noticed that large number of Marines being in that town the night before, and had probably gotten out of there. In any case, we actually found an RPG in somebody's trunk. And we found another car that had a couple of Tommy guns. You know, unusual thing to find. Might find an AK occasionally. It was actually very rare, we did a lot of VCPs, in the city prior to this time. It was actually very rare to actually find a single weapon." He said that word about VCPs on the roads would usually get passed up the road by Iraqis and they would bypass any VCPs.

While manning this VCP, a large crowd of young Iraqi men started coming up from the river area. Soon the Marines were in the middle of a civil disturbance complete with rock throwing. The perception among many Iraqis in the area was that the events in Fallujah at the time were akin to actions by the Israelis in the West Bank with the Palestinians. Humphreys had about 30 Marines, and there was a crowd of about 100 men. Town elders were trying to slow down the demonstrators. Humphreys got the word to break contact. He quickly got a count of his Marines, got them mounted up as the rocks started pelting his men, and broke contact.

Later that day, Humphreys got word to mount up his platoon for another VCP mission. They mounted up in two Humvees and two 7-ton trucks. Staff Sergeant Brodin from Weapons Platoon had recently been sent to 3rd Platoon as acting platoon sergeant. En route, an RPG was fired towards the back of Humphreys's Humvee, but did not hit it. Then a large amount of machine gun fire and RPGs were fired at them along the road. "Your sense of time in these things, everything takes a longer time than you think it does." He said that the radio log of events did not match up with his recollection of how long things took. "There's sort of this extended psychic that takes you to realize that, now that we're outside the wire that somebody could shoot at us."

Lieutenant Humphreys realized that they were in the middle of an ambush. He continued moving his vehicles as he could not tell from which direction the fire was coming. "Sounded like it was coming from several different directions, and we couldn't tell how long the enemy front was." There were buildings near the road. He went about 250 meters beyond the traffic circle, and his Marines had also pulled past it. His Marines then executed their dismount drills as he called in his initial contact report to Echo Company's Combat Operations Center (COC).

He requested the company backup force (BAF) to assist. Luckily, the BAF at the time was just west of this position as they were en route to Husaybah. The BAF came back to them and Humphreys got radio contact. He coordinated with them to set up a blocking position so that 3rd Platoon could assault the enemy shooters. There was a lot of massive radio communications as the company COC tried to coordinate the movement of the BAF, but the BAF was already in position. This finally got straightened out.

Leaders in his platoon also had PRRs (personal role radios). "My squad leader on the left flank, or the north as you look at the situation unfolding, he could hear me on the PRR, I could hear him on the PRR. So, we passed a lot back and forth that way, through the PRRs."

The engagement lasted for over an hour. Most of the gun fire came during the first half hour, then became sporadic.

Then a Marine convoy came through from the south! Humphreys tried to stop them, but they elected to drive through the area. They received some small arms fire and kept going. A number of Iraqi vehicles also drove through the area during this time. Marines would leave covered areas to try to get these vehicles to turn around. They stopped three of these vehicles.

"Searched one of the vehicles [that] we turned into Swiss cheese. We actually only wounded the driver in the arm, which, looking at his car, was surprising. Had holes and stuff coming out all over it. We searched his trunk, and found a number of RPG rounds, a launcher, and machine gun ammunition. So it was obviously involved in what was going on."

The three stopped vehicles all had military-age men in them. Insurgents often traveled without weapons, knowing that they would be supplied when they arrived in an area.

There were several enemy KIA found dead with their weapons. There were also blood trails where wounded had been dragged away. The Marines found a staging area. It was near an auto-repair area on the outskirts of the city.

Every one of Humphreys's four vehicles had its own little fight along its 250-meter front. His Marines in the north were getting fired at from a school building behind the traffic circle. Humphreys said, "I gave the word for them to fire an AT4." The Marines set up a firing position. Humphreys said that this seemed like forever to him as he waited for them to fire the weapon. He heard the AT4 fire, then got a report from Staff Sergeant Brodin that the round had not detonated. (The AT4 is an anti-armor round, and the relatively soft walls of the building apparently let it penetrate without setting off the charge.) The BAF reported seeing the round go over the building. Humphreys did not get permission to fire another of these rounds at the building.

As 3rd Platoon broke contact to continue to the VCP, a section of Marine helicopters came on station. Humphreys was not sure if it was a section of Cobras or a mixed section of Hueys and Cobras. He talked them onto the area, but could not determine any "hot" targets for them to fire on. The helos made several low passes over the area, and then escorted his little convoy to the Mahmudiyah area. The helos then broke contact.

Humphreys's platoon then set up the VCP. They received some ineffective mortar fire from across the river. He noted that the shooters would often fire from across a river since there were limited bridges for the Marines to use to get across and suppress them. There were about eight 82mm impacts that night. "We had dug in by this point, so everybody was pretty safe. We just got in our fighting positions." He said this was the only time that they received accurate mortar fire. The enemy actually "walked rounds" in on them, making him feel that the shooters may have been foreign fighters who had come to Iraq.

Lieutenant Humphreys got word during the night to move to a less exposed position, and packed up his Marines at 0300 to move.

During the Fallujah operations, he saw lots of trucks traveling to that city. They would have banners with Arabic writing on them, and carried mattresses and medical gear. He called reports into higher headquarters. Later it was learned that some of the supplies on these trucks was to supply insurgents in the city.

After six days at the VCP, Echo's company commander Captain Kelley told them that they were to organize for combat operations, a change from the earlier SASO emphasis. They went to Al Asad, and got "meched up" with Amtracs and tanks and got ready for combat operations in the south. There was the possibility of going to Ramadi, Najaf, or Fallujah, and required a refocusing of the Marines to begin offensive operations. 2/7 had the mission of clearing Route Michigan, which had been coded Black. Black meant that control of the road had been taken over by insurgents, and the area was believed to be a safe haven to those insurgents who were fighting in Fallujah. They expected that they would have to assault through areas along this route. They were also expected to have to assault the city of Al Amariyah, a city built for Saddam supporters, and take a hospital in the city that was believed to be treating wounded insurgents.

As 2/7 began to move along the route, they cleared villages without any resistance. They bypassed a strong point that had not been occupied by enemy forces, and went to Al Amariyah. "We didn't fire a shot the whole time, but it's an interesting psychological, kind of, two weeks, mentally. Because almost every day you'd be given a new mission, and every day, something would happen, and, it would turn out there was nothing there."

At Al Amariyah, they lined up in a mechanized force. Four tanks were to lead the way to the hospital, and Humphreys's platoon would come in on Humvees. They would then dismount, assault the hospital, and the rest of the company would arrive in Amtracs. They would then assault through the hospital.

The column moved to the city, stopping about 500 meters from the city, and Captain Kelley met with Lieutenant Humphreys to tell him that intelligence on the city had changed. Humphreys's platoon along with the tanks would enter the city, on more of a SASO-type patrol. They would then set up security so that the command element could go to the hospital and talk to the medical staff there. As Humphreys went back to his platoon and was about to move, he got the word to "Forget the tanks." So they went into the city. Humphreys said, "Probably about the friendliest anywhere we've gotten in Iraq. People in Hit have never been real warm to us." He said that people came up to them to practice their English, and talk about favorite movies. He said it reminded him of when he first went to Russia in 1990.

The Marines searched for weapons, found an air-raid bunker, but no weapons caches. The 7th Marines regimental commander had the entire battalion (2/7) go into the city and patrol as dismounted infantry. They did satellite patrolling throughout the city. The next day, they left the city and continued to Karmah.

Karmah was also expected to be another insurgent stronghold, with reports of 500 to 1,000 insurgents there. The battalion camped outside the city for the night. Tanks would be used only in a limited role. 2/4 was already in a cordon around the city. 2/7 was there with tanks and AAVs, and would be a heavier force to enter the city.

Humphreys described Karmah as a town in a Clint Eastwood movie that had been taken over by the bad guys. "We found dozens of IEDs wired to explode." They began a cordon and search of the city, and confiscated any weapon that they found. They found a lot of AK rifles but no large weapons. There was evidence of fighting with bullet holes in buildings, firing positions for mortars, but no contact with the enemy.

The next morning they went to Camp Fallujah, and were told to prepare to go into Fallujah. Marine artillery on Camp Fallujah was firing into the city, and helicopter gunships were also shooting at targets in Fallujah. 2/7 was preparing to move to Fallujah when the peace agreement was brokered for the Fallujah Brigade to take over security for the city. 2/7 then moved back to the Al Asad area as Operation *Ripper Sweep* concluded with the peace agreement.

Humphreys believed that the sight of the Marine armor (AAVs and tanks) may have dissuaded insurgent forces from engaging them during this two-week period. As it was, his Marines never fired a shot at that time. He said that this was the last time he felt that this part of Iraq might be a center for insurgency. The main threat here continued to be the IED threat.

Since the turnover of sovereignty, the local authorities have taken on more responsibility. The only mission his platoon has had recently has been on an overwatch position on Route Brown. They watch a bypass to ensure that it did not get mined. They have lost a number of vehicles to mine strikes.

His Marines are getting some rest, and catching up on administrative items. Humphreys expects it to either stay very boring, or it could get real exciting real fast.

The experiences have been good for him and his Marines. Things have changed often, and the Marines have responded well to the changes. They now know a lot about fighting in a low-intensity environment. "Basically I had two squads the whole time. Had corporals as squad leaders, both of whom went to SOI together. They now have just over three years in the fleet, so they're coming up on the end of their enlistments. These aren't sergeants who have been in for eight years." He said that they have done very well.

The younger Marines will do well when pointed in the right direction. Humphreys has had four platoon sergeants with his platoon. The first platoon sergeant had 17 years of experience, but had medical problems and was sent home before they had any type of action. For a while he didn't have a platoon sergeant after a squad leader acting as platoon sergeant "didn't work out." Humphreys himself only has three years in the Marine Corps, and most of that had been in training situations. He did call on his experiences in Russia in dealing with differing cultures and personalities.

Staff Sergeant Brodin served as platoon sergeant for a short time during *Ripper Sweep*. Sergeant Brown from Weapons Platoon served for three weeks, then a 15-year veteran staff NCO from outside the battalion was assigned as the platoon sergeant.

Lieutenant Humphreys was proud of the Marines in his platoon. He said that he couldn't think of any other items, but said that he would probably remember some as I drove off in the convoy back to Al Asad.

Captain John Kenneth Kelley
Commanding Officer, Echo Company, 2/7

Originally an enlisted Marine, Kelley received his officer commission after graduation from college. He spent a college year of study in Egypt, and after becoming a Marine officer, was stationed in Saudi Arabia for two years. For much of this deployment, his infantry company operated remotely from his parent battalion near the city of Hit. During Operation Ripper Sweep, *he worked with tanks and Amtracs, east of Fallujah.*

Captain Kelley enlisted in the Marine Corps in 1989, and went through recruit training in San Diego. He was with 2/24 during Operation *Desert Shield/Desert Storm*. While attending college, he said, "I spent a year abroad with the American University of Cairo," and learned a lot about Middle Eastern culture. After commissioning as a second lieutenant, he went to Jedda, Saudi Arabia for two years. "I never made it back to the Middle East until about two years ago. I was one of the junior advisors to the Saudi Task Program."

During OIF1, Captain Kelley was completing Expeditionary Warfare School (EWS) at Quantico, Virginia. He was at 29 Palms when Echo Company returned from its deployment on Okinawa. The company went down to about 60 Marines due to transfers, Expiration of Active Service (EAS), and military schools. By Christmas 2003, he learned that 2/7 would be deploying to Iraq in 2004. In one of the briefs that he gave to his Marines, he told them: "Make sure that you start puttin' your houses in order." That is when he clearly laid it out that they would deploy to Iraq. After Christmas leave, Echo Company began to train for this deployment.

In January 2004, Echo Company began lane training, and continued with Military Operations in Urban Terrain (MOUT) training at March Air Force Base. Its gear came into Kuwait by ship and plane. Some of the gear came from MPF (Maritime Prepositioning Force) shipping. They did some live-fire rehearsals in Kuwait, and did cordon and knock drills, instead of the cordon and search drills. Echo then moved with 2/7 into Iraq by means of three separate ground convoys.

On arrival in the Hit area, Captain Kelley conducted liaison with the U.S. Army units there: Mad Dog Company, 3-3, and 2-5 Field Artillery. He learned a little about the area of operations. The rest of the company finally arrived at Al Asad, and then left for Hit. The Army mission in Hit had been to train the Iraqi Civil Defense

Forces (ICDC) there. On March 6, 2004, Echo Company took over security for the firm base here, and was reinforced by a four vehicle truck detachment of 7-ton trucks, 20 Humvees, a squad of engineer Marines, Human Exploitation (HET) Teams, and Marine snipers.

Starting in March and going right into April, there was lots of activity by insurgents in the Hit area. The Marines made their presence known with their distinctive new digital-pattern uniforms, vehicles that looked different from those of the Army, and more visibility in the area. Enemy activity consisted of stand-off engagements with RPGs, a few bursts of machine gun fire, and mines. "Definitely a shoot and run type of fight."

"We found out right away that one of the things we had to distinguish between [was] celebratory fire and actual attacks." When they go down into the city of Hit on a Friday or Saturday, more often than not they'll hear gunfire, and nine times out of ten it's a wedding or a funeral. The local culture is a gun culture, and automatic weapons are often fired at celebrations of all types! Most civilians in the area have weapons. Kelley noted that this gun culture also existed during the time of Saddam Hussein. Kelley added that a local explained this to him that the policy under Saddam was to arm a large part of the population to fight against an invasion.

Captain Kelley sent out both mounted and foot-mobile combat patrols in the early days to learn the enemy's "Rules of engagement." He explained that he also considered Civil Affairs operations to be a part of the combined arms effort in the area. He told his Marines, "You don't kill anyone who doesn't need to be killed, you don't break anything that doesn't need to be broken." He tried to get with local leadership and work with the Marines in Major Smith's Civil Affairs Group.

The message to local leaders was that he was able to provide grants of up to $10,000 for various projects. "Initially, almost on a daily basis, I was out meeting with someone different. And what I told them was, we're here as an overall approach—I've got Marines on the streets to help protect, but I also want to help the average Iraqi." With approval by battalion, he put together a group of smaller projects. Some of the more visible projects that Civil Affairs sponsored have been successful. These included the rebuilding of a mosque in Mahmudiyah and refurbishing schools. Currently, there were 11 projects underway in Hit, including providing sewage repairs, canal repairs, and money for mosques and schools.

The requisites for the projects were to include local contractors, improve the life of the people, and a limit of $10,000 for each project. Captain Kelley personally met with most of the contractors in the process, and he felt that the money spent has helped the local economy. Major Smith of the Civil Affairs Group was in charge of the Civil Affairs Marines. Kelley insisted that contracts went to local contractors, even without getting the usual three bids needed on Coalition Provisional Authority (CPA) projects. Kelly told the locals that projects had to be under $10,000, local authorities had to prove that they would improve the life of the average Iraqi, and local help had to be hired to do the work. He personally visited all of the local projects. "I couldn't have done any of this without Major Smith and his Marines."

Most of the combat patrols in the area have been Marine-only, even though Captain Kelley attempted to conduct joint patrols with the ICDC. These Iraqis did not yet have the assets to patrol—no vehicles, and their officer in charge at the time was corrupt. This individual was in jail at the time of this interview. The Iraqi police in different areas have done joint patrols on foot with his Marines, however. "We started to do foot patrols with them, which was something they had never done. We tried to work them in with vehicle patrols." The plan was to train these local forces with basic shooting skills, and then the fighting in Fallujah began.

During Operation *Ripper Sweep*, Lima Company, 3/24, relieved Echo here at FOB Hit. Echo Company had to leave with all of its vehicles, not leaving Lima Company much to work with. Echo then went to Al Asad where Kelley's platoons joined up with AAVs from an Amtrac platoon. He mounted his Marines in the AAVs, his own Humvees, and 7-ton trucks. This mechanized force then traveled south with the battalion (2/7) and the regiment (RCT7) towards the vicinity of Fallujah. "Our initial mission at that time was to clear MSR Michigan, between Fallujah and Ramadi, right outside of TQ [Al Taqaddum]. The MSR had been closed there for quite a while, a lotta IEDs, a lotta attacks." LAR (Light Armored Reconnaissance) was out in front of them, and it was mostly a "movement to contact" operation. They moved south from TQ, on the west side of the Euphrates River, but any enemy that had been there was now gone. "We could hear our brothers in Fallujah engaged in firefights, but we weren't really engaged at all."

Kelley said that intel reports warned of enemy resistance at Al Amariyah. He described it as a former Republican Guard walled compound. LAR (Light Armored Reconnaissance) had set a cordon around the compound, and no one know what they would actually find inside. Echo Company was reinforced by a platoon of tanks, and two of his infantry platoons were mounted in AAVs for a forcible entry into the compound. They planned for a lot of fire support including both fixed-wing and rotary-wing assets overhead. "Just as we went into this town that we felt for sure that there was like 200 'freedom fighters' they call themselves, we got word they weren't there. We went in, and it was an amazing thing. We were ready to go, all the Marines ready for forced entry into this walled compound area. There was no area to run, there was no safe area. We rolled up onto it, and no-kiddin', 10 minutes before we went across, through the front gates, we were told to stop, the enemy's all gone, we go into our wave tactics again."

It turned out that there were no enemy forces in the town, so the company instead went to what he called "wave tactics." His Marines searched the whole compound without finding enemy fighters. They searched using cordon and knock tactics. "We spend a couple days there, checking out those streets, and there wasn't anything there."

Echo next went to Al Karmah and was the first company from 2/7 into the city, but they found no enemy fighters there, either. The town seemed "closed."

"We got into Karmah and it was just nothin'. It was the most eerie feeling I think I've ever had in my life. Because, we had good imagery of it, we had a good idea of where fighters would be if they were there. Units had been in contact in Karmah, we had those reports, we knew where the danger spots were. We had good intel on the area itself." But there was no one there. "The entire town was shut down. Closed. Shuttered." He said that he'd be surprised if he saw more than a dozen people in the town during the first 12 hours he was there. This was a large, planned operation, with another infantry battalion along with LAR battalion and 2/7 involved.

Echo Marines did cordon and knock searches, and found evidence of earlier fighting, along with about 100 IEDs along the roads to Karmah. Marines from 2/2 relieved the 2/7 Marines, who then went to Camp Fallujah. After about 48 hours, and the agreement made for the Fallujah Brigade to assume security for Fallujah, 2/7 returned to Al Asad, along with all other RCT7 elements that had been sent to Fallujah. That pretty much ended Echo Company's involvement in *Ripper Sweep*. During this time, they had a lot of combat power, with tanks and Amtracs, fixed-wing and rotary air assets overhead, and LAR battalion as part of the force. With the Fallujah agreement in flux, Echo spent about 36 hours at Camp Fallujah before returning the Hit area in convoy.

Kelley's company stopped briefly at Al Asad to pick up mail and laundry, then went right back to FOB Hit. Hit is a city of about 65,000, and Kelley said that there has never been any hatred shown by the inhabitants to the Marines there. When Echo returned to Hit, the Marines resumed the civil affairs activities it had already begun. The battalion worked with the ICDC (now called Iraqi National Guard) and Echo Company worked with the local leaders, including local sheiks and elected officials, and also local religious leaders. He remarked that this works.

Kelley said, "There has been lots of success here. There has been good guidance from Division on down." He said that General Mattis's motto, "No better friend, no worse enemy," has been good guidance for Echo Company. The locals are grateful as the Marines here have been able to make life a little better for them. Kelley talks with local leaders, and, I believe his knowledge of Middle Eastern culture has made him an ideal leader to have at this remote outpost. In concluding the interview, Kelley said that it has only been in the past few days that he had been able to slow down and look back on all that his company has done to date. He credited the guidance from Division, Regiment, and Battalion for the success his Marines have had. "We've shown restraint and respect. We treated the religion with respect, I've never gone into a mosque unless invited."

Kelley said that this is a long fight, but a good fight. Success was coming slowly. There was hope in Iraq, but it was still a nascent stage and leaving too soon would have bad outcomes.

Not more than five minutes after the interview ended, we heard a large explosion nearby. Immediately Captain Kelley excused himself and went into his Combat Operations Center where all of the key leaders in the company reported in flaks (flak jackets) and helmets with personnel reports, according to company SOP. Kelley then checked via radio the status of Echo Company patrols out in the area—none had been hit in any way. Marines on the wire of this Forward Operating Base reported that the explosion came from north of the FOB. Then patrols reported that the ING (former ICDC) and Iraqi Police were responding in their vehicles to the apparent IED attack. I was still not sure which Iraqi forces were hit, but Captain Kelley said that since the turnover of sovereignty, he had to force himself to let the Iraqi forces respond to this type of attack. It was an attack on Iraqi forces, and we (Marines) were now in this area only as a last-resort backup.

The time for my convoy ride to Al Asad kept sliding back all day long, and this was fine as it enabled me to see all of the Marines that I did today. I met with the convoy commander about 1800, and the convoy finally left FOB Hit about 1945. We returned to Al Asad using roughly the same route that we took to Hit. It got dark about 2015, and the convoy commander gave the OK to use headlights. This time I was in the lead vehicle, and again had my weapon ready. A quiet drive, but I stayed alert the whole time. We got to Al Asad in complete darkness.

CHAPTER FOUR

Fox Company, 2/7, at Korean Village

FOB Korean Village

I met with the Marines of Fox Company, 2/7, at FOB Korean Village on July 7, 2004. I had to be at the RCT7 Combat Operations Center at Al Asad by 0830, so that they could get me to the A/DACG (Airfield Departure Arrival Control Group) for a possible helicopter lift to FOB Korean Village. I got to the building, was manifested, and almost immediately a helicopter was ready. It was a CH53 Echo, and I was the only passenger as it was going to sling-load a large pallet with cases of water bottles for Korean Village. I had never been on a chopper doing that, and while aboard the aircraft as it hovered above the ground, I watched as a crewmember lowered the rig to latch onto the huge pallet of water bottles. After the cargo snatch, I sat near the open floor hatch and could see the land whizzing by during the flight.

This was a direct flight from Al Asad to Korean Village (also known as KV), and took about an hour and a half. During the flight, one of the crew directed me to his window, and pointed out a photo opportunity—two other CH53 Echos also slinging water pallets in the distance.

We got to Korean Village about 1230, and I went inside the compound looking for Marines in Fox Company, 2/7. The camp was tiny—it sits in the middle of the desert about 1,500 meters off a main supply route/highway. Three units shared it—a Marine helicopter aviation detachment, 1st LAR Battalion, and Fox Company 2/7, attached to 1st LAR. I met Major Bodkin, the 1st LAR executive officer, and told him the purpose of my visit. He would check with the battalion commander and get Marines lined up for interviews tomorrow. It turns out that Bodkin went to Council Rock High School in Pennsylvania, and was born in Philadelphia. A lance corporal there was also from Upper Merion High School, also from Philly. They knew about Lansdale Catholic where I taught, and we talked Philly stuff for a short while.

I walked to Fox Company's buildings, and met the Commanding Officer, Captain Donald Shove. He was in the middle of a brief for a raid that was to be conducted that afternoon. Most of the company not on guard duty was to be involved. The 1st LAR Battalion had Humint (Human-based Intelligence information) about the location of a weapons cache in the city of Ar Rutbah. So much for interview plans! I apologized to Shove, then watched them during the brief. A no-nonsense, serious group. I was afraid that I would have little to do this afternoon, and called the air officer at RCT7, Major Adams, to see if I could delay my return to Al Asad (which was scheduled for Thursday). If I did this, I might not be able to get a bird on Friday, and I wanted to be sure to be at Camp Blue Diamond (at Ramadi—site of the 1st Marine Division's headquarters) on Monday for Division interviews.

Fortunately, the platoon that had been on the Syrian Border Check Point until June was now on guard here at KV, so I interviewed the platoon commander, Lieutenant Robert Christafore, and his platoon sergeant. Amazing stuff. This Marine second lieutenant had been the senior Marine on the border, working with Iraqi border police and customs people, as well as officials from Baghdad. Two outstanding interviews!

After about 1830, the raid force returned from the afternoon raid at Ar Rutbah.

I went to 1st LAR's informal debrief, where all the staff and officers went over the raid that they had just conducted. The major leaders stood in a circle outside of 1st LAR's Combat Operations Center (COC) and quickly reviewed what had happened. The raid was successful. They had a tip on a weapons cache in Ar Rutbah. Several LAR elements as well as Recon and part of Fox, 2/7 participated. They found a cache of RPG rounds, recoilless rifle rounds, 7.62 ammo, several rockets, etc. It was their first success in finding a cache in some time.

Fox Company then had several Marines ready for me to interview. I started with the commanding officer, Captain Shove. We conducted the interview on the roof of his command post, where it was cooler and quieter than the company office. It got completely dark, and I had to use a flashlight to take notes. The main highway from Syria was about a click away from the camp, and I watched the lights of the commercial trucks and passenger cars roll in and out of Iraq. I then had several more interviews in the dark, and learned a great deal about Fox Company. It was detached from 2/7, and attached to 1st LAR. Most of the time, one of Fox's platoons was over 100 kilometers away on the Jordanian border, and another platoon was about the same distance away on the Syrian border. These platoons were the only U.S. presence on these critical border crossings. Fox Company also went on Operation *Ripper Sweep* near Fallujah in April, and then returned to the KV area.

Captain Shove suggested that I sleep on the roof after the interviews, since the power was off and on for the air-conditioning in the command post building. I went to the roof and found an empty cot. It was a great sleep. I had my poncho and poncho liner, and gazed up at the Milky Way as I drifted off. I woke up a couple of times during the night, and saw some wispy clouds, and woke up in time to see the dawn. No indirect fire either.

Lieutenant Robert Manuel Christafore
Platoon Commander, 1st Platoon, Fox Company, 2/7

Christafore's platoon was the only Marine presence on the border with Syria from March through June 2004. He had to deal with local Iraqi officials and ever-changing conditions during this time in attempts to control the flow of traffic into and out of Iraq. The remote location required the use of four radio systems to stay in contact with Al Asad and Korean Village. Absence of Marines at the border during Ripper Sweep *created headaches when he returned to the post. He routinely sent patrols along the border areas to limit the flow of illegal good and smugglers. He described his Marines as "Diplomats as well as warriors out there every day."*

Lieutenant Christafore graduated from the Virginia Military Institute, and was entering his second year in the Fleet Marine Force. After graduation from Infantry Officers Course (IOC) at Quantico, he received orders to 7th Marines. Half of his peers sent to 7th Marines went to 1/7, and the other half went to 2/7. He joined 2/7 during the last three or four months of its deployment to Okinawa in 2003. "Got to see a seasoned battalion. A really good, seasoned battalion, how they operated and how they acted." On return to CONUS, he got to attend some military schools, and then got geared up to come to Iraq.

2/7 got a "dump" of new Marines in November 2003. That December, 2/7 got word that it would deploy to Iraq. He outlined some of the training done to prepare for the move. He was at Mountain Leader's Instructor Course at Bridgeport, California, when 2/7 began to go through its Security and Stability Operations (SASO) training. 2/7 had originally been scheduled to do a battalion training package at the beginning of March. 1/7 provided the lane training for the regiment. 2/7 also did some weapons training, then went to March Air Force Base for more training.

About a week before 2/7 left CONUS on February 12, 2004, Fox Company received another small burst of new Marines. Christafore got six new Marines for his platoon.

"We were in Kuwait about three weeks. We didn't do any live fire, we kept screaming for it, and Division kept saying there's no ammo, there's no ammo." He said it was kind of disheartening, because they didn't do any live-fire training with all of the new Marines during the earlier SASO training.

Fox Company went to Al Asad for about a week. Then it moved to Korean Village, and the platoons that were going to the borders went to the border crossings with Syria and Jordan. The Relief in Place (RIP) with the U.S. Army units here was supposed to take two weeks, but only lasted about five or six days. "I have to say, I got a pretty good RIP with the Army units out there. There were two Army lieutenants out there at the border. At one time they had a company, minus, at the Syrian border, the one I took over."

He said that the dynamics of the border crossing there was "nuts." I asked what he meant by this. He responded that the Iraqi government kept sending new ministries there: Trade, Agriculture, Interior, Oil. New policies would constantly be instituted.

One new Iraqi government policy was a 5 percent levy on all incoming goods. And at the time, it was mostly incoming goods crossing the border, so this affected many merchants. "Hardly anything's exported, it's all imported."

On the Syrian border, "It was just my platoon. I had some weapons attachments from Weapons Platoon. I had some assault men, just as extra bodies. I had some truck Marines." Helos would fly there about once a week, but if Christafore's platoon was attacked, they were on their own for a good while. It takes an hour and a half by ground to reach there from Korean Village, and for helos, it was stretching it if a Marine was wounded to try to bring him to a medical facility inside of the "Golden Hour."

Christafore's platoon was on the Syrian border from March through June 2004. "I relied on my small unit leaders to the fullest." Squad leaders took out the patrols and convoys. Christafore was usually dealing with local authorities at the border: The colonel for the Iraqi border Police, the colonel for Customs Police, and officials like this.

Christafore praised his platoon sergeant, Staff Sergeant Daniel Mainville. He had spent time in the sniper "community" as well as at MEF, and knew how to run a Combat Operations Center (COC) and taught the lieutenant how to run a COC. Their small COC had four different types of communications assets because they were in such a remote location.

"These Marines interacted with Iraqis every single day." The Iraqis on the border looked on the Marines as a lifeline in keeping order on the border. The goal, Christafore said, was to enable the Iraqis to run the border on their own without the Marines providing security.

About a week before Operation *Ripper Sweep*, the border crossing was shut down. Christafore said that there were civilian vehicles lined up for 20 clicks (20,000 meters) both ways along the road. He said that at the actual border crossing, there was a "no-man's-land" of about seven clicks before reaching the Syrian border crossing checkpoint. Then he got the word that the border was still shut down, but he had to take his Marines out of there. Once the Marines left to join *Ripper Sweep*, there was chaos at the border crossings. Goods flowed without any checks both ways across the border. The Iraqi border police had to police a border area of about 30 clicks (30,000 meters) each direction with only four vehicles. The area was just too big to control by themselves.

Christafore said that an Iraqi Colonel Maad was in charge of the crossing, and had high praise for this official. He said that this colonel had resisted pressure from some Iraqi officials to allow certain export goods to illegally cross the border. Unfortunately, the colonel was demoted for failing to go along with various government officials.

The Marines at the crossing did get rocketed and mortared a few times, but without any casualties at the FOB.

The lieutenant had an interpreter from Baghdad, and customs also had its own interpreter. "I actually had a great interpreter, a young guy, college guy from Baghdad. A lot of stuff [like bribery and corruption] there he saw pissed him off too, 'cause it was bringing down Iraq instead of supporting Iraq."

As an example, Christafore said that one night he and some of his Marines went into the passport office, and found 15 million Iraqi dinars there. It took them three hours to count it all. This office was there to check on the validity of passports, and this much cash in the office raised Christafore's suspicions about what was actually happening there.

"We had a lot of patrolling operations ourselves up and down the border. We would go out all night, from roughly 2200 at night to zero two [0200], zero four [0400] in the morning. We had our own Named Areas of Interest, and we'd send out squads, and vehicles. And they'd go out and sit, observe. We'd catch a lot of smugglers that way. Sometimes with people."

He said that before *Ripper Sweep*, they were detaining people who were crossing the border on foot or in vehicles. They often had "ungodly" amounts of Iranian money. Once they detained a group of 20 young men, who all had military-style haircuts. They sent them to Al Asad.

From the start of *Ripper Sweep* until the end of April, only commercial vehicles were allowed into Iraq. Men between the ages of 16 through 45 were not allowed to enter. Christafore's Marines dealt with this on a daily basis. "That caused a lot of problems for us at first." At the time of the interview, the border was open to everybody.

He described the small border FOB as surrounded by a small dirt berm about five feet high on the inside part of the base. In June, HESCO barriers arrived and it really started to look like an FOB. Finally, they were relieved by Marines from an artillery unit.

Next to the crossing was a tiny town called Waleed. His Marines patrolled there often and found contraband. They also found old weapons caches in outlying areas. Sometimes while patrolling along the border berm, there would be random, poorly aimed AK fire from the Syrian side of the border. He kept his Marines sharp by changing up missions for them. Sometimes they would patrol, sometimes they would be on OPs, sometimes inspecting the working areas of the Iraqi forces on the border.

Christafore said that during *Ripper Sweep*, his Marines were looking forward to offensive operations. His platoon, with LAR, was the lead for Fox Company. They were supposed to take the first intersection just south of Fallujah. They were expecting to encounter a company of foreign fighters there. But after they crossed a small bridge, they only had a small skirmish.

At Karmah, they drove by a lot of IEDs.

After *Ripper Sweep*, he and his platoon returned to the border crossing area. "It was a mess. A melee. No one was in charge." When the Marines left for *Ripper Sweep*, the border was open. Christafore said that it was a challenge to basically have his own area of operations (AO) there. He personally met with the battalion commander, the regimental commander, and even General Mattis, the division commander, at one time or another.

I asked him to outline some of the meetings that he had with the local Iraqi leaders. "Colonel Aruf, he was basically in charge of all border enforcement in the Al Anbar area. That's Customs Police and Iraq border police. We didn't have a regular relationship at first, as I never saw him. And I'd be saying, no, this is not gonna happen 'cause this is asinine. No, we're not gonna let this go through." Christafore asked questions about why things were happening as they were. Once Colonel Aruf got an office in Waleed, cooperation got better.

"Colonel Maad was the IBP, Iraqi Border Police, battalion commander there. [I] Worked well with him. Colonel Fowad was Customs Police. And we just talked about what training he was doing with his men." They discussed how other border crossings operated, and what stuff to let through the border. For instance, Marines would discover that border guards were taking cash to allow certain vehicles through, even conducting deals over their radios with other crossing guards.

Lieutenant Christafore helped to oversee how coalition money was being spent on facilities for the Iraqi Border Police. He recommended that the Iraqi border police rotate their men on posts so that the same men would not be on the same posts and make arrangements with smugglers.

"I'd get intel there daily about Rutbah, about Ramadi, about Fallujah, because everybody came through there. I had a pretty good relationship with a lot of the workers there, and they'd tell me a whole bunch of stuff that I think helped me a lot." Christafore said that he would often have Civil Affairs Group (CAG) Marines there for a week at a time, and would pass information on to them.

Christafore said that his Marines were "Diplomats as well as warriors out there every day." He said that he had been skeptical about living and working with the Iraqis when he first got here. But he developed good relationships with the Iraqis there. "They're gonna trust you when you're living there every day with them. And they're gonna tell you everything." He felt that we would begin rooting out the insurgents when they begin living with the Iraqis. "I saw it first-hand."

He said that, if possible, he would extend (his tour) to do Civil Affairs Platoon operations in Iraq.

Christafore was just coming back to Korean Village when the turnover of sovereignty took place on June 28. He said that the Iraqi officials on the border were scared to death about the turnover of sovereignty They feared chaos and that the American forces were leaving.

But by the time that the end of June 2004 came, the Iraqis were already starting to enforce policies that were coming from Iraqi authorities.

He said that the Syrian border authorities caused a lot of problems. They allowed many to cross the border, and refused to meet with him. Eventually the Syrians did begin to meet with Iraqi border forces, but on the Syrian side of the border.

Lieutenant Christafore had high praise for his platoon sergeant (Sergeant Daniel Mainville), squad leaders, and the young Marines. They subsisted on MREs (Meals Ready-to-Eat) most of the time they were on the Syrian border, not getting tray rations until late in June. He had the platoon organized into two large squads. One would be either on FOB security, React Force, or rest for two days, while the other was out on operations. He made sure to always talk with his Marines to see how they were doing.

At the time of this interview, 1st Platoon was on camp security duty for FOB Korean Village. That ended the past Sunday. He has also done some "Trojan Horse" operations. This involved about 10 of his Marines and an Iraqi truck. They outfitted the truck to look like it had a load of 50 new air conditioners. They would go on MSR Mobile in this truck, with a squad of Marines in the back of the truck, and Christafore and another Marine in front dressed up like Iraqis, trying to attract an attack. LAR was on overwatch. There were common thieves who hit Iraqi and coalition-chartered vehicles and steal the cargo. So far, the Marines on the Trojan Horse had not been hit by thieves.

In closing, Lieutenant Christafore felt that the Marines needed to get inside the cities and fight alongside the Iraqi forces. Building trust with them was critical. He also felt that the Marine squad leaders need to be given the missions. He has tried to do this in his platoon. If they get the job done, then he has done his job.

Staff Sergeant Daniel Joseph Mainville
Platoon Sergeant, 1st Platoon, Fox Company, 2/7

Staff Sergeant joined Fox Company only weeks before departure for Kuwait, but said that the time there allowed for some valuable training for a company with a lot of new Marines. He outlined the challenges of working on the border crossing into Syria, language challenges using contracted translators, and breaking habits of corruption in the Iraqi border workers. During Ripper Sweep his platoon fought near Fallujah.

We sat on cots opposite each other on the roof of Fox Company's CP building. It was very dark, the only light coming from stars and the headlights of the highway in the distance. I used my Maglite flashlight to illuminate my notebook as the interview proceeded.

Staff Sergeant Mainville began: "I enlisted in January of 1987, after graduating ITS (Infantry Training School) I was put into a line company [infantry] in First

Battalion, First Marines [1/1]. Did one deployment with them. Got a chance to go over to a sniper platoon from there."

After attending sniper school and reenlistment, he was assigned to Quantico, where he was part of Enlisted Instructor Company. He later spent a year as a sniper instructor at Quantico, then a year as an instructor at the Infantry Officers' Course (IOC).

After his second reenlistment, he returned to 1/1 in 1993. He was chief sniper and platoon sergeant for the sniper platoon until 1998. He then went to IMEF (1st Marine Expeditionary Force), where he worked in the G3 shop, then the G7 shop. In G7, he worked in simulation and modeling, to look at situations throughout the world, and figure out how to train Marines for them. They studied convoy operations that occurred during OIF1, and saw how they were taking enemy fire. They designed ways to train convoy and vehicle commanders. They bought a computer simulation program, and customized it for use to train Marines for convoys, crowd control, and dealing with IEDs. He said that they trained 1st FSSG, (Force Service Support Group) and 1st MHG (Marine Headquarters Group). When he left IMEF and came to 2/7, Mainville stayed in touch with his old boss at G7 via email, and now answered inquiries as to how effective the training has been.

Staff Sergeant Mainville joined Fox Company on January 30, 2004, only about 10 or 12 days before they deployed to Iraq. "I was glad to get a platoon after such a long period of time away from the grunts, and now, here I am!"

"When I checked in, we had, I think it was roughly, 20 or 22 brand-new Marines, right out of SOI, all PFCs [Private First Class]. I had one sergeant, and four or five corporals. Total in the platoon we had two squads, plus one fire team. I was a little bit reluctant about taking over the platoon. After seeing the structure of it, because, at first, I started getting that, brand-new, second lieutenant mentality, going to Vietnam. Checking in, getting a brand-new platoon, bein' a brand-new platoon sergeant, not having a chance to go through training with them. Deploying a few days later, into [a] hot zone. I didn't know what to encounter. But, [the] Marines did outstanding. We had a month in Camp Udari. So we got a chance to work on a lot of things I saw them working on."

He said that many of the new Marines had come right from SOI, and after joining Fox Company, they did a lot of SASO training, but had not had the time to work on basic infantry formations and drills. In the time they spent at Camp Udari, Mainville began to work on these basic small unit skills.

Four of his Marines were drivers who drove all the way from Kuwait out here to Korean Village. The rest of his platoon, along with Fox Company, flew out of Kuwait by C130 airplanes. They landed at Al Asad and spent two days there. They then flew on Army CH47 helicopters up to Korean Village. Mainville said that part of the reason for using Army helos was that the Army had worked out the load numbers while in Iraq, and would load up a larger number of Marines onto their helos than the Marine helos were carrying. All of 1st Platoon flew in two Army CH47s.

1st Platoon was assigned to go to Al Waleed on the Syrian border to work on border security, and help train the Iraqi border police, customs personnel, and Iraqi police. The total number of Marines at the small FOB varied, from 42 up to 53, with attachments that included dog teams and machine gunners. They had two squads and a headquarters element when they first got there. One of the squads was on FOB security for two days, and the other squad patrolled, checked on border procedures, and patrolled with the Iraqi border police. They searched for smugglers and also for foreign fighters coming into the town.

On first arrival at the border crossing, they began to teach the Iraqi border police on how to search vehicles and personnel properly. The Marines also taught them to patrol along the border, and better weapons handling.

Staff Sergeant Mainville said that the next order of business was "Putting a foot in the ass" of the Iraqi Police. They had been content to stay in their offices instead of working on the streets of Al Waleed. "Any time we went into east or west Waleed, we stopped into the police department, took one of the police officers, or two of them. We brought them on a patrol with us, so that the people of the town got to see their faces, and they could point out things to us."

After the Marines returned to Al Waleed when *Ripper Sweep* was done, they worked with the Customs Police on the border. The Customs Police had a little bit better training than the Iraqi Border Police. Marines helped with teaching better documentation and record keeping. For instance, when the Iraqi officials would take the tariff money for an incoming cargo, they would give a receipt to the driver, but not log the amount into their own records!

Mainville said that there were two or three Iraqis who always had their hand in the till. "One of the things we did, was, every morning at 0700, we would have one of our Marines go up there and get a basic morning report from them: How many vehicles went in and out of the country, what types of vehicles they were, how many personnel went in and out, and how many monies were collected in the tariffs."

For communications the Marines had an Iraqi translator working with them. Later, the Customs Police had a translator. The Marines also had access to this translator. Mainville said that the hard times were when they were without their own translator. Their translator's contract had him work for a month, then he had a 10-day leave period when he could return to his home and spend time with his family. The platoon would then have to send back to Korean Village to get a translator, or they would ask for a translator from the Food for Oil office, which was right across the street from them. But this translator had to stay close to his office. "We had a few of the Marines, who worked the border points, day in, day out, they got to pick up all the basic [Iraqi] terms: Greeting the Iraqis, opening the doors, closing their doors, [and] general commands for vehicle search."

Before Staff Sergeant Mainville joined the platoon, there had been three Marines sent to basic Iraqi language training. But he said it was really being on the border that forced them to pick up and use these basic terms. Many of these terms were on the laminated language cards issued to all Marines.

Mainville said that there was a Jordanian-American who worked for a trucking company on the border who sometimes helped out when needed for translations. This individual also provided hints on local customs that would ensure better relations with the Iraqis with whom they were dealing. "This is the way the Iraqi people do things, so this is the way you have to do things."

I asked him about the frustrations of working on the border. He responded: "I think some of the biggest ones, sir, for myself and all the Marines, were, if we caught smugglers, we turned them over to the Iraqi Border Police, or the IP, Iraqi Police department. And usually two, three days later, they're back on the streets smuggling again. A couple times we had warnings, or indications, that the Iraqi Border Police were helping smuggle people and benzene into Syria, and we caught them one night. We turned them over to the Iraqi Border Police, and they basically laughed when we turned them back over to them at the border police personnel." Mainville said that these smugglers were back out doing their thing the next night.

About five to ten days before the border was closed for *Ripper Sweep*, Mainville's Marines caught about 20 military-age men. They had crew cuts, Lebanese money, fake passports, and the Marines considered them to be foreign fighters.

"A few days later, the border was declared closed. And, we had a lot of problems with not only the customs personnel, the border police, and people out in town trying to get through the border. They would crowd up around the border checkpoint, we had to go out there, disperse them, and the biggest thing then was trying to get across the border. It was a threat for us, 'cause we only had two squads, a platoon on the border point. And one of them [a squad] was on security. So there were times when we were on 100 percent alert, and, that, lack of sleep, frustrated with the border not being open, having to go out there and deal with it. Deal with it. We started having the Marines starting to get pretty mad. Plus, it was hot out at that time, too."

Another troubling time was when pay from the coalition for the Iraqi Police was late in arriving. If they weren't getting paid, the Iraqi Police stopped showing up for work. On days when there should have been 70 or 80 police on post, they might only have 20 or 30 appear. This meant that the Marines had to help them with security at the borders. This limited the Marines' ability to do security patrols around their FOB.

During Operation *Ripper Sweep* near Fallujah, 1st Platoon had enemy contact at the first town they encountered. He could not recall the name of this town, but said, "After the first 15 minutes we were in town, we actually started receiving machine gun fire. There was AK fire from a gentleman [*sic*] driving a fuel truck. There were two men in the truck. We opened up on it, killed the driver. The assistant driver jumped out of the vehicle, he got away. Vehicle was in flames. Then we had to go house-to-house searching. Then after about four or six hours of doing that, we were relieved by 3rd Platoon, we went into reserve. And we started setting out VCPs [Vehicle Check Points]."

As the company continued on, 1st Platoon served as the lead element, searching for IEDs and possible hostile intent in small towns. Staff Sergeant Mainville had the up-armored vehicles with the Mark 19 (40mm grenade launcher) and .50 cals (M2 Browning .50 caliber machine gun) on them to act as the Support-by-Fire element if needed. He said that they went on a roundabout way to the area of Fallujah, going north first to the area around Al Qaim, then on what he called a "Tour of Iraq" to get to Fallujah.

"The first town we hit was just south of Fallujah, our limit of advance was the bridge that was going into Fallujah. And we met up with, I think it was Echo Company or Golf Company of 2/7 over there. They moved across the bridge with their AAVs, and they were stopped, and we met them, and that was when we set in our defense that night."

Mainville said that most of the time in the Fallujah area consisted of cordon and searches of the villages. They had a big search in Karmah, where they went through every house and business in the city. They also set up vehicle check points. The night they were due to leave Karmah, they got word from some local Iraqis—who'd had their sons killed by foreign fighters when they refused to join with them—about a weapons cache and the bodies of two German contractors. Fox Company's mission was to recover these two bodies. They found one partially decomposed body in a quarry near Karmah. He did not know the identity of the person that they uncovered there.

Staff Sergeant Mainville estimated that they were on Operation *Ripper Sweep* for about three weeks, then they returned to Korean Village. "We sat here for one night, gathered up all our belongings, and we pushed back to the Al Waleed border point."

While Fox Company was first gone from the border crossing point, the border crossing was empty of Marines for a few hours. Then Marines from the Civil Affairs Group and some Air Wing Marines and Camp Guard from Al Asad came out to fill the void because the border crossing had opened up wide without control.

When they got back to the border crossing, things had changed. Mainville said, "One of the biggest things was the border was open 24 hours a day. Not 24 hours a day, but it was open to traffic both coming in and out of Syria. Originally, it was open to just commercial traffic coming from Syria. Now it was open to all traffic going back and forth. That was when IBP [Iraqi Border Police] started losing some of their position out there. Where they were told they were just gonna man the border, do security of the borders, north and south of the point of entry. And Customs Police will man that point itself. Roughly about that time is when the Iraqis started getting a little more, uh, into doing the border crossing. They started building up more offices. Figuring out what they needed to man the border point instead of just having a customs office they needed a Ministry of Transportation there, they needed, a Ministry of Health there. So they started bringing them in." The Iraqi officials started to define the roles for the various Iraqi agencies at the crossing.

Mainville said that this made it a little bit easier for the Marines, but harder for his platoon commander, Lieutenant Christafore, because he was the individual who had to go out there and deal with the Iraqi personnel in the offices. The Marines would not have to do the searches at the border crossing, they could just observe the Iraqis conducting the searches.

The Iraqis also set up a large parking area so that vehicles waiting would not have to do so in the "no-man's-land" for three or four days between the Iraqi and Syrian crossing points. Vehicles would be brought into the parking area and then searched. This put a new burden on the Marines, however, as they needed to show the Iraqis how to provide proper security for the parking area, search vehicles, and have proper documentation done. 1st Platoon spent about a month and a half at the border crossing before being pulled back to Korean Village.

"Echo, 2/11 [Echo Battery, an artillery unit—serving as a provisional rifle company] relieved us. And we sat down with them, explained the procedures, some of the tasks that we had going on, the plans that we had for the border crossing in the small town. We handed all that over to them so that hopefully they can build off that to help the Iraqis build their government right there."

Mainville said that he had about two days to do a turnover with his counterpart from Echo Battery, and Lieutenant Christafore had about four days. Mainville said that he felt a week to 10-day turnover would have been better for him to do. This Marine-to-Marine turnover took place in mid-June.

Mainville noted that (1st Marine) Division did send a request to Fox Company to send one Marine to both the Syrian and Jordanian border crossings to see if traffic levels crossing the border had increased since the turnover of sovereignty. But it did not happen. Mainville told Division that customs personnel had computers to track everything at the border.

He also said that just before Fox left the border crossing, there was an increase in traffic leaving Iraq, as the border crossing at Al Qaim had been closed for a few days.

Once back at Korean Village, 1st Platoon began to work on VCPs (Vehicle Check Points). They would go out for six hours and then come back in for 18 hours. They conducted Snap VCPs east and west of Ar Rutbah, and night Observation Points along "Ambush Alley," an area just east of Ar Rutbah. The night missions would begin around 2200 and end just before sunrise. He said that right now, most of the platoon was on FOB guard duty, and they were also running "Trojan Horse" missions.

"We have an Iraqi truck, 7-ton if you will, and we set it up with a driver and A-driver [Assistant Driver] dressed up in Arabic clothes. The rest of the unit goes in the back [of the truck]. We have it looking like a merchant's vehicle. And we have a QRF of LAR that gets in position, either somewhere behind us, or get pre-positioned somewhere ahead of us. And we drive up and down Ambush Alley, either hoping to get ambushed or, we stop our vehicle and make it look like it's broken down. And just see if we have any thieves that come up and, so we can takedown the thieves that are hitting the KBR and coalition forces, transportation that moves through that area."

He said that the Marines who are the drivers and front seat passengers get permission to let their hair grow longer and go without shaving, so that they look more like locals. He said that a few of them are getting to like this, getting ready to do civilian trucking when they get discharged in the States. Several of his "short timers" will get their discharges about a month after they get home.

Mainville said that the variety of missions his Marines have done have helped them avoid complacency. They now had daily missions, rather than the routine of their role at the border. "One mission after another, sir, it's helping time go by a lot faster."

He said that his young Marines have responded well. When the platoon was at the border, he established a mentor program for them. "One of my taskers to the squad leaders and team leaders, was to start having those junior Marines step up to the plate. And before we did missions, they would do the warning order, the overlay, the operations order. With the oversight of either myself, or the squad leader while they were doing that. And in doing that, we started seeing a lot of the junior Marines step up, and starting to take charge. We wouldn't have seen that if we did things the way infantry platoons do things."

Now, Staff Sergeant Mainville had an idea of who his future squad leaders and team leaders can be when 1st Platoon reorganizes after its return from the deployment.

Captain Donald Louis Shove
Commanding Officer, Fox Company, 2/7

During my visit today Fox Company participated in a successful raid to capture weapons hidden in the town of Ar Rutbah. During the first part of his deployment, Captain Shove had platoons at two different locations on the western Iraqi borders, and his company attached to 1st LAR Battalion. He relied on satellite communications to stay in contact with his far-flung platoons.

My final interview of the evening, also conducted in the dark on the roof of the Fox Company command post.

Captain Shove began, "I went to LSU [Louisiana State University]. I enlisted in the Marine Corps in 1987. Stayed in for three years, got on the GI Bill, I was with 3/6, [as] enlisted. Once I got out, I went to LSU. While I was going to LSU, I stayed in the Reserves. Spent five years in the Reserve program, 3/23. Earned my commission. Went through the PLC [Platoon Leaders Course] program, junior and senior."

After the Infantry Officer Course (IOC), he went to 3/3 as a platoon commander, and later served with Weapons Company, then moved to regimental headquarters as the executive officer. He went to the School of Infantry (SOI) East as a company commander, and later in a variety of billets there. After completing Expeditionary Warfare School at Quantico, he came to 2/7 in June 2003.

Normally, I ask the interview subject to review events chronologically, but since I had seen the briefing about the raid, I asked Captain Shove to outline this fresh operation first before I asked any other questions.

RAID on Ar Rutbah Today (Wednesday, July 7, 2004)

Shove responded, "Okay, single-source intel, led us to a weapons cache site, located in the town of Ar Rutbah. Single-source gave us the information that was accurate, which is a first for us. Fox Company, minus, reinforced, with Dagger [Delta] Company, 1st LAR, and then, LAR headquarters, conducted a cordon and knock on the objective. Came up with a few weapons. 60mm mortars, RPGs, ammunition, some AKs, RPKs, so, it was pretty successful."

The 3rd Platoon from Fox Company, with an element of Showanis (Iraqi Special Forces from the Iraqi National Guard) and an engineer squad conducted the inner cordon and the search. One of his platoons was attached to Dagger that set up Vehicle Check Points (VCPs) for the outer cordon. Another platoon attached to Dagger conducted satellite patrols around the objective to guard against any insurgents from firing off RPGs.

"One RPG came, not from the north, but from the southeast. Actually, it was the first time that we've had an RPG fired at us since *Ripper Sweep*, back in March." Captain Shove said that before that operation, that Fox Company had had two RPGs fired at them at different times. Most of the time they have been dealing with IEDs.

In addition to Dagger Company going with them, Lieutenant Colonel William Richard Costantini (1st LAR Battalion Commander) was along with his Jump command post (CP) that consisted of four LAVs. Costantini's S2 and S3 officers also went along.

I told Captain Shove that when I saw his Marines coming back in late today, they seemed pretty motivated. He responded: "Yes, sir. They were excited because most of the time we hit 'dry wells,' but today was good because we actually came out with what we were looking for."

I then redirected my questions to review how Fox Company prepared for the deployment, and earlier operations.

Captain Shove: "Last summer when I took over, the company had just got back from 10 months in Okinawa. They were extended over there, because [of] Stop-Loss, Stop-Move. I took over, they had leave. We were building the company, it lost a lot of people, we were building the company up. I know, my company, in October, biggest event, training event, that we were training for, was WTI [Weapons and Tactics Instructor course] one tac zero four, down at Yuma, Arizona. We were the rifle company that was supporting the training for MATSS One [Marine Aviation and Training Support Squadron]."

When Fox Company returned from that exercise, Shove learned that they would deploy for OIFII.

After a Block Leave in December 2003, they began training in January 2004 with 7th Marines, doing lane training and SASO training. They went to the Division's training at March Air Force Base. They deployed overseas to Camp Udari, Kuwait in February 2004. After about two weeks in Kuwait, the company split for the move into Iraq.

"Lieutenant Campbell, who is my Weapons Platoon commander, took all of my rolling stock, which is about 23 vehicles. It was Truck Platoon, minus, supporting us, as well as Humvees. He went with Dagger [Platoon], and rolled with them from Kuwait all the way up to Al Asad, and from Al Asad down to here."

"The rest of the company flew from Udari to Al Asad, in C130s. And we flew from Al Asad to here, Camp Korean Village, by Fifty-Threes [Marine CH53 Echo heavy-lift helos]."

He described his mission and this FOB, Korean Village. "Korean Village is exactly what it is. A bunch of Koreans, when they were building the highway, actually lived here. Bunch of structures, actually a development, concrete buildings, homes, that Koreans who were working on the highway lived in. My mission was, I was attached to 1st LAR, my priority mission was to establish the points of entry. One, at Trebil, that's on the Jordanian border. And one at Waleed, which is on the Syrian border. I had one platoon, reinforced, at both those positions. My other missions were, provide camp security for Korean Village, and then finally, limited offensive operations in the city of Ar Rutbah."

1st Platoon up on the Syrian border was his main effort, as there were foreign fighters believed to be coming across the Syrian border. 3rd Platoon was at the Jordanian border, and after *Ripper Sweep*, he replaced them with 2nd Platoon.

"Waleed is 117 kilometers from here. Trebil is just about 100 kilometers from here. It takes us about an hour and a half to both positions."

Shove had to make weekly logistics runs to support his elements on the border. If a Quick Reaction Force (QRF) was needed, the Marine helicopter detachment (two Cobras and one Huey) at Korean Village could get to the borders in about 35 to 40 minutes.

"I would occasionally run border operations. Dagger Platoon [from 1st LAR Battalion] was also stationed out here with me. They would set screen lines and screen the border, preventing any type of infiltration from Waleed all the way to Akashat. Actually, north of Akashat." Apache had the area north of there.

"Finally, about two weeks ago, we were replaced by Echo, 2/11 at both POEs [Ports of Entry]." So now Fox Company no longer had any forces on the border. Its current missions were camp security and limited offensive operations in Ar Rutbah.

He reviewed Fox Company's actions during Operation *Ripper Sweep*. His platoons on both the border crossings with Jordan and Syria were brought back to Korean Village. The crossing at Al Waleed was shut down, and Trebil was allowed to function on its own. Captain Shove said, "We participated in *Ripper Sweep*, attached to LAR. 1st LAR, at some points we attached back to 2/7 during some operations, such as when we went back up to Karmah."

When *Ripper Sweep* ended, Fox Company rejoined 1st LAR, and was told to reestablish the border points.

When Fox's platoons were absent from the border crossings, the truck drivers up at Waleed had started a lot of trouble. What Shove called, "Basically a riot." Finally, the crossing was reopened. At Trebil, some of the truck trailers were set on fire. A platoon from the artillery battery (2/11) was sent there. Finally, Shove sent two platoons back to the two crossings. After another two weeks, these platoons were relieved of their border duties and allowed to return to Korean Village. At the present time, provisional rifle platoons from Echo Battery 2/11 were staffing these crossings.

Echo 2/11 had about a five-day turnover for its own incoming Marine platoons. Shove left some of his key personnel there during this time before all of his Marines were withdrawn from these Ports of Entry (POEs). These artillery Marines acting as infantrymen have also been busy. About a week ago, they were told to reinforce three of their 155mm cannons down at Al Asad, and they had to send some of their Marines to that base to man the guns. Captain Shove believed that these artillery pieces were now in support of operations around Fallujah.

In addition to providing security for the FOB at Korean Village, Fox Company was conducting limited operations, such as the cordon and knocks, and Civil Affairs escorts to different areas for the Civil Affairs (CAG) teams.

Shove said that today's cache raid was successful, but they have had a number of "dry holes" in most raids. They receive intel from various sources, including cell phone calls. The Marines from Fox and 1st LAR would quickly deploy to the area of the cell phone "hits." Once there, they would cordon and knock at houses in the immediate vicinity. Most of the questioning is done by HET (Human Exploitation) teams with 1st LAR, but Fox does have some translators assigned to it.

He described one incident: "We were on our way back from [a] Civil Affairs mission, and upon returning, we had one IED go off. It turned out to be part of a daisy-chain of six IEDs, 60mm mortars, uh, double-stacked, daisy-chained. Which is pretty significant for around here."

"Most of the other IEDs that we've seen have either been makeshift IEDs, putting fire extinguishers, or single IEDs laid on the roadside. And then, just the other day, another platoon was dropping off some detainees that LAR had captured while on

Crews of LAV 25s from Delta Company, 2nd LAR, ready for action at Camp Baharia while a firefight was ongoing in Fallujah on June 25, 2004. (Author's personal photo)

Marines from Delta Company, 2nd LAR, leaving Camp Baharia to reinforce units in action outside of Fallujah. June 25, 2004. (Author's personal photo)

Crewmen from Delta Company, 2nd LAR, share the highlights of their morning-long fight during a rest break back at Camp Fallujah, June 25, 2004. (Author's personal photo)

Camp Baharia. A platoon of LAV 25s from Delta Company, 2nd LAR, wait for word to join a firefight outside of Fallujah. (Author's personal photo)

Sergeant John Denton Leuba, Scout Squad Leader/Platoon Sergeant, 3rd Platoon, Delta Company, 2nd LAR Battalion.

Sergeant Michael Irvin Honigsberg II, LAV Crewman/Gunner, 1st Platoon, Delta Company, 2nd LAR Battalion.

Lance Corporal Keith Allen Bridges, LAV Crewman (0313), Weapons Platoon, Delta Company, 2nd LAR Battalion.

Corporal Jeffrey John Bertch, Scout Leader, Bravo Section, 2nd Platoon, Delta Company, 2nd LAR Battalion.

Sergeant Travis Dean Madden, Vehicle Commander, Alpha Section, 2nd Platoon, Delta Company, 2nd LAR Battalion.

Captain Ladd Wilkie Shepard, Commanding Officer, Delta Company, 2nd LAR Battalion.

Sergeant Gaw Sekou Jones, Junior, Squad Leader, 1st Platoon, Delta Company, 2nd LAR Battalion.

Lance Corporal Robert Anthony DeLuca, Junior, Ammunition Technician, H&S Company, 2/7.

Corporal Samuel Frank Dyche, 3rd Section Leader, 81mm Mortar Platoon, Weapons Company, 2/7.

Gunnery Sergeant Troy Antoine Barlow, Company Gunnery Sergeant, Golf Company, 2/7.

Corporal Christopher Michael Bowles, Acting Admin Chief for 2/7.

Sergeant Lorenzo Mathis Young, Communicator/ Radio Operator, H&S Company, 2/7.

Lance Corporal Craig Richard Bowden, Machine Gunner, 81mm Mortar Platoon, Weapons Company, 2/7.

Captain David Wendell Palmer, S2 Officer, 2/7.

Lieutenant Junwei Sun, 81mm Platoon Commander, Weapons Company, 2/7.

Gunnery Sergeant Bradley Scott Everett, CAAT Platoon Sergeant, Weapons Company, 2/7.

Major John Richard Smith, Junior, Civil Affairs Officer, 3rd Civil Affairs Group, serving with 2/7.

Sergeant Jonathon Jarrett Graham, Backup Alert Force (BAF) Commander, Echo Company, 2/7.

Sergeant Timothy Curtis Day, Mortar Section Leader, Backup Alert Force (BAF), Echo Company, 2/7.

Hospital Corpsman 3 Eric Delano Giles, USN, 2nd Platoon Corpsman, Echo Company, 2/7.

Lieutenant Robert Joseph Gould, MD, USN, US Navy Medical Corps, Echo Company, 2/7.

Gunnery Sergeant Paul Michael McElearney, Company Gunnery Sergeant, Echo Company, 2/7.

First Sergeant Harrison Leon Tanksley, Company First Sergeant, Echo Company, 2/7.

Staff Sergeant Jon Thomas Brodin, Weapons Platoon Sergeant, Echo Company, 2/7.

Lieutenant Brian Edward Humphreys, 3rd Platoon Commander, Echo Company, 2/7.

Captain John Kenneth Kelley, Commanding Officer, Echo Company, 2/7.

Lieutenant Robert Manuel Christafore, Platoon Commander, 1st Platoon, Fox Company, 2/7.

Staff Sergeant Daniel Joseph Mainville, Platoon Sergeant, 1st Platoon, Fox Company, 2/7.

Captain Donald Louis Shove, Commanding Officer, Fox Company, 2/7.

Corporal Jonathon Beowulf Cushman, Squad Leader, 2nd Platoon, Fox Company, 2/7.

Gunnery Sergeant Juan Lopez, Weapons Platoon Sergeant, Fox Company, 2/7.

Lieutenant Colonel William Richard Costantini, Battalion Commander, 1st LAR Battalion.

Gunnery Sergeant Phillip Steven Bemis, Battalion Master Gunner, 1st LAR Battalion.

Lance Corporal Justin Avery Shields, LAV Crewman (0313), Delta Company, 1st LAR Battalion.

Captain Andrew Aaron Manson, Intelligence Officer, 1st LAR Battalion.

Lieutenant Jason Matthew Snyder, Watch Officer, 2nd Battalion, 4th Marines.

Sergeant Lewis William Layton, Squad Leader, Weapons Company, 2/4 (Mobile Assault Company).

Sergeant Jeremiah Lee Randle, Section Leader, Weapons Company, 2/4 (2nd Mobile Assault Platoon).

Lance Corporal Reagan Charles Hodges, Fire Team Leader, 81mm Section, Weapons Company, 2/4.

Corporal Jared Heath McKenzie, 1st Section, 3rd Mechanized Assault Platoon, Weapons Company, 2/4.

Sergeant Damien Ryan Coan, Platoon Sergeant, 2nd Platoon, Echo Company, 2/4.

Corporal Eric Michael Smith, 1st Squad Leader, 2nd Platoon, Echo Company, 2/4.

Corporal Joseph Stephen Magee, 3rd Squad Leader, 2nd Platoon, Echo Company, 2/4.

Lieutenant Tommy Edward Cogan, Platoon Commander, 3rd Platoon, Echo Company, 2/4.

Corporal Caleb Zachary Stefanovich, Fire Team Leader, 4th Platoon, Golf Company, 2/4.

Private First Class Kenny Ray Whittle, Point Man for Team, 4th Platoon, Golf Company, 2/4.

Private First Class Christopher Lee Ferguson, Rifleman and Humvee driver, 4th Platoon, Golf Company, 2/4.

Private First Class Peter Joseph Flom, Rifleman, 3rd Platoon, Golf Company, 2/4.

Private First Class Higinio Antuno Martinez, SAW gunner, 3rd Platoon, Golf Company, 2/4.

On arrival at Combat Outpost Ramadi, Captain Kelly Royer, company commander of Echo Company, 2/4, was warned about regular mortar attacks. After the first attack there, he sent a team that killed the mortar team and captured the 60mm mortar, shown in his company's operations center. (Author's personal photo)

Advanced Combat Optical Gunsight (ACOG) mounted on an infantryman's M16 A4 rifle. (Author's personal photo)

A Marine Staff NCO from 2/7 conducts a pre-convoy brief for a trip from Camp Al Asad to Combat Outpost Hit, July 2004. Instructions included the order of vehicles, radio frequencies, immediate action drills, weapons and support available, and the convoy mission. (Author's personal photo)

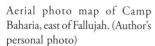

Aerial photo map of Camp Baharia, east of Fallujah. (Author's personal photo)

Corporal Joshua F. Willfong and Corporal Scott Vincent were killed in a vehicle-borne IED attack on April 30, 2004. The Marines of Delta Company, 2nd LAR Battalion, constructed a makeshift memorial at Camp Baharia. (Author's personal photo)

the borders, conducting patrols along the border. They decided to go ahead and release them. While we were dropping the detainees off, and on their way back, the platoon had an IED go off. No injuries. Most of the IEDs, we've been very fortunate. No serious casualties."

The only injury that they have had was to one Marine who was in the turret of a Humvee that had a turnover accident. This Marine was not seriously injured. Fox set up some observation posts (OPs) to overwatch some of these areas, but had not found any individuals emplacing IEDs.

Since Fox Company's March arrival in this area, Captain Shove saw an increase in attacks along MSR Mobile targeting Jordanian truck drivers. IED attacks also increased. Some Marines from a battery in 3/11 hit an IED west of Korean Village, with several injuries. He said, "We've seen an increase in IED activity, and we've seen an increase in attacks on convoys. Most of them Jordanian." He noted that at today's raid was the first time that Fox received any shots (the one RPG) fired at them.

"The target we were going after was a group known to be affiliated with Sheik Haditha. He comes in, preaches, and supposedly has a following group, probably platoon size, that have weapons. And another group that we suspect is attacking the convoys. Trying to shut down some of the commercial traffic along the MSR [Main Supply Route]."

This is the MSR visible from the top of the building where we were doing this interview. This MSR connects with the MSR from the Syrian border about 25 kilometers from here, and then goes to Fallujah. The MSR from Fallujah heads right into Baghdad. Shove said that it was a pretty busy road, and that I would see the tractor-trailers traveling along it during the night hours up until about midnight. The Marines shipped a lot of supplies from Jordan into various camps throughout Iraq along this MSR. Now that his Marines were about halfway through their deployment, Shove kept them sharp by rotating their platoons through different missions.

"Make sure that our pre-combat checks, rehearsals, inspections [are completed]. Marines are motivated. Today was a good boost in their morale, actually coming away with something. I have good platoon commanders, good platoon sergeants. [They] Do an excellent job, focusing the Marines, sailors. They get the job done."

Shove also praised his squad leaders for the job that they were doing.

As the company has been attached to different higher elements, Shove has had a variety of chains of command. He noted, "Our mission has been varied. Focused on a lot of different things. From VCPs to patrolling the desert along the borders, to actually patrolling the border points. At times we've had several different higher headquarters." Working under 1st LAR has enabled him to operate as a highly mechanized rifle company at times. When LAR was pulled out of Korean Village to do sweeps for *Ripper Sweep*, Fox Company came directly under Regiment (7th Marines).

"The Marines and officers have really come to love operating under LAR." This is because of the firepower that LAR carries. Each of his platoons was assigned a section of LAVs. Then they would go out to establish VCPs. The cross attachments have been varied. His Marines liked working for Lieutenant Colonel Costantini, the LAR battalion commander.

I asked Captain Shove if this was anything like he thought it would be when he completed Expeditionary Warfare School (EWS). He replied that it was not at all what he expected. He was glad to have all of his platoons back with him and not dispersed on border points. Now, "I'm able to bring some combat power to bear on whatever task I have."

At times when there were threats at the Ports of Entry (POEs), Shove had to deploy some of his Marines to reinforce the platoons out there. He only had about a platoon to do guard duty here at Korean Village.

Due to the remote location of this FOB, he has often had to rely on tactical satellite (TACSAT) communication to stay in touch with his remote platoons on the distant border crossings, and his own battalion headquarters back at Al Asad.

Corporal Jonathon Beowulf Cushman
Squad Leader, 2nd Platoon, Fox Company, 2/7

Cushman volunteered to join Fox Company after he returned from OIF1 with 1/7. He worked on the border during the first half of this deployment and was on the successful raid to Ar Rutbah today. He has not lost any of his Marines to any serious injuries, and worked to keep his squad alert at all times.

Corporal Cushman is an 0311—Marine rifleman. He entered the Corps in December 2000, and graduated recruit training on March 2, 2001. He completed the School of Infantry (SOI) on the west coast, and went to Security Force Training School. In Spain he was part of Security Forces in Europe, and got to visit a lot of countries there during his 18-month tour. In January 2003 he went to the FMF where he joined 1/7. Shortly after arriving at 1/7, they deployed to Iraq for OIF1.

OIF1

Cushman said, "We [1/7] were there on March 22nd [2003], 21st, when we initially came into Iraq down by Basrah. Took the Ramallah oil fields. Then, progressed up north in Amtracs to Baghdad. We took part in seizing Baghdad. We came back down to Najaf. I spent three to four months in Najaf, basically the summertime. I was there when the large mosque was blown up, in, I believe, September."

He returned to 29 Palms in October 2003. He next spent four or five months as a lane instructor for SASO training for the battalions preparing to deploy to Iraq. He then voluntarily transferred to Fox Company, 2/7.

OIFII

Fox Company left for Iraq in February 2004 and arrived in Kuwait before moving into Iraq. Cushman participated in operations around Korean Village and Ar Rutbah, and during May and June was deployed to the border. There he worked with the Iraqi border police and Iraqi Customs Police. In late June he returned to Korean Village.

Cushman said that when he first joined 2/7 in December, he was impressed with the well-prepared new Marines that he helped to train.

I asked the corporal to describe some of his recent operations. During one operation in Ar Rutbah, his squad was operating in an area where another squad had had several RPGs fired at them a few days before. "And, we went in several days later. Executed operations in Rutbah. I was doing a security presence at the Iraqi police station, while another squad was out on patrol in the city. Once we link back up and begin to retrograde back out of the city, we received RPG fire from across the street. Probably the closest I've ever been to an explosion of that magnitude. About 20 yards away. And, it made me appreciate the perspective of someone who's actually right there when the explosion goes off."

The reaction force arrived shortly after that and helped to search the city.

During *Ripper Sweep*, they went out to Karmah and around Fallujah. Here around Korean Village the area is basically desert. Down near Fallujah, he saw wheat fields, date trees, orange trees and gardens. He said, "We didn't really run into much out there. In one instance, scouts of ours found an ambush before we rolled into it. Some IEDs and some heavy machine guns were just left there and abandoned. There was also an individual in a gas truck who shot at one of the platoons, [and he] was taken care of. Then there was a large-scale sweep of the town of Karmah. There were no major firefights that we took part in."

He described his time on the border: "We spent some time down by Trebil on the Jordanian border. We relieved a platoon there, and took over for a month. We were relieved by 2nd Battery, 11th Marines, I believe. 2/11, it's an artillery unit."

He also got to work with the Iraqi border patrol and Iraqi Customs Police.

Cushman said that the culture of the Iraqi forces was different from the Jordanian forces that he worked with. "The Jordanians run a pretty tight operation. They often complained that the Iraqis were trying to swap favors. You know, 'Do me a favor by letting this guy in here even though he's got bad papers, or no papers.' Something that they [the Jordanians] wouldn't do."

Cushman believed that most of the Iraqis in this western part of Iraq are all part of the same tribe, and are used to doing favors for one another. "It was just frustrating for us. A lot of bribery goes on, things like that, but that's just part of the way they operate."

Cushman added that he spoke with General John Kelly (1st Marine Division Assistant Commander) before. Kelly came down to the borders and they had a meeting with him. And he said in the United States, some of the customs officials and the people who deal with immigration are sometimes involved in some of the illegitimate businesses, so it's tough for us to take the moral high ground in these matters. Corporal Cushman felt that given the security situation, it was important for the Iraqis to be careful about what comes into the country, for their own safety and for that of the coalition forces. He felt that these officials were now going through the basic motions, but that there was still room for improvement.

I asked him to outline what happened today away from Korean Village. When I arrived at the camp, there were very few people for me to interview. He replied:

"What happened today was they got some intel regarding a weapons cache in Rutbah. And, we were mustered to go down to Rutbah. My element of the force was to rendezvous with the ICDC [Iraqi Civil Defense Corps], and get enough of them to come back and execute the actual raid. We went down to the ICDC building to get them. It was the hot part of the day, and they were all asleep. We got four of them there, then went down to the police station and picked up a few more. Then we came back out of the town, went to the objective, and inserted those Iraqi forces, and then pulled slightly farther west, to a position where we could base out of and execute satellite patrols in the vicinity of the objective. At the objective, they found RPGs, RPKs, AK-47s, IED-making material, I believe mortar and artillery pieces. I'm not sure on that. I am sure on the other things, though."

He felt that this was a successful dent in the arsenal of local insurgents in Rutbah.

During the patrols one of the other squad leaders had an RPG fired at them from a considerable distance, and it exploded 100 feet above the ground. No Marines got hurt, but the shooter got away despite a search for him.

This raid today happened on the spur of the moment, as the intel had just come down this morning. However, they have run similar cordon and enter raids in the past, so the Marines were ready to go.

At this point, I asked Corporal Cushman about the local enemy because they were not in uniform. He explained: On the border as well as in nearby Ar Rutbah, the Rules of Engagement were clear when there was a hostile act that showed hostile intent. The SOP was: Shout, show, shove, shoot. First is a verbal command, then body posture and showing the weapon. Shove is a physical action, if possible, then shooting if necessary. Cushman has gotten as far as physically shoving someone, he has not had to fire his weapon.

On the border, at times when there was no translator present, the Marines had picked up enough basic words and gestures to communicate simply at times. "Our role at the border, was to be a presence, a show of force, to support the Iraqi authorities that were there."

When asked if this role was hard for Marines, he said that the whole mission here was hard for Marines, who are trained to "Hit hard, establish a dominant position and accomplish the mission." Here there are people throwing rocks and shooting flares at them, and it is hard to lay down what he called the "Iron Hand."

Cushman said that the training that the company went through before coming over here was super high intensity. There was sleep deprivation, and running through lots of different situations. Once in Iraq, a lot of the time has been waiting for something to happen. They have had to fight off complacency. He said that there was the potential to do what they had trained to do in Ar Rutbah, but the Marines have not routinely patrolled there due to other missions.

With the deployment more than half over, he saw his job as keeping his Marines' minds in the game. Rehearsing and training, when possible, but also allowing time to rest and recuperate. He felt that as time grew shorter, it would be the longest time for the Marines as they begin to get anxious about returning home.

Corporal Cushman said that it was a real long day today, and felt that he would probably remember more about it if he was rested better. But he has not lost anybody, and nobody has been hurt. It has been a good deployment for the Marines in his squad.

Thursday July 8, 2004

I went to morning chow with Gunnery Sergeant Juan Lopez, the Weapons Platoon sergeant of Fox Company. We had a tray rations (tray rats) breakfast together, with real orange juice, then conducted an interview. A very energetic and knowledgeable staff non-commissioned officer (a gunnery sergeant is an E7). This, however, made me late for interview with Lieutenant Colonel Costantini of 1st LAR Battalion.

All interviews today were rewarding. One lance corporal expressed concern that his LAV company had not yet had any action! He said that the LAV 25s scare away many potential enemies.

Gunnery Sergeant Juan Lopez
Weapons Platoon Sergeant, Fox Company, 2/7

Many of the Marines in his platoon were on their first combat deployment. High-intensity training prepared them for SASO operations, and also for taking on security missions on the borders with Jordan and Syria. On an early mission out of Korean Village, Fox Company Marines found a stash of rockets buried in a trash pile near the FOB. Due to differing missions, there has sometimes been friction with the aviation Marines at the FOB.

Gunny Lopez entered the Marine Corps in 1989, going to boot camp a few weeks after high school graduation. He completed TOW (Tube-launched Wire-Guided missile) school and served with 9th Marines in Okinawa. He then served as a Marine Security Guard, first in Hamburg, Germany, and then in Manila, Philippines. He requested orders to 4th Marines in Okinawa, and spent three years there in an accompanied tour. After a tour at Division G3, he came to 2/7.

2/7 deployed to Okinawa for a six-month UDP (Unit Deployment Program) in 2003, but the deployment was extended when the invasion of Iraq took place, as they were a trained battalion ready to deploy from Okinawa. The rest of 7th Marines went to OIF1. Some of the 2/7 Marines stayed on Okinawa from 10 to 12 months. On return to the United States, 2/7 got the word to prepare for deployment to Iraq for OIFII.

Training was Security and Stability Operations (SASO) heavy. Gunny Lopez said that a lot of the older Marines had to get used to a lot of new stuff, such as IEDs, and vehicle patrols, something which infantry companies did not do on a routine basis. They also became familiar with the Rules of Engagement.

After Christmas leave in 2003, they returned for a month of training. Lopez said, "It was a full month of nothing but training. We did day-to-day SASO training on 29 Palms, and then we also did a week-long exercise at March Air Force Base. Pretty much, similar to what we were going to do over here."

He noted that the training really got them ready for the environment in Iraq. The Marines began to provide on-the-ground intel to higher-ups once they got onto the ground here.

He explained that as the Weapons Platoon sergeant, he has 0331 machine gunners, 0341 mortar men, and 0351 assault men.

"They normally attach to the platoons, and they have a specific MOS, or job. In this situation, we were deployed as a Weapons Platoon, and/or, a provisional line company [i.e., an infantry company]. I know my Marines had to learn a lot of new stuff. A lot of Marines come out of SOI [School of Infantry], train for their MOSs, and when they came to the fleet, the immediate things they were doing was 0311 [infantry] patrolling, regular line stuff."

Lopez felt that the SASO training focused everyone's attention, especially the non-infantry Marines. He estimated that about 90 percent of the battalion was made up of new Marines from SOI. They came in groups of 30 and 40 at a time. They even received a group of 50 new Marines about a week before leaving the States. Some of the Marines in Lopez's platoon arrived too late to go through the SASO training, so he had to ensure that they received some SASO training the first week that they got into Kuwait.

His platoon spent about 15 days in Kuwait before moving into Iraq. "During that time we were just doing constant training." He felt that this training has been key to the success that they have had.

Weapons Platoon was tasked with bringing the company's vehicles up into Iraq. The road march to Korean Village took about six days. They stopped at various FOBs en route. He noted that Korean Village was known as FOB Beyers when they arrived. Immediately, two infantry platoons were sent to the border crossings at Syria and Jordan. The Marines at Korean Village then provided FOB security as the Army units left. The Army told them that this was a remote FOB, about a

30-to-40-minute drive away from Ar Rutbah, and the threat levels were very low due to the isolated position. But the Marines didn't know what to expect, and they kept their guard up at all times.

Gunny Lopez described the conditions when they took over the guard of the FOB:

"We took over the guard. A lot of the posts, they were, really didn't have too good posts up there. Blouses [jackets] off, weapons, just staged anywhere, eating chow, water, music on post, not a lot of attention up there, not a lot of on guard up there. So once we took over, and the transition, we had to take all the posts down. We built new posts up there around the FOB. And we started running security up there, keeping in mind that there is enemy out here somewhere."

After a few days at Korean Village, they went on their first mission to visit the town of Ar Rutbah. Lopez said, "Our platoon again was tasked to go in, and I went on that convoy with them. They had pretty good briefs. Army did pretty good briefs. One thing that stood out in my mind about the briefs, right from the start it was sort of a mission, a usual, routine mission. Pretty much how they approached this: 'We've done this a hundred times, we know the drill. This is another routine mission, we're going into Ar Rutbah, coming out.' And that's pretty much it, the whole gist of it."

Lopez noted the different ways that the Army responded to an attack. The Army would mass fires on the suspected origin of the fire, and then drive out of the area. Marines are trained to close with, locate, and destroy the enemy. He wondered what the Marines would be expected do if this Army-led convoy were hit by fire or an IED.

On this first mission, about three to five clicks away from Korean Village, one of the Marines spotted a big trash heap in the middle of the desert.

"He talked [to] the captain that was in charge of the convoy, said, 'Hey, let's go check it out. See what's over there.' Captain said, 'Hey, good to go.'"

"So we went ahead and detoured, and checked it out. And it turned out to be a live missile site! And it was at least, I'd say, 30 maybe, rockets and PVC tube-piping. It was a platform, welded together, and the PVC piping was on steel tubes, and it was pretty much a jury-rigged mortar-type setup. They had rockets in them. Apparently, from looking at the rockets myself, a lot of 'em had been blown up."

Lopez saw big fuse boxes next to each rocket system, with wires leading to each rocket. Each tube had a box. He saw that some of the rockets had blown up in the launchers, and he felt that this may have scared the attackers away from the site, and that some may even have been injured from the blasts. The Marines called EOD to go out and destroy the weapons there.

"Army didn't know how long it was there, and this was like our second day at the FOB."

Lopez said that the next day, Marines walking security inside the security perimeter of the FOB found a couple of rockets that had landed within the security perimeter and had not detonated. They showed these to the Army unit who had not seen them. The Marines had EOD get these rockets out of the ground and destroy them.

Lopez's platoon was tasked with security for the FOB, and to serve as the FOB React Force. The React Force was to respond to any action within five clicks of the base, as a Quick Reaction Force (QRF) for anything five clicks and out. They also did Civil Affairs missions. "To say the least, the Marines that we did have here, we were stretched thin."

He said that at times some Marines would come in off a seven to eight-hour mission, get a couple of hours sleep, and sometimes have to go on company missions as part of the two platoons of the company that were here at Korean Village. Three months like this was wearing on the Fox Company Marines, he said. Assets were also stretched thin, as they had to dispatch weapons, radio assets, and weapons to the platoons on the border posts.

Lopez said that most of the Marines were issued new M16A4s prior to arrival, but some still had the older M16A2s. His armorer said that these older rifles may have malfunctioned if they had to be used in a firefight. He added, "Now that we had Marines EAS-ing [Expiration of Active Service], a lot of Marines leaving theater, they of course left some gear behind. Most of the guys got issued M16s and 9 mil [9mm pistols], they take the 9 mil with them, leave the 16 here. Of course, the new Marines that get here, we give 'em the new weapons."

When Fallujah heated up, the two Marine platoons got pulled from the borders. "We went up there [the border posts] with like five 7-tons [trucks] apiece, took all the Marines off the borders. It was recommended that we leave a presence up there 'cause it's gonna lead to chaos." He said that a small force of about 20 Marines from Division and Wing elements at Korean Village were sent to the borders.

Gunny Lopez said that there had been some friction with the Marine Wing units at Korean Village. These aviation Marines were not allowed to leave the FOB for presence patrols, and could not assist Fox Company on resupply runs to the borders, either. They could not spare their 7-ton trucks for the removal of the Fox Company platoons from the borders. Lopez did say that he understood that the different elements at Korean Village had their own chain of command, and different priorities and restraints.

When Fox Company finally got all of its Marines back from the borders, they convoyed to Al Asad where it linked up with the rest of 2/7 for the move to Fallujah. The night that Fox Company left Korean Village, it was attacked by mortars from a bridge about a click away. From our rooftop vantage point, he pointed to this bridge.

Fox Company went to the Fallujah area for 10 days of operations.

When the company returned to Korean Village, it immediately had to send two platoons back to the border crossings. The Marines there said that things had gotten messy at the crossings. Fox Company Marines resumed their prior missions there.

At this time, Fox Company had all of its Marines at this FOB. It was a large area of operations (AO) to cover, but platoons could cycle better and rest. He said that one of the biggest things that they had learned in SASO training was how to do satellite patrols. British troops provided the classes and training for this. Lopez said that in Ar Rutbah, the Marines were targeted by an RPG. The Marines had set up security around a police station, but did not do satellite patrols. The next day in Ar Rutbah, they did satellite patrols and there was no RPG fire at them. Lopez said that the satellite patrols saturate an area and throw off the enemy. He felt that this type of training can be used in the future for the many different situations that Marines find themselves in.

He said that on the raid yesterday (Wednesday, July 7, 2004) when they went into town, they had good security. This made it harder for enemy to attack them. He was aware that the enemy was always observing and Marines must be alert.

CHAPTER FIVE

1st Light Armored Reconnaissance Battalion at Korean Village

Lieutenant Colonel William Richard Costantini

Battalion Commander, 1st LAR Battalion

Colonel Costantini took over 1st LAR Battalion in June 2003, and by that fall knew he would be leading the battalion back to Iraq. His skills as an Arabic speaker have proved helpful when dealing with local officials. His battalion covered an area of hundreds of square kilometers, and oversaw border Ports of Entry many miles from his command post. During Operation Ripper Sweep, his forces operated in the region between Fallujah and Karmah. The experience has been humbling and gratifying for him.

Lieutenant Colonel Costantini's background includes an MS in Middle East Regional Studies and a rudimentary grasp of conversational Arabic. He can introduce himself and conduct pleasantries without an interpreter. LAR was being used to screen the western borders, and in economy of force missions. He gave a good overview of the huge scale of the area of operations (AO) that his battalion had in western Al Anbar, Iraq.

He began by giving a brief review of his Marine Corps career: "I'm an infantry officer. I served as a lieutenant in 3/8, I was an instructor at The Basic School. Following that I went to AWS [Amphibious Warfare School], then I was a military observer on the Kuwait-Iraq border, after the Gulf War for a year."

He returned to Camp LeJeune and was a company commander with 2/6, then served as S3 officer and executive officer of 1/2.

"I left 1/2 and went to the FAO program, Foreign Officer program, where I got a master's degree in Middle East Regional Studies. Then I learned Arabic at the Defense Language Institute, and then I lived with my family for a year in Egypt. Traveled the Middle East pretty extensively."

On return to the States, he served at Headquarters Marine Corps in Plans, Policies, and Operations (PP&O), in the Strategic Initiatives Group. He was an analyst for U.S. politics and foreign policy.

About six months before OIF1 started he was slated to command 1st LAR. He got his orders modified out of headquarters so that he could report to Division in April 2003.

He said, "I was hoping to leverage some of my experience in the region, my FAO skills, earlier than that. I couldn't get out of headquarters in time for the war. So I spent about seven weeks with the G3, pretty much after the kinetic part of the war, late April until the end of May [2003]."

In May 2003, he went to Kuwait and spent about a week with 1st LAR, and then two weeks with them when they returned to the States before he took command. He was faced with a pretty daunting task that summer, as the equipment had been run pretty hard. The Commanding General—General James Mattis—tasked all elements of the 1st Marine Division to be combat ready by November 10, 2003. 1st LAR's equipment had not gotten off the returning ships until July 2003.

"We spent most of the first two months we were back [in the States], really, just reconstituting LAVs, everything from corrosion control to major repairs. And then for us to be combat capable, we had to get into a training cycle which is focused on gunnery and crew cohesion. I never served in an LAR unit before. So, it was a real learning experience for me, attempting to figure out how to get people, their equipment set up, so they could actually conduct the training they ought to conduct."

Costantini said that in the fall of 2003, they had no idea that the battalion would be re-deploying to Iraq, and the focus was on preparing individual LAR companies to go on WESTPAC (Western Pacific) deployments.

"And then, I started to get an inkling, I would say right about the time of the Marine Corps birthday [November 10, 2003], it was pretty obvious Marine forces were coming back [to Iraq]. It was obvious to me, that at least one LAR battalion, if not more, were gonna come back here."

His only question was whether it would be his battalion or 3rd LAR battalion. The first week in December, Lieutenant Colonel Costantini learned that his battalion would be the one to deploy to Iraq. He said that the battalion had just gotten to the point where all of its forces had been reconstituted, and crews formed. They spent the last week of December and the first two weeks of January doing nothing but embarkation. They actually deployed in February 2004.

"On January 15th, our equipment was embarked, we met our training objectives, we'd done no mission-specific training for this mission here. We had to do that training at Camp Pendleton without the benefit of any of our equipment: No LAVs, little of our rolling stock."

Costantini said that this was a challenge. His battalion was attached to RCT7 on January 20, 2004, and he got his mission assignment. He continued, "Our task was gonna be out here. We were really the economy of force of the regiment, and the regiment was the economy of force for the division."

The 1st LAR Battalion's task was to operate the two Ports of Entry into Iraq, at Trebil on the Jordanian border, and Waleed on the Syrian border. They were to train and supervise four Iraqi border patrol battalions. One of these was north of Al Qaim near the Euphrates River, one was at Akashat, about 80 miles south of Al Qaim, one at the Waleed POE (Port of Entry), and one at the Trebil POE. The battalion also had two Iraqi Civil Defense companies: One at Akashat and one at Ar Rutbah (About 80 miles east of the Syria-Iraq border and along a main highway that runs to the Ramadi-Fallujah-Baghdad areas). There were also some local police north of the Euphrates near Akashat.

"At the same time, we were supposed to do surveillance of the border. We had 317 kilometers of Syrian border, the entire Iraq-Jordan border, and 180-odd kilometers of the Iraq-Saudi Arabian border, and to interdict any cross-border movement that wasn't going through the international POEs."

Costantini's task force deployed with three LAR companies joined by Fox Company 2/7, and other attachments including HET (Human Exploitation Teams) teams and communications assets. Fox Company's mission was to work at the two POEs. He estimated that his task force had a battle of space of 10,000–20,000 kilometers. He said that each LAR company could "look at" about 10 kilometers of border a day, so that he could cover only about 30 kilometers of just the 317-kilometer Syrian border per day.

When 1st LAR arrived in Iraq, the colonel's intention was to not have the individual companies operate from fixed bases. They would go to the field and operate in the field. He had gotten 1st Marine Division directives about setting up camps, and how to contract for local services. "But I told my Marines they should expect to spend 26 out of 30 days in the field. We've pretty much lived up to that from the beginning somehow."

Costantini set up his Weapons Company to the north, Alpha Company in the middle, Delta Company in the south. Delta Company and Fox 2/7 operated out of Korean Village. Alpha Company and Weapons Company operated out of Al Qaim. "I had to split my staff. Operated Battalion Main up at Al Qaim, Battalion Bravo command down here at KV, 120 miles separation between them."

A lieutenant augment from AA (Anti-Aircraft) battalion was tasked as the Detention Facility Officer in Charge (OIC) at Korean Village. A major who had just come from the Air Force Command and Staff College staff became Costantini's Officer in Charge (OIC) of operations here at KV.

"I spent the first month here really runnin' around. My Jump CP [command post] put about 4,500 kilometers on our vehicles the first month we were here." The six different missions of the battalion required him to travel extensively.

Later in the interview, Lieutenant Colonel Costantini explained that his AO was huge, the equivalent of the distance from San Diego to Los Angeles! His forces had to make night movements that would be like moving from Camp Pendleton to the 29 Palms Base using secondary roads, and follow that up with a move from 29 Palms into Arizona.

"Some significant challenges when you talk to a Marine about supervising an international port of entry: Customs procedures, immigration procedures, and that Marine has never traveled outside the United States other than on Marine Corps deployments. So he doesn't have the Western baseline of seeing what immigration and customs are supposed to look like."

When the Marines went to the POEs, they were being run by the Iraqi Border Police, something which was not the police mission. There was significant graft and corruption by the untrained Iraqis. Marine first and second lieutenants were trying to figure this out while over 90 miles from their parent commands. Living conditions for these Marines were primitive, and communications lines difficult, with telephone and fax lines the main method used.

Costantini said that when the Marines worked alongside the Iraqi soldiers, they could get things done. The problems were with the Iraqi bureaucrats from the CPA (Coalition Provisional Authority)—Baghdad regime. Sometimes these authorities wanted to have people that they sent out to be hired, while the Marines there wanted to hire the people that they had been working with. Since the turnover of sovereignty on June 28, 2004, this has changed because these decisions were now all made by Iraqi authorities. The main mission at the POEs was to prevent munitions or equipment from entering Iraq.

Costantini then described the first engagements by his battalion: "For the first month the environment was very benign. The only contact we made, we made about three contacts the first month, all of them north of the Euphrates River. There's a thin green belt up there that's habitable. We hit a couple of mines up there with LAVs. Minor injuries to personnel. The LAV proved to be very survivable with the mines we were hitting. April 8th, we had our first real direct-fire engagement up there. Complex ambush, probably 10 to 12 enemy soldiers, large IED, RPG, machine gun, small arms fire, all at a range of about 75 meters in a built-up area. About 75 meters from a police station. We were actually moving up to that police station, patrolling. We think they [the police] were complicit in setting up this ambush. We had one Marine killed and one Marine wounded in that action. We killed two uniformed, weapons-carrying enemy. We captured nine RPG launchers, two machine guns, couple of other weapons. It was a significant event in the battalion, in an area that we had operated in, people we didn't trust. The police up there, we were trying to build up confidence with them. A company, Weapons Company, had been operating up there significantly for a long time."

"To get into a contact with that kind of area taught us a couple things. The enemy couldn't care less about collateral damage. They were firing RPGs where the backstop was farmhouses 50 meters on the other side of the road. We ended up firing about 75 rounds of 25 millimeter. Two guys were killed got hit with 25 millimeter. With those

75 rounds, zero collateral damage. The second lieutenant, three months in the FMF, who was on top—the vehicle commander of that vehicle—gave precise commands, TRPs [Target Reference Points], to prevent any collateral damage, probably allowing a couple of their guys to escape. He did it to save some of the people [not involved]. Got into a bad situation, his personal action broke an enemy ambush, we think. I mean, he saved the rest of this platoon without a doubt. I recommended him for a Silver Star. He was wounded in the middle of his side, he continued to fight it out. Some other real heroic action by Marines in the battalion, exposed themselves to fire. I'll give you the citations afterwards."

A week after this contact, 1st LAR Battalion received orders to participate in Operation *Ripper Sweep*. Lieutenant Colonel Costantini took his battalion and Fox Company 120 miles to Al Asad. They then went south of Ramadi and operated near Al Taqaddum and Fallujah. 1st Recon Battalion and other units had previously had significant contacts in this area.

"We went down there, 2/7 and 1st LAR, and almost nothing happened. We ended up circling all the way around Baghdad, operated in a place called Karmah with 1/5."

1/5 had been taking daily contact for almost two weeks and was sent to Fallujah. In three or four days, 1st LAR cleared about 60 IEDs in Karmah. But they had no serious contact with any enemy.

"The lesson to me, in that, is that the LAV, en masse, have a real calming effect on the battlefield. There were areas down there that were almost no-go, and when we talked to people who had been operating there significantly, they told us that we were gonna be shooting at people every day. It never came to that. There's some theory that all those guys were attracted into Fallujah. I don't know, I think they saw the mass, firepower, and our ability to move fast around, and maybe they went to 'man dress.' Went to native attire and just avoided us."

When the operation was over, 1st LAR returned to Al Asad and Al Qaim. Costantini put Weapons Company and Fox Company back into their areas at the POEs again, while the battalion operated east of the Euphrates River for about three weeks. This area was east of Al Asad, an area suspected of being the origin of rocket attacks on that base. 1st LAR picked up one weapons cache there, but had no contacts with any enemy forces, not even dirty looks from local inhabitants.

"We went to operations around Rahwah, we had to make a 130-kilometer movement across the desert, two LAR companies. We couldn't start until nightfall, we had to do it and be in position at four o'clock in the morning." This was in desert, with no roads, and they didn't know the area.

Costantini said that these long movements brought home to him that his Marines respond to the environment that they are in. "We had a first lieutenant navigating for the battalion, and I didn't give it a second thought."

He said that the battalion had gone from being not very well-trained, to a unit capable of long-range operations in a variety of situations. They did the maintenance, and exercised small unit leadership. As a battalion commander, he noted that there was not much close supervision that he could do at the small unit level, but the leaders at that level responded well.

1st LAR battalion developed a list of targets in the area, working with RCT7. Delta Company had been out in the field since June 11th, and it was now July 8th.

"We did a couple of operations up here to pick up smugglers. Basically, we get a SIGINT [Signals Intelligence from electronic sources] hit, where this guy was. Move out, get a hit at 2300 at night, he's 80 miles away. Be out the door by 2345, we'll be at the target about 1:30, two in the morning. Go in, pick him up. We've never met any resistance in these cordon and knock operations. We think a lot of this is, everywhere we go, we go in overwhelming force. There's an outer cordon of LAVs, an inner cordon of infantry or Force Reconnaissance Marines. No one's gonna fight back against us."

Costantini expected more activity after the Transfer of Sovereignty, and was now waiting to go back to Al Qaim for some needed maintenance on his vehicles.

In mid-June, he was tasked to send a company to support RCT1, and he sent Alpha Company. They were operating on MSR Tampa doing route security. They have had more direct-fire contacts in those three weeks there than the 1st LAR Battalion has had in its first four months in Iraq. They have captured a few people laying-in IEDs, had one lieutenant wounded, and one vehicle damaged by an IED.

Many of the missions are what the colonel expected, and it has been difficult to develop reliable sources of intel about smugglers. When he meets with members of a city council, he suspects that some of these officials are in with some of the smugglers. Costantini said that his battalion has not done very well at developing these sources. Weapons Company, however, has done this in the built-up area where it operates. Now, he was attempting to take a more "hands-off" approach and allow Iraqi forces to take on more of the tasks.

"The police here are not ready for that. The ICDC [Iraqi Civil Defense Corps], now [called] the National Guard, has had a big leadership change, they are retraining a bunch of their people. And I think they are going to be useful with these things in the future, but our ability to really drive them, it's, the Transfer of Sovereignty really changes the relationship."

Lieutenant Colonel Costantini said that a challenge for the Division was where to deploy 1st LAR. There have not been a lot of direct-fire contacts in the region, but the border area was critical, and forces might be needed to respond quickly.

This week, 3rd LAR liaison personnel would be coming in to begin their pre-deployment site survey. 1st LAR had about another two months of operations remaining. Their goal was to professionalize the Iraqi Border Police as much as possible. One problem for the Iraqi forces was a lack of equipment. RCT7 was also working to professionalize the Iraqi National Guard.

I asked Lieutenant Colonel Costantini about his own language training, and whether it has aided him out here. He said that he was not a great linguist, but his knowledge of Arabic was a great icebreaker when dealing with local officials.

"I can converse in pleasantries very easily. And I can put my message out. I can generate the language in my own head, tell people what I want to tell them. I don't attempt to have detailed conversations. That's when I use an interpreter, when I have to have Air Force people. But it is very handy for me when I want to get my message out."

"Last year when I was on the staff, at the end of the war, I was in Baghdad for about a week, and I worked with the CMOC [Civil-Military Operations Center] that was in the Palestine Hotel. And I worked with the HET [Human Exploitation] team that was with 3/4 right in that area. And I was with another FAO [Foreign Area Officer] who was an Intel officer with that HET team. They would travel out and attempt to talk to people. I was kind of a carnival barker. I could tell people, we're working on the electricity, we're working on the water. We need your help. I would draw a crowd, and give the collectors an opportunity to try and pick people out of the crowd they wanted to talk to. I could get the message out, people were fascinated by a guy, obviously not an Arab, who could speak fairly formal Arabic."

"I came back this time, it's good for me 'cause I could make all my introductions in Arabic, tell them who I am, what I'm gonna do. If I want to get nasty with someone, I know just enough to do that, as well. When I see cowardly actions, by Iraqi security forces, I can talk to them very directly. It's nice for me to monitor the interpreters, 'cause I can, usually track, and ensure the message, if I've got to speak English, what they're translating."

He said that there have been times when it is nice to surprise people with his knowledge of Arabic. His FAO training has also given him a knowledge of the culture. "You know, I can drink tea and eat dates forever!" He's also used to the Arab culture. His master's degree armed him with knowledge of the local history and politics. He said that he had enough knowledge, to "probably be dangerous." He had lived in Egypt and traveled pretty extensively in the Middle East while earning his degree. He was also now able to travel around without an interpreter, thus freeing up an interpreter for someone else.

I then asked Lieutenant Colonel Costantini if he had any thoughts to wrap up the interview. He paused for a moment, then responded: "When I look back at having gained command in June, to the point in February, we've tried to be very self-critical. How we use our time, what we'd do different. I learned a lot from the other battalion commander that came over here."

He said that the enlisted Marines and staff were all high-quality individuals. "We bit off a lot, initially, trying to run two CPs [command posts] 120-odd miles apart. We didn't do it very well. We've changed the way we operated. That's been interesting for me to see us evolve during the operations. It was real hard for me to change some things. I felt that we were gonna see a lot of people coming across the borders. Just didn't pan out that way. Going away from the theory to the reality, is not always that easy. Having a reevaluation mechanism is difficult. The thing I always tell these guys is, you gotta live in the world the way it is, not the way you want it to be. And, it's difficult in a combat environment. You think you know what's going on, you think you know what's happening. And it's somewhat amusing to me sometimes when I read some of the intentions passages and thoughts, and think that's not really what it is."

Costantini said that it took about a month here on the ground to begin to understand how things were in this part of Iraq. He noted that the experience has been a humbling and gratifying experience for him.

Gunnery Sergeant Phillip Steven Bemis
Battalion Master Gunner, 1st LAR Battalion

"We bring the show to the fight." A veteran of OIF1, he joined the battalion as it was preparing to deploy for OIFII. As IMEF was preparing Operation Vigilant Resolve, *1st LAR Battalion moved from Al Asad to the region outside of Fallujah in a day and a half. When the battalion entered the area of Karmah, enemy resistance failed to appear. Several vehicles have survived IED attacks, but several Marines riding in General Mattis's LAV have been wounded, and one killed. With constant missions, time was flying for this experienced Marine.*

Gunny Bemis entered the Corps at MCRD San Diego in June, 1986, and completed infantry training at Camp Pendleton. He was assigned to be part of Marine Security Forces at Yorktown, Virginia, for two years, then served with Fox Company, 2/2. While in Okinawa, he reenlisted and made a lateral move to become an LAV (Light Armored Vehicle) crewman. After schooling, he was sent to 2nd LAI (Light Armored Infantry—former designation for LAR) Battalion and went to the Persian Gulf, serving as a gunner for the company commander of Delta Company, 2nd LAR. From 1993 to 1995, he served on the drill field and then went to the 1st LAR Battalion at Camp Pendleton, with Delta and Alpha Companies. In 1999, he became Operations Chief and Master Gunner for the 4th LAR Battalion (a Marine Reserve battalion). At the start of 2004, he was assigned to join 1st LAR as the Battalion Master Gunner.

OIF1

During OIF1, Bemis served with 4th LAR Battalion. He felt that that was one of the highlights of his career, as he was able to help train these Marines during their Reserve drills. He emphasized the intelligent use of time during Reserve unit training. "The highlight for me was the OIF tour, with Alpha Company, 4th LAR. Where we were attached to 1st Light Armor Reconnaissance Battalion, as an augment/reinforce."

Once their gear arrived, the Reservists fit right in. He explained that all of the LAR battalions "chopped" their Reserve companies to 4th LAR Battalion, and that battalion stayed in Iraq for eight months conducting route and area/zone reconnaissance, security patrols, and SASO operations.

"Other highlights [in his career], I'd have to say, was, my time at 1st LAR, was being one of the members of a 150-man company that took out 25 vehicles on the first MEU deployment, in 1996, to Kuwait and Southwest Asia. The history of LAR, it dates back to the late seventies, seventy-nine, eighty, where the development of the LAV started coming in."

Bemis has spent 14 of his 18 years in the Corps with LAVs, and he calls them remarkable vehicles. They shoot, move and communicate, and drive really far, really fast. They conduct economy of force operations, convoy escorts, and raids.

He outlined his time in Iraq during OIF1 in 2003. He deployed with 4th LAR, a reserve battalion activated in February 2003. Bemis was with Alpha Company, and they were left on their own for a short time while their vehicles arrived in Kuwait. They then caught up with Division a few days later. Colonel Toolan, who Bemis thought was the G 3 for Division at the time, decided to use this LAR company for Division security and MSR (Main Supply Routes) security for Marine units coming to the Division. They also performed route, area, and zone security missions. He said that they operated closer to villages and towns, and went into the international airport at Baghdad. At Baghdad, Bemis ran Vehicle Check Points (VCPs) and Entry Control Points (ECPs), checkpoints, and security. He said that there were thousands of people and hundreds of cars and trucks trying to come south back into Baghdad. "We really didn't think about all of the things that are happening right now, Vehicle-borne, or vehicle-carried IEDs."

(At the time of the interview in 2004, he said that he didn't know when a vehicle or person would come up to them and set off a bomb.)

4th LAR Battalion was reinforced with two Force Recon platoons, and from one to three infantry companies, two full HET (Human Exploitation Teams) teams, two Explosive Ordnance Disposal (EOD) teams, and an area of responsibility over three major cities: Mahmudiyah, Yusufiyah, and Lutafiyah. Gunny Bemis said that supply trucks going into Baghdad were being ambushed, and the LAR battalion began doing "Trojan Horse" operations. This involved taking two five-ton trucks, armor plating them, and putting them into lightly defended Army convoys. Aboard the Marine trucks would be two squads of Marines with machine guns, AT4s, 203's, Squad Automatic Weapons (SAWs) and M-16s. These Marine trucks would be intermixed with the Army convoys. When the convoys got attacked, the LAR Marines would dismount and sweep through enemy attacks.

Some of the Hispanic Marines were also allowed to grow beards and drive around in civilian vehicles to obtain basic intel about areas without being noticed as much.

Bemis said that there was lots of innovation by Marines during the eight months he was here last year. He left Iraq in October 2003, and returned in February 2004, after a four month break.

OIFII

He remarked that when he joined 1st LAR Battalion in December 2003, this was coming back into the LAR unit where he had begun in LAVs.

Currently, 1st LAR was operating in a gigantic area, with hundreds of square kilometers. The vehicles were ready to pick up and assist anywhere in a moment's notice. He said that often when they show up, "Nobody wants to play with us." He was referring to enemy forces, who seem to avoid confrontations with the speedy, well-armed vehicles. "If I can go through this whole deployment without firing a single round, I'm fine with that."

Whenever he sees any of the companies in the battalion, he likes to share his experience with LAR Marines. He noted that one can create a legacy just by a simple conversation with a Marine, be he a lance corporal or a staff sergeant.

As for Security and Stability Operations (SASO), he said that one can't conduct it from inside an LAV 25. These are feared vehicles, given their capability to fire 200 rounds a minute of explosive 25mm ammunition. They also have a 7.62mm coaxial-mounted 240 Golf machine gun. But once Civil Affairs Marines dismount the vehicles, they can begin SASO.

Gunny Bemis said that vehicle maintenance has been a real challenge. He was the gunner for the battalion commander's command, or "jump command post" vehicle. The battalion commander travels with two LAV 25s: one is the communications vehicle, and the other his command vehicle. These vehicles could be called on to move out at a minute's notice. Bemis said that in these four-and-a-half months, the vehicles have clocked over 15,000 kilometers, or about 9,000 miles, by his estimate. The crews have done well in keeping the vehicles maintained. He tells the younger Marines to apply the same care to the LAVs that they do to their own cars back home. These were the vehicles taking them into combat, and they needed to be in top condition so that they could shoot, move, and communicate.

Bemis said that the suspension system of the LAVs has helped them to survive many strikes by mines currently used by insurgents. The suspension helps to absorb some of the blast from the mines. "We've been coming kind of clean when it comes to damage." Tires and drive train components have been destroyed. As for RPGs, he said, "RPGs have been known to hit off the vehicles and just deflect off, based on the angles of the armor."

LAV Marines have also taken to strapping their packs onto the outside of the vehicles to help deflect attacking weapons. Bemis said that the armor on the LAV 25 is only a quarter of an inch thick, and he would like to see thicker armor on future vehicle variations. The Marines also report on improvements that they would like to see on the vehicles to include fire-control systems and better drive systems.

Gunny Bemis said that one of the interesting things about being in LAVs was that one never knew where he would be from day-to-day. They could be east in Baghdad tomorrow or west on the border with Syria. They can live in their vehicles when they move to another mission.

I then asked him to describe recent operations. 1st LAR was involved in Operation *Ripper Sweep* near Fallujah. RCT1 was assigned to go into Fallujah after the killing of four private security contractors there. It was another example of LAVs quickly reacting and traveling quickly to concentrate around Fallujah.

"When *Ripper Sweep* came along, it was a phone call: Saddle up your Marines, get on their gear, and come to Al Asad, and stand by for the brief. Within hours, and I think the total movement took a day and a half. We had every piece of rolling stock, every essential body, whether he was a communicator or repair, a crewman, a tow truck operator, it didn't matter. Everybody was in Al Asad, standing by for the mission. Once the mission came up, we did several cordons, towns and cities I'm pretty rusty with, the only one that really sticks out is Al Karmah. Karmah is just a little south and east of Fallujah, and it was said that they were feeding insurgents, and they were a big hiding point for mujahideen."

Bemis said that as they tightened the cordon around Karmah, when they entered the city there was no resistance. The LAV Marines discovered many IEDs along Route Lincoln. A patrol found six daisy-chained remote-detonated IEDs on both sides of a road. Down the road from this was a 12.5mm machine gun aimed down the road. Bemis noted that had the mujahideen not left the area, this was a sophisticated ambush that would have caused many friendly casualties and vehicle damage. No IEDs were detonated during this two-day sweep. He said that they cleared and conducted 60 IED operations during this two-day period of *Ripper Sweep*. Bemis noted that the IEDs have become more and more sophisticated since he has gotten here: "With a remote control, cell phone, toys, you name it."

They also came across many weapons caches with 82mm mortar ammo, 60mm mortar ammo, 57mm rockets, 120mm mortars, RPGs, AK-47s and ammo, RPKs and ammo.

After *Ripper Sweep* there have been small operations looking for smugglers. There were also sheep smugglers, and cigarette smugglers from Jordan.

Gunnery Sergeant Bemis said that time has been flying this year [2004]. Once in country, it has been 100 percent continuous operations. He was just waiting for a day to just "hang out" at the command post (CP). Because he traveled with the battalion "Jump" group, he was always on the move with the battalion commander.

Bemis said that General Mattis, the 1st Marine division commander, also required a Jump CP, and this involved detaching two LAV 25s to the general's command post. He added, "Our first major losses, was one of the corporals in Weapons Platoon. He was killed in an ambush by RPG and small arms fire." He said that this created a lesson learned for the Marines who maintain the vehicles. The attack caused one KIA (Killed in Action) and three WIA (Wounded in Action) out of seven Marines on the vehicle. That hit vehicle was repaired and put back on the road in a day. A few weeks later, the other LAV 25 assigned to the General Mattis was hit with an IED, resulting in one Marine KIA, and four WIA.

Keeping vehicle repair parts on hand was a challenge. The vehicles were constantly on the move.

Gunnery Sergeant Bemis said that the pre-deployment was mostly geared towards SASO. Since arrival, the Marines adapted to the current threat environment of ambushes and IED attacks. If someone made a mistake, the Marines learned from each mistake. They were learning to always be vigilant, even when it's 110 degrees outside, and 140 degrees inside the vehicles. When on stops, the scout Marines go out of the vehicles, guarding and watching. They were ready to take action at any time.

LAVs were sought-after by all the Marines over here. Wing (Aviation) Marines wanted them, infantry wanted them, and armor units wanted them. As he put it, "We bring a show to the fight."

Lance Corporal Justin Avery Shields
LAV Crewman (0313), Delta Company, 1st LAR Battalion

This young Marine was on his first overseas and first combat deployment. To date, his main missions as an LAV crewman have been on security and anti-smuggling patrols along the border areas with Syria. During Operation Ripper Sweep, *he participated in scouting actions near Fallujah and Karmah, but was not in any direct-fire encounters.*

Lance Corporal Shields joined the Corps in February 2003, and went to boot camp and graduated in May 2003, completed the School of Infantry (SOI) and trained as an 0311 for the first six weeks there. He was then chosen to be an 0313: LAV crewman.

He arrived at 1st LAR Battalion in October 2003. He had gotten promoted to lance corporal so quickly as he was meritoriously promoted out of LAV school. When he joined the battalion, it was just completing a maintenance scheduling on the LAVs. By December 2003, rumors that the battalion might be re-deploying to Iraq turned into fact.

Shields participated in the Security and Stability Operations (SASO) training as well as Vehicle Check Point (VCP) operations and IED training. "After Christmas, we left. February 19th. There wasn't much time to get ready." Their vehicles were sent out in January 2004, and the battalion received some Maritime Prepositioning Force (MPF) LAVs when they got to Iraq.

In Kuwait, they went down to the port facilities to get their vehicles. "We spent several days, prepping the vehicles, making sure everything worked. They had to be able to shoot, move, communicate, and some of the vehicles we brought with us couldn't shoot, move, or communicate!" The Marines also took the LAVs to the firing range to make sure that their guns worked. They then staged the vehicles to move into Iraq. They spent about five days traveling up into Iraq, with only about four hours sleep each night.

He said, "They were long days. We were also accompanying the Air Wing with us. The Air Wing had some vehicles that broke down. We'd spend several hours on the side of the road, waiting for them to get their recoveries done." The Wing units stopped at Al Asad, and the LAV battalion continued to Korean Village.

Shields said that the relief in place with the Army units up here at Korean Village went well. The Army had no armor assets here. The main missions concerned the border areas with Syria and Jordan. Fox Company, 2/7, sent detachments to the border crossings. He said, "We were more worried about the informal border crossings, cuts in the berm. People smuggling anything across the border: Weapons, people. So we concentrated on reconning along the Syrian border, along with some known areas of interest inside of Delta Company's AO [area of operations]." This AO is the largest of the companies in the battalion. He believed that it took several hours to drive across, split into three separate zones so that three LAV companies could scout and one LAV company could provide security for Fox Company.

Lance Corporal Shields said that there was not really a lot of enemy activity in Delta Company's area. They spent a lot of time as Quick Reaction Force (QRF) for Fox Company.

"I guess the most exciting for our platoon, was, we were running a patrol along the border. One click along the border, because that's our limit of advance, so the Syrians don't get happy and decide to shoot at us. And we caught some guys smuggling that night. We had observed them smuggling products. What appeared to us from Syria to Iraq. But it was actually the other way around, it was going from Iraq to Syria. It was a truck full of cigarettes! I think there was 200 cases of cigarettes in that truck. So we caught them early in the morning and were in the process of transporting to Waleed, which is a formal Syrian border crossing. When my vehicle, the platoon commander's vehicle, hit a pothole in the desert, the only pothole in the desert for 50 clicks, and we rolled our vehicle! Tossing one scout out the back, we had another scout in the back with a detainee. And a cut in the driver's face, I believe he had 40 or 50 stitches. That was the only injury, but that was the most exciting thing we had happen in the month of March." That damaged vehicle was still at Al Asad.

In April 2004, he said, "We got involved outside of Fallujah and Baghdad." The whole battalion moved in about three and a half hours. They moved to Al Asad, then on to the outskirts of Fallujah. "They did not let us into Fallujah."

RCT7 was on the outskirts of Fallujah. 1st LAV Battalion sent vehicles with Fox Company into Al Karmah, and Fox Company, along with an LAV platoon from Delta Company, took fire from a small village. But Shields was not involved in these actions. He felt that they were in the area about three or four weeks, and were not sleeping much, and living in the vehicles.

Shields said that he tried to keep a journal of his observations. He said that he has not been involved in any direct-fire engagements, and there have been no mine strikes or IED detonations. He said that many of the Marines are frustrated at not having action. He felt that the locals fear the LAVs and do not want to rouse them. "I don't know, they don't seem to mess with us."

"We'd like to see something, sir. We'd like to see some action. You hear about it all over the country, that's all I hear about when I call my family. 'I'm so worried about you, I'm so worried about you.' And, there's nothing going on in our area. I know some of the Marines from OIF1, they're like, good, I don't want to see anything. But there's a lotta new Marines, that joined the Marine Corps to come to Iraq, to help their country, and that's what they'd kinda like to see."

He concluded, "These are the best guys a man could work with. Grunts in the field, are, a different breed. Some will say 0313s aren't really grunts because they ride in a vehicle. But I don't know of anyone, whether you're an 0311, or an 0313, bind together like a crew of LAV crewmen. The driver, the gunner, the VC [vehicle commander], they work hand-in-hand every day. And sometimes they'll spend 20 hours in close proximity, every day. Marines that are grunts don't get tighter than any family I've ever met with. Packages, they come in, it's like payday. If a Marine doesn't get something, or get a package, there's always his buddy standing there, or somebody there in the platoon, who'll say, I'll share what I've got until yours gets in."

Captain Andrew Aaron Manson
Intelligence Officer, 1st LAR Battalion

During OIF1, Captain Manson was the battalion intelligence officer, and conducted much of his work on the move the entire time. Prior to the return to Iraq in 2004, he contacted Army units operating in Iraq, ordered maps and digital cameras to prepare for actions here. The size of the LAR battalion's area of operations, and the constant moves created challenges for his Intel Section. A tip-off by a local source resulted in the successful raid on a weapons cache in nearby Ar Rutbah. He was also able to utilize multiple-source assets to plan the capture of an individual who entered Iraq.

Captain Manson entered the Marine Corps Reserve in 1994, and after recruit training, attended the University of Georgia. During his college summers he attended the PLC junior and senior courses at Quantico, Virginia, and received his commission as a second lieutenant after college completion. After graduation from The Basic School (TBS), he attended Infantry Officers' Course (IOC) and the Scout-Sniper course, then went to Okinawa for his first FMF tour as an 0203, ground intelligence officer. He worked in 3rd Marine Division G2 for about a year, then spent a few months with 3rd Reconnaissance Battalion. He returned to 3rd Marine Division as a collections officer. After a total of two years in Okinawa, he reported to 1st LAR Battalion in June 2002. He has been with this battalion ever since.

OIF1

During OIF1, he deployed as the intelligence officer with 1st LAR. Captain Manson gave a brief overview of operations during OIF1 in 2003. Most of the LAR battalion came in on ships, but he had flown in earlier. As 1st LAR's intel officer, Manson developed their targets and objectives. After crossing into Iraq, it was basically a nonstop 30-day movement, with short breaks of a day or two along the way.

"Our battalion specifically went past Baghdad. Seized Tikrit as a part of Task Force Tripoli. Task Force Tripoli consisted basically of 1st, 2nd, and 3rd LAR battalions, plus some infantry. Our main objective up there, seize Tikrit, Saddam Hussein's loyal spots. Lot of palaces were up there."

After seizing Tikrit, they moved to the Saudi Arabian border, chasing people that were believed to be crossing over the border into Iraq. The battalion returned to Kuwait, and left for the United States on May 27, 2003.

For that operation, much of his intel operations were conducted on the move. There was not too much contact with enemy forces. There was not too much enemy presence either, mostly insurgent-type resistance involving small ambushes.

OIFII

Manson said that there were lots of rumors about which LAR battalion would be deploying to Iraq for OIFII. In early December 2003, they learned that 1st LAR would indeed deploy. After return from the Christmas block leave, he began to order maps, got computers ready, ordered digital cameras: Still and video. He contacted the Army units here in Iraq to begin doing analysis of their operations. He began to develop a situational awareness and packed up the gear to fly out to Iraq. A major job was ordering and laminating the maps that the battalion would need in Iraq. He noted that vehicles and sections often operate independently, and LAVs need more maps than an infantry unit.

The missions and area of operations (AO) were not firmed up at first, so Manson and his Marines developed a big picture view for the LAR Marines.

Captain Manson ordered a *lot* of digital cameras. "The idea was to have at least one digital camera per platoon, one camera per company, and then one video camera per company. Intel Section itself has a couple of cameras as well. We primarily use those for taking detainee pictures, documenting sensitive site exploitation, when we go in to do a raid. We document the actual location, we document the stuff that was found in it with pictures. But the companies themselves, they do the same kind of thing. When they were out there acting kind of independently of the battalion, or farther away from the battalion, they would still have the same capability to take pictures of suspicious individuals, suspicious areas."

Prior to deployment, Captain Manson developed over 300 NAIs (Named Areas of Interest). These included breaks in the berm along the border with Syria, suspicious houses and buildings, and possible terrorist camps in the middle of nowhere.

The battalion's gear was put onto ships for transport, and the Marines flew over to Kuwait in mid-February 2004. In Kuwait they waited for their gear to arrive so that they could unload from the ships. Manson focused on providing intel products for the route of the four-day ground move into Iraq. At the time, there was little insurgent activity south of Baghdad. Once they approached Fallujah and Ramadi, their awareness level increased, but there were no real problems.

Manson said that the constant movement of the LAR battalion created challenges for him as an intel officer.

"As an intel guy, obviously, we want to be able to fix locations for a while. You know, just have a battle space for a while so we can develop patterns, conduct analysis. It's very, very hard to do at this point when you're moving, literally, from one side of the country to the other side. Or to the middle of the country, the Baghdad area, to conduct any kind of detailed pattern analysis."

Often his section would document events, and attempt to go back later to do detailed analysis. He used a lot of what the Army had previously done. He also drew on resources from Regiment (RCT7) and Division (1st Marine Division).

When 1st LAR first came into the area, Manson conducted a 10-day turnover with the Army forces then operating here. The current area of operations was approximately 40,000 square kilometers. Initial operations were mainly just driving around the area to familiarize themselves with it. Ar Rutbah was the main city that was their focus of operations. Part of their AO was north of the Euphrates River, the Ramana Province, which consists mostly of a lot of little villages.

To gather data, Captain Manson utilized everything from National Assets, down to Dragon Eye UAVs (Unmanned Aerial Vehicles, or drones), and individual Marines in the field. The battalion Intel Section then attempted to focus on areas of interest for the battalion to investigate. A continuing concern was the presence of foreign fighters and weapons coming into Iraq.

"We kind of focused our operations, or our collections, trying to find where individuals or people were coming across the border, trying to interdict them, and find out what they were trying to smuggle across." A lot of this turned out to be sheep or cigarettes.

In March 2004, the LAR battalion had one company operating in Ramana Province, and one company operating here, near Ar Rutbah. A third company, Alpha Company, operated in between these other companies. Fox Company, 2/7, was running the Ports of Entry (POE) along the borders, and operations in Ar Rutbah. Manson said that 1st LAR had just really gotten comfortable about its familiarity with this area and who the key local "players" were, when it was tasked to move to the Fallujah area to support RCT1's operations there in April 2004.

Captain Manson said that a lot of data from RCT1 and Division helped his efforts in this new area. "Initially we had some intel reporting that thousands, or hundreds of mujahideen, anti-coalition fighters were in a certain area. We were going into this area expecting that anyone carrying a weapon was a bad guy. Different type of ROEs (Rules of Engagement). It was taken up another notch, almost going back to OIF1 ROEs, rules of engagement. Literally, the night we were about to come across the LD [Line of Departure], come into our new area of operations, it was just south of Fallujah, our mission was to support operations ongoing in Fallujah by kinda conducting area reconnaissance outside of Fallujah and surrounding areas. Clearing those areas out. The thought was, foreign fighters, individuals, bad guys, were coming into the Fallujah area."

1st LAR went out there, assuming that all individuals with weapons were hostile. However, Manson learned that there were friendly Iraqi forces in some areas, and this affected operations.

After leaving Fallujah, the battalion went back to Al Asad for a short time, then was pulled out again to support operations for RCT7, north of the Euphrates River. They did area reconnaissance again before finally returning to the Korean Village/ Ar Rutbah area.

Since returning to the Ar Rutbah area, there has been an increase in IED and mine strikes. Some of the mines were determined to be old mines in unmarked minefields. There was increased anti-coalition rhetoric coming from local mosques. Captain Manson mentioned a Sheik Haditha, who had earlier been kicked out of the area by the U.S. Army, who was suspected of this type of rhetoric.

There have been some attacks along MSR (Main Supply Route) Mobile on the outskirts of Ar Rutbah, mostly on KBR supply convoys. Generally, this area was considered to be a transit point for individuals going to Fallujah or Ramadi, and there were not a lot of attacks on coalition forces.

Concerning the raid that took place on the day I arrived here, Captain Manson explained: "We had a source tell us that they had some weapons being stored in a storage shed in the city of Rutbah itself. It was on the outskirts on the western side of Rutbah. Basically, this individual stated that the store owner rented out a couple storage sheds to other individuals. Store owner himself probably didn't know what was in there, however, this individual gave us a pretty good description of the actual location, of what was actually in the storage shed. And it was actually very good intel. We pinpointed locations, pretty much exactly how the source described."

"Inside one storage shed we found numerous weapons, munitions. We had grenades, RPG 7s, RPG 9s, 60mm mortar tube, 60mm mortar rounds, some IED-making materials as well. Wires, TNT, PE4, stuff that was used in these IEDs. Just a lot of munitions was found at these storage sheds. So it was very good intel. We conducted the operation, found it, no one got hurt. In addition to that, while searching the area, we had an RPG attack on one of our satellite patrols."

This patrol was north of the storage shed area. The RPG round was fired over the heads of the patrol, and exploded in the air without harming anyone. He added that no crowds formed during the raid. Often, crowds of mostly kids will form and throw rocks.

Another earlier success involved intel from a source about a smuggling network. "So we put together a mission, very time-sensitive. We'd get a report about the individual, and his location. We acted within an hour, hour and a half. We started moving forces to interdict this individual. We also incorporated other assets: P3 [Orion P-3 surveillance plane], we had Harriers on station as well after P3 checked off. Basically, from the time [of] the initial report, we had collection assets on station, collecting on these individuals, focusing on these individuals, providing us that real-time coordinates crucial in, as we were moving towards the objective our ops guys placed us in a great position to interdict him as he was coming from the border. Again, basically what it was, he was out there on the Iraq-Syrian border. They noticed some vehicles on either side, swapping merchandise, didn't know what it was. Followed those vehicles from the Iraq side from the border all the way into ASR [Alternate Supply Route] Silver, which is one of the major roads that, in this area, smugglers, everyone, pretty much have to utilize to get north up to Husaybah, wherever."

"So we had the collection assets follow them all the way down to ASR Silver where we set up a blocking position, a VCP, ended up interdicting them there. So we had these guys pretty much the whole time. A lot of good, real-time collection assets that helped."

"We got the guy, got him back to our higher headquarters, detailed interrogations, and they got the information. Now, they've sent him on to Abu Ghraib, and holding these guys. We've had a couple of operations like that, very similar."

For both of his deployments, Captain Manson felt that there has been good utilization of intelligence assets. "I think, for OIFII, we've been able to utilize more assets. My Marines specifically have been able to utilize their skills. I've been able to utilize them more during OIFII for the simple fact that the tempo's a lot slower. We have the time to do some analysis at the very least. And it's a very good feeling, when you're out there, especially, for instance, the smuggling operation we did. Trying to get the smuggler."

Yesterday's raid was also rewarding for him—getting the intel and operating on it successfully.

1st LAR's Intelligence section consisted of eight Marines. Most were intel analysts. Staff Sergeant Kwashi [sic] was the S2 Alpha, and Sergeant Scofield the S2 Chief. They both could do Captain Manson's job. The Marines actually created the information for the line companies. One of these Marines broke a femur bone when his LAV rolled and had to be evacuated to the States.

Manson said that the Dragon Eye UAV (Unmanned aerial vehicle) has proved very valuable. It can fly 10 to 12 clicks (10,000 to 12,000 meters) ahead of a unit to give real-time intel. His Marines actually control/fly the aircraft. Also, the money spent for the new digital cameras has been a great help. The commanding officer's guidance was to purchase what they needed. The images created would also help the incoming units. Marines who were in Iraq for OIF1 have helped to train Marines new to Iraq this year.

Leaving FOB Korean Village

I finished up Captain Manson's interview about 1300, then checked on the flight time to Al Asad. The helos weren't due for an hour and a half, so I worked on downloading photos and interviews at the Fox Company Combat Operations Center (COC). At about 1400 the Company phone rang and the air boss said that the helos were early and were now at the LZ! I lugged my gear to the LZ, and the Ch53s were there but not yet loading.

It was hot today, nearly 120 degrees! Inside the CH53 was also hot, and due to my rush to get to it, I had not grabbed a bottle of water for the hour-and-ten-minute helo flight to Al Asad. Normally, once a helo is airborne, the inside cools off from the wind blowing through it. Today, it felt like an oven was blowing into the chopper. This was the only time I've felt even a little queasy inside a helo.

Once at Al Asad, I checked on the flight manifests, and saw that I was on the manifest for a flight back to Camp Fallujah tonight. I now had 28 interviews from this trip to catalogue and summarize, so I felt that returning tonight would be a good idea. Plus, Major Adams at RCT1 did not have a firm flight for me for the following night.

Now that I was familiar with traveling in the AO, it was easier to ask people for help and to know where to get it. But before I did anything else, I got a bottle of cold water at the Passenger Terminal (PAX) and practically inhaled it! I then called Major Adams at RCT7 to see if Colonel Tucker, the regimental commander, was available. He was not, so I got a bus ride from Major Biggins at A/GDAG to 2/7 to interview their commanding officer, Lieutenant Colonel Skuta. Guess what! He was with Colonel Tucker at FOB Hit—where I had just left! So I got a ride back to the RCT7 area where I ate in the chow hall, then stopped in the Combat Operations Center. I thanked Major Adams for his help on this trip, and while talking was asked by his lieutenant assistant where I was from. I told her Philadelphia, and she said that's what she thought from my accent. Turns out she was from Cheltenham, Pennsylvania, and went to Gwynedd Mercy Academy, a short drive from where I then taught at Lansdale Catholic in Montgomery County, Pennsylvania! Her dad also directed the school shows there—I was the show director at my high school.

In the evening, Colonel Tucker returned from his afternoon away. I briefly spoke with him, he told me that it wasn't a good time for an interview today, but we'd work on a later date. As it happened, I never got to do this follow-up interview.

I then worked on journals for about an hour and got a ride to the PAX terminal and checked in. It was now dark.

We left for the flight line about a half hour before the helicopters were due in, and loaded onto a CH46 without incident. It was an uneventful ride back to Camp Fallujah.

CHAPTER SIX

Ramadi, Marines of 2/4

This short chapter cannot begin to cover even a small part of the actions of Marines in the Iraqi provincial capital city of Ramadi during the first half of 2004. The plan for Security and Stability Operations by the 1st Marine Division had been foiled by a rapidly growing insurgency movement that took place throughout Iraq in late March and early April 2004. IED threats, constant patrolling, ambushes and firefights became the norm.

My visit to meet with and interview Marines at Hurricane Point Ramadi, and Combat Outpost Ramadi gave me the opportunity to meet with a representative sampling of Marines and officers from three units of the Second Battalion, Fourth Marine Regiment (2/4): Weapons Company; Echo Company; and Golf Company.

The three days of interviews consumed nearly all of the last week of my nearly five-month deployment as a Marine Corps field historian in Iraq. Being based at Camp Fallujah, any travel to camps outside the immediate Fallujah area involved scheduling mostly nighttime helicopter rides after making prior arrangements with receiving staff officers to be sure that I would make maximum use of my time at each camp. It could take the better part of a night to travel to Ramadi, if all connections went well. The return to Camp Fallujah also required another night of travel. The travel had to be coordinated by the staff at a battalion or regiment. This meant that even a few days of interviews could take a week.

Ongoing operations and events always took priority over having Marines meet with me. For instance, I hoped to meet with the commanding officer of 2/4, Lieutenant Colonel Paul Kennedy. However, the day I arrived at his Combat Operations Center at Hurricane Point, he was deeply immersed in meetings with local Iraqi officials while attacks on his men and positions were taking place.

Wednesday July 21, 2004

I attended the RCT1 brief at Camp Fallujah, then finished up with all preparations for the trip to Blue Diamond tonight. At 1330, I attended the Warrior Transition brief in the chapel. It started with a medical questionnaire that I need to pick up on return from Blue Diamond, then the chaplain explained the Warrior Transition. Mostly it applied to combat Marines, but there were situations that will occur in every case of a Marine being away for a long time. All together it took a little over an hour. This is something that is probably long overdue in the services. I know when I returned from Okinawa in the 1970s, I was on my own, even though it was not a wartime situation.

I bumped into Major Willhoite, who asked where I was headed today. When I told him to see 2/4 in Ramadi, he told me that there was another big fight going on there today, and 2/4 was in the middle of it all!

I left for the LZ at 2130, and the flight to Blue Diamond in Ramadi didn't arrive until 2400. I boarded the helo, and we sat at the LZ for a full half hour on the bird! One of the crewmen kept wiping something back by the ramp, and then went back there with a wrench. Just what I don't want to see on a helo! We took off around 0030, and flew to Al Taqaddum. I figured that we were stopping for fuel as usual when they told us to exit the helo. As the 10 Marines from the aircraft watched, the helo then took off with all of our gear on it! What? We sat on the runway for a good 45 minutes with no word from anyone. Then another helo from the flight line taxied over and a crew member yelled over the noise of the props to get on THAT helo. I asked about our gear, and the answer was to get on that helo. We did, it taxied across the runways, and we got off, then onto another helo (which was our first one, with all of our gear). Finally, we were off.

Not so fast! We flew for about 20 minutes, then landed in a field that I recognized as Camp Fallujah! There, the crew chief told us to take our gear and get onto "Dash Two," the helo behind us! We did, and took off one more time. We headed north again, and this time landed at Ar Ramadi, the 1st BCT (U.S. Army Brigade Combat Team) camp, then hopped the Euphrates River and landed at Camp Blue Diamond! It was 0300 by this time. I checked in at the AGDAG shack by the landing zone, walked over to the Transient Tent, and racked out on a cot. A long night of travel for such a short distance! This made up for my last smooth, direct helicopter ride a week prior.

Thursday July 22, 2004

After morning chow I walked to the Combat Operations Center (COC) at Blue Diamond for pickup by 2/4, as per emails from their S3 officer, Major Harrill. After a half hour, no ride, so I went into the G7 office of Lieutenant Colonel Mark Wriggle, and he told me that 2/4 was engaged in combat that morning, and my ride wouldn't be until afternoon. I explained my long night to him, and said that I would go and get some sleep and check back around noon time.

I did get a couple hours of sleep, when at about 1030 Major Judy from EFCAT/ G7 came and told me that my ride to 2/4 was there. I walked over to the Combat

Operations Center (COC), met the staff sergeant who would be taking me to 2/4, and loaded up my gear. It was about 10 minutes from Blue Diamond to Hurricane Point, but a full convoy of at least four armored vehicles was required to travel there across the bridge over the Euphrates River to Ramadi.

On arrival at 2/4's headquarters, I met with several staff officers who made me feel welcome. Major Harrill showed me 2/4's COC, and explained that Lieutenant Colonel Paul Kennedy was in a meeting with local Iraqi leaders, and security officials. Harrill used a tactical map to review for me the major actions that 2/4 has been involved in since March. He then introduced me to Captain Harris, (S3 Alpha) who had organized their extensive battalion historical program. He and Lieutenant Jason Snyder had assembled a treasury of video interviews that were begun after events in Ramadi from April 6 through 10. They also have an animated PowerPoint presentation of these combat operations.

At about 1450, the COC was a hub of activity. There had been three mortar impacts in the vicinity of the Combat Outpost in Ramadi this afternoon, and the battalion commander was in a meeting with the mayor of Ramadi, the chief of police, and some other local leaders. He was keeping the meeting going and, I think, trying to get the explanation from these people as to what was happening near the Outpost. Local leaders usually claim that everything is under control, and trouble is being caused by "outsiders." The result of this is that any chance of speaking with Lieutenant Colonel Kennedy today was just about gone as he would be tied up with these leaders.

After securing me a room to sleep in, Captain Harris walked me around the tiny camp that was Hurricane Point, and then introduced me to the commanding officer of Weapons Company, Captain Weiler. I explained to him what I needed from his Marines, and he agreed to have them meet with me after chow. I had a great set of interviews, and scheduled the last one for Friday morning. One of the interviews I had to do outside of the Company command post at night as it got too noisy inside from Marines watching a movie. So I found a table and benches and did the final interview of the day in the dark, using my flashlight to make notes.

Exhausted, I returned to my rack in the dark, and got a good eight hours of sleep.

Lieutenant Jason Matthew Snyder
Watch Officer, 2nd Battalion, 4th Marines

Lieutenant Snyder was an individual augmentee to 2/4, a watch officer who also served as "kind of battalion historian of sorts" in his words. Using a large map laid out on a table, he outlined the major operations conducted by 2/4 since arrival in the provincial capital of Ramadi, including combat the day of my arrival at the command post.

My recording was not really an interview, but a taping of the overview that he gave of 2/4's operations in Ramadi.

He used a large map fixed onto a table to outline the city of Ramadi and our current location here at Hurricane Point. The Point is the westernmost tip of the city of Ramadi. There used to be a palace here used by Saddam Hussein's sons. There is a helicopter pad at that location.

"Right across Route Michigan, Route Pacer, right across the street, we have the 'Snake Pit' which is another firm base. One company stays there, Fox Company. Their call sign is 'Raider.' At the easternmost part of the city, the most densely populated part of the city, we have another firm base, called the Combat Outpost." There were three outposts in the city of Ramadi.

Weapons Company and H&S Company were located here at Hurricane Point. The Weapons Company was currently being called Mobile Assault Company as they were not using some of their weapons systems, such as mortars.

When 2/4 arrived in Ramadi, they were supposed to conduct a Relief in Place (RIP) with an Army reserve unit, the 1-24, but it had left before 2/4 arrived. So a sort of RIP took place with an Army infantry battalion, 1-16, that had a light presence throughout the city. Each company of 2/4 was given its own area of operations (AO) inside the city. Fox Company had an area with a hospital, which was also a very poor area and has Kurdish ghettos. The south of the city came under Golf Company, also known as "Joker." In this area of operations (AO) there was the government center, the major banks, and the business district. Further east, in the Sofia area in the northeast, Echo Company had responsibility. This was a more rural, more wealthy area, with former Baathist officials and ex-military officials living there. He said, "So, the wealthy people live out of town, and the poor people live in town."

Snyder joined the battalion about a week before they deployed to Iraq, so he was not involved in any of the pre-deployment Security and Stability (SASO) training. "From the get-go, we had dismounted and mobile patrols, 24/7, throughout the entire city, to include all of Sofia. And … there's a lot of the 'wave tactics,' trying to win over the locals. Our CAG Det [Civil Affairs Detachment], which is headed up by Major Lindbergh, they initiated projects. They went out started doing site surveys, things of that nature. We started getting products from Army PSYOPS, talking about 'Don't support the terrorists,' and comic books for kids that talks about personal hygiene, stuff like that. We would go on patrol, talk to the locals, you know, try to assess their needs. And really, three constant themes: Safety, water and electricity, and employment. The unemployment rate in the city's very high. I think it's assessed at somewhere around 60 percent."

Battalion units spent a lot of time on this Civil-Military Operations effort, trying to educate locals on what was happening and how the Iraqi government was going to be taking over power. Some of the documents that they handed out included a timeline of how the transfer of authority would be taking place. Patrolling was constant, and there were some small, mostly uncoordinated attacks from time to time. IED sweeps by the Marines were also constant. Companies would send out platoons every morning to sweep Route Michigan, which runs to Fallujah and on to Baghdad, and another road that sweeps up into Sofia. They were constantly finding IEDs every day, and EOD Marines would come out to destroy them.

Insurgent attacks became more coordinated, where an IED attack would be followed up with small arms fire on the Marines. "A general rule was that if you were out in town for more than four hours, you were expected to be hit." Snyder continued, "An example of that was, I was out on patrol with a Weapons Platoon, 'AP Three' [Call Sign "Apache"]. With Captain Harris, actually, and we were assessing, we had actually gone to the easternmost region, parts of the AO [area of operations]. Spent several hours out there, talking to people. They had never seen Americans out there. They had never seen any coalition forces out there before. We were just sort of assessing their needs. We were out there for at least five hours, and on the way back in, we were hit by an IED. Two wounded, including Captain Harris, shrapnel to the face. And those types of things started to increase."

The battalion had its first major engagement on April 6. Snyder said that he along with many other Marines did not expect any major engagements. The focus had been on SASO. The way they dealt with the city changed on April 6. "It was on April 6th that we took 12 KIA. And something like 25 to 30 wounded." Snyder had a PowerPoint that he showed me later with the exact information. This was at the time that Fallujah was heating up, and the press and media gave little attention to events in Ramadi. Snyder said that Ramadi is the center of government for the Al Anbar Province, and that there were many competing interests here. Many of the wealthy inhabitants, including Baathist officials, ex-military, and tribal sheiks, don't want to see the status quo changed. These individuals and groups felt threatened by the coalition forces and the unknowns that would be caused by the transfer of authority.

Snyder continued, "Also, the battalion commander was engaging the governor, and the mayor, and the chief of police, and sheiks and imams, all the time. Talking to them all the time, trying to develop a rapport with them." 2/4 also provided 24-hour security for the government center in Ramadi. The governor, mayor, and chief of police operated out of there. There have been attacks and riots outside this center.

The Saddam Mosque is in the center of the city. Snyder said that everything south of this area was a "hot spot." On April 6 and 7, there was heavy fighting in this part of town. Most of the firefights took place withing close range, what he described as "hand grenade range." It was house-to-house fighting in a very urban area with close-in streets. 2/4 did not have armor assets during the fights.

Snyder then shifted to the fighting that took place here in Ramadi yesterday, July 21, 2004. "Basically the city erupted in and around the vicinity of the Saddam Mosque. We had three of our companies decisively engaged with the enemy. And Brigade [Army] reinforced us with, I was a watch officer at the time, the Army was pumping in QRFs [Quick Reaction Forces] so fast that we didn't even have call signs for all of them. So we would actually have Army units rolling in."

"And the Brigade would call us and say,
'Okay, you have two Bradleys and four Abrams rolling in.'
'Okay, roger that. What's the call sign?'
'We don't know yet. We'll get back to you on that.'"

"And they were pumping them in so fast. We had QRFs from 134, which controls the AO east of Ramadi. We had QRFs from 116, which is northwest and north of the Euphrates River. We had a QRF from 1-5, which is from west of Ramadi. We had the Brigade QRF. We had 1st Engineers QRF. We had so much air on station [Close air support assets including helos and jets] yesterday that we actually ran out of air. We cycled through all the helos that could be used in the area, all the Cobras. Plus, we had F-16s. That said, the difference between Ramadi and Fallujah, it sounds like, air was used extensively in actually engaging targets. It's been very difficult to engage targets in Ramadi because the fighting is so close. And, this happened on the 6th and the 10th [April] when we had air, and it happened yesterday. Helos would come in and they were getting RPGs and medium machine gun fire. So they were taking fires. They were trying to scan areas for personnel, things like that."

Snyder pointed out major landmarks of the city on the map. Near the Saddam Mosque, the battalion had an observation post (OP) at the Agriculture Center. This OP got attacked daily, usually from a school building to the south. North of the Agriculture Center is a large industrial area, and insurgent attacks often launch out of there. There was also a lot of fighting around a soccer stadium south of the Agriculture Center. The southern part of the city is the poorest, yet Snyder said that it seemed to be the friendliest to the Marines. Fox Company operated in key areas there. Snyder could not say why this area was friendly. People in the Sofia area were often paid to lay-in IEDs or take part in ambushes. The planning seems detailed, but the execution of the attacks was not so coordinated.

Lieutenant Snyder then took me to his computer and showed the PowerPoint that outlined operations by 2/4 since their arrival here earlier this year.

Sergeant Lewis William Layton
Squad Leader, Weapons Company, 2/4 (Mobile Assault Company)

Many Weapons Companies were reorganized for current operations in Iraq. Layton outlined how his section was used as an infantry section for several high-intensity days of combat, especially in April and July. High heat, and an enemy that shoots and runs away were two of the challenges he and his Marines faced in Ramadi.

Sergeant Layton began his time in the Corps at Parris Island in July 2001. While at the School of Infantry (SOI), he was meritoriously promoted to Private First Class. He entered the FMF with 2nd Battalion, 4th Marines (2/4) and received a meritorious promotion to lance corporal. He went to Okinawa for 11 months with the battalion. During about six months back in the States he completed various military schools, and was promoted to sergeant.

I asked him to explain how 2/4's Weapons Company was currently organized, something then common among the infantry battalions then in Iraq.

He replied, "The way our company is organized, we have five platoons. We have Mobile Assault Platoon One, Two, and Three. And 81s Platoon, which I am in, has been broken down into two mobile assault platoons. So pretty much we have five mechanized infantry units, infantry platoons."

Each of these platoons was organized pretty much the same, with gun trucks, Mark 19s, and .50 cals. They did a lot of escorts, stand as the battalion Quick Reaction Forces (QRFs), and man two guard points here at Hurricane Point at North Bridge and South Bridge. Layton's squad consisted of 13 Marines.

The company left the United States in February 2004, not really knowing what to expect in Iraq. They flew into Kuwait, where they spent a couple of weeks before flying up into Iraq. Most came in through Al Taqaddum air base. They then convoyed to Ramadi. Many Marines thought that it would be a lot like OIF1, but it has turned out to be completely different. The most common problems now were IEDs and VBIEDs. They have a lot more armor on their vehicles as a result of this new threat. The current armor was much improved over the vehicles that they arrived with.

"A lot of people were excited to get out there, and see what was going on, and how everything was going. When we first got here, our whole AO [area of operations] was wide open. We traveled many roads."

The Marines saturated the area to get to know where everything was. The IED threat was fairly low, and things were mostly quiet in the area for the first month. "And then April 6th, 7th, and 10th is where it really kicked off."

On April 6 and 7 [2004], Sergeant Layton's platoon was on what he called "day-taskable." He first explained how the company was organized on a weekly assignment schedule: One platoon was on day-taskable, one on day Quick Reaction Force (QRF) (from 0800 to 1800), one night-taskable and night QRF (from 1800 to 0800), and the other platoon would be on guard duty. All had 12 hour shifts on this weekly rotation.

On April 6, Golf Company (Call sign "Joker") and Echo Company (Call sign "Porcupine") got into some pretty severe firefights south of the Saddam Mosque in Ramadi. The QRF went out (3rd Platoon—Call sign "Whiskey Three") and got engaged with the enemy there. Then Layton's platoon got called out since they were now the QRF when 3rd Platoon left the firm base.

"We were going to support Joker, and we're driving along, and all of a sudden we were hit by an ambush from an RPK [machine gun]. So, we got hit, a lot of the rounds into the first and second vehicles, barely dodging our platoon commander and the driver in the first vehicle. We got out, and 1st Squad, was on an alleyway while my squad was on another. And basically, taking pot shots from people around the corners. A few of them were killed."

The Marines then waited for enemy to come out and shoot at them so that they could shoot back. Layton said the most times when he has been engaged in a firefight, "It's not very often you see someone firing at you."

Layton said that the enemy firing pot shots was trying to slow down or stop convoys, and was usually from far away and not well-aimed. "On that engagement [April 6] we definitely saw somebody and we engaged them."

They then went to pick up two casualties from Fox Company (Call sign "Raider") and took them to the Combat Outpost that is about two clicks (2,000 meters) east of the Saddam Mosque (I would visit there myself the next day). After this drop-off, they went back to pick up some casualties from Golf Company ("Joker") to take to the Combat Outpost. While there, Captain Weiler (Weapons Company commander: "Whiskey Six") called for them to go near Route Nova in the Sofia neighborhood, another problem area.

In Sofia, they tied in with 2nd Platoon ("Whiskey Two") and began taking fire. Layton said that his squad was tasked with following a car on a parallel road. They went down the road, got on line and swept through a field where they found lot of .50 cal rounds and weapons. They did not see the car. On the way back, someone in a taxicab shot at one of Layton's fire teams. The team returned fire on the cab, which pulled up to house and the riders went into the house. Layton's Marines got to the house and set up a cordon around it. He said, "I sent a team in. We find out that there's no one in the house, just a family in there, very scared. We checked the cab, we didn't find anything. We did find a blood trail, coming from the cab to the backyard to the field that we had just swept through."

They were then called somewhere else and started heading east along Nova. "That's when we got hit along our left flank, the north, right in between Nova and the river. And that's where basically the whole company opened up with Mark 19s, .50 cals, 240s. Fire lasted for about a minute and a half, two minutes. Fire ceased. Our platoon was tasked with getting on line and sweeping the field [on foot]." He estimated that from Nova to the river was about a click and a half to two clicks. "We found a couple dead bodies, AKs, extra rounds, an RPG. We determined they were dead, so we kept on moving towards the river, sweeping through." They saw a man running towards the river, he got away. They also saw footprints along the riverbank, leading them to believe that insurgents had escaped by swimming. At the end of this day, the Marines were exhausted.

"It's really hard to remember, the turnover between the sixth and the seventh. You know, driving, getting ambushed, shooting people around corners. We do a lot of support for the line [infantry] companies: Grabbing casualties, bringing them to the outposts, evac'ing them."

"Seventh was pretty much the same. Worked hard that day, then I came back, and next day it was pretty quiet." On both days they got back to Hurricane Point around 2100.

It was quiet for the next few days, as they did transportation for Marines. Then came what he called "Operation *Bug Hunt*." He said that they have had a number of "Bug Hunts." On this one (April 10) they went into the Sofia area. Each company was assigned its own area of operations. "We departed here, Hurricane Point, around 0430, to conduct actions on the objective around 0530. We ended up conducting the raid. We had the 120s [mortars] at Junction City firing illum [Illumination mortar rounds]. It started getting light out, all of a sudden we started hearing fire. Pretty heavy AK, RPK fire. [We] Returned with 240 and M16 fire."

They then got word to head up to Apple Street, and then to go to Nova to support the other companies. "Well, once we hit that road, that's when things started getting crazy." Going down the road they began taking AK fire, and they started searching houses. "We had Echo Company on our right flank, we had Fox Company on our left flank. So, we were the only ones that were mechanized, so we kept on pushing up the road."

Their lead vehicle got engaged with a blue van, and hit the van with fire from their 240 Golf machine gun. IEDs started going off at the same time. The company had gotten ahead of the company on their left flank, and had gotten bottled up on the road.

Layton's squad was on the left flank, and started fire team rushes towards houses ahead of them. They stopped at the wall of a house, where Sergeant Layton got his fire team leaders together and told them that they were going to go into the house and go up onto the roof and see what was going on. "So, we hop over the wall, we get into the house. Find the family, they're all in one room, scared. And I'm going to the roof, and that's where we saw two guys running with AKs, towards the north, away from us. They ran into a house, so we couldn't engage. So, after [I] got all of my guys consolidated, and we searched the house, we ran downstairs and started towards the house we saw them run into."

This house was right on the south side of Route Nova. They could see the river from there. They broke down the door and entered the house. It appeared to be the house of a local sheik. When the Marines got to the top of the house, they saw two guys going into a house northwest of them. One of these men ran out of the house and across Route Nova. Layton's Marines engaged this man. The man hid behind a grass hut, but was pinned down by the Marines.

Layton was trying to get radio comm with the rest of the platoon. Then two armed men appeared from the east across Route Nova, heading west. "A few of my Marines engaged them, they both dropped, we assumed they were dead."

The rest of the platoon got up to their position, and then all of the Marines got on line. The insurgent behind the grass hut was wounded, captured, and then evacuated for treatment. Layton's platoon advanced to another house, and one of the two men who had earlier been "dropped" began firing at them with AK fire. The Marines mortally wounded both of them—his partner had already been killed.

The Marines searched other houses in the area. In one, they found what they thought to be a hospital for the mujahideen. There were no personnel there, but lots of hospital supplies. The Marines returned about 1700.

These were to be the most serious engagements of early April. Sergeant Layton said that the weather was not too hot at that time in April. I asked him about his recent promotion to sergeant, and he said that his platoon commander had recommended this as a result of his actions at that time.

The three line (infantry) companies of the battalion were foot-mobile, and get engaged much more often.

Due to all of the IEDs and VBIEDs, his platoon has pretty much cut in half the area it travels. Route Nova and South Canal Road used to be used much more. Currently Layton's Marines only used Route Michigan. All three rifle companies of 2/4 have observation posts all along Route Michigan to keep them open.

His platoon was not involved in the actions in Ramadi that took place about a week and a half ago.

Yesterday, July 21, 2004, he said that Echo, Fox and "Joker" (Golf) companies were heavily engaged. "We had done a raid about noon, going after a high-value target [HVT]. Ended up, he left the country, didn't find him. So we come back, and not soon after that we were called out. We go out, went up Michigan, right past Saddam's Mosque, ended up just about 200 meters just short of Check Point 297." There is a hotel on the north side of the road, they were on the south side. "We'd been called out to pick up two Humvees that were broken down, and tow them back to Combat Outpost." These vehicles had been taking fire from the hotel and returned fire there. Layton said that it seemed like another April 6 and 7. There were sporadic firefights, and Cobra gunships doing gun runs to the north.

Layton's Marines helped "Joker" sweep south to the soccer stadium. When they returned to the Combat Outpost, they got word that there was a mujahideen hospital in the area. So, they went and searched five houses in that area and came up dry. Today, they went back to search the same area with Fox Company. They were moving east on a back road that parallels Michigan, and took fire on a road called Easy Street. A Marine gun truck engaged the shooters in a building, and then Layton's lieutenant engaged the building with an AT-4 round. It was a small building, basically a bunch of small stores. Immediately, Sergeant Layton's team went down to clear the building after the AT-4 went off. No one was in the building.

Layton said, "These guys, that fire at us, it's a lot of hit, they'll fire real quick, and then they're gone. Like the 6th, 7th and 10th, they'll fire, then push to the rear. Fire, then push to the rear."

Once the building was clear, they continued on the road. They then joined up with "Bastard Six," the battalion commander (Lieutenant Colonel Paul Kennedy), and headed back to Hurricane Point.

"The weather now is horrible. We were out all day doing different things, then we finally got called in to do that. You're drenched. You're out for 10 minutes, you're drenched. It's about 115 degrees out, it's very hot. My guys probably go through six to eight bottles of water, and still come back dehydrated. it's horrible out there, it's real nasty." Layton noted that the Marines have flak jackets, Kevlar helmets, "Deuce" gear, and all other needed gear, fighting an enemy with only AK rifles and "man dresses" (Dishdashes).

I asked Sergeant Layton about the pre-deployment training. He said that a two-week period at March Air Force Base was used for mock operations, complete with role players. He said that he would give them some advice now, but it was realistic training in patrolling and moving through a city area. He also went to a SASO training area at Camp Pendleton at Range 31. He said this was also realistic. There was lots of training with live fire, too. He knows that there would be training changes when they return to the States, based on current experiences in Iraq. He said that the IEDs have been a big challenge here.

Sergeant Layton said that his squad has hit seven or eight IEDs. One Marine has been lost, and many hurt by them. When they first got here, they had mostly half-doors on the Humvees, and not many IED attacks. Now the Up-Armored Humvees have saved many lives. There have been minor shrapnel wounds, and temporary deafness from IEDs. There have been many more Up-Armored Humvees, and lots of add-ons. He said that most often, the gunners and drivers and assistant drivers were wounded in early IED attacks due to the gaps in armor. Right now, the gunners don't stand up while the vehicle is moving, and the same for guys in the back of a Humvee. Up-Armored Humvees have continued to arrive. His squad moves out in a high-back and a hard-back Humvee.

Sergeant Layton summed up his feelings: "I guess I'll just give a general perspective of the fighting that's taken place here in Ramadi. Basically, our enemy is just a bunch of cowards fighting for the wrong cause, in my eyes. They shoot. They run. Our battalion's done real well. Our platoon's done real well. Before we came here, it's always a question in your mind, if you haven't been in combat, how your men are gonna perform. And I haven't been disappointed about one of my guys. And, I just go day in, day out, just hoping that I can lead my squad to the best of my ability, and hopefully take them all home."

Sergeant Jeremiah Lee Randle

Section Leader, Weapons Company, 2/4 (2nd Mobile Assault Platoon)

Randle joined Weapons Company in late 2004, and explained how his section of Marines were responding to the guerrilla-style fighting inside the city of Ramadi. He said that he wished that all of his Marines had more time to develop skills with their weapons prior to deployment. (There was a software glitch, so this interview is based on written notes made at that time.)

Sergeant Randle enlisted in the Corps in March 2000. His first assignment was with 2/8. He completed a Mediterranean cruise, and also spent time in Kosovo. He has a language ability in both German and Norwegian, and was stationed for a time in Stuttgart, Germany. From there, he was sent as a tactics and weapons instructor to the Republic of Georgia.

He was transferred to 2/4 in December 2003, shortly before the battalion deployed to Iraq. He said that a training exercise at March Air Force Base was valuable. Once 2/4 arrived in Kuwait, they completed training and convoy rehearsals prior to the two-day convoy through Iraq. He said that there had been conflicting reports about what they would be doing here. They finally discovered that they were facing a guerrilla threat in their AO.

Sergeant Randle noted that the insurgents currently choose the time and place of combat, and the Marines react to them. He also said that the Marines had been made aware of the culture in Iraq, but said that only a few of the Iraqi men actually grow beards, usually the imams and older men. The area around Ramadi is more urban and relatively modern. He said that the religion and culture clash within Iraq. Some insurgents do have a religious motivation, while there was also a general suspicion of American forces here.

Some of the Marines here do not get to see the good that we are doing.

Sergeant Randle explained how the Weapons Company of 2/4 was currently organized and deployed. He said there is a CAAT-like concept. Since April they have used their trucks less. His section has two gun trucks. The sections are kept smaller to avoid IEDs. Leaders look at maps to study where IEDs are more likely to occur. He said that his own anti-terrorism training has paid off for him here. The platoon has used a variety of routes to get to target areas, and this has been successful in avoiding IED attacks. His platoon has only been hit by two IEDs along Route Michigan.

Sergeant Randle outlined a concept that many of the line (infantry) companies have been using. At first, they were using a British anti-IED technique. However, this technique became less effective as the battalion became more vehicle-mobile. More Marine vehicles on the roads created more targets of opportunity for the insurgents.

It was hard to see the IEDs, and the enemy has become better at timing detonations. It is rare to see the IED that "blows you up" when riding in a truck.

The CAAT platoon fills the role of armor in attacks, but Randle said that the Humvees are not the best suited vehicles for this role in the cities. In cities, they are too close to some targets. He said that the up-armored M1114 Humvee, was a good vehicle.

In April, one Marine in the platoon was killed in action. Randle said that during ambushes, the enemy plans escape routes which makes it difficult to find them. Some of the insurgent planning is tactically sound, with every avenue of approach in an area set up for an ambush. The enemy has used Russian-made .50 caliber weapons, also. Their weakness has been that they are not technically proficient with the weapons. They do not like to fight at night, often use AK-47s without a buttstock, and get lazy sometimes when they sleep-in in the mornings. Randle said that although much of the stateside training was good for his Marines, they need to get more time to shoot their weapons during this training. Some of his Marines came to his platoon right out of the School of Infantry (SOI), and needed more training with their current weapons. Sergeant Randle said that it was important for all the Marines in the platoon to be proficient in all of the weapons that the platoon uses.

One sure sign of an attack in Ramadi was when kids leave an area.

When the Army left Ramadi and the surrounding area, Randle said that the insurgents used "Passive Intelligence" to see how the Marines operated, and also began an uptick in activity. From April 5th through the 10th, there were nonstop combat operations here. He described two operations: *County Fair*, a search of the Ramadi area, and *Bug Hunt*, operations in the Sofia area. He said it was a self-test of his Marines that week. It then got quiet for the next three to four weeks.

IED attacks have picked up, and he described current operations as "Quasi Combat." The recent firefights in Ramadi were exceptions to this low tempo. He said that there was some bitterness in the battalion about the lack of media attention to events in Ramadi. There is one infantry battalion covering a city of about 225,000. 2/4 has had more casualties than any other battalion in Iraq to date. There was no fixed-wing support for the Marines here at Ramadi. (Note: There was fixed-wing support in July.)

Close air support has mostly been limited to rotary-wing assets. There has been limited heavy tank or armor support, mostly some Army Bradley fighting vehicles in the April fights. Also, there was no indirect (mortar or artillery) support for Marines engaged with targets in Ramadi. All of the fighting here has been infantry against insurgents. It has not been a combined arms fight. Sergeant Randle felt that there would have been less casualties if the Marines had gotten better training. He said that half of Weapons Platoon has been wounded, and locally 2/4 has had horrific casualties. On this level, it was hard to see the good being done here. He hoped that the current fight does not go down as another Vietnam, but he sees many differences with that conflict and current operations.

Lance Corporal Reagan Charles Hodges
Fire Team Leader, 81mm Section, Weapons Company, 2/4

Since re-enlisting in the Marines in 2001, he has enjoyed his time back in the Corps. Weapons Company provided a wealth of heavy weapons to support the infantry companies in the battalion during combat operations in Ramadi. Their vehicle assets and speedy response time help them to push back insurgent attacks. The heaviest fighting for his section came in early April. He also explained how insurgents terrorized innocent civilians during combat.

"I actually came in the Marine Corps in 1994, I did four years with Third Battalion, Fourth Marines (3/4). I got out of the Marine Corps at that time, not really ready to commit to another four years." He realized that this was a mistake, but he waited around for another four years until: "As soon as September 11th happened, I decided to come back in, and I'm glad that I did."

He enjoys the travel, and training with other Marines. Before this deployment, all of his deployments were for training. He said, "I'd say as far as highlights, it's what I'm doing right now." The battalion left the States in February 2004, and "As soon as we got here, we started doing what they call 'Right-seat, Left-seat' [*sic*] with the Army." This got them familiar with the Ramadi area and what the Army was doing there. In early April, the Marines started running into a lot of ambushes, many in the city (Ramadi) area. "That's honestly the best place for enemy to attack us, due to the fact that a lot of times, in a city, if it's a real congested area, such as a neighborhood. The shot gets rang out, and you know somebody's shooting at you. But it's hard, unless you see a muzzle flash, or see somebody with a weapon, it's hard to tell, at times, where that fire's coming from. The sound echoes off the wall, and if you're in an alley, you pretty much cannot tell. Plus the fact that they have elevated positions."

He felt that the reason the insurgents don't fire at the Marines like this more often is because the Marines will enter the house, find out who is doing the shooting, and will kill them.

"The 6th, the 7th and the 10th [of April] were pretty big days for us." It was when the insurgents started attacking the line (infantry) companies of 2/4 in Ramadi. As the battalion QRF, his section would roll with about 22 dismounted Marines and five trucks loaded with heavy guns, ranging from 240 Golfs to SAWs, M19s and .50 cals. They now even have a TOW launcher. Hodges said that often the infantry companies would have single squads hit by insurgents, and oftentimes be outnumbered in local firefights. The Weapons sections would roll up into an area and gain fire superiority with their gun trucks. "Then after that, we'd send in our own dismounts, and we pretty much could handle any situation that was thrown at us."

Lance Corporal Hodges said that often these fights would start inside the city of Ramadi, and the Marines would push the insurgents out and into fields outside the city. "Once we'd get them in an open field area like that, there was nothin' they could do." The insurgents do not have the firepower or the training to stand up to the force that the Marines place against them. Some fight until they die, some shoot until out of ammo and then drop their weapons and attempt to escape from the area.

During the 6th and 7th of April, when Hodges's platoon would be going to the aid of an infantry unit, they would often get ambushed along the way. These ambushes only slowed them a little.

He described fighting in the area of the Saddam Mosque which is along a main street in Ramadi. There are a lot of back roads and alleys in the area, and many of the buildings are two and three stories tall. It was hard to tell where the small arms fire was coming from. He said a lot of time the only way to find out where the fire is coming from is "kicking in doors and raiding houses." Marines would enter and clear houses, and get to the roofs to have better firing positions.

"We had situations where we had Iraqi police, on more than a few occasions, where we had them taking shots at us." Marines returned fire when this happened.

On April 10, Hodges said a lot more of the infantry skills came into play. Within about a ten-second span, they were hit by two 155mm IEDs on the side of the road, then an RPG, and single grenade attack. The Marines destroyed the trigger vehicle, then proceeded east in support of Echo Company, 2/4. "I was just getting instructions from a Marine who was there, and as I'm talking to him, he gets shot in the leg." He said that this close-in event was a reality check for him.

Weapons Platoon helped to flush the insurgents to move eastward out of the area. Hodges said that these insurgents were using a lot more tactics. They were bounding and covering each other, all signs of training.

One thing that he described as "weird to see" was the way insurgents entered private homes: "A lot of these insurgents would go into houses. And the next thing, you have to be careful who you're shooting at, 'cause, you'd see these insurgents, five or six of them, go into a house. And the next thing you would see, you keep an eye on the house, 'cause you know who's in there, and you're receiving fire from there. But you would see a family in there, of anywhere from three up to ten kids, and a woman, the mother, and the father, running out of the house." The insurgents would take over these houses and use them as a fire base. When the families were kicked out of their houses, they would not be shot at by the Marines. "When they were out of the area we'd light the house up, shoot and maneuver until we can get up to the house. And then we'd raid the house."

When they killed the enemy, they would take their weapons, ammo, and grenades, which would prevent others from using them against the Marines. Hodges noted that the insurgents were also terrorizing a lot of innocent Iraqi families. The insurgents make death threats if locals do not cooperate with them. He said that it also makes him believe that many of the fighters are not from around here.

Hodges said that when there were a lot of kids around, he could pretty much bet that the Marines would not get hit. But lately, insurgents would attack even when kids were around the Marines. "We've had IEDs go off right in front of us, and right in front of a school where there was kids and children around there, with no regard to the safety of the children. We had a vehicle-borne IED, which was a pretty big thing, go off, one day, in front of us right in the middle of town. We seen at least three civilians killed and a lot more hurt." The terrorists show no respect for life.

Yesterday, his platoon brought back two vehicles that had been damaged in fighting. One had been hit with an IED, and one was hit with an RPG. Often the enemy will fire at them as they go to help a unit in need. They started out at 0400, and did not get back until 2400. They were pretty drained.

Today, they did a movement to contact. "We're gonna make ourselves available to them." Hodges felt that the only way to beat the terrorists was to kill them. Today they were doing patrols and searches to find insurgents any way they could. They had a guy driving around in a car taking shots at them, and guys hiding behind fruit stands also taking shots.

Hodges said, "Everybody here wants to go out. And that's what I like about it. Nobody here is wanting to sit back and not do nothing. We've been here five and a half months, we've had people in our platoon killed, we've had a lot of people sent home. Everybody here is pretty much agreed that it's still worth it. Everything you do here, it's needed." Morale is still high. Hodges felt that the Marines' spirit will not be dulled here.

In training the Marines had prepared for a lot of satellite patrolling. However, it is not what they do often. Raids were more common. He said that training helps, but cannot really prepare a Marine for the actual combat reactions that are needed. He felt that drivers and gunners need good training to work as a team.

Lance Corporal Hodges that one day he might be going on a raid, on another setting in on an Observation Post, on another, be part of a reaction team. Sometimes a unit will only get 30 minutes notice that it will be going out the gate on a raid. "We'll go up to a house. We don't know if there's a gate. We don't know if there's a fence. We don't know if anybody's in it. We don't know nothin'. But we pretty much got it down to a "T," know what's gonna happen." When they get to a wall, they might have to jump over it, or get a Humvee to knock it down.

"Actually, on the 10th, had a guy pop out in front of me, nothing in between us, no obstruction whatsoever. He dumped about 25 rounds directly at me. He didn't hit anything. Other than being lucky, the only thing I can say is, another thing that helps the Marines so much over here is, we are a lot better marksmen than they are. We take one or two shots, and we can drop somebody. And they'll dump magazines at us, and pretty much use 'spray and pray' tactics." Marine fire discipline makes every shot count.

I asked about his rank. When he first left the Corps, he was a lance corporal, and he retained that rank when he reenlisted. He said that he was in line for sergeant, when some personal issues caused him to go back to lance corporal. His unit had just returned from an 11-month deployment when he learned that he would be soon deploying to Iraq. Hodges noted that the mission comes first, but it causes some personal problems. Several Marines in his platoon have had children born back home while they have been in Iraq. One Marine who died had four children, and had never seen his youngest child.

Hodges said that he felt good about what he and his Marines have been doing over here. "I'm proud to be over here." They have been in a lot of engagements and have had Marines killed and hurt, but they continue to fight.

Corporal Jared Heath McKenzie
1st Section, 3rd Mechanized Assault Platoon, Weapons Company, 2/4

On first arrival in Ramadi, conditions were fairly quiet and Marines began to fall into a routine. Insurgents studied this, leading to heavy combat starting April 6, 2004. During that fighting, an army colonel in an M113 Fighting Vehicle came to McKenzie's position to help evacuate several wounded Marines. Caught in an IED ambush on July 14, his Marines used M19 40mm grenades to detonate IEDs along the road and push out of the ambush area. Marine helicopters also fired their machine guns at an enemy-infested building.

After basic training and infantry training, McKenzie received orders to 2/4 at Camp Pendleton, California, in August 2001.

After the attacks of September 11, 2001, he was part of a Quick Reaction Force for the Southwest United States for about a month and a half. 2/4 then completed a Combined Arms Exercise (CAX) at 29 Palms prior to an 11-month deployment to Okinawa. While there, the battalion did a Pacific "float," with training stops at Camp Fuji Japan, Guam, Tinian, and Sasebo. On return to the United States, he served with the Military Police for about five months on a Special Reaction Team, SRT, or basic SWAT team. He was planning to extend as a military policeman until he found out that 2/4 was going to go to Iraq. "The SRT training actually helped me a lot when I came over here."

McKenzie came back to 2/4 about halfway through the battalion's training package at March Air Force Base. "After that we deployed, I believe, about February 14th, February 15th, to go to Kuwait." Sergeant Condi was the 1st Section leader at the time. Condi had been in Security Forces earlier. In Kuwait they did close quarters combat drills and practiced patrolling in urban terrain. They convoyed into Iraq, and encountered their first IED outside of Baghdad. McKenzie thought that it was the city of Babylon where this happened. The convoy dropped off some Air Wing Marines at Al Taqaddum, then arrived here at Camp Hurricane Point, Ramadi. Each Weapons Company platoon worked security for different convoys to Ramadi. They did Left-seat, Right-seat patrols with the Army units here for about a week.

"My first time out with the Army, we got hit with an IED, with the Army there, down Route Nova." The Marines dismounted, then started taking small arms fire from their right flank. "That's when I realized that the Army didn't do things the way the Marines did. They didn't actually go after the shooter, which had nowhere to run, because it was abandoned tanks. They called in for their heavy, mechanized units, and their other ground units."

The next really big thing was on April 6. They had already been hit with a couple of IEDs, and McKenzie said that he guessed that the Marines had fallen into a pattern. The QRF got called out to pick up two casualties who had been wounded in action on the south side of Route Michigan. The second casualty was on Easy Street. As they were picking up the first casualty near the government center, they began to draw enemy fire. "Our .50 caliber machine gunner, he saw the enemy from a building, and saw the flash from a rifle. He engaged it with a coupla bursts, and silenced the enemy." They grabbed the wounded Marine from Golf Company.

As they went to the next casualty on Easy Street, the enemy had set up an ambush there. There was a tree laying in the middle of the road. "As soon as we see the tree in the middle of the road, we come in contact with RPK fire. RPK fire from our left-hand side, down our alley. We engaged it, the enemy, he fell back towards a truck the other way. Then we killed him while he tried to get inside the truck. We picked up the RPKs and RPGs, and put 'em in our trucks and pushed to try to get the casualty."

They came around the Easy Street circle, a water tank circle, a turnaround point. They started getting contact from both their left and right sides, and dismounted from their half-door armored Humvees. They pushed forward a couple of blocks to get closer to the enemy. There were insurgents on the rooftops of the buildings along the way. Ahead were insurgents firing at them. McKenzie said that the Marines engaged these enemy fighters, and estimated that they killed at least five of them.

Then another insurgent popped his head out of an alleyway, took a few shots at them, and the Marines engaged him and took him out. Going down Easy Street there was no cover from enemy gun fire, as all houses had walls around them right up to the streets. Insurgents were using taxis to drop-off new fighters and remove their wounded on that street. McKenzie, Sergeant Condi, and Lance Corporal Cox were on foot, some distance ahead of the gun truck. Condi was shot in the left shoulder when he came across an intersecting road. McKenzie and Cox grabbed him and said, "Holy shit, you're shot!" They pulled him back. McKenzie said that he popped a corner, saw three insurgents, one of them about 10 yards from him. Cox took Sergeant Condi to a machine gun truck where they bandaged him up.

Another machine gun truck came down the alley with 2nd Squad and linked up with them. He estimated that they killed four more insurgents and took out a taxicab with three more insurgents inside. "We had helo support, they opened up with their machine guns, nose down, from the alley. It was a breath of fresh air, definitely." They were Marine helicopters.

They swept to the end of the road, then decided it was clear and decided to go back. There were a lot of insurgent bodies everywhere. "We took all their weapons that we could get off them that weren't broke or already dismantled." They brought this gear back to Easy Street.

So far, these firefights had taken about two hours. Sergeant Condi was already up, with his shoulder bandaged, and had made entry into a house suspected of holding insurgents. There were spent machine gun links leading into this house. They had linked up with Golf Company by now. There was a total of two more Marines wounded and one killed in action. Inside the house they found a large weapons cache: Approximately nine RPGs, a couple of heavy machine guns, a lot of AK-47s, blasting caps for explosives and P4 (the German version of the U.S. C4 plastic explosive). They also found a lot of paperwork. (The Marines later learned that some of the paperwork belonged to the son of the house's owner showing that he had graduated from an Al Qaeda training camp.) They detained the owner of the house. This man also had about $5,000 in different currencies.

The Army QRF had now shown up. Corporal McKenzie said that they had a full bird colonel and a sergeant major with them. They had some gun trucks and M113 armored vehicles. McKenzie was amazed to see an Army colonel and sergeant major out there with them, trying to get another wounded Marine out of there.

The Weapons Company forces reached a house with several Golf Company Marines inside. These Marines were glad to see the heavily armed vehicles. The Army M113s took out the seven wounded and one KIA. McKenzie said that things didn't seem "realistic" until he actually saw the Marine KIA. McKenzie said that this Marine had been shot through the leg, and while other Marines were trying to move him, he was shot through the head.

Once the wounded were evacuated, McKenzie said that it was quiet for about ten minutes before another RPG was fired from a side street. It just missed some of the people from his platoon. There was then some sporadic small arms fire. They had run out of water and were low on ammo when the 81mm mortar section showed up. McKenzie's Marines got water from them, and turned over three enemy detainees that they had captured in a house. They then headed back to the FOB, ending the fighting on April 6.

On April 7 they went out with an Army PSYOPS element. "They have these up-armored Humvees, we call them suicide ops, because … they're blasting these Arabic language [messages] on their speakers. I think they were saying, like,

'Thank you for not helping the mujahideen, they're nothing but cowards,' and just basically trying to piss 'em off anyway."

McKenzie laughed and continued, "We were going straight down Michigan, and we have pamphlets, saying IEDs kill everybody. Please tell us if you know where they are. And we're in the back of this high-back [Humvee], five Marines in the back of each high-back, and passing out flyers." He felt that it wasn't a very good idea. They went all the way down Michigan to the Saddam Mosque, and saw people tearing up the pamphlets and throwing them back at the Marines. The crowds were getting closer to the trucks. The Marines were supposed to turn around at this mosque and return on the same route, but because of the crowds that had gathered, and the danger of pot shots, they returned via the back way along Route Nova. On this road, insurgents fired three RPGs at them from two houses on the left-hand side of the road. One house was half-built.

"We open up with the heavy guns. While they're suppressing, Sergeant Condi is still with us, the section leader, we push towards the house. Call cease-fire, start clearing the buildings around that area. Make entry into that building. The back side was wide open. You could actually see where people ran outta the back of the house as soon as there was fire. When we made entry into the house, there was a wife and three children in the bathroom. And I still remember thinking, 'Thank God they survived.' Because the house looked like Swiss cheese from .50 cal and Mark 19 rounds."

They cleared the house, and put some designated marksmen on the roof, because there was a little housing area behind this house. One of these Marine marksmen saw and took out one of the enemy shooters from there. A call came on the radio to leave the house. At the half-finished house, there were two dead insurgents with their AKs still strapped to them. As the Marines pushed back to the trucks, Lance Corporal Cummings got shot in the back. "Heavy guns opened up again. The insurgent showed his face. Bad idea, with Mark 19 rounds."

There were three insurgents in nearby trees. They fell out of the trees. One got a Mark 19 round to the stomach, the other two were detained.

McKenzie picked up the wounded Cummings and brought him to a truck. A Corpsman bandaged him up, and they too off took to Junction City. Cummings was medevacked and it was found that he had a punctured lung. He was treated and returned three days later.

On the evening of April 7, Golf and Echo Companies were pinned south of Michigan in the Easy Street area. McKenzie's platoon was sent to help extract them. They got there and were taking small arms fire from down alleys. "Basically, anybody in black robes, they're the bad guys. If they're in black robes, engage the enemy. Everybody that we saw in a black robe usually had a red headdress, some of them had AKs, most of 'em had AKs and RPGs." They engaged many insurgents while pushing through the alleys. They then linked up with Whiskey 2 and helped link up both Golf and Echo Companies.

The next big action day was April 10. Sergeant Condi's arm got so numb that he couldn't move it anymore, so he let McKenzie take over as section leader. Condi stayed back on the 10th. Lance Corporal Cummings returned to the section, but could not go out on operations yet.

Weapons Company went out on Operation *Bug Hunt*, which was cordon and knocks, and searches in the Sofia area of Ramadi. Things began quietly, then Golf Company got into a firefight. "We hear the rounds, we can hear them in the distance. And then after a while, we heard them actually coming towards us. They were pushing the insurgents towards us, or pushing the Marines towards us, we didn't know which."

Weapons Company pushed towards the firefight and then stopped at a berm where they watched the helicopters light up a building in the distance. They got word to go and support Golf Company. One of the trucks "ran out of road" in a swampy area and drove into a muddy ditch. The Marines had to set up security around the truck for about an hour while they dug it out. Moving again, an insurgent sniper engaged them from about a building about 700 meters away. He "pinged" close to some of the Marines in a gun truck. The heavy guns engaged the sniper.

McKenzie took his squad and Sergeant Williams took some Marines from his squad. They went to sweep the area from where they were taking contact. They found one body that had had a Mark 19 round go through, killing him without detonating until it hit behind him. They continued to take pot shots from their left. McKenzie found a loaded RPG and other RPG rounds around it. They then went into a building where they found a sniper rifle, a man in a "man dress" and a man in a jogging suit. Both men were sweating, and one had grass stains on his knees. These men had the sniper rifle, an AK, and a couple of shotguns. The Marines detained both men. There was another man who had fired at them from the right side of the road, but the Marines could not catch up to him.

Since April 10 things mostly settled down, but IEDs were now the norm. He estimated that his platoon has been hit by 12 IEDs. They finally received new up-armored trucks. Sergeant Condi, who returned to full duty, was killed by an IED on July 1 while riding in a high-back Humvee. One lance corporal had a softball-size chunk taken out of his leg from the blast, while the other Marines in the vehicle were injured. These Marines took shrapnel to hands and legs. The other Marines swept the area, but couldn't find anything.

On July 14, a week before this interview, they went on a QRF call to help Golf Company and Whiskey 1 near the Saddam Mosque on Route Michigan. They began to raid houses, and Golf Company went to a building that had a bunker on the roof. They killed about 15 insurgents, and found computers, walkie-talkies, binoculars, sniper rifles, a Maxim gun, about 30 AK-47s, three submachine guns, and about a dozen medium machine guns, grenades, and body armor vests. In all, a large cache of weapons.

"We heard a IED blast. A very loud IED blast. Maybe 500 meters away from Combat Outpost. We went there, and that was where we shot a Javelin [missile] at a possible VBIED that they left in front of Combat Outpost." Things were then calm for a couple of days, with sporadic fire or IEDs.

On Wednesday of this week, July 21, he was on QRF. The battalion sergeant major was with them. They went to support Golf Company, which was taking small arms and RPG fire. "As soon as we went out the gate, a mile down Michigan, probably not even a mile, a vehicle-borne IED goes off to our right flank. Hits the tail end of our convoy. We dismount, everybody's okay." They kept pushing to support Golf and Fox Companies, down to right in front of Saddam's Mosque.

"My truck gets hit with an IED on the side. Soon as the IED went off, [I] yell at the driver to push through. Gunny's vehicle getting shot through with small arms fire and I see RPGs flying across the hood of my truck and the tail end of his truck. Where there's about a four to five round volley of RPG fire and rifle grenades, that they're shooting at us. Since we're still in the kill zone, I kick open my door, trying to do like a drive-by shooting. I could see where the small arms fire's coming from. And I'm shooting, showing my gunner where the fire's coming from. We finally come to a stop, we couldn't push forward anymore, it was just gunny's vehicle and my vehicle. We were basically trapped. There was another IED set that was blocking off our battalion commander's vehicle and the rest of my platoon's vehicles from us. I just get out of the truck, get out of the back side of the truck. Take cover. Get the guys out. And, start firing at personnel in the buildings, and the personnel that were shooting RPGs at us down an alley."

The Marines at the tail end of the convoy were also providing suppressing fire on the enemy. "Still, RPGs flying at us. One barely misses my gunner, while he's trying to do a reload. He takes flash burns to the eyes. He falls out of the turret. I put Lance Corporal Brown up in the turret. And they do an ammo exchange and start enveloping the enemy. We started moving towards where we received the fire from. It's mostly wide open, so it wasn't the very best idea. Came back. It could be more IEDs set there. Still had gas cans sittin' everywhere. They like to use gas cans and anything else they can find. We already shot a AT4 at the building, I know of at least three people [enemy] that I saw that were actually killed in the building that we shot."

McKenzie said that the battalion commander decided to push through. The Marines tried to shoot at the gas cans to make them explode. But he noted that this will not detonate military explosives. So the Marines shot a Mark 19 round at them, and then a really big IED buried by the side of the road, covered with gas cans, detonated. The Marines engaged a couple of this type of IED with Mark 19 rounds.

As they pushed past the Saddam Mosque, they continued to take small arms fire from the left-had side again. The Marines engaged the enemy here with Mark 19s and .50 cals while the battalion commander and sergeant major continued their movement. Some enemy were in alleyways here. The company commander pushed up to some Army Bradley fighting vehicles, and there were also helicopters on call and fixed-wing aircraft on station.

McKenzie's platoon went on to Easy Street near the Saddam Mosque. They acted as security, sweeping houses there. He and Lance Corporal Cox began receiving small arms fire as they did this. McKenzie had two injured Marines back in his truck: Brown and the truck's driver. So he and Cox continued to sweep houses. A furniture store caught on fire, and McKenzie estimated that he and Cox killed two or three insurgents in this engagement. The company gunny called him back to serve as the headquarters security element. They brought up a Mark 19 gun truck which began firing down the alley, and quieted down enemy shooting.

McKenzie saw some Bradleys taking small arms fire, and Huey helicopters came in and used their chain guns on the enemy building. "It was the craziest thing I even seen, because, the helos were, just complete stop in front of the building. And fired a good, I don't know, 10,000 rounds into that house. It was about a four-story building." He said it was about three minutes of this firing, a long time for solid fire. He laughed, and said, "I was just sittin' there in amazement of that."

After firing several .50 cal bursts down the alley, McKenzie led his squad down the alley. "It was a car on the left-hand side, we already shot it all up. And pushed down. There's an open, like, parking area back there. We found three RPGs, [one] RPK, couple boxes of ammo for the RPK, a couple AKs, and four grenades. We saw blood trails, but no bodies." They took a couple of pot shots from over a wall, so McKenzie threw a grenade over this wall and killed a couple of insurgents on the other side.

They pushed down a side alley from here. They could see Fox Company on their right flank. Golf was to their front, so things were now more secure. He believed that Golf Company brought in about 14 or 15 insurgents, as well as grenades and RPGs and some RPKs. When the 7-tons rolled in, they loaded the captured insurgents onto the trucks. McKenzie could hear shooting in the distance, but things were basically quiet for the rest of the day. They returned to the camp about 2100.

McKenzie said that the next day (yesterday), as they went down the same street, local people were there in the street, acting as if nothing had happened. There were still blood stains on the streets.

I then asked him about the training he had received as a Military Policeman. He said that SWAT training taught concepts such as use of sectors of fire, how to make entry into rooms, and searching and clearing rooms.

He also commented on the early April fighting, the heaviest in the time he has been in Iraq. He said that there was a four-and-a-half-hour, stand-up firefight for them in Ramadi, and another element of Weapons Company was engaged in a five-and-a-half-hour fight. Since then, the enemy has preferred to "gun and run," using IEDs and engaging the Marines from a distance. "There are very few insurgents, people, who will actually stand up face-to-face in the streets that they did in April. Also, it was our first engagement in April, so, it was a big eye-opener for a lot of us." McKenzie estimates that his platoon has been engaged in about eight firefights. This past week was the closest fighting to the fights in April. The enemy stood up and didn't try to run. The enemy has used IEDs to start ambushes.

The enemy has kicked people out of their homes in order to use these houses to shoot at the Marines.

McKenzie noted that the training had prepared the Marines for what he called a "Heart and minds" campaign, not for the insurgency that they have faced. The Marines were trying to help the people here, but some of them are shooting at the Marines. The enemy does not wear a uniform.

Combat Outpost Ramadi, Friday July 23, 2004

I woke, showered, then had chow in the Hurricane Point Mess Hall. Food was served from vat cans from Camp Blue Diamond, but it beats MREs. I went to Weapons Company for the final interview there, then returned to the battalion's Combat Operations Center (COC) to speak with Major Harrill about today's schedule.

Problem—real world situation. 2/4 had gotten intel reports that a big fight was expected in Ramadi today. Lieutenant Colonel Paul Kennedy and Major Harrill were studying the map of Ramadi on a situation table at the COC, and Harrill was on the radio with one of the infantry companies. I stood aside and watched and listened, figuring that this would end my prospects of getting off Hurricane Point today. When I finally had a chance, I asked Captain Harris about where I would be able to go today. He arranged for me to visit Echo and Golf Companies out at the Combat Outpost in Ramadi, going right past the area where there would possibly be an ambush later in the day, if the intel panned out.

I grabbed my gear, and got into one of the up-armored Humvees outside the COC, and was off to Combat Outpost in a convoy through downtown Ramadi. Definitely a nerve-racking ride, even though I was in one of the brand-new, up-armored Humvees with thick armor all around. I loaded my pistol before we left the gate, and I got a look at the main street of Ramadi, which we call Route Michigan. The town is dilapidated and scruffy, even in the downtown area. Most shops are ramshackle affairs. It makes many slums back home look cosmopolitan and modern by comparison.

I took some photos as we traveled down the main drag, and did not like it when we had to slow down or stop for any reason. However, the sidewalks were crowded with people, mostly men and boys, and the Marines had said that usually means that nothing is going to happen. When the insurgents get ready to start something, they put the word out, and the shops will close down, and people disappear from the streets. I noticed on this short drive that there were almost no women visible anywhere, either young or old. I don't know if it was because this is the Muslim holy day of Friday, or if this was the normal state of things in Ramadi.

We reached the Combat Outpost in just a few minutes, and pulled up to a large warehouse where both Echo and Golf Companies have their command posts (CPs). I met Lieutenant Colonel Dan Colgan, USMC, an instructor at the Army Command and Staff College who was visiting combat units in the field here. He was hanging out with Golf Company, so I decided to go to Echo Company to start my work. I met with the company first sergeant, then finally with the Commanding Officer, Captain Kelly Royer. The intel from this morning had rolled over here, and Echo Company was preparing to react to an attack in downtown Ramadi today. 2/4 had prepared a plan which involved Weapons Company creating a diversion to trigger the attack and the Echo and Golf Companies would move in to attack from north and south of Route Michigan. Platoons were readying to launch out of the Outpost, and Captain Royer was monitoring the radios for updates. I did manage to speak with him, and he agreed to make arrangements for me to speak to Marines as they became available.

I decided to watch events unfold in the company COC (Combat Operations Center). There were two Marines on a small bank of radios, one a corporal and one a staff sergeant. Message traffic flowed, all the while Captain Royer was ensuring that a thousand and one details were being taken care of. Was the ammo resupply truck loaded up with the right ammo? Did the guard posts at the Outpost have proper equipment and weapons (including AT4 rounds)? Were all platoons properly briefed? He did this in a calm, controlled manner. I could see that the company has done this type of thing many times before, but still needs someone in the center of it all to ensure that all of the details are attended to.

2/4 had arranged to have helicopters on call, and fixed-wing aviation was also on station. All was in readiness, and observers reported via radio on events in the part of town where trouble was expected. At about 1400, I heard the boom of a large explosion near the front gate of this Outpost. Was it a mortar round? A rocket? An RPG? It was loud, and I felt the vibration from the blast in the building where I sat. The guard posts reported an impact near the front gate, and we felt this might be the signal for the enemy to begin the attack. But the message traffic on the radios continued to report calm in the downtown area, and people continued to mill on the streets there. After about an hour and a half, Captain Royer felt that the fight would not take place today. Perhaps the intel was wrong, or maybe the enemy saw that the Marines were ready to mix it up with them. There had been that big fight in Ramadi on July 21, so the Marines were ready for anything again today.

I started interviews about 1530, went until about 1745, took a 30-minute dinner break, then continued until 2130. One of the most touching interviews was with the 3rd Platoon Commander, Lieutenant Tommy Cogan (from Philadelphia—he attended Central High School). His platoon was hit heavily on April 6, losing five

Marines in a single ambush, and one of the Echo Company Marine snipers recently killed was also from his platoon. All together he has lost seven Marines out of a platoon of 38 that came to Iraq. After the taping was done, I spoke with him about coping with losing this many Marines. I know that so far this was the worst hit platoon of any grunt platoon during this conflict. (2nd LAR had a platoon that has lost four Marines). I listened to him for a while, and then urged him to talk with people about it when he gets back home after the deployment. He had the usual questions about second guessing decisions that he made at various times. He also noted that the actual firefights are "fun." It's what Marines train for. I made a note on the interview spreadsheet to ensure it gets the attention it warrants.

My last interview subject didn't show at 2130, which was fine, since I used the time to catch up on my journal.

Sergeant Damien Ryan Coan
Platoon Sergeant, 2nd Platoon, Echo Company, 2/4

Early on during the deployment in Ramadi, Coan's platoon was heavily involved in counter-IED patrols of the area. A squad in his platoon successfully found the insurgent mortar team that had routinely targeted the Combat Outpost. They killed four insurgents and captured one member of this mortar team. Heavy fighting began the morning of April 6 after he had returned from an all-night ambush mission. His platoon commander, Lieutenant John Wroblewski was one of the 10 Marines killed later that morning from a well-planned ambush by insurgents in Ramadi. During Operation Bug Hunt, *he was platoon commander during a search for high-value targets and led the platoon in a high-intensity firefight. To get a wounded Marine to a helicopter landing zone, he led his platoon across an open field being raked by RPK fire.*

Sergeant Coan joined the Corps in 1996, and went to Security Forces school after boot camp and the School of Infantry (SOI). He was stationed in Bangor, Washington for two years. He joined 2/4 in July 2001 and during OIF1, 2/4 spent 11 months in Okinawa during the initial invasion of Iraq.

Around February 17, 2004, Echo Company left the United States and flew to Kuwait. The company conducted drills and training for about three weeks. In early March, they flew on C130s into Al Taqaddum, and went by convoy into Ramadi for the Left-seat, Right-seat turnover with the Army. Commanders at all levels rode with their Army counterparts to get familiar with the area. These vehicle and foot patrols lasted just a few days. The Army had armored Humvees.

"Once the Army left, we were really busy the first three weeks. We took over the AO [area of operations] on the 19th of March, and we started doing MSR [Main Supply Route] sweeps. Sweeping the MSRs for IEDs, trying to locate them, to control-detonate them with EOD, or engineers if possible. And those were tedious, and a lengthy process. Every morning a platoon went out, and did their sweep on MSR Michigan from Combat Outpost down to about the arches, which is approximately four clicks to the east of Combat Outpost. Then from there, you'd go up Route Gypsum, and you'd start your sweep on MSR Nova." He said that this route traces the south side of the Euphrates River. They would sweep back down to the hospital and then walk about a click to the Combat Outpost. "The MSR sweeps was what was wearing everybody out." These sweeps were foot-mobile, with vehicles riding along for medevacs. The Marines would walk on both sides of the roads, along with engineers and mine detectors.

"Aside from the MSR sweeps, we were doing local security patrols, ambush patrols at night, trying to catch these guys setting all these IEDs along the road. And we're doing information/observation patrols, where we'd patrol through the neighborhoods with pamphlets and coloring books, just all sorts of things for the locals to look at." These explained why the Marines were there, and information about the transfer of authority. Many locals had no idea that the new government would be taking over at the end of June.

They conducted squad and platoon-size patrols. When not on patrol or MSR sweeps, Marines would be on QRF (Quick Reaction Force) duty. For example, on March 25 there was a QRF that went out looking for enemy mortarmen that had been shelling the Combat Outpost every Thursday night at 1900. Coan said that these mortar attacks were like clockwork while the Army was here. "The first Thursday night we were here, we got mortared at 1900. So the second Thursday, Captain Royer sent out the QRF to try to locate these guys. Gave them a route and they actually messed up their route and went up the wrong street, and right into these nine individuals with a 60mm mortar tube. And they had AK-47s and I believe they had one RPK. That was 1st Squad from 3rd Platoon. Ran into those guys and killed four of them. We detained one. There were blood trails and reports of guys checking into the hospital with multiple gunshot wounds, who died in the hospital. Which we presumed [they] were the remainder of the nine mortarmen. We recovered RPGs. Two RPG tubes, four or five RPG rounds, three or four AK-47s, one RPK, and a 60mm mortar tube and several rounds. EOD came and blew up all the mortar rounds and RPG rounds. We collected up all the weapons, hauled them back here. That was our first major contact, it was the 25th of March. We didn't get mortared at 1900 on Thursdays after that!"

On QRF missions, they were frequently finding unexploded ordnance (UXO). They would escort EOD (Explosive Ordnance Disposal) Marines from Blue Diamond or Junction City to blow up UXO or IEDs. NCOs told their Marines to get sleep when they could, as the operations were nonstop in March. Sergeant Coan said that he was not sure how things were going to be when they got to Iraq. He expected to deal with IEDs, but did not anticipate how big Echo Company's AO would be. "When we got out here, I was a little bit shocked to see how large it was."

Then came early April 2004. "The 5th, I was out with one of my squads, they were doing a night ambush. I decided to go out with them. We sat in an ambush all night, right off the side of MSR Michigan. Looking for these guys putting in IEDs.

And the other two squads in my platoon were back here, 'cause they were gonna do the MSR sweeps the next morning." Sergeant Coan came back in with the squad, which was Corporal Joseph Steven Magee's squad, at about 0700 on the morning of April 6. They got chow and then rested. His platoon commander at the time, Lieutenant John Wroblewski, had already taken out the other two squads to do the MSR sweeps. The lieutenant completed the sweeps with the two squads, and they were now the QRF.

3rd Platoon was doing a patrol down by the arches and began taking fire. The QRF under Wroblewski was called out to reinforce them. 1st Platoon was conducting a patrol up north. The QRF with Wroblewski checked out buildings near 3rd Platoon, then went to join up with 1st Platoon which was now in contact. The QRF got ambushed at the intersection of Route Gypsum and MSR Nova. "And that's where we lost 10 Marines killed that day, including my platoon commander, Lieutenant Wroblewski. The ambush was well-organized, and, uh, well executed by the enemy. They had heavy machine gun set up right at the intersection. It's a DShK 12.7mm machine gun. Very similar to the .50 cal. They had guys on rooftops, with RPKs, AK-47s. They had guys on the ground with grenades. They had a guy on the west side of Gypsum with RPGs. It was a very intense gunfight."

"I got out there, with the rest of the company. The gunfight was just about over when I got out there with the remainder of my platoon, and the remainder of the company. A few shots got fired when I got out there, but it was pretty much over. Started cleaning up the mess left behind."

"We know for a fact we killed four. There were four bodies, four enemy bodies at the intersection there. There were several more that were killed or wounded, but the enemy surprisingly, surprised everybody, they were picking up their bodies, picking up their weapons. 'Cause there were blood trails and drag marks on both the east and west side of Route Gypsum. When we searched the area we found a tan, two-door hatchback, that had multiple weapons in the trunk, as well as explosives. The DShK (heavy machine gun) was left in place right at the intersection of Gypsum and Nova." They also found some AK-47 magazines. All of the other weapons were taken by the enemy.

The enemy had broken contact when the Army Bradley fighting vehicles began to show up.

Sergeant Coan paused, then summed this action up by saying, "The 6th was … a pretty bad day."

They stayed at the intersection, searched houses, talked to locals, and salvaged damaged vehicles. They stayed in the area until about midnight. Sergeant Coan said that he learned of the total company casualties from Captain Royer when he got back to Combat Outpost, including the death of his platoon commander, Lieutenant Wroblewski. Royer then gave Coan a "Frag" Order to conduct a platoon-sized patrol around Fish Hook Lake.

"So, after all of this was done, take my boys, give them an hour or so rest, and we conducted a nine-hour foot patrol around Fish Hook Lake, trying to locate some of these insurgents that set up the ambush." The patrol was uneventful, but they brought back some intel about foot and vehicle traffic in the area. They rested on April 8, and did two platoon patrols on April 9.

On April 10, Coan was acting platoon commander for Operation *Bug Hunt*. (He would continue acting platoon commander until April 26). "April 10th was almost fun, as strange as that might sound. We were doing Operation *Bug Hunt*, which was a coordinated raid on multiple houses. Each platoon had a house we're hitting. We had mortars firing into an open field, right at the same time we were kicking doors in. And we were looking for, there were three different targets." His platoon's target was an ICDC (Iraqi Civil Defense Corps) member who had supposedly buried weapons in his yard, and was selling them to insurgents. They hit a house, but it was the wrong house due to an error in the grid reference that they had.

"So we hit the house, and there were seven Iraqi males in there, four females, coupla kids. Went through all their stuff in the house, found nothing but one AK-47, coupla magazines, which is typical." Sergeant Coan said that just about any house in Ramadi will have at least one AK-47 in it.

They then searched other houses. One had an old man and his daughter in it. A third house had an older farming couple.

"We were getting ready to move to the fourth house, when shots started." They started taking shots from the west, and they looked for the shooter. Shots started coming in from the north. "Then one of my Marines sees the individual from the west shooting at us. So, I got one squad facing to the west, doing suppressive fire on the one or two individuals shooting at us from the west. I had 1st Squad go back to the first house that we entered. It was a large house, very solid house, bigger frontage, and our vehicles were staged right in front of it."

"I put 1st Squad up there, under Corporal Smith who was acting platoon sergeant, and he set up a casualty collection point in that house. And, got overwatch security for us, on the rooftops. And provide security for the vehicles. So I had 2nd and 3rd Squads with me. I sent 3rd Squad around, pushing them north, and then west, trying to set up a maneuver element. I had 2nd Squad suppressing, and 3rd Squad moving to maneuver on the enemy to the west. We started taking shots from the south, as well. RPK fire from the south."

Corporal Magee's 3rd Squad was trying to hit the two AK-47 shooters in the house, but trees hindered their view. Corporal Lenze, a machine gun squad leader who was attached to the platoon, manned the vehicle-mounted Mark 19 back at the house and began shooting at the building with the two shooters inside. The building stood up well to the 40mm grenades hitting it. Sergeant Coan said that the main effect of this grenade fire was to keep the shooters inside of the house.

Then Coan got a call that Captain Royer was pinned down back across the field where they had come from. "So, I sent another squad back that way across the field to grab Captain Royer and his crew. 'Cause they were stuck, basically, in a trench. A sewage run-off, that's what it was. Captain Royer, and his radio operator, and his S2 rep, [and] a reporter from the *Philadelphia Inquirer* [David Swanson], was there. And a company Corpsman. They were all stuck in that shit trench, basically. One of my squads went back there, picked him up. Brought him back to the house that we were sitting in. Suppressing the enemy, Captain Royer's trying to assess what's going on. Trying to talk to 3rd Platoon, where are they at. What's going on with them. What's going on with 1st Platoon."

"We kept suppressing that target to the west, that building. Lance Corporal Musser had his AT4s. So we took an AT4 shot into the window. Musser hit that thing, right through the window from about 200 meters. It was a really good shot. It silenced the gunman inside the house for a few minutes. It didn't kill him, because the guy was upstairs, but I guess the concussion from the blast, or whatever, messed him up long enough for us to get out of that house and push to the west. Maneuver on it with both squads."

"3rd Squad made entry. First guy in the stick was Corporal [Logan J.] Degenhardt. They threw a frag in, frag goes off, he opens the door to clear the room, this [insurgent] guy's on the stairs, which leads up to the roof. He emptied a 30-round magazine at Corporal Degenhardt. And Degenhardt pinned himself up against the wall, right next to the door frame. And, out of those 30 rounds, Corporal Degenhardt got one round in his hand. Right here [he pointed to his own hand]. And that was it, right on his left hand. And that was the second time he got shot that day. He had already gotten a ricochet bullet in his shoulder. So he had a ricochet shot in his right shoulder and he had a round go right into his left hand. He was having a bad day!"

"We pulled him [Degenhardt] out. Lance Corporal Musser, same kid that did the AT4 shot is also a combat aidsman. So he was patchin' up Corporal Degenhardt while we restacked. Threw another frag [grenade] in there, kicked the door open and saw the guy on the stairs. He picked up his AK and Corporal Magee shot him four times in the chest. Killed him. Pretty much instantly. There was another individual in there who dropped his weapon, threw his hands up. So, we put him on the ground, put flexi-cuffs around him. And the whole time we're doin' this, we're still taking RPK fire from the south, was hitting the house. That guy saw us come in. There were several more people further west, two, three hundred meters to the west. We had rounds goin' off all over the place. There had to have been 15, 20 people shooting at us. At least that many. And that was just shooting at my platoon. And, 3rd Platoon was just a couple hundred meters southwest of me and they were taking fire from their south, and their west, I believe."

Once they cleared that house, Sergeant Coan got a call from Corporal Smith on a PRR (Personal Role Radio). Smith told Coan that he had Lance Corporal

John T. Sims from 3rd Platoon who had been shot to the back and needed to be medevacked. They needed to secure a helicopter landing zone (LZ), and Smith did not have enough Marines to do this. Coan had his Marines strip the bolts from the RPK and AK-47s in the house so that they could not be used again right away. Coan also told his Marines to leave the RPG rounds in a shed, that they would come back and get them after the helo medevac was done.

"So I push one squad across the field, and as they ran across, RPK rounds were hitting the ground all around them. So the next squad, I'm like hey, you guys need to freakin' go across that field. Link up with Corporal Smith, I need you to set up an LZ right across the road from when I pointed the field. And it was a large field, large enough to land at least two, maybe three Forty-Sixes [CH46 Helicopters]."

"So, I push them over that way, and, the fire team leader of the first squad, the second squad that went across. He kinda looked at me, he saw 2nd Squad run across. Saw the RPK rounds goin' off. And I told him to go and he kinda looked at me, 'Like, are you fuckin' nuts? I just saw the RPK rounds hit the deck.' And I'm like, okay, go over there! And he's like, 'Well, how 'bout if we just go this way?' I say look, we need to get the quickest route, get over there, secure this LZ, 'cause Sims is not doing good at all."

"So I said, I tell you what. I'm gonna run across the field. And you're either gonna follow me or I'm gonna kick the shit outta you when we get back to Combat Outpost! And I ran across the field. They followed. Behind me. And the squad leader was trying to grab his fire team, and that's why he wasn't there pushing them across."

"We got across the field, nobody was hurt. Coupla dead cows. Set up the LZ. And then the Army [helos], of course, wouldn't land, 'cause the LZ was too hot. So they refuse to land. So we got some Bradleys. It was a Bradley ambulance, basically, that rolled up about 30 minutes later. We got Sims placed in the Bradley. It was pretty much too late for him, they had already been doing CPR on him for like an hour. Sims didn't make it," Sergeant Coan paused. Then added, "Probably because the Army wouldn't land in a hot LZ."

Sergeant Coan said that his platoon then stayed focused on the house they had left. In about 30 minutes, Marine Huey and Cobra helicopters came on station and made about three gun runs at enemy that were visible to them. Coan said that as soon as the air support got on station, the enemy broke contact. "They're definitely afraid of the helicopters." Coan said that Captain Royer had requested the helos through battalion, and once they were on station, he had communication with them.

After the firefight, Coan's Marines went back to sweep the houses.

"The bodies were gone. The guy that Corporal McGee shot, his body was gone. There was a guy right outside that same house that Lance Corporal Maxwell shot with a SAW, right in the face. Just tore that guy's head apart. But, his body was gone. All the RPGs were gone. They left the RPK and the AK-47s that we took the bolts out of. They left those there. But the place was amazing how fast there were people, there were women, and teenagers, picking up bodies in the middle of a gunfight. It was very hard for me to understand, why these women would come outside their houses, pick these people up in the middle of a gunfight." This meant that the Marines did not have any captured weapons or pictures of the enemy when the firefight was over.

They continued the sweep through houses in the area for the next two to three hours. They did find some IED-making materials, including blasting caps, plastic explosives and wire switches. Sergeant Coan noted that the whole area was filled with residences of ICDC and IPs (Iraqi Police). He estimated that five out of every seven houses they entered had uniforms for one of these uniformed services in them. He said, with a hint of irony, that it was amazing that these officials can live in the same area with all of the insurgents present.

Sergeant Coan said that many of the ICDC/ING soldiers lacked training. The IPs go through a three-week course that the Marines have set up for them. He says that they need to be forced to do anything. Also, they needed to be trained properly and given better equipment. More now had bulletproof vests, Glock 9mm pistols, and other issued equipment. More were staying on their posts during the day. They now had checkpoints along MSR Michigan that were better manned.

After April 10, there were no more gunfights until a few days before today. After that time, IED sweeps were discontinued, and the Marines conducted MSR ambushes. Starting in mid-May, MSR Nova was made a Black Status, meaning that it could not be used by the Marines without permission of the (Army) brigade commander. Patrols were scaled back the closer the transfer of authority date approached. Since then, Coan's Marines have pretty much stopped patrols except for local security patrols around the Combat Outpost. They have set up an Observation Post out by the graveyard near the arches. There were also two posts near Lake Habbaniyah. One platoon goes out and sets up Marines in one of the several fortified positions. Occasionally they receive random small arms shots or poorly aimed mortar rounds, but there have been no full-scale attacks on these positions. Yesterday, three mortar rounds landed about 150 meters from the post near the graveyard. Coan said that only a very large, say, battalion-size enemy force would be needed to attack the outposts across Route Michigan because of the firepower that the Marines have.

Sergeant Coan said that Marines from Golf and Fox Companies who are at the Agricultural Center in Ramadi get shot at almost every day.

Coan then outlined the fighting on July 21, which centered around the Agricultural Center. "My platoon was the only platoon that had contact. The whole company went out. It was, Weapons Platoon was out at the OP [Observation Post], at the graveyard. 1st and 2nd Platoon, and 3rd Platoon, we all went out to reinforce Golf Company, who was being attacked at the Agricultural Center. And the neighborhood around that. So we went out to reinforce them. We basically did a sweep, and we went to contact, from the stadium across the street from the Agricultural Center on the north side of the MSR. We swept west, all the way to Y Road. Approximately 1,000 meters or so."

Coan's platoon swept west about 300 meters, and a squad north of them got shot at from several houses. The Marines shot and killed two insurgents, and wounded another who hobbled away. Coan's platoon commander did not pursue this man because the mission was to push west, and Golf Company had a platoon up in the area where the man was headed. The platoon continued moving west, with squads bounding ahead. One squad would bound ahead and put Marines on the roof to cover the next squad's bound. Once at Y Road, they secured rooftops for observation and the battalion continued its mission. When the sweep was done, Echo Company made its way back east to the Combat Outpost.

Coan said, "So the 21st of July was nothing like the 6th or the 10th of April. In fact, Echo Company hasn't seen anything to compare to the 6th to the 10th of April. Honestly, I think that the insurgents got a message, especially on April 10th. We unleashed every weapons system in the battalion's arsenal on the 10th, with the exception of the SMAW. We fired Mark 19s, 240s, TOWs, 203s, SAWs, 240 Golfs, and after that, the insurgents really haven't stood their ground to fight. They'll start a firefight down by the Agricultural Center, those Marines'll return fire with 240, M16 and some 203, even a couple of AT4s." The enemy will break contact and take off. When they did attack on July 21, the battalion responded quickly.

On July 21, four Marine snipers from Echo Company were killed at their position. Sergeant Coan did not know the details of how these Marines were ambushed on their rooftop. That day he was out at the graveyard with a mobile QRF, and the company called and told them that they hadn't had communication with the snipers (Call sign: "Headhunter 2") for about an hour. The company gave the grid position of the snipers' "hide," and the QRF went there. Coan said, "We went down there and found the bodies." Coan was with 3rd Squad that found the Marines there. "We found the bodies. All their gear had been stripped. Enemy took their weapons, took their frags, took their bayonets, NVGs, took their sniper rifles, M16s, 203s. The only thing they left was one radio, one frag grenade, and that was it." The enemy did not take their helmets or flak jackets. All their gear had been gone through. The company has done several missions trying to get the guys who did this.

IEDs continued to be a constant threat. There have been four VBIEDs found in the company area. One had blown up on them, one had blown up on ICDC. Engineers went out with Weapons Company a few days ago to blow up a VBIED. They hit it with a TOW missile, and felt that that was not good enough. So they hit it with another TOW missile, and there was a huge secondary explosion from the vehicle. Coan said that it was a fireball at least three stories tall. "We were two clicks away from it when they hit it with the second TOW rocket, and that explosion was huge." He later saw the remains of the explosion and said that there was nothing resembling a car left there.

I asked Sergeant Coan about what training has been the best for coming over here. He said that the SASO training at March Air Force Base was realistic. There would be a lot of activity, then things would get real quiet. That is pretty much how it has been for him and his Marines here in Iraq. He learned how to deal with the frustrations due to the language barrier. The role players at March Air Force Base were good.

However, he said that they practiced Satellite Patrolling for hours and hours in the States, but conditions here were different due to the walls around houses in Iraq.

He concluded, "I think that what we're doing in Iraq is right. I think that we're doing the right thing and we're doing a good thing over here. The only problem that I have is, it seems like, we're out here, sweating, bleeding, and dying for people that don't want to be helped. That's how it seems, a lot of times out here." The Marines have given food, money for schools, and money to replace property damage and damage to farm animals. Sergeant Coan said that it was frustrating at times.

Corporal Eric Michael Smith
1st Squad Leader, 2nd Platoon, Echo Company, 2/4

During the initial invasion of Iraq in 2003, Smith and Marines in Echo Company were training on Okinawa, and were frustrated that they were not able to contribute to the fighting in Iraq. In late 2003, they learned that they would deploy to Iraq to relieve Army units and began training for the mission. He led his squad during the ambush attack on Route Gypsum on April 6, and he ran to mortally wounded Lieutenant John Wroblewski to help administer first aid and arrange a hasty medevac back to the Combat Outpost. The fighting continued during these actions. Without the platoon commander or platoon sergeant present, he led the 2nd Platoon Marines for an hour and a half until soldiers in Army Bradley fighting vehicles arrived.

Corporal Smith began, "I joined the Marine Corps on May 28th, 2001. Went to boot camp, like many other people knowing there was a journey ahead, and here is my journey."

After completing recruit training at San Diego and the School of Infantry (SOI), he couldn't wait to get back home and see his family. He joined 2/4 in November 2001 and got his first taste of life in the Fleet Marine Force (FMF). The battalion was a QRF (Quick Reaction Force) for the entire United States after the events of September 11, 2001. After about two months, the battalion was replaced as the QRF, and began its regular work-up for a deployment. Smith was radio operator for 2nd Platoon of Echo Company. 2/4 then deployed to Okinawa in July 2002. They began a MEU(SOC) (Marine Expeditionary Unit, Special Operations Capable) work-up, a normal deployment cycle for the time. About the time that the deployment was scheduled to end, he began to see news reports about the buildup in Kuwait for the invasion of Iraq. 2/4 was on ships in the middle of the Philippine Sea.

"I remember at that time, we shoulda felt good for our comrades, that they were out here [Iraq] defending the freedom of the United States. At the same time, we felt really left out. 2/4 at that time, was left out in a way." Corporal Smith said that 2/4 wanted to be the Marines in the front lines, even though they were filling an important role as the 31st MEU. "So we felt pretty upset that we weren't there. Especially as the war progressed in the first days, and we were on the ships watching CNN and the casualty reports, and how far they made it." They felt helpless that they couldn't help these Marines out.

2/4 was extended in Okinawa for another six months, for a total deployment of about 12 months. They returned to Camp Pendleton on June 13, 2003. The other battalions in the regiment were returning from Iraq around the same time. 1/5 was already home, and 2/5 and 3/5 returned after 2/4. Then rumors began circulating that a battalion from the regiment would be sent to Iraq to help relieve the Army units there. The Marines in 2/4 felt that they would probably be the ones to go to Iraq.

Corporal Smith then became an NCO and a squad leader in September 2003 as 2/4 began its deployment work-up. At the time, the Marines remaining in the squad were all senior, so Smith was leading his peers as he waited to receive new Marines coming out of SOI. "It proved to be a pretty big challenge, especially when we know what was coming ahead."

"We started with basic MOUT [Military Operations in Urban Terrain] tactics, Urban Warfare town training. We did that for a couple of weeks. We still had people going to school, life didn't stop and just revolve around pointing to Iraq." Many Marines went to schools to learn how to run rappelling and helo fast-rope descents, the martial arts schools, and squad leaders' courses. A lot of the younger leaders like Smith had just become the leaders themselves as older Marines went to other units, or left the Marine Corps. Smith said, "It was our turn to take over and lead." He said that he was nervous, knowing that wherever he would go, he would be tested as a leader.

The new Marines from the School of Infantry began to arrive in November and December 2003. 2/4 went to train at March Air Force Base in February 2004. Smith said that this training was very realistic, including a lot of elements of what they now were doing in Iraq. Instead of the normal 6-to-12-month time frame to train new Marines in a unit, they only had about two to three months to get them ready. Some new Marine joins arrived about two weeks before Echo Company deployed to Iraq!

The move to Iraq began on February 15, 2004. It was the day after Valentine's Day. He laughed, "The wife, she really liked that!" He said that it was not her first long deployment, and may not be her last. Echo Company went to March Air Force Base and boarded an Air Force C17 transport. "We immediately realized the difference between what we were doing—the deployment to Iraq, and the deployment to Okinawa." When they had gone to Okinawa, it was a charter flight with flight attendants bringing meals and in-flight movies. Now on the C17, their cargo was stowed on large pallets at the back end of the military plane. "It became real. We had a long flight to think about it. We came into Bangor, Maine. Landed there, an hour or so there. Landed in Frankfurt, Germany, and had a pretty long delay in Frankfurt." They spent a day there, and many Marines thought about future events. "You know, we're going to war." Even though the large ground attacks were done, there was lots of fighting going on and people dying.

They finally flew to Kuwait and went to Camp Victory, spending about a month there. They resumed training once they got all of their gear. They trained daily from 0530 to 2200 at night. They did squad and platoon operations, convoy ops, cultural classes, and basic Arabic language training. They also had lots of sleep deprivation to get them ready for long operations. Many Marines were anxious to get to Ramadi as soon as they could and get into real operations. He described the mood in Kuwait as one of anticipation.

Elements of 2/4 convoyed into Iraq. Echo Company left a week later than everyone else, flying into Al Taqaddum. After a night there, they convoyed to Combat Outpost Ramadi. "I remember getting into the back of those 7-tons [trucks] at Al Taqaddum. And, I could see the desert sands, I could feel it, even at that time, it was around March, March 12th. It was still warm at that time. The wind was blowing, the sand was blowing. And it's just like, it really hit me then, that, here I am. And I'm in Iraq and there's no turning back now." He knew he needed to do his job. "Throughout the whole time, I didn't worry about myself, but I did worry about my Marines." He wondered if he would make the right decisions for his Marines. Would he bring them all back?

As they convoyed to Combat Outpost, he felt looking at the houses that the lifestyle was very different. As the convoy went to the Outpost, he saw kids and grown men showing them disrespectful signs such as showing the bottom of their feet, while others gave the "thumbs up." The feelings of the Iraqis seemed mixed. Living conditions in Combat Outpost were Spartan, and it was very crowded due to the presence of the Army units still here. Also, at that time there were 100 Iraqis coming into the camp to clean up and get electricity working.

The first night here, Corporal Smith went along with Lieutenant Wroblewski on a Left-seat, Right-seat ride into Ramadi with an Army lieutenant and some of his small unit leaders. The Army leaders shared some of what they now knew about the city. The next day the Army brought some of their Humvees over and some of the leaders of the platoon went out on the different roads and action points in the city. The Army left after about a week.

Then Echo Company Marines began to flood their area of the city with mostly squad-level foot patrols. In the late evenings, after 2300 or so, they would also do curfew enforcement patrols. On daytime security patrols, they began to learn the area. Back at the Combat Outpost, some units would be on camp guard, others waiting as the QRF, and by mid-to-late March, almost got into a routine. "We started company-level missions, doing cordon and knocks, going after enemy targets [individuals]." They also did MSR (Main Support Route) sweeps looking for IEDs. They would walk the roads looking for bombs. "Many times we found them, and many times they found us!" He said that the Marines had to look for these IEDs to make it possible for the convoys to travel the MSRs.

"And then April the 6th, 2004 came across." As 1st Squad leader, 2nd Platoon, Corporal Smith was assigned as the Quick Reaction Force. Around 0900, a large firefight began taking place west of Combat Outpost in Golf Company's area of operations (AO). One of their squads was pinned down. Smith's squad was going to take out a platoon from Golf Company to the area. Golf Company decided to send its platoon by foot, so Smith's squad came back to its own company area and waited to see what was going on. Shortly after this, a squad from 3rd Platoon was near the arches east of Combat Outpost and received small arms fire from enemy on the north side of Route Michigan. This platoon engaged the enemy and waited for the QRF to arrive. "We were called up, and we were quickly loading out the gate. We headed out, along with QRF Bravo, which was the rest of 3rd Platoon." They headed to the arches, which form the entrance to the eastern part of Ramadi.

Smith's squad and the squad from 3rd Platoon dismounted their vehicles and began searching houses in the area on MSR Michigan and along Frontage Road. They didn't find anything, and felt that the enemy had fled to the north, northeast. They soon heard gunshots from the area northeast of them, along Route Gypsum. Captain Royer decided to send two squads from 3rd Platoon to sweep up parallel to Route Gypsum on foot, while Corporal Smith's squad and another squad from 3rd Platoon would remount their vehicles and go down Route Michigan and then head up Route Gypsum.

1st Platoon was doing an IED sweep on Route Nova, and had made contact and was now in a firefight of its own. Now Smith's squad and the squad from 3rd Platoon were to go to 1st Platoon and help them out. "We had four Humvees and three 7-tons. The four Humvees were in the front, the three 7-tons were in the rear." The first two vehicles carried the squad from 3rd Platoon, and Smith's squad was in the rest of the vehicles. They began rolling to the north up Gypsum, and got about three-quarters of the way up Gypsum when Lieutenant Wroblewski called over his PRR to stop the vehicles there to dismount the Marines and continue on foot. The first two vehicles that had the Marines from 3rd Platoon along with two of Smith's Marines (drivers) continued driving as the rest of the vehicles stopped.

"And not so much as I open the door, and step my foot on the ground, and Route Gypsum became hell on earth. That's the best way I can describe it. There was just … a wall of lead that came flying at us, and just immense gunfire. I, I don't know how to describe it. It was just a lot of emotion at one time. And just thinking at one time, all right, for a second, you know, you can't hesitate. But, at the same time you do in a way want to verify whether this is real or not. Because at that time we had received no, at least in my unit, my platoon, we hadn't received fire before. And this was our first major engagement. So we, initially, muscle memory kicks in. And you know what you're doing when you're in the heat of an ambush. You regain fire superiority, you cover, and you push through the enemy. So, that's what we did. We began firing back at the enemy with our heavy weapons that were on the vehicles. While the foot-mobile troops move in to cover."

Corporal Smith said that his Marines got off their vehicles and engaged the enemy. "I remember it was a weird location, it was an open field. It was about 75 meters across, by 50 meters long, right next to the side of the road. And there were some driveways, cinderblock walls that lined the driveways, so we go and get into this little courtyard area of this house. Taking cover from the enemy fire. We see some enemy moving around and we begin engaging targets, by priority, or the ones that we can see, pretty much. So we fought back. First thing that myself as a leader I start thinking about: Where are all my people? Where's the enemy? What am I gonna do about the enemy where they are?"

"The first thing I do is, I put an overwatch up on top of the roof of house to give us a higher vantage point and we can gain a little bit of the high ground. So they can pick out enemy and see them better than we can, 'cause we were in a semi-urban environment. I say this 'cause it was kind of a rural area with a little bit of room between the houses." There was about 75 meters around these houses and he could see when the enemy moved around them. They took down one insurgent who was behind a wall about 50 meters away.

"And almost simultaneously I hear this yell from the street. And it was a blood-curdling yell. And, I turned and looked back. And my lieutenant, Lieutenant Wroblewski, had been hit, and was laying on his back in the middle of the road. Lieutenant Wroblewski had stayed in the middle of the road, for the benefit of my squad. We had no radio operator with us at that time. The radio operator had been used in a different area, he had gone with the CO [Captain Royer]. So, the only [tactical] radio that my unit had was the VRC-88 vehicle radio. So [Wroblewski] had stayed in the road next to the vehicle in the heart of the ambush to call up to high [higher command] and let them know that we had made contact. Like I said, I looked back and see that he had been hit, and Sergeant Valerio, a Motor-T driver, was over there by him, and trying to help him out. So MC [Muscle Control] kicked over, I didn't think about anything other than, that's my lieutenant and I need to help him."

So Corporal Smith now took off from where he was under cover and ran across the field to aid the lieutenant. He didn't know how bad the officer's wounds were, but knew that he had to get him out of there. Smith's squad had the situation under control in its area.

"Running across that field, we took heavy enemy fire. They were aiming and trying to take us down. It was me and the Corpsman. I remember I was really impressed with my Corpsman, HM 3 Guttierez, 'cause when I turned around to yell for the Corpsman, he was about to pass me! So, he was already there. We run out to the lieutenant and rounds were pinging off around our feet, off the road, off the vehicle. And we initially get there, and I see he took an AK round to the face. It entered the right side of his face, in his jaw area, and exited on the left side of his face, in the lower jaw area. He was bleeding pretty bad, I knew it was real serious. We needed to get him out of there. So, I drag him by the drag strap on the back of his flak, and start dragging him back out of the road. I guess we had to drag him about 50, 75 meters before we got him outta the way. But, we drug him back to another Humvee and myself, along with Doc Guttierez, loaded him up into the vehicle. And Guttierez was doing first aid, trying to stop the bleeding. And treating the wounds. Ah, tried to get on the radio to call to high that my lieutenant was down, and, I pick up the handset, and I go to key the handset, to call and, it feels weird. I look down at it, and it had been shot. Lieutenant Wroblewski was talkin' on the handset and an actual round went through the handset first, and then into his face."

"I felt, like, what am I gonna do now? I got the lieutenant, shot through the face. I'm in the heat of an ambush, and I have no, I have no comm. So, I shoot up my [inaudible], let everybody know where I'm at. Make the decision that I don't got time to wait for anything. I send that vehicle back. I send one Humvee back with 240 Golf, mini-machine gun, and the Corpsman, and the driver. I tell the driver, don't stop for nothin'. And drive as fast as he can, get back to Combat Outpost. The lieutenant needs to get back to the docs pretty quick." The driver took off south on Gypsum, and had the lieutenant back there in about 10 to 15 minutes.

Corporal Smith then started to refocus on finding the enemy and deciding what to do about it. With the platoon commander down, and the platoon sergeant not there, Smith essentially became the platoon commander on the scene. He had his squad, plus the Motor-T elements, plus the Weapons attachments, about 22 to 25 Marines all together. They continued to engage the enemy, taking down targets as they came, and moved through houses. About an hour and a half into the gunfight, two Army Bradley fighting vehicles showed up, went past them, and continued north up Gypsum. Smith needed some support in his area. Soon the Bradleys returned, and soldiers told Smith that there were wounded Marines at the intersection of Nova, and the Marines needed to get up there.

"We load up the vehicles, and we push up about 200 meters. And, I dismount the Marines. I didn't want to drive straight into another ambush. We dismount and set up full security around the vehicles, and we push up to the corner of that street. When we get in the corner, it turns again into another large-scale gunfight, right there. Initially, I can see one Humvee has been hit with an RPG. The front of it was scorched, and just shot all through it. I also see some members from 3rd Platoon, that squad from 3rd Platoon, and [I] ask them what's been goin' on. They said they were the first two vehicles in the initial line, kept going, and once they got up to that intersection, they had been hit pretty hard with automatic weapons fire, RPK fire, AK, RPG, they even had DShK, which is a 12.7mm round. And, they were in the second vehicle, and the driver and A-driver had got out and were running to a house, and the last of the people in the back were getting out when it was hit by an RPG. There were two people still in the vehicle. They were thrown out, and they just received minor shrapnel wounds." These Marines moved into a house and used it as a staging point to fight out of.

"So, when we get up there, we link up with them. I ask them what's goin' on. He said that they had been ambushed, and that the first vehicle, I remember it was Corporal [Marcus D.] Waechter I was talking to, was the squad leader. [He] Says, I don't know if they made it, man. They're all dead. And, I'm, 'Uh, what are you talkin' about?' He said, 'The first vehicle's up there, and, I don't think they made it.' I look around the corner and I can see another Humvee, right at the intersection, it's sittin' there next to a row of buildings. And there's two bodies laying in the back of it. And there's bodies around the buildings around it."

Smith's Marines pushed up to the area of this vehicle, while still engaging targets on rooftops about 100 to 150 meters away. The enemy was egressing from the area. Smith believed that the arrival of the Bradleys caused this retreat. The Marines continued to receive fire from the enemy, including RPGs and automatic weapons. "We set up security, and began loading the bodies into the vehicles."

They loaded up. Smith remembers thinking that these dead Marines were his friends and guys he had entered the Marine Corps with, and some were new Marines. All were his brothers. "We were loading them up, and seen what they had gone through in the area they were in. How many bullet holes were all around, and it was, an emotional time. Loading them up, we're still taking fire as we're loading comrades into the vehicles."

Once they had loaded the dead and were turning around, Smith realized that his Marines were starting to get low on ammunition and water. He made the decision to return with the bodies to Combat Outpost and refit his Marines. The dead included: Staff Sergeant Allan Walker, 3rd Platoon's platoon sergeant; Lance Corporal Kyle Crowley, Smith's 3rd team leader who was driving the first vehicle; PFC Ryan M. Jerabek, a mortarman who that day was on a machine gun on the back of the vehicle; PFC Travis Layfield; PFC Anthony Roberts; and the Corpsman, HM3 Fernando A. "Doc" Mendezaceves.

Once he got back to Combat Outpost, Smith's Marines delivered the bodies of the KIAs, resupplied ammo and water, got the rest of 3rd Platoon and left to return to the scene of the ambush on Gypsum. Things were quiet when they got back to the intersection, all the enemy had left the area. The Marines searched the area and found some weapons, and also picked up many of the enemy KIAs. Smith said that there was evidence that some enemy KIAs and weapons and ammo had been "police called" (cleaned up). Combat engineers came to detonate some found RPG rounds and dud grenades. All then returned to Combat Outpost.

"We get back to Combat Outpost. First thing I want to do, I go to the BAS [Battalion Aid Station] and I ask, 'How's lieutenant?' And they say, 'Well, he made it back to Combat Outpost, and he was medevac'd by CH46 to Baghdad.' And, it ends up Lieutenant Wroblewski didn't make it all the way to Baghdad." Smith paused. "He passed away in-flight. And, we'd also lost in my platoon, Lance Corporal Corrado. So, it was pretty tough. They took us into the cafeteria, the mess hall, told us our lieutenant had passed away. And then, you know, all the Marines didn't know what to think about that. It was steps. We were taking steps of reality, almost." He said that reality hit when they first got to Al Taqaddum that they were "here." When they got into their first firefight, it was reality. And now, the reality that there is enemy here who wanted to kill them, and *had* killed some of them. There were friends who weren't here anymore.

"It was tough on a bunch of Marines. You could see it. And, they were having trouble dealing with that. So, but everybody dealt with it in their own way. We moved on. That's what Marines are good at. They still kept moving."

The next morning, April 7, at 0300, 2nd Platoon headed back to the site of the ambush, this time on foot. They also patrolled up around Fish Hook Lake. The patrol was quiet with no contact.

Planning continued for more operations. On April 10, Echo Company was conducting a company-level cordon and knock in several areas around Fish Hook Lake and Route Nova. Smith could not remember the name of the operation. The Marines had grid locations of houses suspected of harboring enemy personnel, possibly to include the planners of the April 6 ambush. 2nd Platoon got up around 0300 to begin preparations, and left Combat Outpost at about 0400. Each platoon had different target houses, and began the actual cordon and knocks at about 0500.

"We searched through the houses. Our first house didn't yield anything significant, so we started searching systematically around that grid." The grid designations of possible high-value targets were accurate to about 200 meters. After searching another house, they found a guy with a permitted AK-47.

"We were en route to our third house, and we cross a little irrigation ditch. We're walking up to this third house. We have one squad that's already around the house and setting up the cordon. About to go in this house, and all of a sudden, we start receiving small arms fire from our south. We turn, engage that, and once again, we start taking fire from all over the place. Just little groups. That's the way I've seen the enemy fight here. They don't mass their troops and fight force-on-force. They'll fight you in ones and twos. They'll have one guy on a rooftop with an AK, firing down at you, or an RPG, or whatever." The Marines engaged these one- and two-man groups in all directions.

On April 10, Corporal Smith was acting platoon sergeant for 2nd Platoon. With Lieutenant Wroblewski's death, the platoon sergeant (Sergeant Coan) moved up to take command of the platoon and Smith moved up into Coan's billet. As they engaged the enemy, Smith took a squad back to the first house that they had searched and got up on the rooftops into overwatch positions. He also set up a casualty collection point there.

As Marines moved into the other house, one was shot in the arm, another (a Corpsman) in the leg. Both stayed in the fight. "I got the call from another platoon on the radio, actually. Just like us, they were en route to another house, when the fire started, [and] they had become separated from this element from their unit which was across this big field. They were taking a lot of enemy fire." The separated element was sniper attachments and a security element for this team. One of these Marines had taken a bullet in his back that entered through a gap in the SAPI plates. They did not have a Corpsman there to treat him.

"They asked me, since I had my CCP [Casualty Collection Point] set up pretty close to them, only about a hundred meters away, if I had any Marines, any Corpsmen that I could send to that area. I said, 'Yes, I do.' That's what I did. I sent my 1st Squad leader with a fire team and a Corpsman over to that area. And they treated that Marine, Lance Corporal [John] Sims. They brought him over to my area, he had collapsed lungs. The round had entered in his left shoulder blade, but had not exited. So, [they] started working on him." Sims had a faint pulse. Corporal Smith called in for an air medevac for Sims. But he said "The air medevac wouldn't come. They said the area was too hot. I was gonna have to move out of that area." This was an Army medevac unit. Smith said that the Marine air casevac had not taken over yet. Smith said, "There were some upset Marines when that took place."

They kept working on Sims while still engaging the enemy. For about an hour and a half they performed rescue breathing and kept Sims's pulse going. An Army Bradley fighting vehicle then arrived to take Sims. Sims died en route to higher medical care.

The rest of the platoon continued to engage enemy targets. The fighting cooled down, and then Marines swept the houses in the area. They eventually left. His Marines did well on this day, as they had on the 6th. "You didn't have to tell them to do something twice, and they never hesitated."

On May 22, Smith was on a QRF that went to pick up a unit that was returning from a foot patrol and was next to the power plant. Smith's vehicles had earlier dropped this patrol off at the power plant, and were now there to pick them up. They got to the parking lot, loaded the Marines, and left the parking lot. As they passed an area there that they had only recently gone through, an IED exploded on Smith's vehicle. The IED was made from three artillery shells: Two 105 rounds and one 155 round all daisy-chained together. Smith said, "They were spread out the length of a 7-ton. So, the two 105s were at the front and the back of the 7-ton, and the 155 blew up right next to my door. [I] Took shrapnel to the face, lost hearing in my right ear, fractured my jaw, and I had pulls and muscle injury to my neck. Also, the machine gunner that was on the turret of the 7-ton took shrapnel to his face and hands, and some debris in his eye. We're both still here. We were some of the lucky ones with IEDs. We have some that aren't still here."

Smith said that there were engagements, but the IEDs were a constant threat. Marines never knew when they would hit an IED. At 40 miles per hour on a road, it was hard to see a few inches of copper wire sticking out of the ground. "It blows, there's nothing you can do about it but try to punch out of the kill zone and take care of your wounded, and search for trigger men." Smith said that more often than not, they don't find the triggerman who was often hiding in a house somewhere.

Smith was in the hospital receiving treatment for his wounds, when two days later, on May 24, another IED hit. "Corporal [Misael] Nieto, my 1st team leader, who had taken over while I was in the hospital, he was on QRF again and went out to pick up another platoon. On their return route, the last Humvee, he was in a four Humvee convoy, in the last Humvee, which was a ten-man Humvee, high-back, was hit with a vehicle-borne IED. Outta that Humvee was four Marine KIA and there was several WIAs. Everyone in that vehicle was either wounded or killed." Corporal Nieto was still being treated in a hospital. That was the first VBIED that hit them. It was located in a white taxicab with its hood up. It looked like a taxi that had engine trouble, nothing out of the ordinary.

The most recent engagement was July 21, two days before today. 2nd Platoon was QRF Charlie. Smith said that this was considered an "off" day, and they would be the last to leave the Combat Outpost. "We got the call, probably about 1500, that the battalion commander's convoy was in a firefight in town. Around the Agricultural Center. And, to get everybody dressed and ready to move. We get everybody up and ready to move. And shortly after they come out, hop in our vehicles and the whole company leaves, that was here." One platoon was out on an observation post.

They got word they're headed to the stadium and to stage there before moving west. Corporal Smith's squad was tasked with security to the north of the stadium. The stadium stands, made of concrete, provided some cover. Golf Company had a squad to the south. 2nd and 3rd squads from 2nd Platoon faced to the east of the stadium. They took some small arms fire from the north, and 3rd Platoon sent an element to sweep that area. Then automatic weapons fire began coming from the south. "And then a red four door hatchback sedan starts coming at a pretty high rate of speed. Same time we're taking small arms fire. And, that vehicle was engaged, and it was engaged heavily. All of our automatic weapons were used, we had M16s, 240 Golfs, all firing at this car. And there were two Iraqi males in that vehicle, and both of them were killed."

The Marines then left the stadium and moved through Ramadi, from Checkpoint 297 (by the stadium) west on Route Michigan. They took a few pot shots from the enemy, but no significant action. They went to Checkpoint 296 by Y Road. Each squad went into a different house along Route Michigan, facing north. Corporal Smith said that throughout the day, the biggest enemy was the heat. He heard that it was upward of 140 degrees that day during the firefight. And the Marines carried a lot of weight, including their ammo, water, flak jackets with SAPI plates, helmets and other gear. They had a few heat casualties that day. Later they moved back to the stadium positions and waited about 45 minutes for the rest of Echo Company to move back there. He said it was a one-sided firefight that day, as the enemy did not stand and fight. Corporal Smith said that this has mostly been the case since the fighting after early April.

For the rest of Echo Company's time here, Corporal Smith said that he planned to keep up the surveillance along Route Michigan from observation posts. They would keep the roads safe for convoys moving in and out. "I have faith that whatever comes up, in the future, that my Marines will be able to handle it. And they've seen a lot, and been through a lot, and they're all looking forward to going home. I think everybody's really, most Marines are appreciative of the commandant and his seven-month deployments, instead of 12 (as per the Army's). You can see that time is starting to take its toll on Marines. They're ready to leave. They know they still have a job to do, and that's the difference between the Marines and the other services. They will continue to do their jobs until their time's up."

Smith said that his Marines can see the light at the end of the tunnel, and talk about WHEN they get home, not IF they will make it.

Corporal Joseph Stephen Magee
3rd Squad Leader, 2nd Platoon, Echo Company, 2/4

During the heavy fighting in Ramadi on April 6 and 7, Magee led his squad as part of a Quick Reaction Force (QRF) for Echo Company. Also in April while searching one house, he shot an insurgent who was reaching for an AK-47 and flexi-cuffed another. He described much of the fighting in Ramadi this year as "A squad leader's fight."

Corporal Magee joined the Corps via the Delayed Entry Program in June 2000, at the end of his junior year in high school. A year later, he left for recruit training at Parris Island, and went straight to the School of Infantry at Camp Geiger, North Carolina. His first duty station was with Echo Company, 2/4 at Camp San Mateo inside of Camp Pendleton, California.

He went with the company to Okinawa last year for its nearly year-long deployment, and learned a lot from the more senior Marines. He tries to pass this on to the junior Marines now under him. "After that, we came back, took a little bit of leave time. I ended up getting married. I've been married for about eight months now." He has only spent about two and a half months with his new wife due to this deployment, though. But he has known her for seven years. He left for Kuwait the night of her birthday.

Magee estimated that Echo Company spent about one month in Kuwait conducting more training in tactics and cultural awareness. "We trained for a lot of the kind of missions that we'd be doing out here as a company. Mostly, cordon, knock, and searches. Searches of detainees." He said that he had two senior Marines in his squad, and the rest were junior. These newer Marines have done well and impressed him. He said that normally a work-up for a deployment is about 18 months, but his newer Marines only had about four or five months of preparation once they joined Echo Company.

"From Kuwait, we were the fly-in element, to get here last. It was kind of like a rear party element to tie up loose ends and then come into Iraq." They landed at Al Taqaddum, about 20 miles from Ramadi, then after a one-night layover, moved to Combat Outpost in a combat convoy. "The first night here, there was a gunfight. It was pretty hectic, I knew we were in for a rough time here." The Army units here did the gunfight.

For about a week in early March, they went with Army leaders to do Left-seat, Right-seat rides with key leaders to learn key terrain features: where the mosques were, which areas in Ramadi were hostile, and where they had received fire. Key leaders who went included platoon commanders, platoon sergeants, and squad leaders like Magee. Since taking over, the Marines have doubled the size of their area of operations (AO). "We ventured out into an area where some people had never seen a U.S. coalition force member the entire time they've been here."

Echo Company's first tasks included curfew enforcement, security patrols, ambush patrols, Main Supply Routes (MSR) clears, and Information Operations (IO) to pass out pamphlets explaining what the Marines were here to do and to counter anti-coalition propaganda. Magee said that he was expecting more hostility from the people here. "There are nice people here, they're pretty decent people. And they're just people just trying to make their living off their own farmland, just like anybody else would. It's actually sad that a few bad apples spoil the dozen."

Then came early April. Corporal Magee explained: "April 6th they kind of drew us into an ambush, when 3rd Platoon launched out on a MSR clear, and they received fire. And the QRF reacted, went out there. And then they heard fire from the top of [Route] Gypsum and [Route] Nova. Which is an area where there's been multiple IED detonations, and just a lot of hostility's come from there. The QRF rolled up, and they [insurgents] ended up having a DShK down the main avenue of approach, which is kind of like an American .50 cal [machine gun]. They had a DShK right on the main avenue of the road, started opening fire. They had men on the roof, and cross fire. They had them on both sides of the roof, and downward. Fire was coming from all over the place."

Magee's squad got there as part of the QRF. Most of the gunfight was over by the time they arrived. "It was just a police-up, the bodies of Marines, and the bodies of the dead [Iraqis], drop 'em off at the IP [Iraqi Police] station. Let them take care of it." He estimated that his squad was there about an hour to an hour and a half.

"April 7th, I reacted as a QRF force again, for 1st Platoon." This was at Gypsum and Nova again. "Their machine gunner got hit, shrapnel to the head, their 7-ton driver was KIA, their Corpsman had a dislocated shoulder. They took an IED detonation, small arms fire from a fire team-size element. My squad, along with fire teams from multiple other squads reacted to it. We went out, secured the area, picked up the casualties, came back, brought 'em off here, Combat Outpost. Went back out there, got the rest of the guys. 1st Platoon continued on their MSR clearing, we came back."

To this date (July 23, 2004), Corporal Magee's squad has not had any casualties.

On April 10, they had a company mission to seek out some corrupt ICDC (Iraqi Civil Defense Corps) who were letting enemy flow through checkpoints into Ramadi. "We got to our target house. We waited until approximately 5 a.m., zero-five. Mortar HE [High Explosive rounds] started impacting on an open field. And illum [illumination rounds] started getting popped, also. And then, that's when we conducted the raid. At first, we detained nine males in the household. It was a very big family in the household. We found one AK-47, which is what they were supposed to have. No ICDC uniforms." They went to another house about 200 meters away with similar results—no uniforms and one AK-47 rifle.

They were about to go south to another house, but 3rd Platoon called them and told them that they had already searched there.

"That's when we received the initial contact from the enemy, which was, I would like to say, about a platoon reinforced. I don't feel it was all enemy personnel, I feel it was some people who were opportunists at the time." He said this firefight lasted about four hours. 1st Squad went to the top of the first house that they had searched to act as overwatch. 2nd Squad secured another house, while Magee's 3rd Squad was running back and forth the whole time: Securing a Landing Z one (LZ) for a helo that never landed, and bringing casualties back out. "That's when one of my Marines, Corporal Degenhardt was shot in the shoulder by a ricochet. Still has the round in his arm." He was still with the squad.

"After we secured that house, we shot an AT4 into a building where we were taking RPK and AK fire from. The AT4 impacted directly in the window. From then, 2nd and 3rd Squads launched out, started to secure the area that we called 'The Alamo,' because it was a bunch of hollowed-out buildings. Some of them barely had roofs."

"We went into one building, we fragged the first room. Came in and cleared it. Nothing happened. We went into the second room, it was Corporal Degenhardt and Lance Corporal [Patric B.] LeBlanc, which were two of my team leaders, platoon's kind of mixed up right now. We fragged the next room, went to go make entry again, and Corporal Degenhardt was shot in the hand. Same corporal was shot in the hand! He was pretty angry at that. Ran outta the room pretty upset. And, we fragged the room again, and we made entry again. This time it was myself and the platoon sergeant, Sergeant Coan. There was one guy on the stairs, he had an AK-47 at his feet. And, he put his hands up. I told him to get down off the stairs. And he reached down for his AK-47, that's when I just, I shot him there. I traversed over to the other guy, told him to get down on the ground. He wouldn't go down, so I swiped him down to the ground, flexi-cuffed him, threw him in the corner." Magee said that he shouted the commands in both English and Arabic.

Corporal Magee said they stayed in the house for about 30 minutes, and then began to receive heavy fire from the east. So they secured the rooftop and began returning fire. Now Captain Royer was trying to consolidate the company into one area, a more defendable position.

They bounded back to the original target house. Magee said, "That's when I found out that my best friend was a casualty. Was, uh, killed that day. The only one." I asked if this was the Marine that they were trying to medevac by helicopter that day. "Yes sir, it was Lance Corporal John Thompson Sims, Junior." He then paused for a few moments.

The firefight pretty much was over by the time they got to this house. They launched patrols to see the damage in the area and to get any loose weapons or intel. Marines found four rice bags, commonly used in the area, but these were filled with IEDs, weapons, ICDC uniforms, and IP uniforms. The company finally went to the convoy area, loaded up into their trucks, and returned to Combat Outpost.

Things were mostly quiet after that, although Magee said that recently the Combat Outpost has been getting mortared more, with some rounds landing inside the firm base.

One big operation in late May was to clear IEDs on MSR Michigan from Combat Outpost down to the 530 grid line. Once this was clear, Echo Company established an Observation Post in the cemetery. Things were quiet in July until the 21st, when they reacted as a Quick Reaction Force for Golf Company and the battalion commander who had just received fire on the MSR by the Agricultural Center.

"We got to the soccer stadium, 1603, I'd like to say. We set up in a 360, 2nd Platoon occupied the twelve to six. There was a car rolled down the MSR, was a possible VBIED. 3rd Squad opened up and let it rock on that car."

They used M16s, SAWS, and Golf Company fired 240 Golfs. Magee's squad then moved out to the northwest area and then moved west towards where they heard firefights. They received some small arms fire, returned it, then continued west. They occupied several rooftops as observation posts (OPs) to cover Marines on the ground who conducted searches. Later they returned to the stadium and Combat Outpost.

Asked about the value of the training given to his Marines before coming into Iraq Corporal Magee said he felt that Marines should be taught how to operate the AK-47, the RPK machine gun, and the RPG 7. They did a company-level all-night operation, learning how to operate with NVGs, including how to place their feet. They learned how to identify buried IEDs or buried trip wires with a laser. They reviewed basic patrolling fundamentals. "I also focused a lot on mostly close-quarters battle things: Speed reloads and tactical reloads, different positions to shoot from, shooting from behind barriers." Marines in his squad picked it up well. NBC training was mostly on how to don and clear the gas mask, and how to decontaminate things with kits. They learned Satellite Patrolling in California from a British Marine training them.

Magee described a technique for clearing buildings that he called "Hasty front, detailed back." This means that, "You hasty clear everything, make sure all the family members are in one room. The men are separated from the women with the senior, eldest man with the women at all times. One guard on the women, one guard on the men. Search teams will move in. There's one talker with the head of the household, which would normally be me. One talker would talk to the head of the household, see what he had in his house."

"Ask him, for example, if he had six AK-47s, 'What's up with these over here?' 'Ali Babi leaves that.'

'Okay, well we're gonna take these off your hands.'"

Magee said that often this would cause them to cough up some other weapons.

Searchers would hasty clear all rooms in a house, then they go back through and search drawers and closets for the detailed searches.

I asked about much of the fighting this year as a "Squad Leader's Fight." He responded, "A squad leader's fight? I definitely feel it's been a squad leader's fight. They're kinda like my little brothers. Pretty soon they're gonna be all alone in the world someday. I'm trying to do that the best that I can while keeping 'em safe."

Corporal Magee said that he felt that he has done his job over here. We've turned over a free and stable Iraq, and Iraq needs to train its people up. "Freedom doesn't come free. It always has a cost. It's cost many Marines' lives. Which, it's tragic. But, it's the line of work that we choose. It's what we love to do."

He also said that sometimes here it has seemed that the people didn't want to help us at all. They will need to defend themselves when American forces pull out. Currently the Marines were mostly off the streets to give the Iraqi army and police the chance to enforce their new laws. "I hope that one day they can all just live free."

Lieutenant Tommy Edward Cogan
Platoon Commander, 3rd Platoon, Echo Company, 2/4

After arriving in Ramadi, Lieutenant Cogan's platoon began patrols in the area. The intense battle on April 6 claimed the lives of five of his men, including his platoon sergeant. A request for an Army helicopter medevac for one badly wounded Marine was denied as the only landing zone close by was still "hot." Seven of the original 38 Marines in his platoon have been killed in action, the most of any Marine infantry platoon in Iraq to this date.

Lieutenant Cogan attended Niagara University, and entered the Marine Corps via the PLC Combined program. He graduated from the university and accepted his commission on September 5, 2002. He entered The Basic School in January 2003. After completing a martial arts course and Infantry Officer's Course, he joined 2/4 in November 2003. Shortly after this, 2/4 received the warning order that it would deploy to Iraq in 2004. He deployed to Iraq along with Echo Company on February 16, 2004.

When Cogan first joined Echo Company, his platoon consisted of only 12 Marines, due to post-deployment transfers and changes. Many new Marines from the School of Infantry soon joined the company. Some senior NCOs and staff NCOs came in at the last minute to become squad leaders and platoon sergeants. When he left for Iraq, the platoon totaled 38 personnel, including himself and his Navy Corpsman.

They first went to Kuwait: "Kuwait, we basically trained every single day. Basically [from] 0700 to 2200 we were always doing classes and stuff." They did a lot of SASO training during the three weeks in Kuwait. They reviewed the training they had done in the two months prior to deployment. He had many junior lance corporals and PFCs.

Cogan's platoon flew out of Kuwait into Iraq, landing at Al Taqaddum airfield. After a day there, about half of the platoon rolled into Combat Outpost, Ramadi, and the rest of his platoon followed in the next day. "Then we linked up, were doing 'Left-seat, Right-seat,' with the Army for, I guess, about a week, before we took over operations."

Cogan noted that the Army used different tactics here. "They weren't primarily foot-mobile like we were. They just drove around a lot. It was okay, we got to see lots of the area that we were occupying. Our AO [area of operations] actually, was a lot bigger than their area was, so we only got to see part of it. And a lot of different tactics than what we did. So it was good to get eyes on the area, but it really didn't help us with any tactical development." He said that the Army rode around the area in Bradleys and Humvees, and their ideas of infantry tactics were very different from the Marines. "So we were basically foot-mobile, and basically, we take our fight a little bit different than they do. And the way we attack things."

Lieutenant Cogan said that the Army unit that they were replacing had only been in this area for about three months, and that they had replaced another Army unit that had been here for about 10 months. They were living out of Camp Ramadi, what the Marines call Junction City.

"Primarily based on intel, we did a lot of squad-size patrols. Every once in a while, we'd mix in platoon operations. Because the primary threat was, anywhere, attacks from fire team to squad-size elements to the max." Based on this, Echo Company did small unit ambushes and IED sweeps, along with recon patrols in the area.

As he only had two squads at the time, Cogan would usually go out with one squad, and his platoon sergeant [Staff Sergeant Walker] would go out on another at least once every day. At first, they kept the clamps on the squad leaders, but as time went on, they allowed the squad leaders to lead the patrols. By the end of March, they were still figuring out the area, trying to get Security and Stability Operations (SASO) going. "Every time we went out, it was a learning experience." They did a lot of route reconnaissance east of Fish Hook Lake because the Army units did not have that as a part of their area of operations.

The Marines kept reacting to new things, and the enemy also continued to adapt to the Marines' actions. "We had to keep modifying our routines constantly."

"The 6th of April was the first major contact that I was a part of. It was the second one for my platoon." (The platoon's first contact was on March 25 as part of a reaction force.) "About 1300 or so, that afternoon, one of my squads was out on patrol. They were actually egressing back towards the firm base. They were at the far eastern end of the AO [area of operations]. On the way back in, they were on the south side of Route 10. They took some RPG fire, some small arms, didn't take any casualties at that point in time. Estimated there was a fire team force on the north side of the road. They attempted to secure the area, but the area was pretty expansive out there. They called in for support. I launched out with one of my squads, plus, another platoon went out to cordon off the area. We started sweeping through, searching all the houses."

"While we were doing that, while we had that area cordoned off and were searching houses, [we] heard some gunfire to the north. I asked the CO [Captain Royer] if we could check it out. Punched up, couldn't really see anything. Heard some more, punched up a little further, and then saw somebody smokin'. At that point we were up far enough, my one squad with me, my other squad was down with my platoon sergeant, with the cordon on still. And, it was too far up for the vehicles to drive. Again, I thought it was the snipers at first, but apparently it was our 1st Platoon engaged way up the road a couple clicks."

Cogan's Marines needed to "marry up" with their vehicles to get there fast, and the closest checkpoint that they all knew was Check Point 338. Cogan called back to his buddy Lieutenant Wroblewski of 2nd Platoon, and his other squad with Staff Sergeant Walker, and told them that he'd link up with them and the vehicles they brought out at Check Point 338. "They began to punch up to 338, we started on foot towards 338, moving east. As we ran east, cutting close to the road where the vehicles were driving on, we got eyes on the vehicles in front of the formation. Called them over the inter-squad radio, 'Stop!' So we just stop the vehicles right there. First couple vehicles just shot past. Don't think they heard me. Then the CO called over the 119 [radio] for them to stop. Vehicles start slowin' down. So we hit the road, rounds start coming, all sorts of directions. We punched across the road, behind a house."

Cogan said there was a field, a house to the north, and a house to the east. They pushed to the east to try to get close to the intersection. He and his Marines started taking heavy fire from rooftops from the north and east. "So we run across the field, starting shooting at the guys on the rooftops. Started clearing houses."

Cogan continued: "I had one squad with me, the initial one that pulled up. Plus, there was another squad from Weapons Platoon. And upon contact, since there's an open area where we start taking fire, everybody dispersed and started taking cover. So I basically grab any Marines I could find. First four, made a fire teams out of them, started clearing houses. To the north, we cleared the house. And start punching to the east. As we punch to the east, start taking heaving machine gun fire, RPG fire."

The enemy had a heavy machine gun position about 500 meters east of them, so he pulled his Marines back. Cogan put Marines on rooftops, but they could not get good visibility on the machine gunner. Cogan was going to try to send some Marines to flank the position, when a 7-ton truck mounting a Mark 19, manned by Corporal Smith, pulled up. Smith asked if he could pull the vehicle up the road a little and engage the machine gunner with the Mark 19. Cogan said that he couldn't see it, but heard that the grenades from the Mark 19 were not having much of an effect at that range (500 meters). He linked up with Captain Royer and told him what they were doing. He had some Weapons Platoons Marines about to attempt to flank the enemy machine gunner. Then some Army armor assets showed up. These vehicles moved north on the road, and the flanking movement continued and found the machine gun, but no enemy bodies. Cogan noted that it seemed bizarre that there was no spent brass or bodies there. They found some grenades set up on trip wires.

Cogan then got to Check Point 338. Five of his Marines who were in the lead Humvee were killed in action by enemy machine gun fire. His platoon sergeant, Staff Sergeant Walker, was among them. A 12.7mm machine gun had chewed them up. Marines in the second vehicle survived. This was a long day for the Marines in the platoon, and they did not return to Combat Outpost until about 0200.

Prior to April 6, the Rules of Engagement had Marines allowed to fire on enemy who were carrying weapons. The insurgents had figured this out, and would often drop weapons and go to another area where weapons were staged for them.

On April 10, Echo Company began conducting a cordon and knock operation, looking for a high-value target (individual). On entering one house, they took gunfire from inside. The Marines killed the enemy inside this house. Enemy then approached from the east and west, mostly carrying AK-47s, but also RPGs. During this fighting, Lance Corporal Sims was wounded in his shoulder, but Lieutenant Cogan could not get the Army medevac helicopter to land. A Corpsman arrived, and Sims held on to life for a while. He soon died after the ground medevac came to get him to Combat Outpost Ramadi.

2nd Platoon continued to clear houses. Finally, Echo Company's first sergeant arrived, and so did several Army 113 Bradley fighting vehicles. One Bradley was the medevac vehicle for Sims. Some of the Bradleys rammed walls of some compounds. Fighting finally ended, and the Marines found four enemy KIA, as well as 14 AK-47s, ammo and magazines. They also took about 14 detainees from houses in this area. The fighting lasted about four to five hours. Finally, Echo Company returned to Combat Outpost.

Since April 10, there have been more of the platoon-size operations. In many of the areas where they operate, the local people are apparently friendly. However, the picture of the area changed after April 10, and it became apparent that there were more FRE (Former Regime Elements) becoming active in the insurgency. For the past month and a half, Main Supply Route (MSR) security has been the main mission for Cogan's platoon.

On July 21, 2nd Platoon was called to react to the firefights that had broken out that day, but by the time his platoon could react, most of the fighting was over. His Marines did engage and kill one insurgent. They also got intel about a VBIED, and destroyed the vehicle with an AT4 shot. Cogan said that there were many secondary explosions when the AT4 round hit the vehicle.

Cogan talked about "BOLOs" or "Be on the lookout for" missions based on intel briefings. He said that this, his first deployment has been quite an experience. His Marines have been awesome in firefights, but it has been hard to accept the losses—seven of the original 38 Marines in his platoon have been killed in action in Ramadi. There was not a day when he could relax.

Saturday July 24, 2004

I slept until about 0700, then found the Combat Outpost shower area for showering and shaving. I went to morning chow, served in vat cans prepared at Camp Blue Diamond at the other end of Ramadi. Then I walked over to the Golf Company area to check on the schedule of interviews with their commanding officer, Captain Christopher Bronzi. I noticed on their Read Board a notice for a raid by Golf Company that was supposed to take place early tomorrow (Sunday) morning. Turns out that the raid was moved up to this afternoon due to a tip that the targets have moved building(s). So it looked like I stumbled into another big operation and might not have any Marines from the company to interview. But Captain Bronzi told his master gunnery sergeant to send over some Marines to meet with me. I met with them and set up times to meet individually. All told, I interviewed five Marines from Golf Company.

Corporal Caleb Zachary Stefanovich
Fire Team Leader, 4th Platoon, Golf Company, 2/4

Corporal Stefanovich was in the middle of the intense fighting in Ramadi in early April. His infantry platoon was formed from elements of the Weapons Platoon in Golf Company. In mid-April, his squad was near the explosion of a Vehicle-Concealed Improvised Explosive Device (VCIED), but none of these Marines were injured. (There were technical issues with the recording. Written notes were used for this interview.)

Corporal Stefanovich joined the Marine Corps in June 2001, and after the School of Infantry he reported to 2/4. He explained that during this deployment to Iraq, the company's weapon platoon was split up, and made into a provisional rifle company.

On arrival in Kuwait in February 2004, they conducted lots of additional training. They then convoyed up to Combat Outpost Ramadi, and did the Relief in Place with Army leaders here.

Their first casualty happened around March 6 or 7 during a mounted patrol. It was an IED attack. The company then settled into missions involving Information Operations (IO) to give out materials to the Iraqis in the area of operations (AO) explaining what the Marines were doing here. They also conducted Security Patrols at night.

They had a quiet routine. Then came April 6.

Corporal Stefanovich was in bed (the "rack") when another platoon in Golf Company came into contact with the enemy. Stefanovich's team was part of a foot-mobile Quick Reaction Force (QRF). During the day they found a small weapons cache, and returned to Combat Outpost by mid-afternoon. April 7 started the same way. Golf Company responded in force, with a movement to contact. They found many weapons in houses during searches. The company linked up at the soccer stadium in Ramadi. During fighting that day, Stefanovich found himself pinned up against a wall at one point by enemy fire. There was fighting throughout Ramadi.

They got ammo and water resupply, and continued on foot accompanied by Humvee gun trucks. Golf Company sent platoons down every street, and fought to cross side streets. Finally, heavy guns from Weapons Company came and relieved Golf Company. Golf Company found multiple weapons on this day before returning to Combat Outpost around 1700. Several Marines were killed during the fighting.

For the rest of April, Golf Company routinely found IEDs. In early May, Echo Company came across a VBIED near Check Point 297 in Ramadi. Stefanovich saw a fireball and heard the explosion from this VBIED that hit Echo Company. He volunteered to help with the massive casualties that came into Combat Outpost.

In May, Corporal Stefanovich said that the commanding general's (General Mattis) convoy was hit by an IED, and the Quick Reaction Force from Golf Company was sent to help.

Marines at observation posts (OPs) looking for IED emplacers started operations in June. Towards the end of June, the new Iraqi governing body took over in the country. During this time, snipers with Echo Company got hit and were killed. When a fight broke out near the Agricultural Center, 4th Platoon returned fire there. Insurgents fired RPGs at the Marines. The 4th Platoon Marines employed SMAWs, and other weapons systems against enemy, some who were using a taxi stand as a firing position. When the fighting ended, the enemy had suffered 11 KIA. Now when OPs are attacked, they fight back with force.

During a patrol on April 12, Stefanovich's squad was hit by a VBIED hidden in a brown car on a road. Fortunately, none of the Marines suffered any serious injuries. They returned to Combat Outpost after the blast.

Two days before today, on July 21, 2004, 10 mortar rounds impacted inside the walls at Combat Outpost. At the same time, RPGs and RPG7s hit the Agricultural

Center in Ramadi. The Marines expected an ambush. "Bastard," the call sign for battalion commander Lieutenant Colonel Paul Kennedy, rolled to Main Supply Route (MSR) Michigan. The commanding general's convoy was hit also. Bastard's convoy was hit by an ambush, and rolled through it. The Army then rolled in with armored vehicles. Corporal Stefanovich's team was on security at the Agricultural Center. He described Cobra helicopters that made gun runs and "lit up" areas. The whole battalion was in the fight that day, and then swept through the city. It was very hot, and several Marines became heat casualties.

On July 22, the Marines attempted to take the fight to the enemy, and conducted sweeps in Ramadi. They did find some rocket launchers, but did not get engaged in any firefights. Yesterday, July 23, Stefanovich and Golf Company expected contact, but did not get any.

Corporal Stefanovich said that there were many new Marines in Golf Company, and they were doing well. 3/5 conducted training for them before they left the States, and much of it has proven valuable. He did, however, expect more of a "stand up" fight here in Iraq. The fighting was not at all like that from OIF1. He felt that the Marines need to show force. He said that the enemy knows our tactics, and we Marines need to execute better against them.

Private First Class Kenny Ray Whittle
Point Man for Team, 4th Platoon, Golf Company, 2/4

During his first day on a convoy in Ramadi, the Humvee he was in was hit by an IED, severely injuring several of the Marines in the vehicle. During the April 6 and 7 fights, he lost several friends during hours-long firefights. He praised the leadership in his platoon for taking decisive actions during the fights.

PFC Whittle entered the Corps on June 16, 2003, and finished recruit training on September 11, 2003. After completing the School of Infantry, he joined Golf Company, 2/4. He trained with the company for about three months before deploying to Kuwait. Training continued for several weeks in Kuwait. He explained that Golf Company took the Weapons Marines from its Weapons Platoon and spread them out among all of the platoons in the company due to the threat here in Iraq, becoming a fourth infantry platoon. He is an 0311 infantryman.

To move from Kuwait, "We took a convoy, lasted about three days. We slept out in the desert for a couple of nights." They went through Baghdad, stopped in Junction City in Ramadi for a few hours, then came to Combat Outpost via Route Nova, because MSR Michigan was too dangerous due to IEDs. Leaders in the platoon went out on familiarization rides through the area with Army personnel already here. Once they started going into the town on their own, Whittle said that they were going out "blind." He was point man at the time, and he did not know the city he was walking into.

Right off the bat, things began happening to 4th Platoon.

"The day before we took over the AO [area of operations], we were driving down Route Michigan, where Corporal McPherson, he did pick up corporal, he was a really good guy, PFC Zimmerman, Lance Corporal Harrison, got hit with an IED. Corporal McPherson lost his lower jaw. PFC Zimmerman lost his eye. And Lance Corporal Harrison had a piece of shrapnel about the size of a ChapStick tube through his leg. And it blew those three people out the back. So, we were pretty much the first ones to get hit with an IED."

About a week later, "2nd Squad, 4th Platoon was walkin' at the government center, back, and they got ambushed that night. PFC Yancy got shot in the back of the arm. So, we were the first platoon to get ambushed. We pretty much so far led the way in everything!" Things then quieted down for a while in Ramadi.

"April 6th and 7th, which everybody's heard about now, were the most heinous days in my life, at the time. It just started out [as] a simple distress call, like, 'Hey we're getting shot at, we need QRF.' So we responded, and we just, like, like, going right into fire."

Before they even got to the platoon they were trying to help, Lance Corporal Cantu got hit in the ankle. "And we're coming in on 7-tons [trucks], and we just got hit. We ended up fighting our way all the way. Lance Corporal Cantu, we got him in the back of the truck. And then just had the drivers leave. They left us there to fight. And it was all day fighting. It was crazy. Just bullets everywhere, you didn't know if you were gonna get hit or not. Impacts all around you. I watched my pretty good buddy Weber almost get shot. That day, one of my really good friends did get shot. He died from that—PFC [Deryk] Hellal. That hit pretty hard, 'cause he was a good friend of mine. Lost a couple [of] other good friends that day. We thought it would be over. That day was like six, seven hours straight. And we raided this house. We got suppressive fire at the house. Found these guys with all these weapons, and had a grenade thrown at us in the house. That was pretty intense! It wasn't what I expected it to be like. I really thought, like a big opposition, they can't do it two days in a row." Whittle said that when they got here, the Marines had been expecting to do mostly Security and Stability Operations (SASO), helping Iraqi civilians.

"Well, the next day was even worse. We went out there on foot, ran out the rear gate. Came around, through the palm grove. Ran down the road, tracks to the back of the Al Farouq area, the bad area here in Ramadi. And, that was nonstop fighting all day." He said that people shot at them from moving vehicles, and from windows all over the place. "It was confusing, nobody here really experienced that kind of combat, just to be hit like that, all at once, going from little, small stuff that we can handle to [a] full-out hit."

"We ended up fighting through, then we go to an ammo resupply point [ASP]. Which I'm glad we did, 'cause at that time, I had, not even half a magazine left. And, we loaded up on ammo. We went back out there. And we're walking down the street, where Lance Corporal Elmgreen [*sic*], actually, ended up gettin' combat stress from this, and had to go away for a little bit, 'cause it kinda messed him up. He was on the 240 [240 Golf machine gun], and we were getting hit so hard. Just whole groups of people shootin' at us. He musta shot at least 50 people that day. And it weighed on him pretty bad. And it was like that for all of us, 'cause we were at one point, we were going down the street, and we're suppressing fire down all the streets. Just to run across them, we had to. 'Cause they were shooting at us from both sides. And I remember at one point, our company had TOWs, 'Like sergeant [inaudible], there's nobody shootin' at us.' And he's standing in the middle of the road, so, we let up off the triggers, rounds just started impacting all around him, hitting the Humvees. Then he just screamed out, 'Suppress fire!' Kinda what we were already doin'. Just shootin' down that road. And shootin' down that road. And, just, people fallin' everywhere."

"We get back to the firm base [Combat Outpost Ramadi], and I remember saying out loud, to my squad leader, 'I'm ready to get back out and get some more shit.' And we cleared our weapons, pulled out my magazine [from his rifle]. I had one magazine left, and I had two rounds left in it! So, I went through quite a few rounds that day!" PFC Whittle said that he had not just been spraying rounds either. He had targets for every round that he fired. He said that people were running around all that day shooting at them. One of the biggest things was guys who would drive up in vehicles and shoot RPGs at them. "They were gettin' pretty ballsy, stuff they were doing was pretty crazy. It was like they almost knew they were gonna die too. They pull up to us, and we were supported by .50 cals, and 240s, and they pull up right beside the convoy. They *knew* they weren't gonna make it outta there. And none of 'em did!"

After this, things were quiet for a couple of weeks around Combat Outpost Ramadi and the area of operations except for a couple of sporadic, small fire fights. Then, they were walking on a Main Supply Route (MSR) sweep. He was not sure of the date. He said that the Iraqi Police told them about an IED, but let them walk right into it, which turned out to be an ambush. "I honestly think these guys were ambushing the road, because they didn't hit a single one of us. I think they're ambushing the road and we just happened to be there."

They get fired on from the rear. Whittle said that a lance corporal who was the SAW gunner, turned around and started spraying the area with rounds from his weapon. Whittle said that it was kind of a "C" shape or "L" shape ambush. A lot of people were shooting at them from all over. They had to run about a click, and he said that it was hot, running with all of their gear.

Another incident was when another friend of his, PFC Rossman, got shot through his armpit into his lung. PFC Whittle was part of the QRF for that day, and they were told that the medevac area was all secure.

"What the enemy did, was, they shot him in a place where they'd have to go in this one building. And there was a school right there. It was a pretty coordinated ambush.

They [the insurgents] knew the Marines were gonna come get him. And soon as we pull up, we park our Humvees, they pop out of every damn window there was! And they just started lightin' us up. [They] Did not accomplish the mission, though. My team leader that day was Lance Corporal Leerah [*sic*]. He was my team leader. He ended up getting put out, so it was kinda hard, 'cause I didn't really have a team leader. He was just directing what to do, so I had to do it myself. Pretty big step up from what I was used to doing. They were shooting from one building. A room where they had a big steel door. And he [Leerah] stuck the butt stock of his weapon through the window, and shattered glass, and slit his wrist pretty bad. He's going home soon."

When Leerah pulled his hand out of the broken window, he was disabled from the wound. He still ran from building to building during the short ambush. Then a Marine unit, he didn't know which, rolled up with .50 cals and lit up the building. Whittle and the Marines in his team then swept through the building. He said the sweep continued pretty smoothly until they came to a lady curled up in a ball at a door. "And she's screaming, 'No! No! No! Mister!' and she wouldn't let us in. Can't figure out why. Eventually she opens up the door, runs back in the room, she pulls out a 9 mil [pistol] and sticks it right to my team leader's face. She was gonna shoot him! And, we were just hopin' that women don't do that here; they're peaceful, they're not gonna fight us. And she tried to shoot him. She didn't accomplish her mission. [He] Just took the weapon from her, pushed her on the bed."

"Later on that day, walking down the street, [there's a] guy sitting on a roof. Starts shooting at me. I'm standing across the street, so I shot him a couple times and that was pretty much the end of that." Later on another guy shot at Whittle, and he shot back and ended that little firefight.

Not using any notes, PFC Whittle sometimes jumped back to earlier events. One was a VBIED attack on a convoy along "No-Name Road." He said it happened before the big attacks in April. 155mm artillery rounds were placed under a car, destroying the car, but not did not damage any Marine vehicles nearby.

Another IED explosion came when he was returning from the Agricultural Center. He saw a patrol from Echo Company in the area. They heard a large explosion, and saw a huge fireball. They then just ran back to the hanger bay. He helped some of the wounded Marines, one of them was seriously mangled. He had never seen wounds so severe on another Marine. Some had bad facial wounds, others had chunks of metal sticking out, and then came the body bags of the dead Marines.

With pride, PFC Whittle noted that 4th Platoon rarely calls for a QRF when it gets into contact, preferring to suppress the enemy by itself. One day they were called out, and he saw an orange vehicle with no seats, and said, "That vehicle looks really suspicious." His team leader looked at him like he was stupid, but Whittle said to him, "I think that's a vehicle-borne IED. 'Says, like where?' Turns his head, and like two seconds it [the VBIED] blows up." No one was hurt except for the Corpsman who had a small piece of shrapnel in his lower lip. They went to the area, and saw a guy dressed in all black standing in a grassy field. They suspected that he might have been the triggerman for the VBIED. Whittle was told to fire a warning shot at the man, and he did. The man did not move from the spot. He fired another warning shot at the man, who ducked, then stood back up.

They went back to their Humvee, and found a chunk of metal the size of a basketball stuck in the vehicle. It should have hit one of the Marines, Gianalla [*sic*], but did not. Whittle said that a small piece of shrapnel from the VBIED stuck in that Marine's personal bible that he carried with him. Whittle himself has been struck by small pieces of shrapnel, but none required serious medical treatment.

Another Marine at an Observation Post (OP) was hit and knocked back by a small arms round that hit his SAPI plate. Whittle said that he could hear this Marine saying, "What the fuck! What the fuck!" as he was stunned into full awake mode. He said, "Man, it doesn't even hurt, it just pisses you off!"

Currently 4th Platoon had a schedule that included Day Operations, Night Operations, QRF, Security, and Day Off. They were supposed to get a day off every eight days. When out on Day Ops or Night Ops, they are out for 24 hours. In the last few weeks, he said that the Marines are getting "Ran down" from the tempo and lack of sleep. They man an OP at the Agricultural Center and the Echo OP, and sometimes an OP at the Agricultural Center. They share turns at the government center OP with Fox Company and Weapons Company.

He said that sometimes calls come in from the Iraqi Police (IPs) alerting them to IEDs which may be setups for ambushes. What the Marines have done on occasion is to call the Iraqi Police and tell them to check out a suspected IED in an area where the Marines have an OP. The call will come back that the IPs have checked out the site, even though the Marines on the OP never saw the IPs there. The Marines then know that the first call was a setup for a possible ambush.

PFC Whittle said that on the other hand, he has met IPs who really do care about doing their job correctly, and who want a better life in Ramadi. At the government center, the Marines in Golf Company there had gotten shot at from the street. "And, they [insurgents] start shooting at this IP. And this IP chases this guy down, and he starts beating him in the back of the head with an AK." Another time, an IP chased a guy dressed in black down an alleyway, and came back with two guys. He told the Marines he didn't want their help. Whittle said this made him feel that some Iraqis do care.

On top of their "house" here at Combat Outpost, Golf Company Marines constructed six really good observation posts, complete with sandbagged walls. They joked that they would never use them. Then on July 21 the insurgents began to shoot at them from buildings across the street. The Agricultural Center got attacked, and mortars struck Combat Outpost. The enemy knew that the QRF could not launch out under mortar fire. The Marines there ended up shooting lots of ammo, including several drums of SAW ammo. On security that day, Whittle got to shoot a .50 cal machine gun for the first time. He did not go out and fight in Ramadi. There were also many IEDs set out along area roads. Many Marines became heat casualties that day.

Yesterday, when I got to Combat Outpost, the Marines here got intel reports to expect a big attack today. Whittle said that every time they get intel that something's going to happen, nothing does!

He praised the leadership in the 4th Platoon. One of the sergeants picked up his rank in less than two years. "We got luck 'cause we have outstanding squad leaders." He described an incident that happened on April 7: "There was an ambush set up for us. And we see the ambush, and we know we're about to get hit really hard. My squad leader looks back at us, and everybody's thinkin', 'What the hell are we gonna do?' We know we're gonna run across this field and get ambushed so that, we had to get to the MRE [Meals Ready-to-Eat] supply point. I just remember Sergeant looking back, with his devilish smile. He looked forward, looked back. He says, 'We're assaulting through. Run like hell!' And we just took off running across this damn thing. We were getting, they're shooting at us. Rounds impacting everywhere. It was a long, it was about 300 meters we had to run through this ambush. And then a huge ambush. We get in the thing, he just got this smile, like, 'Yeah, I told ya!' Somehow he knew we were gonna make it across that, even though we didn't think so! Everybody made it. It was a good day!" Whittle, the point man, didn't think they would make it.

PFC Whittle personally has not seen much use of the helicopter gunships. On April 6 and 7, and July 21, he has seen them, but felt that they should be used more. He also felt that he could have used a lot more training for himself before he deployed. He spent a week training in Military Operations in Urban Terrain (MOUT), but over here as point man, by his estimate he has been involved in clearing at least a thousand buildings. "Now I know a lot about MOUT. I've actually done it in a combat zone, and been shot at while doing it." He said that some of the trainers did not really know how things would be here. Also, the Army units did not give them a lot of intel about the area. Now they know what they are doing, but the enemy is also adjusting on the fly to the Marines. He also said he would like to have had more PT back in the States. They did run in their gear, doing at least three miles a day. He said that the heat factor here adds a lot of stress in any movement. He says that even trying to run around inside this firm base in the heat was draining, and he is a good runner.

Private First Class Christopher Lee Ferguson
Rifleman and Humvee Driver, 4th Platoon, Golf Company, 2/4

Ferguson described the intense fighting in Ramadi on April 6 and 7 and how the platoon later changed its tactics during patrols and convoys as they adapted to the techniques of the insurgents in Ramadi. En route to a fight near the Ramadi Agricultural Center, his Humvee passed an abandoned car that was actually a VBIED. The car detonated as two other Humvees behind Ferguson's passed it, but no Marines were seriously injured at that time.

PFC Ferguson joined the Marine Corps on June 2, 2003. After recruit training and the School of Infantry (SOI), he arrived in the Fleet Marine Force to join Golf Company, 2/4, on December 12. He trained with them for about two months prior to deploying to Iraq. He referred to this time of training as a privilege for him, as there were "drops" of brand-new Marines just out of SOI within weeks of Golf Company's deployment. He noted how Golf Company reorganized to have four line (infantry) platoons by dividing up Weapons Platoon. He said, "It's a good idea. It's worked out great here." Ferguson is an 0311 (infantryman), but he was also trained as an Assault Man, and served as a Humvee driver for 4th Platoon.

When they arrived in Kuwait, they continued training until crossing into Iraq. They rehearsed Military Operations in Urban Terrain (MOUT) and convoy training. "I look at when we first came up here, how naive we were. None of us had been in combat before. Or what it was like. We trained real hard on figuring out what to do, but we didn't know what to expect until the actual time came."

They sandbagged their 7-ton trucks for the trip, and painted wooden panels green to look like armor. It was a long, hot convoy. They rode high in the vehicles, and really did not know what to expect. They had no enemy contact on the convoy. They expected to spend a day or so at Junction City in Ramadi, but when they arrived, they were sent over to Combat Outpost Ramadi within hours. 4th Platoon was the advance platoon to the Combat Outpost. Ferguson said that they were supposed to take over security before the rest of Golf Company arrived. He said that the Marines had strict Rules of Engagement, but when they did the first Left-seat, Right-seat rides with the Army, all of the Army observation posts (OPs) would "open up" when taking even a few "pop shots." When the Army hit an IED, they would spray the area with gunfire. Marines had been trained to look for specific targets. Now, after almost six months here themselves, the Marines find themselves responding with overwhelming force at times.

Two weeks after arrival in Ramadi, they did their first operation, a government center security convoy. Ferguson explained, "We were in four Humvees, high backs, which were lightly armored. They had the sandbags and wood, pretty much. We didn't have a lot of armor. It was an IED behind a brick wall. I believe it was a brick wall, or bicycle IED. It hid, can't remember how many 155 rounds. We started using the benches on the Humvee, we didn't know what to expect, we got no contact. It was the Humvee behind me that got hit. We stopped, ran out, and ... everyone was pretty shell-shocked. 'Cause that was three or four casualties: Corporal McPherson, PFC Zimmerman, and Lance Corporal Harrison. They all got hit." That made them realize the dangers of an IED. They wanted to improve the protection on their Humvees.

Ferguson said that 4th Platoon was slow getting into its first contact. Their first big contact came on April 6 and 7, when they were the company's Quick Reaction Force (QRF). 3rd Platoon was out on patrol and had gotten hit really bad, were pinned down and taking massive casualties. Echo Company was also taking casualties in their area of operations. "We proceeded to fight our way through to get to 3rd Platoon." The firefight was ongoing. 4th Platoon finally got to the area and the enemy was still shooting at 3rd Platoon. Then the enemy got up and left.

"Our platoon had to go out that night. And it was a Contact Patrol, just to see if we could get contact, just to see how the enemy would do at night. We went out there, and that was just the most gnawing feeling. You didn't even hear a dog bark out there. It was dead, there was no one out there. Lights were dim. Walking, and all you can hear is the grass, kick the grass, and you didn't hear nothing. We set in at a cemetery, see if we could hear any noises, gunshots, or anything like that. But we didn't hear nothing. So it was a gnawing feeling."

Ferguson said that on April 7 the Rules of Engagement (ROEs) changed: "Anyone on a roof with a weapon, you kill. Anyone that seemed hostile, you shot. And pretty much the entire city, I'd say, was hostile. It was pretty tense, [we'd] never felt so scared in our lives. There were bullets everywhere. Not one single casualty that day." Some Marines suffered shrapnel wounds, and many won Purple Hearts. Lance Corporal Miller took a round to the back that hit a SAPI plate, and he had some shrapnel to his Achilles tendon, but he kept fighting the whole day. Ferguson heard reports of hundreds of enemy killed during these two days of fighting.

After these two days, Golf Company did lots of *County Fair* and *Bug Hunt* Operations. They would go into houses and search for weapons. Each house was allowed to keep one AK-47. The city of Ramadi got quiet after April 10, he felt that the people there were in shock at the violence of those days.

Another day of contact happened when they were patrolling up towards the government center in Ramadi. As they were going through the cemetery, machine guns opened up on them. Marines hid for cover behind tomb stones. The enemy had set into an L-shaped ambush, shooting at the Marines from the east and north. Enemy shooters were on top of four-story buildings. Ferguson said that half of his squad was in the cemetery, and the other half was on the road. The other squad from 4th Platoon was behind the building and began to clear this building where that the enemy was using to fire from. The enemy escaped from the building.

PFC Ferguson also had pictures of a Humvee that was destroyed by a VBIED. The driver was a good friend of his, but was uninjured by the blast. He said that now when traveling in the Humvees, they no longer sit on the benches. They ride on the floor, with just their eyes looking out over the sides. He also said that Marines noticed that IED blasts would often come in through the wheel wells.

Since then, they have taken some of the older armor from vehicles and placed it over the wheel wells.

Ferguson said that the Marines have also adapted their patrolling techniques based on experiences here. "You get contacts. What was hurtin' us most was, we were out in the open. And they were in elevated positions. So, when you're foot patrolling and you get contact, I mean, where are you gonna go? Hide behind a pile of rocks, a door in the alleyway. So we changed our tactics to: We get contact—take cover, fire back, breach the nearest house. Fortify the house, go to the top of the roof, shoot back that way. And then go in the next house. That's how we gained our ground. Move up, get back on their level." He said this helped to minimize casualties.

Patterns were often hard to avoid. He said that on the day of the VBIED, the Marines had passed over the same route many times. Marines reacted well, but it was a shock to see the casualties that day.

Currently, 4th Platoon mostly covered the observation posts along the Main Supply Routes. They only do patrols to and from the OPs, and have largely stopped the presence patrols in the city. One OP took an RPG attack from a taxi stand. The shrapnel from one RPG wounded one of the Marines. One day, two RPGs and lots of small arms fire came from a corner by the taxi stand, so the Marines hit it with four SMAW rockets and three rounds from an AT4. They had about eight enemy killed there. The taxi stand was used again by enemy to shoot at the Marine OP. Eventually, Ferguson said that the locals moved the taxis away from the stand, as they apparently were getting fed up with the damage brought on by the insurgent fighters. Some civilians even began to call in with information about planned attacks.

The enemy observed that when they would shoot up the Agricultural Center, a Marine QRF would come out in Humvees. After weeks of this, they shot at the Agricultural Center, and a QRF went out via the shortest, most often taken route there. "They set off a VBIED, and I was the lead vehicle on that. Come off the Round, 297, where we cut across, going the oncoming lane. 'Cause we try to do different things. Well just before the end of our road here, there was this taxi just sittin' on the side of the road. And, I thought in my mind, you know, car's kinda outta place, there's no one around. Just broke down. There's no one in it. And I pass it, we're gonna take this corner kinda sharp, get away from this car. Any parked car is suspicious. So we took the curb a little bit, turned sharp, continued on. Was like, well, maybe it wasn't nothin'. They were waiting for the third and fourth vehicle. And they detonated it. And there's nothin' left of this car but the engine block. And it blew up right next to our Humvees. All we got was a total of four tires blown out on both Humvees. And some eardrums. And some whiplash. That was about it. I mean, no one got hurt." Only one Corpsman got some debris to his eyelid.

One of the Up-armored Humvees, called a "Cadillac" by the Marines, had three tires blown out, and another Humvee had one flat tire. The bulletproof glass protected the driver and assistant driver.

Meanwhile, back at Combat Outpost Ramadi, two guys drove up near the front gate and got out and left the vehicle there. The Marines there blew up the car with a Javelin missile. Ferguson said that all of these actions in a single day showed how the enemy had planned a large, coordinated attack on the Marines operating out of the Combat Outpost. "Only thing that made that day fun and exciting was that no one got hurt." Ferguson said that all the Marines knew that they should change up routes that they take, take different routes for even routine missions.

The fighting on July 21 began when the advance party and incoming commander from 2/5 was doing a leader's reconnaissance of Ramadi. He was videotaping routes and areas, and an IED hit his Humvee. That attack was now on tape.

The QRF left Combat Outpost, and had contact as soon as they passed the gate. Soon, Weapons Company told 1st Platoon that enemy fighters had gone into a particular building. According to Ferguson, on clearing this building, 1st Platoon found windows that had been sandbagged, and they found about 20 AKs, 12 RPGs, and five wounded insurgents. They also found some flak jackets, a .30 caliber machine gun and a .50 caliber machine gun. There were also thousands of rounds of ammunition. He said, "Holy cow. Glad they got them before they got to use it."

Finally, Golf Company had use of some air power. They used Cobra gunships in support of some of the fighting on the ground. Marines on the ground marked targets with smoke grenades so the Cobras could shoot. He said that we need to use more air power.

PFC Ferguson said that he expected to go to war when he joined the Marine Corps. "I was just tired of watching the news, and seeing all of those soldiers getting hurt. All this stuff. I was like, can't wait to go." After SOI, only 12 of these graduates went to 2/4. And 2/4 was scheduled to deploy to Iraq.

When he returns home, he was scheduled to go to MOUT school. Many of the senior Marines in the company would be leaving active service (EAS). He sees himself as using much of his experiences here to make him a better instructor. He felt that even some of the training not directly used was useful in preparing the Golf Company Marines for what they have done here.

Living conditions at Combat Outpost Ramadi have been spartan, and they were looking forward to going home, much as the Army units that were here when they arrived. Ferguson anticipated getting home and going deer hunting.

Mortar hits on the camp have gotten more accurate lately. There were already rumors that 2/4 would return to Iraq in September 2005.

Golf Company shared this Combat Outpost with Echo Company. Echo has had worse experiences with explosions according to Ferguson.

He also noted that in April, the fighting in Fallujah got all of the press coverage, yet here in Ramadi, 2/4 fought door to door through the whole city. The Marines here wanted everybody to know about what they were doing. Ferguson said that the press always emphasizes the negative, for instance when a Marine is killed, and does not mention the large number of enemy fighters killed. He said that former Marine officer Oliver North, then working for Fox News was here a few days ago. (I briefly met North that week at the battalion CP at Junction City.) North rode in a Marine convoy hit by an IED, and the Marines fought a firefight. His report gave the total results of the fight, including the number of enemy that the Marines killed. Ferguson was glad to read that account.

This was his first deployment, and PFC Ferguson was glad to have this as his first. He felt that this would help him to lead the Marines who will be under him. He also liked the fact that the Marines here have access to the internet, and often get to call home on a satellite phone. When talking to his mom, she tells him that the news reports talk about the fighting, but Ferguson told her that the Marines with him have not been seriously hurt. Ferguson remained a motivated Marine. He wanted to kill the enemy so that he can stop them.

He described an incident when a sniper was shooting at him when he was in a 7-ton truck. He and several Marines were shot at, but not hit, by this shooter. He noted that the day the Army left Combat Outpost, they got hit by an IED. Ferguson said that everyone here remains alert at all times, even as they begin to look forward to leaving.

Private First Class Peter Joseph Flom
Rifleman, 3rd Platoon, Golf Company, 2/4

This young Marine was on his first combat deployment. In March he participated in security and route recon patrols on foot in Ramadi without enemy contact. Full-blown urban combat hit on April 6, and he described the difficulty in finding enemy who were shooting from positions hidden in city buildings. He had the M203 40mm grenade launcher on his M16, and used "Kentucky Windage" to hit targets. Several Marines in his squad were killed that day. In July he was in a Humvee with his platoon commander and had an RPG rocket skid under the vehicle without detonating.

PFC Flom enlisted on April 16, 2003, and graduated recruit training on September 11, 2003. He did the School of Infantry (SOI) at San Diego and then reported to 2/4, just before the work-up to Iraq began. The last big train-up was at March Air Force Base. He flew into Kuwait for a few weeks where they did lots of immediate action drills to prepare for the convoy into Iraq, and reviewed some other training.

Despite his relative youth, he was actually more experienced than some of the brand-new Marines who joined the battalion less than a month before the deployment.

For the move into Iraq, he said, "Actually, our platoon was tasked with security for the Air Wingers [Marine Aviation units]. It was us and Weapons [Company], I think it was just a platoon from Weapons. We were separated from our company. We were like the mobile security in case they got hit with an IED or anything like that. So we moved by 7-tons up here." It took about a day and a half on the road. They first went to Al Taqaddum Air Base, then came to Combat Outpost Ramadi.

As the leaders did the Left-seat, Right-seat turnover rides with the Army here, the Marines in Golf Company prepared to take over the observation posts and switch out the security. Once the Army left, the platoons and squads began to take over the patrols in March. Flom went out mostly on security patrols and route recon patrols. They did these patrols on foot.

His first contact with the enemy came on April 6. "It was an ambush, sir. It was at least a three-way, if not a 360 ambush. Small arms at first, later on in the engagement, maybe a half hour, RPGs started. At first, we were doing a foot patrol to the government center. It was just a squad-sized element. We were pushing down side streets in the residential areas. We received first contact from the front. They just opened up with AKs. We immediately took cover. Suppressed fire. Got accountability of everyone. Just continued to fight for an hour and a half, two hours, at least, before the QRF [Quick Reaction Force] got there. Everyone was getting hit that day, sir. It was like a jihad or something. So that's why QRF was tied up. Battalion QRF was getting hit; Porcupine, Echo Company was getting hit. That day was crazy. We took two KIA and three WIA." These were casualties in his squad alone! "There was already one WIA from 3rd Squad. They were at the government center, which is where we were going."

Flom believed that 3rd Squad got hit first, and his squad was almost doing a movement to contact to go out and help them.

"Finally, the QRF got there. I think actually the Army got there first. Bradleys rolled up and the enemy egressed to wherever they go. [We] Loaded up the casualties and continued on. For the greater part of that day, just searching houses, trying to find weapons, enemy." They had no enemy contact during these searches. His squad finally returned to Combat Outpost in late afternoon. The initial contact had started at about 1100.

I asked if he could see any of the shooters. "At first all I could see was the rounds impacting all around us. It's a damn miracle I wasn't hit, sir. That was the initial contact. After that, I finally saw some of these ... guys. Obviously, took 'em out. What I could. I mean, urban warfare's tough. It's so hard to get good 'eyes on' 'em, 'cause they can just be shooting from any window or any balcony area. Definitely any time I could acquire a target I did so, and took care of it. But, it was tough, sometimes."

I noticed the M203 grenade launcher attachment on his rifle. I asked about if he sometimes acted as a grenadier. "That's correct, sir. I love that thing. It's a good weapon." At first on April 6, he engaged only with his M16. Later when he had some time, he loaded the breach and took on some enemy on rooftops with the 40mm grenades out of the launcher. He did not use the grenade launcher's sight. "It was definitely 'Kentucky Windage.' I wasn't about to take the time to look down the sights on that." He said that after that the grenade launcher sight broke, he took it off the launcher and hasn't used it since. He says it usually takes about one round to get onto a target.

When the remains of the squad returned to Combat Outpost on April 6, PFC Flom said, "It was weird, sir. There was about six of us left, with our platoon sergeant.

We just kinda ... we were in shock, I suppose. Just kinda ... I don't know ... sat there, had a cigarette and looked at each other. I think we talked about it a little bit. But we didn't go in any deep conversation. Just kinda small talk."

The next day, April 7: "I believe that [was] the day we did a *County Fair*. It was a battalion-size, basically just a sweep through the whole city. I believe it was just south of the MSR [Main Supply Route], which is where we were hit. Was three companies, I believe, and Weapons was in support or cordoning off. Us [Golf Company], Fox, and Echo, we just swept through the city. Clearing houses, just a big chunk of the city, just cleared that solid chunk. Looking for weapons, IED-making material, insurgents, anything like that."

He believed that they found some weapons caches. Some individuals were also detained.

Golf Company continued on a four-day rotation: Day Operations, Night Operations, QRF or Quick Reaction Force, Security when they took the posts. During the Day Ops, they did IED sweeps along the roads, using attached engineers up front. They have gear at the government center. For Night Ops, they did mostly security patrols. QRF duty allowed them to wait at Combat Outpost. One squad gets stood up and waits at the company command post while the rest of the platoon goes out on a mission or patrol.

Things quieted down for a while, with only an occasional IED hit or ambush. The Outpost sometimes got mortared.

Then three days ago, July 21, the company got into a big fight. Since the turnover of sovereignty the Marines had turned over most of the street security to local Iraqi forces. Golf Marines have mostly gone out to man OPs and watch for IED emplacers along the MSRs.

"I guess this one building, they don't like us being in there. Every day they'd hit it with an RPG. One of our guys from our platoon was out on a balcony and gets hit by a sniper. So every day this place gets hit. Other day [July 21], a convoy's going by and it gets hit by an IED and small arms, so we went out to react to that. Turns out it was a full-blown ambush. We pulled up, we kinda, we pulled off the MSR, it was kind of a diagonal alley that came into the MSR there."

An AK kicked off the ambush. "I could see the muzzle flash coming right at us. It was probably the most helpless I've ever felt. And bein' in the Humvee, seeing that happen. And, uh, before you knew it, guy pulled front of the apartment with an RPG. Fired that at the Hummer." There were two Humvees: Flom's with the driver, the lieutenant, his squad leader and him; The 1st Squad was in the other Humvee, abreast of them. "And the RPG was fired, I think it bounced off the deck, kinda bounced right up underneath the Hummer right next to us, to the left of us. After that happened, finally got the Mark 19 cooking, firin' down that alley. We dismounted, laid down a base of fire down that alley. We ran across, busted in some gate, and we used that house as a casualty collection point."

He believed that out of the five Hummers there, three did not get hit. The Mark 19 gunner kept firing down the alley, and wound up blowing up a car. There were weapons on the car. "I think we musta got 'em as they were setting up or something. Because we lit this car on fire, because for the next 10 or 15 minutes you hear 'Boom!' You hear explosions. It musta been full of RPGs, mortars, grenades, whatever. And you could just hear the small arms cooking off in there, also. We definitely messed that up for them good there. The only casualties we took there was two, two wounded, had some pretty good shrapnel to the elbow and got peppered in the leg. Another was just kinda peppered in the arm there." They cas-evac'd these Marines right away. The initial contact lasted about 10 minutes.

3rd Platoon then did a mini sweep to the east. 2nd Squad found a huge weapons cache. They found 120mm mortar tubes, aimed at the Combat Outpost, and some RPGs launchers and AK rifles. They detained some Iraqis there and took the weapons and personnel back to Combat Outpost. He summed this up: "That was a lot of fun that day."

I asked him what changes he would recommend in training. He said that the immediate action drills are good. This makes actions instinctive, creating "muscle memory." There was not much to do to prepare for actual combat.

Also, this deployment was supposed to be a postwar operation, helping to get the populace back into the swing of things. The insurgents disrupted this. As for SASO efforts, PFC Flom said, "We definitely try to conduct some of that. Handing out soccer balls. I know our XO's been working with the governor, [or] whoever, givin' 'em money for their soccer stadiums and cleaning up their city. Trash disposal, and we're definitely trying to help these guys out."

Flom said that once when 1st Platoon was conducting an Information Operation, handing out soccer balls and pens, and pencils, when a guy popped up with an RPG and blew guys' legs off. That put a damper on these efforts.

PFC Flom did say thanks to all of the people back home who have been writing to him. "It's something me and the guys really look forward to is mail call. Just hearin' what's goin' on back home. Even if it's from somebody you don't know. Just a good uplift."

Private First Class Higinio Antuno Martinez
SAW Gunner, 3rd Platoon, Golf Company, 2/4

Martinez saw his first combat in Ramadi on April 6, 2004, when he was on a patrol that was drawn into a 360-degree ambush. His squad fought for hours while waiting for a Quick Reaction Force to get to it. For the rest of the month, Golf Company suspended squad-size patrols, and only sent platoon-size patrols into Ramadi.

PFC Martinez began, "When I came in first, sir, I planned on just being part of the infantry. I didn't really know that I was gonna end up here in Iraq." He knew that they would end up in Iraq, but not that it would be a war zone. He said that at boot camp, and additional training, he didn't think it would be as hard as it was, but felt now that it was worth it. He also said that the infantry is not for everybody, but it is for him. He started recruit training on June 23, 2003, and graduated September 19, 2003. During the School of Infantry (SOI) training, the instructors told them to train as if they were in a combat zone, because they soon would be in a combat zone. He then joined Golf Company, 2/4, and on March 19, 2004, he was in Kuwait, en route to a combat zone!

He arrived with Golf Company at Camp Wolverine, Kuwait, on March 20, 2004. The next day, they went to Camp Victory, and began lots of training to include immediate action drills, Military Operations in Urban Terrain (MOUT) training, ambush reaction drills, and convoy operations. Instead of the normal year-long work-up training for a deployment, Golf Company did it in three months.

"Our platoon was tasked on the convoy up here to escort the Air Wing. So we convoyed to the Air Wing Unit, then convoyed up here, which was a three or four-day convoy." When Golf Company got to Combat Outpost Ramadi, the NCOs and officers of the company went on familiarization rides to learn the area. Then the Marines of the company began to take over responsibility for security and patrolling. They went out into town to ensure that the locals knew that the Marines were here to replace the Army. He called it "A presence of force."

"The first encounter we had was on a Night Operations mission. There were said to be enemy insurgents coming in with weapons, so we patrolled south of the MSR [Main Supply Route] around the canal area. And north of the MSR to a bush line by the soccer stadium. We were gonna set up snap VCPs, search vehicles. That's when people started firing—it wasn't heavy fire, just a small contact. But that was our first enemy contact here."

The worst encounter here began on April 6. "We were patrolling down to the government center. The south end of Ramadi, south side of the MSR, by the soccer stadium. It was just a routine patrol to the government center. We had done it many times before. We started receiving pop shots, and we decided to chase the guy, see if we could catch him. And, he led us into a 360 ambush. We were pinned down, I'd say, for a good two and a half, three hours." 1st Squad was the only Marine element engaged at this point. He estimated that they faced a platoon-sized element. The enemy fired RPGs, grenades, small arms at them. "It was one of the biggest, if not the biggest firefight in Ramadi."

I asked about the use of his Squad Automatic Weapon (SAW). He replied, "It was difficult to see targets, but it was a very efficient weapon as to suppressing in order to move to a safer place." They moved into a house for cover.

"We had called out the QRF [Quick Reaction Force], and on the way out there, the QRF had also gotten contact. And they had also gotten pinned down. So, we had to wait for reinforcements."

At first, they were on the street there, and when they figured out the enemy contact came from the streets and rooftops, they planned to move down the streets and get to the government center. But every area was covered by enemy. "We'd try to move down one street, and, we'd get engaged. We'd try to move down an alleyway, and we'd get engaged. We were just pinned down in the middle of the road at first. And then, we just decided to break down a door, set up inside a house, see what we can do from there."

They had to set up a casualty collection point (CCP) because one of the Marines on their side of the squad's fight had gotten hit. On the other side of the road, they had one KIA and two other Marines wounded. "We had to set down some type of CCP so we can treat 'em. And that's exactly what we did."

Finally, another platoon from Golf Company showed up, clearing the roads and clearing houses. "They showed up about half an hour after we had called out QRF, 'cause they had also gotten pinned down. There were also Cobras [attack helicopters] flying around, supporting us. They [ground vehicles] came out, they picked up casualties. We came outta the house, and we started clearing down the road. While we're still clearing down the road, we're still receiving small pop shots."

Going down the road, Martinez saw the damage to cars and buildings that had been hit by both sides during the fighting. "There were bodies lying on the ground. It looked like all hell had broken loose. As we were moving down, we had vehicles with us as well. There were still pop shots going on, down alleyways. We still continued to take it to the enemy." They finally started loading up on vehicles and began to leave this area. They got back to Combat Outpost about 1800. The fighting had begun around 1130. They had left the Outpost at 0800 on foot that day.

On April 7, Martinez said, "We all went out as a company, see if we could get enemy contact. The enemy was still there, trying to give us all they got. But, we still took it to them, sir. We went and started clearing all areas, finding big weapons caches." He said that the fighting on the 7th was big, but not as big as on the 6th of April. Enemy fighters used small arms, RPGs and heavy machine guns, but the Marines killed many of them. Golf Company left around 1100 and returned about 1700. 3rd Platoon did not have any fighting on April 10.

After these days, squad patrols ended and instead they did platoon-size patrols. They stopped doing satellite patrolling too. If they got contact from a platoon-size element, they would respond with a platoon-size element. He said that about a month ago, they stopped the foot patrols in the area and have gone out to observation posts to keep observation on MSRs for convoys.

Two days ago, July 21, 2004, Marines at the Agricultural Center came under fire. Martinez said, "We went out there, about 1430, and came back at 2100. They [insurgents] were shooting all kinds of weapons. They were shooting RPGs, small mortar rounds, RPKs. Basically, we took it to the enemy once more, sir. Shooting enemies on rooftops, inside of buildings. Then we started clearing houses, finding weapons and men who were involved in the firefight, trying to hide." Marine helicopters again flew overhead, north of the MSR, looking for enemy on rooftops.

His platoon has been hit by IEDs. They have not been able to find the triggermen. Once when an IED went off near railroad tracks, they went to a berm and saw a group of men in an open area about 300 meters away. These men were hiding behind a tractor. They began running towards a canal area when the Marines shot at them.

Golf Company has been on standby for the past two days, anticipating a possible large attack. But things have mostly been quiet except for an occasional mortar round hitting outside the Combat Outpost.

PFC Martinez noted some Marines who have fought on, even when wounded during a firefight. On April 6, "There's some Marines there that got hit with a frag grenade, and also got hit with an RPG. Those Marines, to me, have set the example. One of 'em being Corporal Hayes, he was the 1st Team Leader, 1st Squad, 3rd Platoon. He had gotten hit with a frag, shrapnel, to the arm, the back, and the leg. And he still managed to bandage himself up, before the doc helped him. And he was still able to get up and get back in the firefight. Another Marine as well, one of our fallen Marines, PFC [Deryk L.] Hallal, who passed away on the 6th. He also put up a real good fight while he was gettin' bandaged up from the first shot he had gotten to the leg. He was still lying down while being bandaged up, and shooting at the enemy."

"Those Marines, for me, have really set the example. They made me realize that we are fighting for a reason, not just to fight."

"If there's one thing I've learned from everything here, [it's that] there are little things in life that we take for granted. People in the States should realize that we have it a lot easier than people do here. Freedom is a great thing, and it's part of the cause for us fighting."

He now realized that fighting for our country was a big cause, and he would not give it up for anything in the world.

I then met with Captain Kelly Royer. It was so rewarding to listen to this commander recount all that his company has been through. Echo Company, 2/4, has suffered 21 Marines killed since April 2004—the highest losses of any company over here to date in 2004. The city of Ramadi was not what intel had advised the Marine Corps it would be … An outstanding interview, and a great way to close out my interviews here in Iraq.

Captain Kelly Dean Royer
Commanding Officer, Echo Company, 2/4

On his arrival in Ramadi, departing Army forces warned Royer about a routine once-a-week mortar attack on the Combat Outpost. In his first Thursday here, mortar rounds hit the outpost, right on schedule. The next week he sent a force out to the origin of the mortar fire, which killed or captured the mortarmen and additional weapons.

Royer gave a detailed description of the intense fight that took place on April 6, 2004,
where one of his platoon commanders, a platoon sergeant, five junior Marines, and a
Navy Corpsman were killed in a single well-planned ambush by insurgents in Ramadi,
as well as two other junior Marines killed while reinforcing an attached Scout/Sniper
team that was under enemy attack as they lay in a covert Observation Post (OP). The
challenges of coordinating his dispersed platoons and working with other units from 2/4
were a clear example of the "fog of war." During another fight on April 10, his helmet
was forcefully hit by an enemy bullet. He borrowed an M203 launcher using its smoke
grenades to mark targets for Marine helicopters to hit.

Captain Royer had an unusual path to commanding a Marine Rifle Company.
"Originally I signed up for the United States Air Force back in 1985, the
enlisted program. Actually joined in 1986, served for six years on active duty.
Then served two years in the California Air National Guard. I had about a
two-year hiatus, with a civilian job and then considered the Marine Corps. I
was enlisted in the Air Force, I had finished my degree, and was excited about
an opportunity to command Marines. So, I went and spoke to the OSO, Officer
Selection Officer, and here I am today." He joined the Marine Corps in 1996
when he went to the Officers' Candidate School (OCS). He then completed The
Basic School (TBS), then the Infantry Officers' Course (IOC), and became a
platoon commander with Kilo Company, 3/5. After eight months as a platoon
commander, he became the executive officer for the Company for the remainder
of this two-year tour with 3/5.

Captain Royer then served at the School of Infantry on the west coast for three
years. He completed Expeditionary Warfare School (EWS) and joined 2/4. He
augmented the Division staff during Operation *Iraqi Freedom* in 2003 at Al Hillah,
also known as Camp Babylon. On return to CONUS, he became headquarters and
service company commander at 2/4 for four months. At the request of the battalion
commander, Lieutenant Colonel Paul Kennedy, he took command of Echo Company
only one week prior to deploying for OIFII.

"I really didn't know a lot about the company. I hadn't been with them, hadn't
trained with them." Captain Royer had helped facilitate some of 2/4's training
back in the States. After picking up command of Echo Company, he focused on
fundamentals he felt were important to success in Iraq while training in Kuwait.
These were things he had witnessed during his time in Iraq during OIF1: Things
like casualty evacuations, Rules of Engagement, Urban Patrolling, Low and High-
Intensity Room Clearing, and martial arts takedown techniques.

This led to a lot of high-intensity training during Echo Company's three weeks
in Kuwait prior to entering Iraq. Captain Royer said, "Didn't know much about
these boys, I had to test their mettle, and I had to ensure that they had the skill
set to accomplish the mission and survive in a combat environment, as I knew it."

To move into Iraq, Royer said, "We were part of a fly-in echelon. The bulk of the battalion, the main body, came up in two serials of a convoy. We departed about four days later on the fly-in echelon. Wherein I brought the remainder of H&S Company, elements of Weapons Company, and my entire company. We flew into Taqaddum Air Base, and from Taqaddum we were trucked over to Combat Outpost. Those elements that are not at Combat Outpost were trucked over to Hurricane Point."

I asked about briefings and turnover with the Army here. "The turnover with the Army was minimal. They were on their way out, virtually, on the night we made our leaders' recon. All the commanders came up, the battalion operations officer came forward, I believe the battalion logistics officer as well. We came forward, about a week, week and a half prior to the main body leaving, at Camp Victory, Kuwait. We spent hours with the gentleman whose area of operations, I understood, I would be taking over." Royer said that in fact he would eventually take over an area that had only been partially patrolled by the Army.

With Echo Company still in Kuwait, the Army 1st of the 124th, an infantry unit out of Florida, arrived there. Captain got Echo Company together long with the Army company commander, their Civil Affairs captain, as well as some squad leaders to address Echo Company and explain what Combat Outpost was about, the situation in Ramadi, and what they could expect on the ground here. Royer said, "It wasn't exactly what it turned out to be." For instance, this company commander told Captain Royer that the Army battalion had taken 50 casualties in the six months they had been here, none KIA. But it did not pan out this way for either Echo Company or Second Battalion, Fourth Marines (2/4).

Once here at Combat Outpost, Royer said, "Primarily, we focused on Main Supply Route [MSR], Improvised Explosive Device [IED] Clearing Operations. And we had about 15 kilometers of roadway that circled our area of operations. And early in the morning, we'd kick off the IED sweep. And we'd sweep the entire roadway for bombs that the insurgents might have placed during the day or at night."

"Along with that we conducted security patrols twenty-four-seven within our area of operations. Primarily boots on the ground, not in vehicles, which is something different from what the Army had conducted." The Army was mainly in vehicles. Royer said that the Marines wanted to meet the locals, and carry out the "No better friend, no worse enemy" slogan of the First Marine Division. "Also, understanding the IED threat, I didn't really want my men in vehicles. The temperatures weren't very high at that time, and I figured one of the best ways to stave off that type of threat is just not even be along the roadways. It's a pretty big task when you consider that the AO [area of operations] is 27 grid squares. [Each grid is 1,000 meters on a side.] My company AO, which is three times the size of the next company's AO, which geographically is the size of Fallujah. We also conducted what's called cordon, knock, and searches. It's basically a cordon and search, with the exception of kicking in the door. You'd knock, give them an opportunity to come to the door, and ask to come in the house. And, we've never been turned down. In those cases where they don't answer the door, then we have an alternate entry, say a secondary door, so that we don't go barging in the door we just knocked on. Because, you anticipate that someone's prepared to engage that 'fatal funnel.' So we'd go in that alternate hatch [door]." He said those were the primary taskers at that time. This lasted for about three months.

They changed the tactics for the IED sweeps, and then stopped them completely about a month and a half after arriving in Iraq.

He then outlined the fighting at the beginning of April.

"The deadliest day for Echo Company was the 6th of April. And I might add, it was one of the deadliest days for the enemy, as well. We had been taking IEDs in the western part of our AO, area of operations. So, I figured the enemy was putting these IEDs in at night. I reasonably assumed that the locals wanted us to be here, like they had in Hillah [in 2003]. So no way would they tolerate somebody putting bombs in, in broad daylight. Well, as we continued to conduct our sweep, and have eyes on that section of the roadway where they predominantly put the IEDs, they weren't putting in those IEDs at night. On the 5th [of April] I assigned a four-man sniper team to stay out for 48 hours, so they could actually see what was going on during the day. As well, that morning, I had sent the 1st Platoon minus to conduct the IED sweep. They conducted that sweep from the south, to the west, to the north, and then back to the south, and to the east. They had just, probably an hour before the first contact had passed by where the scout-snipers were. They didn't even see the scout-snipers when they passed through that area. They did find some IEDs, and waited EOD's [Explosive Ordnance Disposal] detonation of 'em. Then they [1st Platoon minus] pushed to the very northern portion of our AO, which is approximately five clicks [5,000 meters] from Combat Outpost. And they found some more IEDs. I think it was a 155 round and two 82mm rounds. So they were waiting there for EOD to show up."

"Meanwhile, I had a squad conducting a security patrol approximately four and a half kilometers due east of Combat Outpost. They had been out for approximately four hours, and were egressing back to the Combat Outpost, when they took some small arms fire from across the main road, which is Highway 10. We call it MSR Michigan. They took fire, they contacted my Combat Operations Center, or COC. I gathered together a Quick Reaction Force. I already had one Quick Reaction Force that was going to assist Golf Company. They were engaged in a firefight and needed a resupply of ammo and water. So I had two QRFs, Alpha and Bravo."

"On hearing that we were in a firefight, the platoon commander, Second Lieutenant John Wroblewski, came around the corner and asked what was goin' on and I told him. He said, 'Hey sir, I wanna get in the fight. I want to get down where I can give 'em a hand right now!'"

"I said, 'Okay, drop what you're doing, I'll let Golf Company know, and punch out the gate, and we'll be right in trace of you.' And it worked just like that. They punched out the gate. I got my QRF ready, and launched that QRF. So it was eight vehicles worth of men headed down there. We linked up with that squad, we cordoned the area with two QRFs and began to sweep through. As we swept through, on the northwestern portion of the cordon, Lieutenant Cogan, Tommy Cogan, who was on that portion of the cordon, said he needed the interpreter. I only had one at the time. So I ran down there with the interpreter to interrogate some suspects."

"As I got down there, I heard that my 'Headhunter' team [Scout-snipers] was coming under fire. I only had eight vehicles at that time. And, knowing it would take a long time to get this widely dispersed force back together, get 'em loaded into vehicles, get accountability, and move to the aid of Headhunter, I contacted my COC, spoke to my XO [executive officer], and said you have to get the battalion's QRF. Request battalion's QRF and send them out there to Headhunter."

"What ended up happening, the insurgent force, of approximately 12 to 15 men, I don't think they knew where my Headhunter team was, but they knew they were out there. Somebody had obviously reported it to them. And they began, on line, basically, to strafe the ground with their AK-47s. Scout-snipers engaged them, and started to kill them. At that time my XO ordered one squad from 1st Platoon minus to come from the northern part of the AO, and push down to the southwest to assist. Which they did. And they engaged in the fight. It was at that location, however, that I lost two of my Marines. And had three more injured."

Battalion sent "Whiskey" (Weapons) Company, 2/4's QRF, known as "Reaper," to assist. Captain Royer believed that they came up a southerly route. Also, the Army Brigade (1st BCT) commander with a QRF had also shown up on the scene. Golf Company's executive officer had sent the remainder of headquarters platoon, and an ambulance, and one other Humvee for the rescue. When they got on scene, however, all of the enemy fighters had been either killed or repelled, so they assisted in sweeping the area.

Then Captain Royer heard additional gunfire where the initial squad had been engaged. "So I then instructed Lieutenant Cogan along with his QRF, to search to the northwest, about 750 meters, which is the area we thought the fire was coming from. So we pushed to the north, northwest, and searched that area out to about 800 meters. And realized that the fires that we heard were more than likely the fires that were being engaged by the Scout-snipers, the squad from 1st Platoon, at that point probably Reaper and Brigade."

"So, with nothin' up in that area, we began to push back to where the initial cordon was, by the arches. Which is where the squad initially took fire. We were moving back, I got a call on the radio that that remaining squad in the northern part of the AO that was sitting on those IEDs, basically in a 360, waiting for EOD. That they were under a severe enemy attack. So, I got on the radio, and I contacted

Lieutenant Wroblewski, and I told him to gather up all eight vehicles, and the remaining men that were on that cordon. To link up with us at Check Point 338, which is the intersection of Routes Gypsum and Nova. Meanwhile, myself and Lieutenant Cogan and his QRF, we ran, to the northeast. To that linkup point. And just as we were heading northeast, uh, I saw vehicles starting to go by. And I contacted Lieutenant Wroblewski and told him to stop. Well, in the amount of time it took me to get him on the radio, communicate to stop, and for him to get on his PRR, which is a little, tiny, like, walkie-talkie, and talk to those in the lead vehicles, it was too late."

"The first two vehicles in that eight-vehicle convoy, which were Humvees, and they did not have ballistic windshields. They had the makeshift armor on them. They had ended up at the checkpoint, which is a marketplace. That day there was no one in the marketplace but insurgents. And, that's when the tremendous, intense, enemy fire picked up. It was the loudest thing I've heard since I've been a Marine. You could hear machine guns all over the place, and explosions. It was just an incredible volley of fire. We, at this point, were running as fast as we could, to directly across to the east in order to flank whoever they were engaging."

"As we crossed the road, we started taking fire from, uh, basically all directions. That's when I realized, this was something huge. This was, I mean, all said and done, it was an enormous kill zone: Approximately 450 meters long, by 200, 250 meters wide. And they had men all over the place. Primarily, we were taking fire, as we crossed the road, from the rooftops. We began, I began to push Lieutenant Cogan to the north, to secure some houses and some high ground. As he pushed to the north he began taking fire. Returned the fire, but was able to close on and secure a house. And then basically move house-to-house towards the east. As he pushed through about three houses, we started detaining individuals. Came under an intense volume of machine gun fire. And as I moved upstairs, to establish a COC, CP [command post], whatever, I looked to the front where there was a yard. It looked like we were taking mortar rounds, but in fact, it was RPGs."

"All the while I'm on the radio trying to gain comm [communications] with higher [battalion], and gain comm with that platoon that's in the kill zone. It was extremely difficult, being as far away as we were, with a man-portable PRC 119 [tactical radio]. Comm was intermittent, at best."

"I then tried to get a hold of that platoon commander, Lieutenant Wroblewski, via PRR. I couldn't get a hold of him. I then heard over the radio, over the PRR, they had taken, the platoon commander was hit. I tried to get more information, was unable to get any comm at that point. With that unit, it took, probably, 40 minutes to an hour. We continued to push east. When we started taking that heavy volume of machine gun fire and the RPGs, I grabbed Sergeant [Ronnie G.] Ramos, who was with Weapons Platoon. And I had Lieutenant Cogan provide him with suppressive fires to the east, while I sent him [Ramos] to the north to envelope the machine gun position. When he arrived there though, the [enemy] machine gun was gone, the [enemy] machine gunner was gone, and there was just brass [shell casings]."

"So we continued, he pulled back to my position, we pushed to the north, and then pushed back to the east. It was sort of like a stair step—step to the east, step to the north, step to the east, step to the north."

"There was some suspect houses to our eastern flank once we secured a couple of houses, and established a CP. I sent Lieutenant Cogan's QRF to investigate these houses, from which we had taken fire earlier. As he swept through the houses, he was unable to find any insurgents or really any weapons. But what he did find were anti-personnel IEDs. They were in the trees. And they [the insurgents] had taken hand grenades at about face level, and place them by string from tree to tree, with a trip wire. I think he found three of those. We continued to push through to the north again, through some houses."

"What I forgot to mention, probably 30 minutes prior to us establishing that final OP [Observation Post], that final CP on that northernmost house, we had heard tracked vehicles coming up from our rear. I believe they were [Army] Bradleys, the armored personnel carriers, not infantry fighting vehicles. They pushed through the kill zone and engaged the enemy. And, assisted the Marines that were on the scene with the fight, as well as collecting up any casualties."

"We then secured the entire market area, which is what's at 338. Good 360 perimeter security, and began to push through to identify if there were any enemy KIAs, WIAs, or still any insurgents in the area. As well as locate any weapons that they may have left behind. We did find a DShK, basically an enemy .50 caliber machine gun. Found vehicles loaded with RPGs, RPG boosters, PE 4 explosives, thousands of rounds of AK-47 and RPK, PKC ammo. What we really didn't find a lot of, was brass. Until we started to look on rooftops, which is generally how they like to fight."

Royer explained some traits about the enemy here. "There's three things the enemy here likes to do: Number one is, they like to catch you in an ambush. Wherein they have the advantage of surprise, at least the initial volume of fire; They like to engage you in a cross fire, so you have rounds coming all around you and you're not really certain where they're [the insurgents] at; And lastly, they like to engage you from the high ground. Most of the houses in the area, in Iraq, have a patio upstairs. A walled patio upstairs. And they use that to their advantage."

Captain Royer said that some of the things that intimidate the enemy fighters are: Tracked vehicles; Anything that sounds like armor; And any air assets, whether fixed-wing or rotary-wing.

"In talking to my men though, they said that it was approximately 90 men, enemy insurgents that established that ambush. They said that they saw many of them with bags attached to their AK-47s, as though to catch the brass after they fired their weapons."

"I think that the enemy that day, there were definitely some who were professionals. They were trained. I say that by the depth of their kill zone. There was definitely a focus to their kill zone, but they also had security for their ambush. The fact that they had their heavy machine gun ... along the axis of the kill zone was impressive. They engaged from the high ground. They had put engine blocks up on the roof to hide behind. Also, they swept through a portion of the kill zone, and were actually able to take weapons from my Marines. Though, they didn't mutilate the bodies, they didn't disrespect the bodies at all. They knew what they wanted, they went down as close as they could, and were able to take some of the weapons off the Marines. Other things like bayonets, compasses, and night vision devices."

The enemy also had a plan to egress from the area. Not all of their people or vehicles were able to leave, however. Royer felt sure that the enemy's vehicles were staged and ready to go. He was not certain how many enemy they killed that day, saying, "I do know we collected four bodies. And we detained one non-injured individual who I believe was one of the insurgents. But, my men told me as the insurgents would die, that somebody else would come up and grab their weapon and begin to engage. And that as they pulled out, they took the bodies with them." Captain Royer said that at first it was hard for him to believe this, but on reflection said that we take our deceased as well. Also, he has seen this happen himself. In another big fight on April 10, he saw four dead enemy. An hour later, when he returned to the same area, those bodies were gone.

Echo Company cleaned up the ambush area, and Captain Royer heard from the battalion operations officer that the enemy liked to egress to the east. Some of Royer's Marines also confirmed seeing fighters moving east and going into some houses about 500 meters from the ambush site. The Marines searched these houses, but found nothing. They came back to Check Point 338 to wait for EOD to dispose of ordnance and ammo. Up north, one of Echo's squads fought with some enemy. EOD disposed of some IEDs for that squad, then came back to Check Point 338 to detonate some unstable enemy munitions. This done, Echo Company returned to Combat Outpost. From the time of the first shots that day until returning to Combat Outpost was about eleven-and-a-half-hours.

Royer paused and then said, "On that day ... I took 10 friendly killed, the battalion took 12."

He paused again, and then said, "I had ... two that were killed reinforcing scout-snipers, and eight, in Check Point 338. It was primarily the lead vehicle. He got hit by that heavy machine gun, the initial barrage of fire. There were eight friendlies in that vehicle, and two men that we had detained down by the arches. Three individuals were able to get out of the vehicle, three were able to fight their way out of the vehicle. Two were killed after they exited the vehicle. One survived the day. The remaining five friendlies that were in the vehicle were killed in action.

And the two detainees that were in the back of the vehicle were killed by the insurgents as well."

"The eighth individual that was killed that day, started out as a wound, to the face. He was shot in the face. It was the platoon commander [Lieutenant Wroblewski]. He tried to get on the radio, contact me. The only word he got out was 'Six.' Which, the commanders are usually known, like I'm, call sign, 'Porky,' I'm Porcupine Six. He was shot in the face. He was medevacked … but later … died of his wounds that evening."

"So it was a, it was one a hell of a day, in the Porcupine AO. We got hit in the very southernmost part of our AO, then the southeastern part, then the western part, then the northern part, and then the far eastern part. Weapons [Platoon], I believe, was engaged in the west as well. And, uh, that's the 6th of April, sir."

I asked about fighting on April 7. Captain Royer said that it was a day of intense fighting for Golf Company, which also operates out of Combat Outpost. "But for us, it was a day to reset. We still had missions we were conducting, security patrols. You know, after that day, we didn't conduct squad-sized security patrols. One of the things I have yet to mention, you talk about the intel. There's a lot of talk, prior to us coming over here about the ten-second fire fight. And, sure, that happens. But no one anticipated, through intelligence sources, that a fight like that [on April 6] was gonna happen in Ramadi. In fact, upon our leaders' recon, one of the company commanders from our battalion, had commented that he thought Ramadi was sort of the model city leading towards democracy. The one key phrase that I still remember to this day was, 'Ramadi is a benign environment.' Well, nobody feels that way anymore."

"Our next major contact would be on the 10th. That was a big fight as well. On the 8th we conducted a sweep of Golf Company's AO, where they had taken contact on the 7th. That was known as *County Fair Two*. The 9th [April] was a refit day for everybody from *County Fair Two*. The entire battalion was involved in *County Fair Two*. Then on the 10th, we conducted Operation *Bug Hunt*." The entire battalion came into Echo Company's area of operations, assigned areas to sweep, and Royer said they swept every house that day.

They had targeted houses to kick off *Bug Hunt*. "My company had three targeted houses, as well as, we were going to employ indirect fire assets to sort of intimidate the mujahideen. So I left one platoon, my Weapons Platoon, which is really a platoon minus, at the very southern part of my AO, near the major cemetery that's here in my AO. They launched mortars from that position just as we were kicking in the doors of these houses. And these [houses] were geographically separated, so I had one platoon hit each house. They were all probably 500 meters to a kilometer from each other. One house was IED-making insurgents. One house contained criminal ICDC, Iraqi Civil Defense Corps insurgents. And one house was the house of, purportedly, corrupt sheik. That day I went with 3rd Platoon. Being that we're culturally sensitive, I wanted to ensure that since they were taking down the sheik's house, that it was done in the proper fashion."

The Army Brigade fired artillery illumination rounds, and Captain Royer had his 60mm mortars and 81mm mortars fire HE (High Explosive) rounds into an unoccupied swampland area, known as the Fish Hook. The shooting was designed to intimidate. All of the platoons in Echo Company kicked in the doors of the target houses at the same time and began to search for them. "The sheik's house didn't exist, not by the grid, so we picked houses we thought a sheik might live in. Nicer houses. We searched about eight houses." They did not do cordon, knocks, and searches. Instead, the Marines kicked in the doors.

Royer now mentioned the role of the Army PSYOPS detachments in the area of operations. Initially, they blared the group AC/DC's "Hells Bells" song via loudspeakers. Then they attempted to get the mujahideen to come out and fight.

After searching the eight houses without finding the sheik, Captain Royer decided to tone down the effort and make the searches cordon, knock, and search. 3rd Platoon was moving to the northwest, and 2nd Platoon was moving towards the north. "It was at that point that we linked up both 3rd and 2nd, that I switched over to 2nd Platoon to sort of observe their actions. As my headquarters element left 3rd, and crossed an open field, to link up with 2nd ... we heard shots fired. I immediately instructed everybody to take a knee, and the phrase we got from the Brits, from the training we received from them down in Kuwait based on their experiences in Northern Ireland, [I] immediately announced the phrase 'Go Firm!' It was basically, get in a security posture, get some cover, and uh, make sure you got good 360 security. And then start doing checks around you for potential threats like mines, or booby traps, IEDs, so forth."

"As we took a knee, [we] started looking for where the fire was coming from. Sounded like it was coming from all over. Which it was! There just so happened to be a foot-high trench right beside us, and we were along a wall. It was the wall to the north, and then a little trench, and then an open agricultural field. We decided to take a knee right there, by the trench. As I heard more rounds, I told everybody 'Get in the trench!' It was like an irrigation trench, but it had oil in it, and probably feces, urine. It was disgusting! But, by then, safety was more important. So we got in the trench, we started looking around for where we were taking fire. And, trying to ensure we didn't engage friendly forces, 'cause at this changeover, this transition, it became kind of dangerous because, it's not like everybody's on line. They're moving from house-to-house, conducting cordons. We realize the largest volume of fire came from the east. So we turn to the east."

"Next thing I know, my head kicks back, and I was hit by a bullet right to the front of my Kevlar [helmet]. I said, 'I'm hit!' Immediately put my hand up there, feeling for a hole in my brain. At that point, even though we were taking fire, my Corpsman, my company Corpsman, jumped out of the trench, we called the 'shit trench.' Jumps out of the shit trench, exposes himself. About the time I pulled my hand down, there's no blood, and I'm like,

'Doc! What the hell are you doing?'

[He] Says, 'Sir, I'm just doing my job!'

I say, 'Yeah, but I'm not hit.' And I grab him, threw him back in the hole."

Captain Royer kept this damaged Kevlar helmet after the firefight. He had it in his Combat Operations Center, and he showed me the nasty gash cut into it by the rifle bullet.

"And I try gaining comm with my 3rd Platoon. I couldn't get comm. I wanted him to provide us with suppression. I got a hold of my company [COC] and told them we were, of course they could hear it all the way back at the Outpost. Told them we were taking fire. I estimated to be a fire team on each flank. [They] Asked if I needed reinforcements. I told them, 'No, I got two platoons on deck, we can handle this fight.' But I had to get my headquarters element out of this open area."

"So we began to engage to the east. Then we picked up some machine gun fire, some RPG fire from the west. We began to engage to the west. There happened to be two Marines in the shit trench with me from 2nd Platoon. I ordered them to roll over, turn around, and start to low crawl out of this trench. It was about a 125 meters we crawl out of this thing."

A reporter with them from the *Philadelphia Inquirer*, David Swanson, also got hit while in the shit trench. It was only a flesh wound. Royer said when Swanson got back home, his newspaper buddies gave him a "Purple Camera" award, since he's not eligible for the military Purple Heart. (Note: Swanson later produced a photo essay DVD on his deployment with Echo Company entitled *Echoes of War—Ramadi Iraq, Echo 2/4 Marines*)

Royer had an S2 representative from 2/4 assigned to Echo Company who got hit by gunfire. Fortunately, it turned out to be only a flesh wound. When the firing first started, a HET (Human Exploitation Team) Marine with Royer had jumped out of the trench and went behind a wall to try and provide suppressive fire. "He begins taking more fire, comes back. Jumps *over* the wall this time. Comes down in the hole, says he's hit. Which he wasn't, as he landed on his foot and broke his ankle." So all of the Marines with Captain Royer low-crawled out of the trench, providing suppressive fire as they went. 3rd Platoon provided suppressive fires also, helping them to get out of the trench.

Now Captain Royer was with 2nd Platoon on the other side of the wall. 3rd Platoon had a fight towards the east. They moved to the south, then in a counterclockwise motion to go to the east then the north. Royer directed Sergeant Coan, now leading 3rd Platoon, to take a house to the west of there. Once 3rd Platoon took the house, Royer used it as a base of fire against a house to the south that was now firing at them. They also fired towards the west. They had stopped firing to the east.

Royer continued: "We were taking *heavy* machine gun fire from the house to our south, as well as RPGs. We engaged the RPG—one of my SAW gunners got ahold of the RPG guy and just routed his face. It was just unbelievable." Royer said that this RPG gunner was one of the bodies that were gone when they went back over the area later.

"At this point, one of my Marines, Lance Corporal Musser, asked if he could fire his AT4. I'm like, 'Hell yeah!' So, he goes running out the door to fire the AT4 at the target house, and I grab him by the back of his flak jacket and I said, 'What the hell are you doing? Get back in here!' And I told the sergeant, 'Hey, get some suppressive fire on that house!' So he stuck two SAWs out the window, this huge window. Broke the glass, and began firing on the building with those SAWs. Musser goes running out. First time he's ever fired an AT4. Boom! Right on target!"

"We didn't take any more fire from that house, so I ordered him to close on the house. Which they did. As we close on the house, we took a little bit of fire, from the west and the south. There was some machine gun fire from the south. As we closed on it, I was running by, and that's when I saw that RPG gunner, and his face was just gone. And there was a machine gunner on the left, and there was another guy with an AK-47 in between those two. We closed on the first house, and as we open the door, we saw a guy running down from the roof entrance. He was running down the stairs to grab an AK-47. And, one of my Marines said, 'Don't go for it! Don't go for it!' And of course, [the] guy doesn't understand English. And the guy went for his weapon, so they threw a hand grenade and closed the hatch [door]. And it exploded. They opened it up again, and the guy was standing there with the weapon. Put *another* hand grenade in there, exploded, as well as fire rifle fire at him. And the guy fell on the stairs."

"They [Marines] charged in, did some room clearing. We found an older man in there, probably in his sixties along with an older woman. Took the man to the ground, and began searching back towards the west, in a couple of other houses. In one house we found, and these were small houses too, we found a bag of RPGs and I think it might have been some hand grenades. In the house just to the south of that we found a room that there was probably 20 children and five women huddled in." As best as they could, the Marines tried to calm them down.

This area now secured, Royer got a report that a stay-behind squad establishing a helicopter landing zone for wounded Echo Company Marines was now under fire. Royer got in touch with "Bastard" (Battalion) and they told him that air was coming.

"So I rolled over [on his radio] to the appropriate CASTADNET, that's Close Air Support, Tactical Air Direction Net, and began moving back to that house. We were still taking fire now from the north and from the west. So, I was waiting for air to come on station. My men continued to engage. At that point we heard the sound of mechanized vehicles. Army engineers had come up to assist us. They took some of our casualties out. I had to go link up with them and show them exactly where we were. As I did that, air came on station so I went back over to the west and called some CAS [Close Air Support] targets. Unfortunately, there was some friendly forces, apparently, I couldn't see and didn't know they were there. At least that's what the helicopters reported. So I told them to abort, that there were some [enemy] forces to the north and I knew who was to the north and who they were."

Royer then went to the top of a house, borrowed an M203 grenade launcher, and got some violet smoke grenades to mark targets for the helicopters. He told the Cobra and Huey helos where his forces were, and told them to engage the mark [smoke mark]. The helos made their first pass, and AK-47s fired at them. However, the helos lit that place up.

Royer said, "It was incredible. They came around for a second pass, and then finally a third pass. And I gotta tell ya, sir, after that, I didn't hear *shit* in that neighborhood for the rest of the day!"

Echo Company lost one Marine KIA that day. Captain Royer estimated that his Marines faced a platoon-size force of about 40 to 60 fighters in his area. The enemy began the attack right as the sun came up. Royer felt that when the Marine attack kicked off at 0500, it gave the insurgents time to get on their cell phones and arrange a hasty ambush. Generally, the enemy does not like to fight at night.

Royer noted that sometimes the Rules of Engagement work against the Marines. Marines were in uniform, ride certain types of vehicles, and are visible. The enemy fighters blend in with the populace, and wear no uniforms. Civilians are also allowed to have weapons. He said that he saw this after the ambush of April 6. Shortly after the ambush he saw men of military age, but without weapons, in the immediate area. "I didn't allow my Marines to engage them, because it wasn't within the Rules of Engagement. Because the guy wasn't armed, I wasn't certain that he was a combatant. Unfortunately, because of the dispersal of forces, I didn't have a team to send out there to detain him. And so, he was able to walk free, to this day it bothers the hell out of me."

Captain Royer said that on the 10th of April they began taking that massive volume of fire from AKs and machine guns. His platoon that was to the north of that firing began to move towards the fight. Six times they found weapons pre-staged, each time about 100 to 150 meters apart. "The enemy would hit us, and then they would drop their weapons, and move back to fallback positions. What 1st Platoon was able to actually see was this in reverse order. They were actually walking up on these fallback positions. It was strange over here, because whenever there's a gunfight, there always seems to be a whole bunch of tourists around. I don't mean tourists from out of country, I mean the locals here, they watch it! It's amazing! So that's another reason why it's difficult to determine who's a bad guy and who's not. So what the bad guys would do, they would engage us, and they would drop their weapons. You know, if you rapidly engage somebody, by the time you look around and figure out where the fire's coming from, you may not even see the guy.

But if he's already dropped his weapon, and he's blended in with the locals, you *don't know* who that is!"

Royer said they had trained for that, to do discriminant shooting, but it's easier said than done.

The house searches on April 10 continued. They did not find much, other than the fact that most of the houses in that area were homes of ICDC or IP personnel. They found uniforms and ID cards in the houses. They also detained two Iraqi policemen who claimed that they did not help because they did not have any weapons.

Fox Company was in the north of the AO, and got engaged, as did some elements of Weapons Platoon. Royer estimated that they detained 70 people that day. "Don't know, for certain, how many we killed. About an hour after the firing had stopped, we heard a loud wailing. Sort of lamentation by the women type thing, from a compound to our northwest, approximately 200, 300 meters. I had sent a squad to check out the area that the helos had engaged. While over there, they noticed the compound, and that there were bodies upon bodies stacked up in the compound."

That day, Echo Company Marines fired M16s, M203, AT4s, Mark 19s, grenades, and used Close Air Support (CAS), basically everything that they had. "I know there were a lot of insurgents killed that day."

For the rest of April, Captain Royer sent out platoons for operations, not just squads. After about two weeks, he did conduct squad operations in the western part of the Fish Hook area, a swampy area in his area of operations. He used platoons for operations on the eastern side of the Fish Hook. Soon, they ended the Main Supply Route IED sweeps.

Echo Company had not had a lot of enemy engagements for the past month. Golf Company has been engaged in their AO. Many of these fights originated from an industrial area in the southern part of Echo's AO. Echo has not been involved in most of these fights.

A few days ago, on July 21 (Captain Royer's birthday, he noted), Echo Company did get called out when battalion needed additional forces. He called in and said he had three platoons ready to go.

"They got us in the fight, and we cleared that south, western portion of my area of operations. Which isn't very far from the firm base, it's probably about 600 meters from the firm base. But, it extends about two kilometers from the firm base. I got the company, we launched out the gate. Went to Check Point 297, what we also call the Tear Drop, because it's like a "Y" intersection. We rallied at the northern stadium. We're getting ready to launch our clearing operations, and CAS was called on station. We took some fire from [the] north, but that had subsided. Battalion asked me to call in some targets. I told them essentially I didn't have any targets, because there was no more fire. Then they decided they were gonna strafe the area, which they did. We popped smoke, they came to the forward area of our smoke and strafed the area with both a Huey, and, I think it was a Super Cobra. Then we took fire from the south, in the vicinity of the Al Haq Mosque. There was a vehicle that was driving up, there was a specter of potentially a VBIED, but the Marines took it under fire. I think that damn near half the force that was out there engaged this vehicle. I think it was three guys in it, they were all killed."

Once Captain Royer learned that air support would no longer be in the area, he asked if Echo Company could sweep to the west, which they did. His northernmost element began to take sporadic fire from the north. Echo continued west, getting about halfway through the zone they were assigned to clear. They came upon a "BOLO" (Be On the Look Out for) vehicle: A white, four door Oldsmobile, suspected of being a VBIED. He got the okay from battalion to engage it, and hit it with an AT4 round. The vehicle blew up, and then three more explosions followed. Echo continued moving west without any large engagements. They killed four enemy, and detained nine. Finally, the battalion operations officer told him to move south and secure the area near the MSR. They were out for about four to five hours on July 21.

In its time here, Echo Company has been mortared 41 times, had 73 IEDs, around 19 firefights, and about a dozen RPG attacks. The Marines have found 10 weapons caches, two of which were very large—one in a cemetery and one in a target house. Neighboring Golf Company also found a bicycle IED. One of the weapons caches Echo found had 36 82mm mortar rounds, IED-making materials (wire, glue gun, motorcycle batteries), a Dragunov sniper rifle, a can of 500 rounds of ammo, two improvised rocket launchers. In the next yard they found 12 120mm artillery shells, a pistol, a shotgun, some PE4 explosives, and RPG boosters.

Royer said that his current focus was MSR security, firm base security, and raids. "Initially we were stretched about eight kilometers of the MSR to provide security. Now, we've ceded some of that to a fellow company. So now the distribution throughout the battalion's a little more equal." Echo is now responsible for about five kilometers of the MSR.

They have an Observation Post in the cemetery, on the highest ground in Ramadi. Some of his Marines had gone south, and found bags with weapons in the cemetery. There they found eight SA-14 surface-to-air missiles, seven 155mm artillery rounds (four of which still had explosives inside), three RPG launchers, two RPGs, four PG 9 anti-tank rounds, about 20 hand grenades, other explosives in canisters, and about fifteen 2.2 Italian plastic land mines. About 15, sort of like the American "Bouncing Betty," Italian-made anti-personnel mines. There were also two Soviet-made light anti-tank weapons similar to the old American LAWs (Light Anti-Tank Weapon).

Marine combat engineers searched the cemetery for more caches there, and Royer invited the Army engineers from Brigade to search there also. Neither have found any more weapons caches.

Outside of the big fights in April and last week, mostly only occasional small arms or a random RPG gets fired on his outposts. However, IEDs have been a continuous threat and have gotten larger including VBIEDs also called VCIEDs

(Vehicle-Concealed Improvised Explosive Devices). Three of these have detonated in his AO, and two or three were destroyed. "There was a VBIED, VCIED, detonated on the 29th of May that killed four of my Marines, and injured another three more."

As a wrap-up, I asked Captain Royer for some final thoughts. He responded:

"Not too long ago there was a meeting of all the officers in the battalion. We had a guest speaker come from Division, who's senior in rank. He addressed us, and he said there were two things where, things that may have been underestimated, prior to our arrival. He said that, and I don't know at what level this originated, but certainly felt here, at our level, they had underestimated the threat by a pretty good amount. Based on intel that we had received on those we had replaced. Based on intel from intel agencies. That was the case. As well the second significant thing was we had overestimated the capabilities of the Iraqi security forces, meaning the police and the ICDC. I would concur with both of those assessments."

Royer noted that Pattern Analysis is extremely important. Once either side establishes a pattern, the other side can use this to their advantage. This brought him back to an earlier fight here: "The enemy had been mortaring the Army at this outpost every Thursday. You could set your calendar by it. Every Thursday, just after it got dark, they would mortar the outpost. I experienced that when I came up here on my leader's recon. I was here one night, and they started taking rounds. That was the first time, I'd ever realized, that somebody was 'No shit!' trying to kill me. We were here, we took over, and, 'No shit,' on that first Thursday, soon as it got dark, we got mortared. Well, I wasn't gonna take that!"

"So, the next week, I launched a QRF in a counter-mortar ambush role to find these guys and kill 'em. Well, they did. 'Cause they were out there. And that's why, you've been in my COC, you've seen probably displayed there in the center, that 60mm mortar tube. [I took a picture of Captain Royer next to this captured mortar tube.] That's what we found on the 25th of March."

I pointed to the mortar tube and asked, "That's it?"

Royer replied, "Yes, sir. That's the bad guys.'"

"They [his QRF] were going down the MSR. Doubled back on a parallel street. They were going east on the MSR, doubled back towards the west on a parallel street. Came under intense volume of machine gun fire and RPG fire. Exited the vehicles. Laid down their base of fire. At that point, the enemy fire ceased, the unmanned Humvee continued to roll. The enemy just lit it up. Well, that allowed us time to not only identify their exact locations, but to maneuver on them. And my boys just destroyed them! Walked up on the scene and found four dead, and one who appeared to be dead, but was really unharmed. The attitude of this kid was amazing. He was like, 18, 19. His only concern was how long we would be detaining because he needs to get back and finish his final exams! Incredible! I mean, the absolute aloofness of this kid."

"After they swept it, we had taken three casualties that day, we'd swept it back. Once they took fire, then we launched a QRF. I went out with that QRF, and we linked up with them. By then the firefight was over. But I still wanted the area swept. That's when we found the four dead bodies and the one enemy prisoner of war. We found four RPKs, two PKCs, two AK-47s, three RPG tubes, about six rockets, hand grenades, ammunition, and the 60mm mortar tube with baseplate and bipods, as well as six prepped mortar rounds."

Two weeks after that came the events of April 6.

Captain Royer concluded: "Throughout this whole ordeal, throughout combat, throughout casualties, caused by small arms or IEDs, ambushes, throughout the heat, and the workload, and some of the mundane tasks, my men have continued to be honorable, and courageous. They continue to be warriors. My boys, they're fine men. And I'm proud to serve with them."

Final Thoughts

The meetings with the Marines at Combat Outpost Ramadi marked the last field history interviews of my tour in Iraq. My meetings with the Marines of LAR and infantry units during the spring and summer of 2004 showed the great flexibility of Marines working together. Much of their work went unnoticed by major news media outlets, especially for those Marines operating in Ramadi and remote western areas of Al Anbar Province in Iraq, far from Fallujah.

Many of the Marines interviewed had been involved in the invasion of Iraq in 2003. I included their recollections of those events, as well as short bits of their military backgrounds to give a fuller picture of their perspectives on more recent operations in 2004. Often I did not get the correct spelling of names, nor the first names of many Marines mentioned during interviews, and I apologize to these Marines for this shortcoming.

The tours of Marine units in Iraq during 2004 lasted seven months. These deployments were shorter than the U.S. Army's deployments of 12 months, but Marine leadership felt strongly that this allowed the Marines to remain focused and fresh throughout their tours. It also allowed the Marine Corps to maintain its worldwide deployment obligations.

The border crossings from Jordan and especially Syria were very critical during that time. Tiny elements consisting of two different Marine infantry platoons were tasked with supervising potentially volatile situations at these areas. They assumed their missions with a can-do attitude typical of all Marines I met during my time there. The provincial capital of Ramadi was the scene of high-intensity combat actions that resulted in many Marine deaths. Ramadi would continue to be a hot spot for insurgent actions for the next several years.

I remain inspired and humbled after meeting so many of these dedicated young men who placed themselves at the "tip of the spear" while in Iraq. I shared in their sorrow at the loss of comrades.

Currently, all of the 190 interviews that I conducted during my deployment are in storage at the Marine Corps' Historical Center in Quantico, Virginia. The slow process of transcribing them, along with several thousand other interviews done by members of the Field History detachment during Operation *Iraqi Freedom* in 2003, continues. All interviews have succinct summaries of their contents, and are available to researchers there. My hope is to continue to tell more of the stories of the Marines and sailors I met, and to make the public aware of this valuable resource: The Marine Corps Oral History Program.

Glossary

0311	Military occupational specialty code for a Marine infantryman
0313	Military occupational specialty code for an LAV crewman
29 Palms	Marine Air Ground Combat Center in California
240 Golf	M240 belt-fed, gas-operated machine gun firing a 7.62mm round. Rate of fire 650 to 950 rounds per minute
.50 caliber machine gun	Browning M2 machine gun
7-ton MTVR	Medium Tactical Replacement Vehicle. Tactical truck with a 7-ton capacity
8th and I	Marine Barracks in Washington, DC. The oldest post in the Marine Corps. Supports ceremonial and security missions in the nation's capital
9 mil	M9 Beretta semi-automatic pistol
AAV 7	Amphibious Assault Vehicle. AAV P7. Fully tracked amphibious landing vehicle. Armament includes Mk19 40mm automatic grenade launcher, and M2 .50 caliber machine gun. Also called "Amtrac" or "Tracs" by Marines. See Amtrac
Abrams	M1 Abrams tank
AC130 Spectre	Heavily armed ground-attack variant of the C130 Hercules transport aircraft. Had one 20mm GAU-equalizer cannon, one Bofors 40mm cannon, and a 105mm M102 howitzer
ACOG	Advanced Combat Optical Gun sight for the M16 and M4 rifles
ACR	Armored Cavalry Regiment of the U.S. Army
A-driver	Assistant driver in a vehicle
AK/AK-47	Avtomat Kalashnikova. Soviet-designed assault rifle firing a 7.62mm round. Also called a Kalashnikov
Amtrac	Nickname for the Amphibious Assault Vehicle, LVT 7. See AAV 7
AN/PVS-17	A lightweight scope for night vision

AO	Area of operations of a military unit
ASR	Alternate Supply Route
Asad	Al Asad Air Base. Large air base 100 miles west of Baghdad. Second largest U.S. air base during Operation *Iraqi Freedom*
AT4	84mm unguided, portable recoilless smoothbore rocket. Common anti-tank weapon
AWS	Amphibious Warfare School. See: Expeditionary Warfare School (EWS)
BAS	Battalion Aid Station. Medical section within a Marine battalion's support company. Led by battalion surgeon, a Navy medical doctor, and staffed by Navy nurses and medical Corpsmen
Basic School	The Basic School at Quantico, Virginia. A 26-week course. Provides training for all newly commissioned Marine second lieutenants prior to further MOS training. Also "TBS"
Bird	Helicopter
BLT	Battalion Landing Team. Smallest of the Marine Task-Organized operational forces, consisting of an infantry battalion and attachments, including elements from H&S Battalion of a regiment, and aviation assets (Usually rotary-wing)
Bradley Fighting Vehicle/Bradley	(BFV) Family of U.S. Army armored fighting vehicles with a crew of three and room for six soldiers
Brigade	U.S. Army maneuver element. The U.S. Army 1st BCT, 1st ID (First Brigade Combat Team, First Infantry Division), was the senior U.S. combat team in Ramadi during much of 2004. Marine battalions 2/4 and 3/11 augmented this Army command
BZO	Battle Sight Zero. Adjusting the sight settings for the rifle
C-130	"Hercules" Turboprop multi-engine multi-mission airplane used by the U.S. Air Force, U.S. Marines, U.S. Navy and U.S. Coast Guard. Marines often referred to both the C-130 and AC-130 by this term
CAAT	Combined Anti-Armor Team. A platoon from a Weapons Company task-organized to support infantry operations in Iraq in 2004. Employed armored vehicles with heavy machine guns and TOW missiles

CAG	Civil Affairs Group. Plan and execute civil-military operations while serving as the liaison between military forces and civil authorities, local population, and non-governmental organizations. All Civil Affairs Marines come from Marine Corps Reserve forces
Cammies	Marine camouflage uniform. Desert MARPAT design newly issued in 2004 (see MARPAT)
CAS	Close Air Support. Air-to-ground actions by military aircraft against enemy forces close to friendly forces
CASEVAC	Casualty Evacuation that may use non-standardized vehicles to provide movement to medical care, may or may not provide en route care
CAX	Combined Arms Exercise. The Marines' program at the Marine Corps Air Ground Combat Center (MCAGCC), 29 Palms, California, is the Marine Corps' most advanced live-fire unit-level combined arms training program for ground and air fire support with maneuver at the tactical level
CCP	Casualty Collection Point. A temporary location to bring wounded to while waiting evacuation for further medical treatment
CEB	Combat Engineer Battalion. Provides Marines to emplace obstacles, conduct breaching operations, and reduce explosive hazards
CERP	(Commander's Emergency Response Program) funds for local projects
CH46	Boeing Vertol Sea Knight helicopter. Medium-lift tandem rotor transport helicopter used by U.S. Marines and U.S. Navy. Nicknamed "Phrog." Retired in 2014. Replaced by the Bell Boeing V-22 Osprey tilt-rotor aircraft
CH47	Boeing Chinook helicopter. Twin-engine, tandem rotor, heavy-lift helicopter used by U.S. Army aviation
CH53 Echo	Sikorsky CH53 Super Stallion, heavy-lift helicopter of the Marine Corps
CHS	Pronounced "cash." Combat Support Hospital. A U.S. Army field hospital
Claymore	A directional, command-detonated mine that fires steel balls in a 60-degree arc about 100 meters

Click	1,000 meters measured on a tactical map
CO	Commander Officer of a Marine unit at the company level and above
Cobra Helicopter	The Bell AH-1W Super Cobra Attack Helicopter. Weapons Systems can include 20mm M197 3-barrell Gatling gun, 2.75mm Hydra 70 Rockets, 5" Zuni Rockets, TOW missiles, AGM 114 Hellfire missiles, AIM-9 Sidewinder anti-aircraft missiles
COC	Combat Operations Center
Combat Outpost (Ramadi)	Outpost in the eastern sector of Ramadi. Served as the outpost for both Golf and Echo Companies, 2/4
CONEX	Large intermodal shipping container
CONUS	Continental United States
Corpsman	U.S. Navy enlisted Hospital Corpsman assigned to Marine units. Provides emergency and first aid care
CP	Command post of a military unit
CPA	Coalition Provisional Authority. A transitional authority over the Iraqi government during the first half of 2004. Abolished June 28, 2004
CSSB	Combat Service Support Battalion. The main mission is to provide supplies and other support to IMEF operating in western Iraq, though the unit also planned to conduct a variety of humanitarian projects to assist with reconstruction efforts
Delta Force	Officially the 1st Special Forces Operational Detachment-Delta. One of the U.S. Army's special missions units, focused mainly on counterterrorism
Det Cord	Detonating Cord. A thin, flexible tube filled with PETN that detonates at a rate of 6,400 feet per second. Used to detonate high-explosives and multiple charges
Dishdash	Long-sleeved, traditional robe worn by many men in Arab countries. Also called "Thawb"
Doc	Nickname for a Navy Hospital Corpsman
Dragon	Man-portable wire-guided anti-tank missile, retired in 1999. Replaced by the Javelin missile
Dragon Eye	Small reconnaissance drone airplane, range of 3.1 miles
DShK	Soviet-designed heavy machine gun. Roughly equivalent to the U.S. M2 .50 caliber Browning machine gun. Rate of fire is 600 rounds per minute

EAS	Expiration of Active Service. When a Marine is discharged after completing an enlistment contract
ECP	Entry Control Point. An entry to a facility or base
EFCAT	Enduring Freedom Combat Assessment Team. Based at Quantico, Virginia in 2004. Sent teams to Iraq and Afghanistan to collect Lessons Learned relating to Marine Corps participation in Operation *Enduring Freedom* and Operation *Iraqi Freedom*
EOD	Explosive Ordnance Disposal
EPW	Enemy Prisoner of War
EWS	Expeditionary Warfare School. A 41-week resident course for company grade officers at Quantico, Virginia. (Formerly AWS—Amphibious Warfare School)
F16	General Dynamics "Fighting Falcon" of the U.S. Air Force. A single-engine supersonic multirole fighter aircraft
Fallujah Brigade	Formed in April 2004, composed of local Iraqis under the command of a former Baathist officer named Muhammed Latif that attempted to take control of the city
FAO	Foreign Area Officer. Officers who receive regionally focused training to serve in allied nations
FAST	Fleet Anti-terrorism Security Team. Marines who guard a variety of installations like naval bases and areas too sensitive to leave without an armed presence
Fedayin	Arabic term for "one who sacrifices himself" for a larger campaign
Fire	Generally referring to gun fire in combat
Fire Team	A rifle fire team is made up of four Marines: A team leader, rifleman, automatic rifleman, and an assistant automatic rifleman
FMF	Fleet Marine Force. The operational forces of the U.S. Marines
FOB	Forward Operating Base
Frag	Fragmentation grenade. An anti-personnel hand-thrown grenade
Frag	Fragmentary order. A partial operations order. Often given during contact with the enemy

GBU	Guided Bomb Unit, also called a "smart" bomb
Grunts	Nickname for Marine infantry
Gunnery Sergeant	A Marine staff non-commissioned officer, rank E7
Gunny	Nickname for a Marine gunnery sergeant
Harrier Jet	McDonnell-Douglas AV 8B single-engine jump jet capable of short takeoff and landings
HE	High Explosive artillery round, with fragmentation and blast effects
Helos	Slang for helicopters
HESCO Barrier	Barrier made of collapsible wire mesh filled with earth, gravel or rock, to create a defensive barrier. HESCO is the company that manufactures these barriers
HET	Human Exploitation Team that includes translators, provided by U.S. Army
HETs	U.S. Army Heavy Equipment Transporter System. A tractor and trailer system that can carry up to 140,000 pounds on- or off-road
H&S	Headquarters and Service support element of a Marine unit
Huey Helicopter	Bell UH-N helicopter used by U.S. Marines
Hurricane Point	Location of 2nd Battalion, 4th Marines, Combat Operations Center, on the banks of the Euphrates River in Ramadi
HVT	High-value targets (individuals)
IBP	Iraqi Border Police
ICDC	Iraqi Civil Defense Corps, became the Iraqi National Guard (ING) after the turnover of sovereignty at the end of June 2004
IDC	Independent Duty Corpsman. Enlisted sailor with extensive medical training. Duties similar to a civilian physician assistant or paramedic
IED	Improvised Explosive Device, using available explosives and a wide variety of triggering devices including cell phones, doorbells, and batteries. Some devices are wireless or radio-controlled
IMEF	1st Marine Expeditionary Force, a task-organized force composed of elements of Marine Ground, Aviation, and Combat Service Support elements
IOC	Infantry Officer Course, at Quantico, Virginia. Challenging course to screen Marine second lieutenants seeking the infantry MOS 0302

IP	Iraqi Police
IPAC	Installation Personnel Administration Center— Provides administration support for commanders, Marines, and family members
ITB	Marine Infantry Training Battalion, for graduates of Marine recruit training prior to assignment to operational units
JDAM	Joint Direct Attack Munition. A guidance kit that converts unguided bombs into all-weather precision-guided bombs, dropped from fixed-wing aircraft
Jump CP	A mobile command post, in 2004 often utilizing Light Armored Vehicles.
Junction City	Large camp in Ramadi on west bank of the Euphrates River, Combat Outpost for U.S. Army's 1st BCT, 1st ID
KBR	Kellogg, Brown, and Root. A civilian company contracted by the Department of Defense to help supply units deployed to Iraq
Kentucky Windage	Adjusting the aim of a weapon without using the sights
Kevlar	Material used for combat helmet. Nickname used by Marines for the helmets
KIA	Killed in Action
KV	Korean Village. Name for the Forward Operating Base in western Iraq near Syria. So-called as it was built to house Korean workers who were building a highway in the area. Used as the Combat Operations Center for 1st LAR Battalion in 2004
LAR	Light Armored Reconnaissance. Armored mobilized land reconnaissance unit. Used to gather intelligence and for screening. Marines use the LAV 25 (Light Armored Vehicle) as its main vehicle. Previously LAI—Light Armored Infantry
LAV	Light Armored Vehicle. The LAV 25 is the main variant of this wheeled armored vehicle used by Marine LAR forces
LAV AT	Mounts a turret with two TOW long-range anti-tank guided missile launchers, plus 14 more missile reloads
LAW	M72 portable anti-tank weapon firing a 2.6 inch unguided rocket.

Left-seat, Right-seat	Technique used to familiarize incoming units with an area. The combat veteran takes the left seat of a vehicle first and the new arrival rides in the right seat. Within days the new arrival will take charge in the left seat
LeJeune	Marine Corps Base Camp LeJeune, located in Jacksonville, North Carolina
Line Company	A Marine infantry company
LOG	Logistics
LOI	Letter of Instruction. Where a senior commander prescribes broad aims, policies, and strategic concepts for operations in a large area for an extended period of time
M16 A4	Standard infantry rifle in use by Marines in 2004
M19	Belt-fed 40mm grenade launcher. "Mark 19"
M203	Single-shot 40mm grenade launcher, under barrel attachment to the M16 rifle
M242	Bushmaster 25mm chain-driven autocannon used on LAV 25
MAGTF	Marine Air Ground Task Force. A task-organized self-contained Marine Expeditionary Force
MARPAT	Marine Pattern multi-scale camouflage uniform. Designed in 2001, issued to Marine forces in Iraq in 2004.
MCRD	Marine Corps Recruit Depot. The Marine Corps has two basic training bases: San Diego, CA, and Parris Island, SC
MEF	Marine Expeditionary Force. See IMEF
MEU	Marine Expeditionary Unit. Composed of a Marine infantry battalion with attachments and supporting elements. Deployed worldwide on Navy shipping
MHG	Marine Headquarters Group
MOS	Military Occupational Specialty
MOUT	Military Operations in Urban Terrain
MPF	Maritime Prepositioning Force. Strategic power-projection capability to provide most of the combat equipment needed for two Marine Expeditionary Brigades (MEBs)
MRE	Meals Ready-to-Eat. A variety of dehydrated meals in plastic pouches
MSR	Main Supply Route

Mujahideen	Guerrilla fighters in Muslim countries, especially those fighting against non-Muslim forces. One engaged in Jihad. Also "Mujh"
MWR	Morale, Welfare, Recreation. In deployed areas, often providing phone and internet services for Marines and sailors
NAI	Named Areas of Interest for a military unit. (Examples include suspected enemy training camps, cuts in border sand berms, and buildings)
Navy Shower	A method of showering that conserves water: Short flow of water, then lathering with soap, then rinse. Originated on Navy ships to conserve valuable fresh water
NBC	Nuclear, Biological, and Chemical weapons. Also, CBR—Chemical, Biological, and Radiological weapons
NCO	Non-commissioned officer. In the Marine Corps, corporal and sergeant, E4 and E5
NVGs	Night Vision Goggles
OIC	Officer in charge
OIF	Operation *Iraqi Freedom*. In 2004, Marines referred to the 2003 invasion of Iraq as OIF1, and the return by Marine Corps Forces to Iraq in March 2004 as OIFII or OIF2
OP	Observation Post
Operation *Ripper Sweep*	During the April 2004 cease-fire in Fallujah, General James Mattis ordered the 1st Light Armored Reconnaissance Battalion (1st LAR) and 2/7 Marines into the farmlands around Fallujah to neutralize insurgent gangs to allow supply lines to remain open. Simultaneously, 3/4 Marines conducted raids into Al Karmah
Operation *Vigilant Resolve*	Operations against insurgents in Fallujah. April 4 to May 1, 2004. Also, "The First Battle of Fallujah"
Op Order	Operational Order for a unit to go into an engagement or action
Overwatch	A force protection tactic where one military unit supports another unit, executing fire and movement tactics
P 3 Orion	Lockheed four-engine turboprop surveillance aircraft developed for the U.S. Navy
PCR	Personnel Casualty Report

PE 4	British term referring to a common variety of plastic explosive. Similar to the U.S. C4 explosive material
Pendleton	Marine Corps Base Camp Pendleton, located in San Diego County, California
PFC	Private First Class, E2 rank
PKM	A Soviet-designed 7.62mm machine gun. Also Kalashnikov PK/PKM
PLC	Platoon Leaders' Course. An officer screening and selection program for college students. Held each summer at Quantico, Virginia. Successful candidates receive Marine officer commissions after college graduation
POE	Ports of Entry into Iraq along the border area
PP&O	Plans, Policies, and Operations at Headquarters Marine Corps. Two missions: 1) Serves as the focal point for interface between USMC, and joint and combined activities of the Joint Chiefs of Staff; 2) Coordinates the development and execution of service plans and policies related to the structure, deployment and employment of Marine Corps forces in general
PSYOPS	U.S. Army Psychological Operations. Specialists who assess the information needs of a local population and craft messages to influence them
PT	Physical Training
QRF	Quick Reaction Force. Any task-organized unit ready to respond to another unit in contact with enemy forces
Quantico	Marine Corps Base Quantico, Virginia. The "Crossroads of the Marine Corps." Marine Corps Combat Development Command
RCT	Regimental Combat Team. Task-organized regimental-size combat force of infantry battalions, attached and supporting units
RCT1	Built around the 1st Marine Regiment based out of Camp Pendleton, California. Headquarters in Iraq at Camp Fallujah in 2004
RCT7	Built around the 7th Marine Regiment based out of the Marine Air Ground Combat Center 29 Palms, California. Headquarters in Iraq at Camp Al Asad in 2004

Recon	Reconnaissance unit of a Marine Infantry Division
RIP	Relief in Place. An incoming military unit taking over for an outgoing unit
RPGs/RPG	Shoulder fired Rocket-Propelled Grenades
ROE	Rules of Engagement to be followed in an area
RPK	Soviet-designed light machine gun, fires a 7.62mm round
SA7	Soviet-designed, man-portable shoulder fired air defense missile
SAM-R	A specially modified M16 with optical sight
SAPI	Small Arms Protective Insert. Placed into ballistic vests (flak jackets) to intercept projectiles and some explosive fragments
SASO	Security and Stability Operations. In 2004, Marine units originally planned to oversee the peaceful reconstruction of infrastructure in Iraq
SASR	Special Applications Scoped Rifle. M107 recoil-operated anti-material sniper system. Fires a .50 caliber round, has a range of 1,800 meters
SAW	Squad Automatic Weapon. M249 Light machine gun. Belt-fed, firing a 5.56mm round, has a quick-change barrel
Showanis	Special Forces from the Iraqi National Guard
SIGINT	Signals Intelligence. Intelligence gained from monitoring electronic messaging
SMAW	Mk 153 Shoulder-Launched Multipurpose Assault Weapon. A shoulder-launched rocket used primarily to destroy bunkers and fortifications
SOI	School of Infantry. Second stage of military training for Marines who have completed Basic Training
SOP	Standing Operating Procedures
Squad	A Marine rifle squad is made up of three four-man Fire Teams and an NCO squad leader
STA Platoon	Surveillance and Target Acquisition Platoon. Also provides scout-snipers
Staff Organizations	S1 Personnel/manpower
	S2 Intelligence or security
	S3 Operations
	S4 Logistics or supply
	S5 Plans
	S6 Communications

TACC	Tactical Air Command Center, a mobile Combat Operations Center
Taqaddum	Al Taqaddum air base located about 55 miles west of Baghdad. See TQ
TBS	The Basic School at Quantico, Virginia. A 26-week course that provides training for all newly commissioned Marine second lieutenants prior to further MOS training
TCP	Traffic Control Point. Temporary position to examine vehicular traffic
TOW	Tube-launched, Optically tracked, Wire-guided anti-tank missile. The BGM-71 TOW has a 3,000 meter range
TQ	Slang for Al Taqaddum air base
T-RATs	Tray Rations. Food in prepared aluminum trays heated in portable heaters
Trojan Horse Missions	Disguising a civilian truck apparently carrying merchandise to entice thieves to attempt to stop and seize the merchandise. However, the trucks were loaded with armed Marines and in touch with a Quick Reaction Force. The goal was to stop thieves from hitting KBR supply convoys
TRP	Target Reference Points that allow a weapons system to find a target
TTP	Tactics, Techniques, and Procedures
UAV	Unmanned Aerial Vehicle or type of drone
UXO	Unexploded Ordnance
VBIED	Vehicle-Borne Improvised Explosive Device. An explosive in or near a car, bike, wagon, or truck
VC	Vehicle Commander in the LAV 25
VCIED	Vehicle-Concealed Improvised Explosive Device. See VBIED
VCP	Vehicle Check Point
WIA	Wounded in Action
Wire/The Wire	Refers to the boundary of a camp or base
XO	Executive Officer of a Marine unit at the company level or above

Sources and Further Reading

Field History Journal of Lieutenant Colonel David E. Kelly, USMC, March–July 2004 (On file with U.S. Marine Corps History and Museums Division).

Interview Notes of Lieutenant Colonel David E. Kelly (Author's collection).

Field History Interviews by the Author

Lieutenant Colonel William Richard Costantini, USMC, FOB Korean Village, Iraq, July 8, 2004.
Major John Richard Smith, Junior, USMC, Camp Al Asad, Iraq, July 5, 2004.
Lieutenant Robert Joseph Gould, MD, USN, FOB Hit, Iraq, July 5, 2004.
Captain John Kenneth Kelley, USMC, FOB Hit, Iraq, July 6, 2004.
Captain Andrew Aaron Manson, USMC, FOB Korean Village, Iraq, July 8, 2004.
Captain David Wendell Palmer, USMC, Camp Al Asad, Iraq, July 5, 2004.
Captain Kelly Dean Royer, USMC, Combat Outpost Ramadi, Iraq, July 23, 2004.
Captain Ladd Wilkie Shepard, USMC, Camp Baharia, Iraq, June 28, 2004.
Captain Donald Louis Shove, USMC, FOB Korean Village, Iraq, July 7, 2004.
Lieutenant Robert Manuel Christafore, USMC, FOB Korean Village, Iraq, July 7, 2004.
Lieutenant Tommy Edward Cogan, USMC, Combat Outpost Ramadi, Iraq, July 23, 2004.
Lieutenant Brian Edward Humphreys, USMC, FOB Hit, Iraq, July 6, 2004.
Lieutenant Jason Matthew Snyder, USMC, Hurricane Point, Ramadi, Iraq, July 22, 2004.
Lieutenant Junwei Sun, USMC, Camp Al Asad, Iraq, July 5, 2004.
First Sergeant Harrison Leon Tanksley, USMC, FOB Hit, Iraq, July 5, 2004.
Gunnery Sergeant Troy Antoine Barlow, USMC, Camp Al Asad, Iraq, July 4, 2004.
Gunnery Sergeant Phillip Steven Bemis, USMC, FOB Korean Village, Iraq, July 8, 2004.
Gunnery Sergeant Bradley Scott Everett, USMC, Camp Al Asad, Iraq, July 5, 2004.
Gunnery Sergeant Juan Lopez, USMC, FOB Korean Village, Iraq, July 8, 2004.
Gunnery Sergeant Paul Michael McElearney, USMC, FOB Hit, Iraq, July 5, 2004.
Staff Sergeant Jon Thomas Brodin, USMC, FOB Hit, Iraq, July 6, 2004.
Staff Sergeant Daniel Joseph Mainville, USMC, FOB Korean Village, Iraq, July 7, 2004.
Sergeant Damien Ryan Coan, USMC, Combat Outpost Ramadi, Iraq, July 23, 2004.
Sergeant Timothy Curtis Day, USMC, FOB Hit, Iraq, July 5, 2004.
Sergeant Jonathon Jarrett Graham, USMC, FOB Hit, Iraq, July 5, 2004.
Sergeant Michael Irvin Honigsberg II, USMC, Camp Baharia, Iraq, June 21, 2004.
Sergeant Gaw Sekou Jones, Junior, USMC Camp Baharia, Iraq, June 28, 2004.
Sergeant Lewis William Layton, USMC, Hurricane Point, Ramadi, Iraq, June 22, 2004.
Sergeant John Denton Leuba, USMC, Camp Baharia, Iraq, June 21, 2004 and June 28, 2004.
Sergeant Travis Dean Madden, USMC, Camp Baharia, Iraq, June 21, 2004.
Sergeant Jeremiah Lee Randle, USMC, Hurricane Point, Ramadi, Iraq, July 22, 2004.

Sergeant Lorenzo Mathis Young, USMC, Camp Al Asad, Iraq, July 4, 2004.
Corporal Jeffrey John Bertch, USMC, Camp Baharia, Iraq, June 21, 2004.
Corporal Christopher Michael Bowles, USMC, Camp Al Asad, Iraq, July 4, 2004.
Corporal Jonathon Beowulf Cushman, USMC, FOB Korean Village, Iraq, July 7, 2004.
Corporal Samuel Frank Dyche, USMC, Camp Al Asad, Iraq, July 4, 2004.
Corporal Joseph Stephen Magee, USMC, Combat Outpost Ramadi, Iraq, July 23, 2004.
Corporal Jared Heath McKenzie, USMC, Hurricane Point, Ramadi, Iraq, July 22, 2004.
Corporal Eric Michael Smith, USMC, Combat Outpost Ramadi, Iraq, July 23, 2004.
Corporal Caleb Zachary Stefanovich, USMC, Combat Outpost Ramadi, Iraq, July 23, 2004.
Hospital Corpsman 3 Eric Delano Giles, USN, FOB Hit, Iraq, July 5, 2004.
Lance Corporal Craig Richard Bowden, USMC, Camp Al Asad, Iraq, July 4, 2004.
Lance Corporal Keith Allen Bridges, USMC, Camp Baharia, Iraq, June 21, 2004.
Lance Corporal Robert Anthony DeLuca, Junior, USMC, Camp Al Asad, Iraq, July 4, 2004.
Lance Corporal Reagan Charles Hodges, USMC, Hurricane Point, Ramadi, Iraq, July 22, 2004.
Lance Corporal Justin Avery Shields, USMC, FOB Korean Village, Iraq, July 8, 2004.
Private First Class Christopher Lee Ferguson, USMC, Combat Outpost Ramadi, Iraq, July 23, 2004.
Private First Class Peter Joseph Flom, USMC, Combat Outpost Ramadi, Iraq, July 23, 2004.
Private First Class Higinio Antuno Martinez, USMC, Combat Outpost Ramadi, Iraq, July 23, 2004.
Private First Class Kenny Ray Whittle, USMC, Combat Outpost Ramadi, Iraq, July 23, 2004.

Other Books by the Author

Kelly, David E., Lieutenant Colonel USMC (Ret.), *First Fights in Fallujah: Marines During Operation Vigilant Resolve, in Iraq, April 2004*. Havertown, PA: Casemate Publishers, 2023.

Kelly, David E., Lieutenant Colonel USMC (Ret.), *Hell in the Streets of Husaybah: The April 2004 Fights of 3rd Battalion, 7th Marines in Husaybah, Iraq*. Havertown, PA: Casemate Publishers, 2022.

Further Reading on Conflict in Iraq

Camp, Dick. *Operation Phantom Fury: The Assault and Capture of Fallujah, Iraq*, Minneapolis, MN: Zenith Press, 2009.

Estes, Kenneth W., Lieutenant Colonel, USMC (Ret.), *U.S. Marine Corps Operations in Iraq, 2003–2006*, Washington, DC: History Division Marine Corps University, 2009.

Estes, Kenneth W., Lieutenant Colonel USMC (Ret.), *U.S. Marines in Iraq 2004–2005 Into the Fray*, Washington, DC: History Division Marine Corps University, 2011.

Lowry, Richard S. *New Dawn: The Battles for Fallujah*, New York: Savas Beatie, 2010.

O'Donnell, Patrick K. *We Were One*, Boston: Da Capo Press, 2006.

Reynolds, Nicholas E., Colonel, USMC (Ret.), *Basrah, Baghdad, and Beyond: The U.S. Marine Corps in the Second Iraq War*, Annapolis, Maryland: Naval Institute Press, 2009.

Schlosser, Dr. Nicholas J. *U.S. Marines in Iraq 2004–2008: Anthology and Annotated Bibliography*, Washington, DC: History Division Marine Corps University, 2010.

West, Bing. *No True Glory: A Frontline Account of the Battle for Fallujah*, New York: Bantam Books, 2005.

Online Sources

Swanson, David. "Echoes of War" Ramadi Iraq, Echo 2/4 Marines. November 20, 2013. https://www.youtube.com/watch?v=an9wYgePsuk.

About the Author

Lieutenant Colonel David E. Kelly retired from the Marine Corps Reserves in 1999 after a 29-year career, both active and reserve. His last assignment prior to retirement was as operations officer for the Marine Corps Field History Detachment that operated out of the Washington, DC, Navy Yard. In that billet he planned training for Marine Corps field historians, and also contributed to the Marine Corps 1998 commemorative anthology, *Marines in the Spanish American War*.

In late 2003, he agreed to return to active duty in order to deploy to Iraq as one of only two Marine field historians there. During the planning stages that year, the Marine Corps trained for Security and Stability Operations, but events would overtake this planning as a full-scale insurgency began in the spring of 2004. During a five-month deployment, Lieutenant Colonel Kelly and Major John Piedmont traveled to interview Marines in all areas of Iraq.

Upon completion of the deployment, all oral interviews and photographs were downloaded onto CDs and filed at the Marine Corps Oral History department. The collection is now located at Quantico, Virginia.

He "re-retired" on the completion of his deployment, and returned to civilian life in the fall of 2004. He then began to review his copies of these interviews to create this and other books. He has published two other books based on his field history deployment: *Hell in the Streets of Husaybah* and *First Fights in Fallujah*.

Lieutenant Colonel David E. Kelly retired in June 2017 as a high school history teacher at Cardinal O'Hara High School in Springfield, Pennsylvania. He lives with his wife Terrie, and both of his married daughters live nearby.

Index